German Literary Culture at the Zero Hour

Studies in German Literature, Linguistics, and Culture

Edited by James Hardin
(South Carolina)

German Literary Culture at the Zero Hour

Stephen Brockmann

CAMDEN HOUSE

First published 2004
by Camden House

Camden House is an imprint of Boydell & Brewer Inc.
668 Mt. Hope Avenue, Rochester, NY 14620, USA
www.camden-house.com
and of Boydell & Brewer Limited
PO Box 9, Woodbridge, Suffolk IP12 3DF, UK
www.boydell.co.uk

ISBN: 1–57113–298–8

Library of Congress Cataloging-in-Publication Data

Brockmann, Stephen.
German literary culture at the zero hour / Stephen Brockmann.
p. cm. — (Studies in German literature, linguistics, and culture)
Includes bibliographical references and index.
ISBN 1–57113–298–8 (hardcover: alk. paper)
1. German literature—20th century —History and criticism. 2. Lit-
erature and society —Germany —History —20th century. 3. Authors,
German —20th century —Political and social views. 4. Germany —
Intellectual life—20th century. I. Title. II. Series: Studies in German
literature, linguistics, and culture (Unnumbered)

PT405.B683 2004
830.9—dc22
2004004013

A catalogue record for this title is available from the British Library.

This publication is printed on acid-free paper.
Printed in the United States of America.

Contents

to the memory of my grandparents
Sam and Betty Samuelson
and
Harry and Maria Brockmann

Acknowledgments

I WOULD LIKE to express my deep thanks to Frank Trommler, who first suggested to me a decade ago that I should investigate the culture of the German zero hour, and who has provided support and encouragement to me throughout the long process of work on this book. I also owe a great debt of gratitude to Erhard Schütz, who has helped me in numerous ways with this project, particularly during several study visits I made to Berlin. My gratitude also goes to Christine Lubkoll, Ursula Heukenkamp, Ursula Reinhold, Leonore Krenzlin, and Helmuth Kiesel, who have all helped me in various ways during my visits to Germany. In addition, I am grateful to Michael Markert in Leipzig, who helped me with research for parts of chapter seven, as well as with previous research; and to Rita Wegner and Thorsten Hinz in Berlin, who have been a constant source of support and encouragement. Claus and Erika Keiper lived through the zero hour itself as young people in northern Germany, and I am grateful to them for sharing their sometimes very difficult memories with me.

I spent the year 1999 working at the Institut für Deutsche Literatur at Berlin's Humboldt-Universität, and during that year I lived in a beautiful apartment in Berlin-Schöneberg that belonged to Half and Susanne Zantop. Both of them were leaders in their respective scholarly fields: Half as a geologist and Susanne in my own field, as a Germanist. The completion of this book is made much sadder than it should be by the untimely death of the Zantops in January of 2001. I cannot help but remember the wish that Susanne expressed to me when she visited her Berlin apartment in 1999: that she would soon get a chance to spend real time there herself. It is outrageous and horrible that she was deprived of that chance. I would like to express thanks to both of the Zantops, even after their deaths, for providing me with an excellent working and living space in 1999. I remember them not only with sadness, but also with great fondness and affection, and I am grateful for having had the opportunity to know them.

At my own university, Carnegie Mellon, I owe thanks to a great many people. In particular I would like to thank my two colleagues in the German program, Christian Hallstein and Anne Green, who have continued to support me and to help the German program grow and thrive. Dick Tucker, the head of the Department of Modern Languages, has, as always, provided support and encouragement, as has John Lehoczky, Dean of the College of Humanities and Social Sciences. Without the help of Jean Alexander, Joan

Stein, and the staff at the Hunt Library my research on this book would have been far more difficult. My scholarly work continues to intersect in sometimes surprising ways with the questions and interests of my students, and so I would also like to express my thanks to them. Scholarly work can sometimes lead one into unusual and even arcane paths of research, and more than anything else it is my continuous contact with students, their questions, and their responses that helps me to bridge the gap between my own work and the interests and concerns of a larger community. I am very lucky and privileged to have lively and intelligent students who constantly challenge me to probe, explore, and explain.

For generous financial support, I would like to express deep thanks to the Alexander von Humboldt Foundation, which supported both my research visit to Berlin in 1999 and my follow-up visits to Berlin in 2002 and Erlangen-Nuremberg in 2003. I also gratefully acknowledge support from the German Academic Exchange Service for an initial study visit to Berlin in 1996, during the early stages of my work on this project; to the Berkman Faculty Development Fund and the Falk Grant program at Carnegie Mellon University, which provided support for travel and research; and to the Friends of the Libraries at the University of Wisconsin-Madison, who supported my work at the Memorial Library in the summer of 2000.

My thanks go to Sabine Hake, a close personal friend and also a respected scholar and colleague, who provided not only support and encouragement but also valuable critical readings of the manuscript. April Eisman also gave me important advice on the manuscript. I thank Keith Bullivant and Bernhard Spies, who enabled me to develop some of the ideas in chapter seven in their volume *Literarisches Krisenbewußtsein: Ein Perzeptions- und Produktionsmuster im 20. Jahrhundert* (Frankfurt: Iudicium, 2001); Neil Donahue and Doris Kirchner, who invited me to contribute an early version of chapter three to their volume *A Flight of Fantasy: New Perspectives on Inner Emigration in German Literature 1933–1945* (Providence: Berghahn, 2003); and Manuel Köppen and Rüdiger Steinlein, who allowed me to contribute an earlier German translation of parts of chapter four to their anthology *Passagen: Literatur-Theorie-Medien* (Berlin: Weidler, 2001), a Festschrift in honor of Peter Uwe Hohendahl, to whom I am also indebted for his wisdom and teaching. I developed some of the ideas from this book in an essay entitled "Heroes of the Zero Hour," published in *Heroes and Heroism in German Culture: Essays in Honor of Jost Hermand* (Amsterdam: Rodopi, 2001), a book I co-edited with the inimitable Jim Steakley. To both Jost Hermand and Jim Steakley I would like to express my thanks; and also to Marc Silberman, who helped organize the conference on which that volume was based.

I was born in 1960, and hence I am very much a child of the postwar period. Although my own father was fortunate enough never to have to fight in a war, I had many friends whose fathers were veterans of the Second

World War, and the culture in which I grew up was steeped in the lore of that great conflict. As I worked on this book the lives and experiences of Germans one, two, and three generations before me were very much on my mind: the lives of people born between 1880 and 1940. In reflecting on the situation of Germans in the difficult postwar years, I was also, of course, very much cognizant of the experiences of their American counterparts. It is to some of those American counterparts that I would like to dedicate this book: to my grandparents Harry and Maria Brockmann and Sam and Betty Samuelson. Harry Lyndon Brockmann (1898–1971), a physician, was old enough to be a veteran not of the Second but of the First World War, although he served not at the front but in the decidedly more comfortable environment of Washington, DC; Gilbert Justus (Sam) Samuelson (1907–73), as a petroleum chemist, was lucky enough, during the Second World War, to be deemed more crucial as a researcher than as a soldier. Maria Butler Brockmann (1900–1976), a homemaker, was the daughter of an admiral in the United States Navy; Ida Elizabeth (Betty) Frey Samuelson (1912–88), the daughter of a Nebraska farmer, became, like her husband, an excellent chemist; like so many women of her own and of later generations, she gave up her professional career to become a homemaker. I cherish and honor the memory of all four of my grandparents and hope that this book is at least in some respects a fitting tribute to them.

S. M. B.
April 2004

Introduction: The Zero Hour

ALTHOUGH THE IMMEDIATE postwar period known to Germans as the "Stunde Null" (zero hour) laid the foundation for the subsequent development of literary and political culture in the two German states that emerged in 1949 and the reunified Germany that succeeded them in 1990, it has received surprisingly little attention in literary scholarship, particularly in English. Most literary histories of the postwar period tend to stress the importance of figures like the later Nobel prizewinners Heinrich Böll and Günter Grass, who emerged as major writers over the course of the 1950s, while eliding the complex and contradictory literary-cultural situation of the zero hour itself.

Contemporary scholars are in broad agreement that the absolute break in continuity denoted by the concept of a literary zero hour simply did not take place, at least in West Germany, and probably not in East Germany either. Franz Schonauer, for instance, begins his examination of postwar literature with the programmatic statement that "neither in the east nor in the west did the history of German literature after 1945 begin with the so-called 'zero hour.'"[1] Heinrich Vormweg places the negation of the zero hour into the very title of one of his own contributions.[2] As Stefan Busch observed in 1998, "since the 1970s no work dealing with the topic of postwar literature has failed to point out . . . that there was no such thing as a 'zero hour.'"[3] And yet the ongoing and almost ritual debunking of the zero hour has, paradoxically, contributed to its dominance as a concept. Because contemporary literary histories of postwar Germany frequently begin with the invocation of a radical historical discontinuity that did not happen — why, one wonders, *should* it have happened? — that absence tends to color the interpretation of subsequent history.

At the same time, as Schonauer acknowledges, much of the literary material that actually dominated the immediate postwar period is now, like Hermann Kasack's once famous novel *Die Stadt hinter dem Strom* (The City Beyond the River, 1947), "well-nigh forgotten."[4] Even in Germany, formerly well-known names like Kasack, Elisabeth Langgässer, Rudolf Alexander Schröder, Reinhold Schneider, Werner Bergengruen, Hans-Egon Holthusen, Marie Luise Kaschnitz, and Ernst Kreuder are now rarely mentioned. And yet most of these names would have been familiar to Germans with literary interests during the period 1945–1949.

It is not only these authors — seen during the immediate postwar period as belonging to the elite of German literary talent — who have been forgotten, however. Even authors like Hans Werner Richter, Gustav René Hocke, Wolfdietrich Schnurre, Walter Kolbenhoff, and Wolfgang Weyrauch, perceived in literary history as founding spirits of a purportedly new West German literature associated with the Gruppe 47 (Group 47) after the zero hour of 1945, are now rarely mentioned, and most of their books are long out of print. If authors like Kasack and Langgässer are largely absent from German memory, they were seldom present in English-language depictions of postwar German literature, which tend to begin with the failures and triumphs of self-styled revolutionaries like Richter — figures who, as Schonauer rightly notes, were a "marginal phenomenon" in the years of the zero hour itself.[5] One telling measure of the invisibility of Langgässer and authors like her in the English language is that Langgässer's magnum opus *Das unauslöschliche Siegel* (The Indelible Seal, 1946), celebrated at its publication as a major work of twentieth-century German prose, has never appeared in English translation.

It is difficult to assess the reasons for the neglect, in both popular memory and scholarship, of German culture and literature in the immediate postwar period. W. G. Sebald's suggestion that the repression of memory is a response to the pain and helplessness experienced in Germany at the end of the war is convincing.[6] Perhaps given the dictates of cold war politics and the horrific memories associated with the destruction of the nation, the relative absence of analysis of the immediate postwar period becomes easier to understand. Another possible explanation for the neglect of zero-hour literature is simply that contemporary mentalities are significantly different from those prevalent at the zero hour. For instance, one of the primary intellectual phenomena of the immediate postwar period, described in the seventh chapter of this book, was a Christian revival present in both literature and politics; this revival led to the birth of Germany's dominant postwar political party, the Christian Democratic Union (CDU), and of its Bavarian sister party the Christian Social Union (CSU), which governed the Federal Republic of Germany for most of the postwar period. If Botho Strauß is correct in contending that many contemporary German intellectuals now insist on a materialist worldview and reject anything connected to "the transcendental and the theological," then this difference in mentalities may further complicate any understanding of the German zero hour.[7] Perhaps Reinhold Schneider was right when he argued in 1946 that "no epoch, if it is to be understood, is dependent to such an extent on metaphysics as this epoch, which has denied the metaphysical with such bitterness."[8] However over half a century later, in what many observers now view as a post-Christian era in Germany, the postwar religious revival may seem profoundly alienating.

Both of these reasons — the need for repression and the sheer alterity of zero-hour mentalities — would in and of themselves help to explain the neglect of zero-hour literature. However another powerful reason for the neglect of zero-hour literature is that in West German literary history the absent zero hour ultimately became part of a mythic prehistory. The supposed blankness of the purported zero hour served as a foil against which the supposed founders of West German literature could shine brightly in what Stuart Parkes and John J. White have called "the 'heroic' early period" of postwar West German literature.[9] The zero hour became necessary not as literary-historical specificity but as the background of ruin from which a triumphant literature and culture emerged.

In West Germany the study of postwar literature did not begin in earnest until after the student revolts of 1968, at which point the critical deconstruction of the zero hour concept became one of the most important thrusts of progressive *Germanistik*. It was in this period that concepts of restoration became particularly important, developing what Helmuth Kiesel has called "an effectiveness that can now hardly be contained."[10] When, in 1967, Hans Mayer declared that "there was nothing to the year zero," and when Vormweg asserted four years later that "there was no 'zero hour,'" they were not simply reinforcing and echoing earlier assertions by Gruppe 47 writers and others about a postwar German restoration.[11] In addition, and far more important, the demonstration of continuities between postwar German culture and the culture of the Nazi period was thought to prove the need for a radical progressive change in German culture.

Literary-critical deconstructions of the zero-hour myth in the late 1960s and afterward were part of a widespread effort on the part of postwar intellectuals to contribute to democratic consciousness by demonstrating ongoing continuities between postwar West Germany and the Nazi Reich. In the view of left-liberal critics, the myth of a zero hour — originally created by left-liberals like Richter — now provided German conservatives with a kind of fire wall that protected them from guilt by association with the Nazi period. The concept of a zero hour seemed to imply that postwar West Germany had emerged out of nowhere, without a past and therefore unencumbered by the problems of that past. During the early 1970s literary historians were able to demonstrate convincingly that, at least in the realm of literature, there had been no absolute zero hour and that West German literature after the end of the war continued with more or less the same personnel and in more or less the same styles as before. In particular, the continuity of literary existentialism throughout the 1930s, 1940s, and 1950s led critics like Frank Trommler and Hans Dieter Schäfer to speak of the entire thirty-year period from 1930 to 1960 as one of largely apolitical existentialism.[12] In such a scheme the year 1945 appeared not as a zero hour but rather as the chronological middle of a literary period that predated the Nazis' rise to power and lasted for another

decade and a half after their defeat. Thus the 1960s appeared as the true turning point in German literary history, dominated by the writers of the second
postwar literary generation, in particular Böll and Grass — both of them, as
Schonauer has noted, still marginal figures in the years immediately following
the end of the war. As useful as it was, however, the deconstruction of the
zero hour concept not only left unchallenged but actually reinforced the
claims of Richter and others to have fought a largely heroic, albeit unsuccessful fight against political restoration. Moreover, the literary-critical deconstruction of the zero hour seemed to render any critical reconstruction of the
zero hour itself unnecessary.

One measure of the power exerted by the impulse to exclude the authors of the immediate postwar period from the literary history of postwar
West Germany lies in the fact that even scholars who question Trommler's
and Schäfer's demolition of the zero hour myth tend to uphold the notion
that the literary culture of the immediate postwar period is a *quantité
négligeable* in the cultural history of the Federal Republic. Bernd Hüppauf,
for instance, writes that figures like Alfred Andersch and Richter, the founders of Gruppe 47, may have failed in the crisis after 1945, but he adds that
their efforts were "not lost, but remain present as underground streams and
subcultures."[13] While the immediate postwar period may have been dominated by figures like Gottfried Benn, who, in Hüppauf's words, "experienced his greatest influence after the Second World War," Benn himself
cannot, in Hüppauf's view, be seen as an author of the Federal Republic.[14]
Rather, it was only the Gruppe 47 and the writers associated with it who
truly initiated postwar West German literature.

While Hüppauf is no doubt correct in pointing out the strength of conservative pre-1933 culture in the late 1940s and 1950s, his approach con-
signs the literature of the immediate postwar period to a historical void. The
implication of his argument is that there is no specifically West German cultural identity at all in the late 1940s and the early 1950s, and that only progressive literature produced at the end of the 1950s and later can be seen as
part of West German literary history. Hence, the literary history of the Federal Republic can only have begun at least a decade after the state itself was
founded. David Roberts is even more forceful in denying the literature of the
zero hour a place in postwar West German literary history. It is only with
Böll's *Billard um halbzehn* (Billiards at Half Past Nine) and Grass's *Die
Blechtrommel* (The Tin Drum), both published in 1959, Roberts argues, that
"a West German literary public sphere" emerges. Fifteen years after the end
of the war, such works are "the first true challenge to the repression of the
past as the foundation for the West German political restoration."[15] The
power of this historical narrative is evident in the fact that even critics of
Gruppe 47 subscribe to it. For Klaus Briegleb, for instance, Gruppe 47 is essentially identical with postwar West German Literature, and therefore the

failings and obfuscations of Gruppe 47 are the failings and obfuscations of postwar German literature as a whole. On the one hand Briegleb attacks the dominance and self-celebrations of Gruppe 47, but precisely in making it the centerpiece of his attack, while ignoring other literary figures, he paradoxically helps to cement the ex post facto dominance of Gruppe 47.[16] In the same manner a conservative critic like Frank Schirrmacher, who wishes to attack what he sees as the politicization of postwar German literature, assumes that it was only with Gruppe 47 that postwar West German literature really began. These authors, Schirrmacher claims, formed "one of the production centers" of West German consciousness.[17] If they were the consciousness of the Federal Republic, however, then the largely forgotten authors of the zero hour are surely its unconscious. It is precisely the systematic neglect or even repression of the zero-hour authors that suggests the need for a reexamination of them.

Roberts's invocation of a "repression of the past" sounds a common theme in discussions of the immediate postwar period in Germany: one of the reasons for its purported inadequacy and failure is that authors and other intellectuals in the defeated nation supposedly sought to avoid discussions of the Nazi past. Two recent studies suggest that such accusations against zero-hour literature still have credibility. In a 1999 study of the East German writer Christa Wolf, Gail Finney claims that "in the years immediately following the war, fascism was a taboo topic in both East and West Germany; the horrors were simply too close and too immediate to contemplate."[18] And in a study of the thematization of the Holocaust in West German literature published during the same year, Ernestine Schlant asserts that "early postwar literature . . . focused predominantly not on the Nazi atrocities but on the wartime and postwar travails of the German population." In Schlant's view, this focus, while "legitimate," nevertheless "carried within it the burden of an ominous silence."[19] In accordance with other histories of West German literature, Schlant begins her study with the works of Böll and Wolfgang Koeppen, discarding prior literature as "mystical journeys of quest" by writers like Langgässer and Kasack.[20]

There is no doubt more than a grain of truth in the assertion that many authors of the immediate postwar period avoided direct discussions of the Nazi past. If Finney's contention that there was a "taboo" on such discussions means simply that intellectuals who focused on Nazi crimes may have had to pay a price for their bravery, then her statement is probably accurate; however if it means that there were no such discussions at all, then the statement is false: on the contrary, a multitude of philosophical and historical as well as literary works demonstrate that there were many such discussions.[21] The historian Jerry Muller has argued that "the intellectual life of the years between the defeat (of Germany) and the *Wirtschaftswunder* (economic miracle) remains underilluminated by historical research," and he has rightly criticized the myth that the immediate postwar years were intellectually bar-ren and characterized solely by attempts to ignore or repress the awful past.[22] In fact the problem of German guilt for the crimes of Nazism was one of the fundamental literary-political discussions of the immediate postwar period, as I seek to demonstrate in the first chapter of this book. While Schlant is cor-rect in pointing out that the idealistic or "mystical" aspect of much zero-hour literature frequently obscured discussions of the Nazi past, this was not always and everywhere the case. As Ruth Rehmann accurately notes, in addi-tion to silence "there is also the other side, full of sparks, shimmering, fasci-nating." Rehmann describes the immediate postwar period as one in which "there is open, critical, angry discussion, complaint, mocking."[23] There is far more going on in postwar Germany than just silence.

Langgässer was herself defined by the Nazis as "half-Jewish," and her daughter had survived the Auschwitz concentration camp. She was one of the first and most forceful writers to address the most massive of the Nazis' many crimes, their systematic murder of European Jews, directly in litera-ture. Nevertheless, Schlant unfairly includes her among the authors partici-pating in the obfuscation of the past. Langgässer's novel *Das unauslöschliche Siegel* concludes with a lament for the murdered Jews of Europe; and her *Märkische Argonautenfahrt* (The Brandenburg Journey of the Argonauts, 1950) features a passage at the core of the novel in which a woman mur-dered as a Jew in a German concentration camp speaks directly of her own history. In addition, the latter novel even thematizes the denial of Nazi crimes. One Nazi character in the novel claims: "These pictures of Auschwitz on every bulletin board — any reasonable person can imagine how that came about. Propaganda, nothing more."[24] When confronted by another character who has herself personally experienced a concentration camp, the Nazi pro-claims: "Until and unless I can . . . make our dead heroes come to life, it's all one to me if a few scumbags were gassed in Auschwitz. Gypsies and Jews, Poles . . . and trash like that."[25] This literary Nazi thus reveals a dialectic of public denial coupled with secret affirmation and even celebration of mass murder that characterizes the radical right in Germany and the United States to this day. Langgässer's treatment of Nazi crimes is certainly mystical and informed by her deep Catholic faith; and many of her characters are baptized Jews. Such depictions of the Holocaust as part of a Christian history of struggle between God and the devil may now seem offensive to many, and they may even be perceived as silencing the specifically Jewish dimensions of the Holocaust. However no matter how inadequately, they do thematize the Holocaust, even if they do not use that word — itself a product of cultural history after the zero hour. In the immediate postwar period, such themati-zations were tremendous accomplishments. To ignore or elide such achievements is a kind of silencing that is perhaps itself part of Sebald's al-leged taboo on the specificity of the zero hour.

Langgässer's novels clearly demonstrate two things: 1) that silence about what we now call the Holocaust was by no means universal in postwar German culture; and 2) that the approach taken to the Holocaust, when it was dealt with, was not necessarily consistent with the approaches taken today, over half a century later. Another good case in point is the Austrian writer Ilse Aichinger's semi-autobiographical novel *Die grössere Hoffnung* (The Greater Hope, 1948), which in spite of its romantic, anti-realist style clearly addresses the Holocaust, anti-Semitism, and the destruction of German cities in the air war. For the Nazis, Aichinger was a "half-Jew" because her mother, but not her father, was Jewish; Aichinger's grandmother and some of her mother's siblings were murdered in Nazi concentration camps. The Nazis did not allow Aichinger herself to study because of her "half-Jewish" status. Ellen, the fifteen-year-old girl who is the heroine of Aichinger's only novel, is, like Aichinger herself, a "half-Jew" and hence not as vulnerable to Nazi persecution as her young Jewish friends or her Jewish grandmother. But far from rejoicing in her fate, Ellen wishes she could wear a yellow star like her Jewish friends; when she does wear one, she suffers the same kind of discrimination and racism that they suffer. In this novel Aichinger goes into specific detail about Nazi racial designations of Jewishness, which for the Nazis was defined by one's grandparents: with four Jewish grandparents one was fully Jewish, with three Jewish grandparents one was 3/4 Jewish, with two Jewish grandparents one was one-half Jewish, and with one Jewish grandparent one was one-fourth Jewish. One child in the novel introduces Ellen thus: "This is Ellen! . . . Two wrong grandparents and two right ones! A tie game!"[26] Over the course of the novel all of Ellen's young Jewish friends are taken off to concentration camps, and Ellen's own Jewish grandmother commits suicide in front of Ellen's eyes before she too can be taken away by the Nazis. All of this makes Aichinger's novel an important early statement about the Holocaust and anti-Semitism. However, like Langgässer Aichinger is profoundly influenced by Christianity, and she views the Holocaust from the perspective of the Christian message of salvation. This becomes clear when, just before Ellen's Jewish grandmother dies after having swallowed an overdose of pills, Ellen baptizes her:

> And she poured the rest of the water over the white, gnarled forehead, over the neck and the breast . . ., and she spoke into the middle of the last, solitary gasp: "Grandmother, I baptize you in the name of the Father, and of the Son, and of the Holy Ghost. Amen."[27]

Today such a death-bed baptism would likely be seen as yet another injustice and outrage against a poor old Jewish woman whose Christian granddaughter does not even allow her the dignity of dying as a Jew. However, in the context of the novel it is clear that Ellen is trying to help her grandmother, not to dishonor her. Likewise, when Aichinger portrays Jewish children performing a kind of Christmas pageant shortly before they are hauled off to a concentration camp, she does so not to show that the children have betrayed the religion of their parents and their grandparents, but that they have come to a greater understanding of the truth; it is this truth that Aichinger considers "the greater hope." For Aichinger the suffering of Jews in concentration camps, far from being unique, is one part of a much greater story of suffering and martyrdom. In a bizarre sense the concentration camps allow their inmates to achieve their fully human potential, as one allegorical figure in the novel declares: "crystals — the enlargement of value in that which is smallest. Concentration, you know, concentration of the human being."²⁸ Such a story of triumph over adversity and betterment through suffering, while not fully foreign to today's sensibilities, would now more likely be consigned to popular than to elite culture.

No doubt one of the reasons such depictions of the Holocaust could be incorporated into a more general understanding of the supposed postwar "silence" about the past is their radical difference from contemporary notions of how to treat the Holocaust. That difference certainly needs to be acknowledged, and the reasons for it need to be explored. In the immediate postwar period what is now called the Holocaust was seen as one particularly horrific part of a general panoply of horrors, not as a unique and incomparable event. It was seen not from the perspective of late twentieth-century identity politics, but from the perspective of a generally idealistic universalism that potentially included all human beings. And it was generally seen from the perspective not of the Jewish but of the Christian religion. Such ways of approaching the Holocaust may now seem outdated or wrongheaded, but they do not constitute silence. And it is quite likely that by exploring them further we may come to understand more about our own approaches to and preconceptions about the Holocaust.

This raises another question: how can one now treat the Jewish aspects of the zero hour? Some of the major German-speaking intellectual figures of the period were or at any rate were perceived to be fully or partially Jewish: Anna Seghers, Victor Klemperer, Arnold Zweig, Max Horkheimer, Ilse Aichinger, Theodor W. Adorno, Paul Celan, Elisabeth Langgässer, Alfred Döblin, Hans Mayer, Nelly Sachs, Hermann Broch, and Ernst Bloch, among others. There is no question that in both East Germany and West Germany, as well as in Austria, Jews and people of Jewish ancestry played an important role in the intellectual rebuilding of the country. However it is also safe to say — as the preceding discussion of the Holocaust has shown — that sensitivity to and interest in Jewish questions was significantly less acute then than it is now — in both Central Europe and the United States. In fact, given the Nazis' own obsessive interest in the "Jewish Question," it might be argued that postwar Germans' relative lack of interest in specifically Jewish questions was itself a kind of passive and perhaps not even an entirely condemnable response to those obsessions. Nor did all of the postwar figures now perceived as Jewish actually perceive themselves as such. Victor Klemperer, for instance, who is now generally perceived as a Jew, at least in Germany, saw himself as a German Protestant who happened to have Jewish ancestors. He insisted that he was more German than the Nazis, whom he viewed as "un-German."[29] Elisabeth Langgässer, in spite of two Jewish grandparents, was a devout Catholic; Alfred Döblin, although certainly "Jewish" for the Nazis, converted to Catholicism during the Second World War. Anna Seghers, Arnold Zweig, and Hans Mayer were Marxists and went to live in the German Democratic Republic; as Marxists, they were not religious and did not see themselves as religious Jews — although Seghers's autobiographical short story "Der Ausflug der toten Mädchen" (The Excursion of the Dead Girls, 1946), certainly one of the most moving literary statements on Jewish-Christian-German history in the twentieth century, concludes with the narrator's invocation of her dead Jewish mother, murdered by the Nazis in a concentration camp. Arnold Zweig had actually emigrated to Palestine in 1933, but he returned to Germany in 1948 because as a German Marxist and an anti-nationalist he felt more at home there than he did in non-German-speaking, Zionist Israel. In the German Democratic Republic (GDR) Zweig served as president of the Academy of the Arts and won numerous awards. Max Horkheimer, who had four Jewish grandparents, and Theodor W. Adorno, who had two, returned to West Germany from exile in the United States in 1949 and helped to lay the foundations for postwar German sociology and philosophy. Both Horkheimer and Adorno were products of the history of Jewish assimilation in Germany during the nineteenth and early twentieth-centuries; both probably saw themselves primarily as Germans, not as Jews; neither was religious. In fact Adorno's father had converted to Protestantism before Adorno was born, and therefore neither of Adorno's parents was a religious Jew. In the general turn to religion after the Second World War, it was primarily Catholicism and Protestantism, not Judaism, that predominated. Those writers, such as Paul Celan, Nelly Sachs, and Hermann Broch, who became more interested in questions of Jewish tradition and Jewish identity generally did not return to live in Germany, either East or West. Hence although it is accurate to say that Jews and people perceived as Jews played a significant role in postwar intellectual reconstruction, it is important to understand that many of these intellectuals did not see Jewish identity as a primary category for their self-understanding, and that the intellectual climate in Germany at the time was not particularly conducive to explorations of Jewish identity. Klaus Briegleb is entirely correct in stating that for the most part "the *German-Jewish difference after the Shoah* was not thematized" by postwar German writers.[30] However the notion of a well-defined "German-Jewish difference," which he reifies and places in italics, like the notion of the Shoah or the Holocaust itself, is a historical construct that emerged well after the zero hour. The fact is that many intellectuals of Jewish ancestry who remained in

Germany during the war or who returned to Germany after the war saw themselves primarily as Germans and not primarily as Jews. Hitler's determination to rob them of their status as Germans made some of them even more determined to claim it as their own. If one fails to recognize that contemporary notions of "German-Jewish difference" or even of identity itself do not necessarily reflect the consciousness of German intellectuals in the immediate postwar period, then one will have a difficult time understanding their motivations. Like all other notions, concepts of "Germanness" and "Jewishness" are historical constructions that evolve and change over time. They are not ahistorical or in some way natural; to posit them as such would, paradoxically, mirror Nazi notions of racial essences.

The result of the deconstruction of the zero hour myth in the late 1960s and 1970s was that German literature of the immediate postwar period — the literature produced by Langgässer, Kasack, and others — appeared not as a triumphant and positive new beginning but rather as part and parcel of the discredited past. It was only with the advent of Richter's supposedly nonconformist Gruppe 47 in 1947 and its growing public recognition throughout the 1950s, it seemed, that a truly new and progressive West German literature had emerged, one willing to confront the demons of the Nazi past. In effect, Richter and others in the first postwar generation had laid the groundwork for the emergence of what were only later to become the dominant voices of postwar literature. In order to create what Parkes and White have called "a skillfully orchestrated public image," Richter and his associates painted a largely heroic picture of themselves and their unsuccessful struggle against the German — and Allied — restoration in the immediate postwar years; this picture was to a large extent accepted by subsequent literary critics.[31] The French scholar Jérôme Vaillant has suggested that Germanists in the late 1960s and 1970s sought to create for Richter and Andersch a past in accordance with the significance later ascribed to them, thus overemphasizing their importance for the immediate postwar period itself.[32] What resulted bore the attributes of a heroic myth. In that myth, even if the Davids of Gruppe 47 had failed to triumph politically over the Goliaths of conservative restoration during the interregnum period, at least they could continue the struggle more successfully later in the realm of culture. Dagmar Barnouw writes that Gruppe 47 "in a sense 'created' postwar German literature,"[33] while Wolfgang Schivelbusch suggests that the authors of Gruppe 47 embodied the "energy for renewal" of a generation that sought to attack the "literary accomplishments and moral position" of "the unified front of the grand writers," represented above all by great literary emigrants like Thomas Mann.[34]

Such descriptions encapsulate the view of Gruppe 47 as an essentially heroic, idealistic group fighting against the forces of restoration. In this view, as the writer and scholar Hermann Kinder has written, the history of West German literature "becomes the history of a victorious program."[35] Even more than battling Schivelbusch's "unified front of the grand writers," Richter and others sought to distance themselves from the nonemigrant writers like Benn and Kasack who largely dominated West German literary culture in the first decade after the end of the war. In his book *After the Fires: Recent Writing in the Germanies, Austria and Switzerland* (1986), an analysis of postwar German-language literature, Peter Demetz writes accurately about Richter's and others' "strong disinclination to work with authors of the self-proclaimed 'inner emigration'" (authors who remained in Germany but claimed to have distanced themselves spiritually from the Nazis). Because Richter and most of his other colleagues in the first generation of Gruppe 47 simultaneously kept their distance from writers who had emigrated to other countries, Demetz views Gruppe 47 as "a kind of third literary force" separate from both the inner emigration and the German emigrants.[36]

There is no doubt that this is the way Richter and Andersch wished to view themselves and to be seen by others. And yet the line between Gruppe 47 and the inner emigration is by no means as easy to draw as Richter and Andersch would have wished. Andersch's own famous statement, with respect to the Nazi dictatorship, that "my answer to the total state was total introversion" could easily have been used as a slogan for the entire inner emigration.[37] Moreover, in spite of their zero-hour pathos, the major figures in the first postwar literary generation in West Germany — Richter and Andersch — were not blank slates. During the last decade and a half, literary historians have uncovered considerable evidence of conformism and complicity during the Nazi period on the part of some of the very writers later celebrated as the heroic nonconformists of the zero hour.[38] Richter and Andersch had both lived in Germany during the Third Reich, both had sought membership in the Reichsschrifttumskammer (Reich Chamber of Literature), the writers' organization controlled by the Nazis, and both of them had already engaged in writing and publication. Far from being the youthful writers invoked in their own prose, they were nearly middle-aged by the time the war ended. As Trommler had already noted in 1991, at the beginning of a decade that witnessed a gradual deconstruction of some of the myths of postwar literature, the resistance of Gruppe 47 was in some ways a "nachgeholte Résistance" (post-facto resistance).[39]

As early as 1966 Urs Widmer demonstrated that many of the supposedly youthful revolutionaries of the immediate postwar period used the same kind of language as many of the pundits of the Third Reich.[40] Even if one accepts Vaillant's point that this language was to a large extent strategic and intended to win over a specific group of former German soldiers and Nazis, the fact remains that it was not as new and uncompromised as its users frequently claimed.[41] In spite of Richter's 1947 invocation of an "absolute fanaticism for truth" and his declaration that "we must learn again to be

simple, genuine . . . and, when necessary, cruel to ourselves," these authors
tended to paint their pasts in the most positive possible light after the end of
the war, ignoring or eliding compromises with Nazi power politics.[42] Sebald
has described this process as one that transformed literature into "a means of
straightening out one's curriculum vitae," in much the same way that Nazi
retreats from the Red Army after the defeat at Stalingrad were often euphe-
mistically referred to by the Nazis as a straightening out of the front (Frontbegradigung).[43] Stephan Reinhardt writes that for Andersch "literature
offered the possibility of telling one's life story in a new, different way" and
of correcting "what Andersch had neglected."[44] As Schäfer puts it, "the now
largely accessible papers of the zero-hour authors document their beginnings
and sometimes shed light on the darkness of their entanglements."[45] In a
1989 study of the poet Günter Eich — who had married Ilse Aichinger in
1953 — Glenn Cuomo noted that, like Eich himself, "members of Eich's
generation had been willing to make many more compromises than has generally been believed," including specific compromises with Nazi ideology
and its propagators.[46] As a culmination of such reexaminations of Gruppe 47,
Klaus Briegleb proclaimed in 2003 that "nothing positive can be seen any
more" in these writers' attempts to come to term with the German past, and
that "this literary agency has no right to claim authority on the subject of the
German past."[47] These revelations and reexaminations suggest that the linguistic ambiguities identified during the 1960s by Widmer were symptomatic of deep personal associations with an undesired past, and that the
supposed zero hour was, among other things, frequently an attempt to
white-wash individual histories. Hence the line between the supposedly
youthful and untouched zero-hour writers and the "inner emigration" from
which they sought to distance themselves is not as easily drawn as Richter
and others would have liked. It is not just Andersch who was, in the words
of Margaret Littler, "more firmly rooted in the specifically German tradition
of *Innere Emigration* than has hitherto been acknowledged."[48] When confronted with five prose works he had written and published during the Nazi
period, Richter himself admitted that he and many of his colleagues had
been active as writers prior to 1945, "because otherwise they could not suddenly have surfaced. No one falls from heaven."[49] Thus at the end of his career Richter was essentially admitting the emptiness of his own zero-hour
pathos decades earlier. And yet this fundamental debunking of the zero hour
concept by one of its own primary proponents has not yet been absorbed in
a broader scholarly understanding of zero-hour literature. Richter, Andersch,
and their associates are still for the most part accepted — even by critics like
Briegleb — as the founders of postwar West German literature, while their
inner emigrant colleagues are still largely ignored. Friedrich Denk has gone
so far as to call this the "censorship of those born afterwards" ("Zensur der
Nachgeborenen").[50] Hermann Kinder complains that the dominance ulti-

mately achieved by Gruppe 47 is projected backwards onto the 1950s and even the late 1940s, when the Gruppe 47 was a marginal phenomenon.[51]

Far from being accepted at face value, notions of a zero hour as well as subsequent complaints about a postwar restoration must be understood as profoundly strategic, part of a largely successful attempt by Richter and others to elide the issue of their own junior membership in the inner emigration. It was not just with respect to society at large that the zero hour failed; the zero hour was also not a zero hour for Richter and Andersch. In a sense, they were themselves part of the postwar restoration. If this is true, however, then our picture of the emergence of postwar West German literary culture becomes more complex than it had previously been, with once "clear distinctions" blurring "into a grey," as Cuomo has written.[52] Instead of the brave and ultimately successful struggle of Gruppe 47 against cultural reaction — the dominant narrative in scholarly treatments to this day — we have a broad spectrum from the literary emigrants all the way to Nazi collaborators, with Gruppe 47 as an initially marginal phenomenon of more or less younger authors seeking to distance themselves both from their own pasts and from the presumably discredited members of older literary generations.

In a study of the zero-hour myth completed fifty years after the end of the Second World War, I suggested that if the year 1945 is denied the status of a zero hour, then German cultural history is faced with a fundamental dilemma, forced to explain how a supposed restoration could ultimately result in the most liberal and open society Germany has ever known. "If 1945 was not a break, then at what point did the break come? At what point did the National Socialist Germany become the democratic Germany Germans and others know today?" I asked in 1995.[53] Kiesel has identified the same fundamental dilemma with respect to postwar literary history, suggesting that because of their reliance on the theory of restoration to discredit cultural development in West Germany during the immediate postwar years, literary historians have boxed themselves into a corner. The ultimate dominance of Gruppe 47 and a literature "which was both aesthetically and politically progressive" becomes virtually inexplicable if one relies solely on the theory of restoration, Kiesel believes.[54] While such arguments ignore the complex way in which Richter and Andersch may themselves have been implicated in any postwar literary restoration, they are nevertheless a useful corrective. In Kiesel's view, the collapse of the GDR has made it essential to take a new look at the early cultural history of the Federal Republic, freed from myths and preconceptions about cultural restoration.

Another fundamental complication in any attempt to reexamine German literary culture of the zero hour is the division of Germany. The two postwar German states — the Federal Republic of Germany in the west and the German Democratic Republic in the east — were not created until 1949, and yet subsequent political and literary histories have tended to deal either

with West Germany or with East Germany, not with the muddled and inchoate Germany that existed between 1945 and 1949. Literary critics and
scholars have tended anachronistically to project the subsequent history of
German division onto a period in which neither the Federal Republic nor the
GDR existed. This complication is no doubt reason enough to leave the
1945–1949 period out of postwar literary histories. However with the reunification of Germany such an approach is no longer tenable, and it becomes
crucial to examine the zero hour period as a kind of prehistory to the reunified Germany of today.

In what follows I will explore the German literary situation of the immediate postwar years neither as a radical zero hour nor as a restoration but rather
as a complex, ambiguous, and productive period in which German authors in
all four occupation zones and in both the east and the west sought to respond
to specific challenges, to engage in concrete debates, and to position themselves for the future. Because Austrian writers like Ilse Aichinger and Swiss
writers like Max Frisch were also part of literary discourse in Germany during
these years, I will not exclude them, but they will not be my main focus. Likewise, since many German-language writers living outside German-speaking
Europe at the end of the war, such as Thomas Mann, were nevertheless directly or indirectly involved in literary discourse in Germany, they are an important part of the story. I am less interested in institutional history than I am
in the concrete discourses that writers and other literary intellectuals engaged
in during the immediate postwar years. This is partly because good institutional histories are already available, and partly because, aside from broad cultural histories of the postwar period such as those by Hermann Glaser and Jost
Hermand, there has been remarkably little systematic study of literary discourse during these years.[55] Implicit in my approach is the conviction that what
writers were talking about is more important than the cultural and literary institutions in which many of them were organized. One of my primary conten-
tions is that the substance of literary culture was surprisingly similar in both
east and west during the Nuremberg interregnum, in spite of all institutional
and political differences, and it is precisely such discursive similarities that tend
to be obscured by institutional history. Moreover a focus on institutions can
hardly capture the flight from politics that was one of the dominant trends in
literary culture at that time.

In exploring the literary culture of the immediate postwar period, I draw
on novels, plays, poems, essays, speeches, and reports. Rather than focusing
primarily on certain genres, authors, or regions, I organize my material around
seven primary thematic problems, which correspond to some of the most
pressing cultural-political questions faced by Germans in the postwar period.
To each of them I devote a chapter. The most pressing was the problem of
German guilt. Although my primary interest is in the period from 1945 to
1949, I occasionally include material written and/or published in the first half

of the 1950s, through 1954. Given the necessary belatedness of literature, such inclusion is reasonable; after all, Langgässer's *Das unauslöschliche Siegel* and Kasack's *Die Stadt hinter dem Strom*, both primary works of the immediate postwar period, were in fact originally written but not published during the years of the Third Reich. In examining the literary culture of the immediate postwar period, I am in agreement with Ursula Heukenkamp's specific understanding of the literary and "cultural public sphere" as "the essential forum of communication" about matters of public importance during this period as well as, more generally, with Schlant's invocation of "the privileged position of literature as the seismograph of a people's moral positions."[56] As Schlant argues, literature frequently succeeds better than conventional historiography or political science at "exposing levels of conscience and consciousness that are part of a culture's unstated assumptions and frequently unacknowledged elsewhere."[57] Schlant's reflections point to moral and ethical dimensions of literature that will play an important role in my analyses. Beyond the level of moral thought, however, my approach is governed by the conviction that, as Walter Delabar has suggested, "literature is one of the essential media for the recognition, reflection, and depiction of reality which human culture has developed."[58] But since social reality is by definition constructed by human beings, their reflections upon and understanding of that reality cannot fail to affect it. Thus literature is not simply a reflection of social reality; it also participates in the creation of that reality. Within the context of the present study, what this means is that the literary-cultural developments and debates that form the subject matter of this book are a fundamental part of the history of postwar Germany. From the perspective of a West German culture of the 1960s and 1970s in which the national unity still envisioned by most of the zero-hour authors was largely repressed, much of postwar literary culture appeared old-fashioned and even discredited — part of an unpleasant and unwanted past that had supposedly been overcome. In the context of German culture after reunification, these authors and debates may well have acquired a new relevance — a relevance to which I will return in the postscript. The once famous authors and intellectuals of the postwar period and their then marginal opponents were doing more than just writing about Germany; they were, through their writing, seeking to recreate the nation itself and their role in it. Of course Germany was not a blank slate, even in 1945. But writers' invocations of a "tabula rasa" were probably more than just passive wishful thinking; in attempting to erase their own and others' previous traces, they were actively trying to make room for new, and different, signatures.

Notes

[1] "Die Geschichte der deutschen Literatur nach 1945 hat — weder im Osten noch im Westen — mit der sogenannten 'Stunde Null' begonnen." Franz Schonauer, "Die Prosaliteratur der Bundesrepublik *Literatur nach 1945 1: Politische und regionale Aspekte*, ed. Jost Hermand, 195–272; here, 195 (Wiesbaden: Akademische Verlagsgesellschaft, 1979). Unless otherwise specified, all translations from German in this book are my own; the German appears in the notes, followed by sources. I have added the notation "my translation" in a limited number of cases where confusion might otherwise occur.

[2] Heinrich Vormweg, "Deutsche Literatur 1945–1960: Keine Stunde Null," in *Deutsche Gegenwartsliteratur: Ausgangspositionen und aktuelle Entwicklungen*, ed. Manfred Durzak, 14–31 (Stuttgart: Reclam, 1981).

[3] "Seit den 70er Jahren unterließ es keine Arbeit, die sich mit dem Thema der Nachkriegsliteratur beschäftigte, darauf hinzuweisen, daß von einer 'Stunde Null' . . . nicht die Rede sein konnte." Stefan Busch, "*Und gestern, da hörte uns Deutschland*": *NS-Autoren in der Bundesrepublik: Kontinuität und Diskontinuität bei Friedrich Griese, Werner Beumelburg, Eberhard Wolfgang Möller und Kurt Ziesel* (Würzburg: Königshausen & Neumann, 1998), 10.

[4] "nahezu vergessen." Schonauer, "Die Prosaliteratur der Bundesrepublik," 204.

[5] "Randerscheinung." Schonauer, "Die Prosaliteratur der Bundesrepublik," 210.

[6] W. G. Sebald, *Luftkrieg und Literatur* (Munich: Hanser, 1999), 18. English translation as "Air War and Literature" in Sebald, *On the Natural History of Destruction*, trans. Anthea Bell, 1–104; here, 10 (New York: Random House, 2003).

[7] "ans Transzendente und Theologische." "Am Rand. Wo sonst," interview with Botho Strauß, *Die Zeit*, 31 May 2000, 55–56; here, 56.

[8] "keine Epoche ist, wenn sie verstanden werden soll, in solchem Maße auf Metaphysik angewiesen wie diese, die das Metaphysische mit Erbitterung verleugnet hat." Reinhold Schneider, *Der Mensch vor dem Gericht der Geschichte* (Augsburg-Göggingen: Johann Wilhelm Naumann, 1946), 23.

[9] Stuart Parkes and John J. White, "Introduction," in *The Gruppe 47 Fifty Years On: A Re-Appraisal of its Literary and Political Significance*, ed. Parkes and White, i–xxiii; here, iv (Amsterdam: Rodopi, 1999).

[10] "kaum mehr zu unterbindende Wirkungskraft." Helmuth Kiesel, "Die Restaurationsthese als Problem für die Literaturgeschichtsschreibung," in *Zwei Wendezeiten: Blicke auf die deutsche Literatur 1945 und 1989*, ed. Walter Erhart and Dirk Niefanger, 13–45; here, 14 (Tübingen: Max Niemeyer, 1997).

[11] "Mit dem Jahre Null war es nichts." Hans Mayer, *Zur deutschen Literatur der Zeit* (Reinbek: Rowohlt, 1967), 300; "Es hat auch für die deutsche Literatur keine 'Stunde Null' gegeben." Vormweg, "Deutsche Literatur 1945–1960: Keine Stunde Null," 30.

[12] See Frank Trommler, "Der 'Nullpunkt 1945' und seine Verbindlichkeit für die Literaturgeschichte," in *Basis: Jahrbuch für deutsche Gegenwartsliteratur* 1 (1970), 9–25; and Hans Dieter Schäfer, *Das gespaltene Bewußtsein: Über deutsche Kultur und*

Lebenswirklichkeit 1933–1945 (Munich: Hanser, 1981), particularly the chapter "Zur Periodisierung der deutschen Literatur seit 1930," 55–71.

[13] "gehen nicht verloren, sondern bleiben als Unterströmungen und Subkulturen präsent." Bernd Hüppauf, "Krise ohne Wandel: Die kulturelle Situation 1945–1949," in *"Die Mühen der Ebenen": Kontinuität und Wandel in der deutschen Literatur und Gesellschaft 1945–1949,* ed. Hüppauf, 47–112; here, 111 (Heidelberg: Carl Winter, 1981).

[14] "Benn hat wohl seinen größten Einfluß nach dem 2. Weltkrieg erlebt." Hüppauf, "Krise ohne Wandel," 112.

[15] "eine westdeutsche literarische Öffentlichkeit," "die erste wirkliche Herausforderung gegen die Verdrängung der Vergangenheit als Basis der westdeutschen politischen Restauration." David Roberts, "Nach der Apokalypse: Kontinuität und Diskontinuität in der deutschen Literatur nach 1945," in Hüppauf, *"Die Mühen der Ebenen,"* 21–45; here, 42.

[16] Klaus Briegleb, *Mißachtung und Tabu: Eine Streitschrift zur Frage: "Wie antisemitisch war die Gruppe 47?"* (Berlin: Philo, 2003).

[17] "einer der Produktionszentralen des bundesrepublikanischen Bewußtseins." Frank Schirrmacher, "Abschied von der Literatur der Bundesrepublik," *Frankfurter Allgemeine Zeitung,* 2 October 1990: L1–2; here, L1.

[18] Gail Finney, *Christa Wolf* (New York: Twayne, 1999), 49.

[19] Ernestine Schlant, *The Language of Silence: West German Literature and the Holocaust* (New York: Routledge, 1999), 24.

[20] Schlant, *The Language of Silence,* 23.

[21] Michael Schornstheimer demonstrates in his study *Bombenstimmung und Katzenjammer — Vergangenheitsbewältigung: Quick und Stern in den 50er Jahren* (Cologne: Pahl-Rugenstein, 1989) that even the popular press in Germany during the 1950s was filled with — highly problematic — depictions of the Nazi years, not with silence.

[22] Jerry Z. Muller, *The Other God That Failed: Hans Freyer and the Deradicalization of German Conservatism* (Princeton: Princeton UP, 1987), 362.

[23] "Aber es gibt auch die andere Seite, funkelnd, schillernd, erregend." "Es wird offen, kritisch, rabiat diskutiert, geschimpft, gespottet." Ruth Rehmann, *Unterwegs in fremden Träumen* (Munich: Carl Hanser, 1993), 65.

[24] "Diese Bilder von Auschwitz an jedem Brett — jeder vernünftige Mensch kann sich denken, wie sie zustande kamen. Propaganda und weiter nichts." Elisabeth Langgässer, *Märkische Argonautenfahrt* (Hamburg: Claassen, 1959), 160.

[25] "Und ehe ich nicht unsere toten Helden . . . lebendig machen kann, ist es mir einerlei, ob ein paar Lumpen in Auschwitz vergast worden sind. Zigeuner und Juden, Polen — und solches . . . solches Zeug." Langgässer, *Märkische Argonautenfahrt,* 161.

[26] "Das ist Ellen! . . . Zwei falsche Großeltern und zwei richtige! Ein unentschiedenes Spiel!" Ilse Aichinger, *Die grössere Hoffnung* (Amsterdam: Bermann-Fischer/Querido, 1948), 51.

[27] "Und sie goß den Rest des Wassers über die weiße, eckige Stirn, über Hals und Brust . . ., und sie sagte mitten in das letzte, einsame Röcheln: 'Großmutter, ich taufe

dich im Namen des Vaters und des Sohnes und des Heiligen Geistes, Amen.'"
Aichinger, *Die grössere Hoffnung,* 275.

[28] "Kristalle — die Vergrößerung des Wertes im Kleinsten. Konzentration, wissen Sie, Konzentration des Menschen." Aichinger, *Die grössere Hoffnung,* 241. This passage was eliminated from later editions of the novel.

[29] Joachim Garbe, *Deutsche Geschichte in deutschen Geschichten der neunziger Jahre* (Würzburg: Königshausen & Neumann, 2002), 177.

[30] "Die *jüdisch-deutsche Differenz nach der Shoah* wurde nicht thematisiert." Briegleb, *Mißachtung und Tabu,* 12.

[31] Parkes and White, "Introduction," vi.

[32] Jérôme Vaillant, *Der Ruf — Unabhängige Blätter der jungen Generation (1945–1949): Eine Zeitschrift zwischen Illusion und Anpassung,* trans. Heidrun Hofmann and Karl Heinz Schmidt (Munich: K. G. Sauer, 1978), 149.

[33] Dagmar Barnouw, *Germany 1945: Views of War and Violence* (Bloomington: Indiana UP, 1997), 197.

[34] "Erneuerungsenergie," "literarische Leistung und moralische Position," "Einheitsfront der Großschriftsteller." Wolfgang Schivelbusch, *Vor dem Vorhang: Das geistige Berlin 1945–1948* (Frankfurt: Fischer, 1995), 289.

[35] "zur Geschichte eines siegreichen Programms wird." Hermann Kinder, *Der Mythos von der Gruppe 47* (Eggingen: Edition Isele, 1991), 18.

[36] Peter Demetz, *After the Fires: Recent Writing in the Germanies, Austria and Switzerland* (San Diego: Harcourt Brace Jovanovich, 1986), 8, 9.

[37] "Ich antwortete auf den totalen Staat mit der totalen Introversion." Alfred Andersch, *Die Kirschen der Freiheit: Ein Bericht* (Zurich: Diogenes, 1972 [originally 1952]), 46.

[38] See, for instance, Glenn Cuomo, *Career at the Cost of Compromise: Günter Eich's Life and Work in the Years 1933–1945* (Amsterdam: Rodopi, 1989); Stephan Reinhardt, *Alfred Andersch: Eine Biographie* (Zurich: Diogenes, 1990); and Friedrich Denk, *Die Zensur der Nachgeborenen: Zur regimekritischen Literatur im Dritten Reich* (Weilheim: Denk, 1996), 432–45.

[39] Frank Trommler, "Die nachgeholte Résistance: Politik und Gruppenethos im historischen Zusammenhang," in *Die Gruppe 47 in der Geschichte der Bundesrepublik,* ed. Justus Fechter, Eberhard Lämmert, and Jürgen Schutte, 9–22 (Würzburg: Königshausen & Neumann, 1991).

[40] Urs Widmer, *1945 oder die 'Neue Sprache'* (Düsseldorf: Schwann, 1966). For a critique of Widmer, see Walter Dieckmann, "Diskontinuität? Zur — unbefriedigenden — sprachkritischen und sprachwissenschaftlichen Behandlung der Nachkriegssprache in Deutschland 1945–1949," in *Nachkriegsliteratur in Westdeutschland,* ed. Jost Hermand, Helmut Peitsch, and Klaus R. Scherpe, vol. 2, *Autoren, Sprache, Traditionen* 89–100 (Berlin: Argument, 1983).

[41] Vaillant, *Der Ruf,* 139.

[42] "unbedingten Fanatismus zur Wahrheit," "wir müssen wieder lernen einfach, echt . . . und, wenn es not tut, gegen uns selbst grausam zu sein." Hans Werner Richter, *Briefe,* ed. Sabine Cofalla (Munich: Hanser, 1997), 13; also cited in Parkes and White, "Introduction," iv.

[43] "Literatur als Mittel zur Begradigung des Lebenslaufs." W. G. Sebald, "Der Schriftsteller Alfred Andersch," in Sebald, *Luftkrieg und Literatur,* 121–60; here, 157. Alternative English translation: "Between the Devil and the Deep Blue Sea: On Alfred Andersch," in Sebald, *On the Natural History of Destruction,* 105–42; here, 139. The word "Begradigung" implies a comparison to "Frontbegradigung" (straightening out the front) the Nazi euphemism for military retreats.

[44] "Literatur bot die Möglichkeit, Lebensgeschichte anders, neu zu erzählen. Mit ihr ließ sich korrigieren, was Andersch versäumt hatte. . . ." Reinhardt, *Alfred Andersch,* 61.

[45] "Die nunmehr zum großen Teil zugänglichen Nachlässe der Stunde-Null-Autoren dokumentieren ihre Anfänge und bringen zuweilen Licht in das Dunkel ihrer Verstrickungen." Hans Dieter Schäfer, "Kultur als Simulation: Das Dritte Reich und die Postmoderne," in *Literatur in der Diktatur: Schreiben im Nationalsozialismus und DDR-Sozialismus,* ed. Günther Rüther, 215–45; here, 228 (Paderborn: Schöningh, 1997).

[46] Cuomo, *Career at the Cost of Compromise,* 136.

[47] "nichts Positives mehr zu sehen ist," "Diese literarische Agentur beruft sich zu Unrecht auf ihre Autorität in Sachen deutsche Vergangenheit." Briegleb, *Mißachtung und Tabu,* 320–21.

[48] Margaret Littler, *Alfred Andersch (1914–1980) and the Reception of French Thought in the Federal Republic of Germany* (London: Edwin Mellen Press, 1991), xii.

[49] "denn sonst hätten sie ja nicht plötzlich auftauchen können. Vom Himmel fällt keiner." "Exilautoren und Aussenseiter in der frühen Gruppe 47 und Hans Werner Richters Schreibanfänge im Dritten Reich," interview with Volker Wehdeking, in Wehdeking, *Anfänge westdeutscher Nachkriegsliteratur: Aufsätze, Interviews, Materialien,* 173–91; here, 180 (Aachen: Alano, 1989). Cited in Schäfer, "Kultur als Simulation," 231.

[50] Denk, *Die Zensur der Nachgeborenen,* 10.

[51] Kinder, *Der Mythos von der Gruppe 47,* 16.

[52] Cuomo, *Career at the Cost of Compromise,* 136.

[53] Stephen Brockmann, "German Culture at the 'Zero Hour,'" in *Revisiting Zero Hour 1945: The Emergence of Postwar German Culture,* ed. Stephen Brockmann and Frank Trommler (Washington: American Institute for Contemporary German Studies, 1996), 8–40; here, 26.

[54] "die in ästhetischer wie in politischer Hinsicht progressiv wirkte." Kiesel, "Die Restaurationsthese," 40.

[55] Hermann Glaser, *Kulturgeschichte der Bundesrepublik Deutschland: Zwischen Kapitulation und Währungsreform 1945–1948* (Munich: Carl Hanser, 1985); Jost Hermand, *Kultur im Wiederaufbau: Die Bundesrepublik Deutschland, 1945–1965* (Munich: Nymphenburger, 1986). For institutional histories, see, among others, David Pike, *The Politics of Culture in Soviet-Occupied Germany, 1945–1949* (Stanford: Stanford UP, 1992); Jost Hermand, Helmut Peitsch, and Klaus R. Scherpe, eds., *Nachkriegsliteratur in Westdeutschland 1945–1949;* Schivelbusch, *Vor dem Vorhang;* Harold Hurwitz, *Die Stunde Null der deutschen Presse: Die amerikanische Pressepolitik*

in Deutschland 1945–1949 (Cologne: Wissenschaft und Politik, 1972); and Gerhard Hay, ed., *Zur literarischen Situation 1945–1949* (Kronberg: Athenäum, 1977).

[56] "kulturelle Öffentlichkeit," "das wesentliche Forum der Kommunikation." Ursula Heukenkamp, "Vorwort," in *Deutsche Erinnerung: Berliner Beiträge zur Prosa der Nachkriegsjahre (1945–1960)*, ed. Ursula Heukenkamp, 7–10; here, 8 (Berlin: Erich Schmidt, 2000).

[57] Schlant, *The Language of Silence*, 3.

[58] "Literatur ist eine der wesentlichen Wahrnehmungs-, Reflexions- und Darstellungsmedien für Realität überhaupt, die die menschliche Kultur entwickelt hat." Walter Delabar, *Was tun? Romane am Ende der Weimarer Republik (Opladen: Westdeutscher Verlag, 1999)*, 25.

1: The Consciousness of German Guilt

IN A 1946 ARTICLE in the *Deutsche Rundschau,* Rudolf Pechel suggested that the question of German guilt "is perhaps the most difficult problem, faced by us all, without exception."[1] Whether explicitly articulated or not, the problem of guilt lay at the root of many intellectual debates in the postwar period, from the dispute between "inner emigrants" and exiles to discussions of German youth and their predicament; it was, as Barbro Eberan has suggested, "a mirror of German self-understanding" in the years after the war.[2] Martin Niemöller declared in 1946 that the problem of guilt "is the real question behind all our disquiet, our coming and going, our innermost dissatisfaction."[3] In her novel *Die grössere Hoffnung* Ilse Aichinger asked: "Where does it end, the path of this guilt, where does it stop?"[4]

The extent to which the more general problem of German guilt — whether differentiated or not — became associated in the immediate postwar period with the undifferentiated concept of collective guilt (*Kollektivschuld*) requires explanation, since virtually none of the major participants in the debate, even Germany's staunchest foes, subscribed to the notion that every single German was equally guilty for the crimes of the Third Reich. It is true that during the war Henry Morgenthau, Jr., the U.S. Secretary of the Treasury under President Franklin Delano Roosevelt, and Lord Robert Vansittart, a senior British diplomat, took a negative view of Germany and favored harsh political and economic sanctions against the conquered nation during the postwar period, up to and including deindustrialization and a partition of Germany. Vansittart argued that Germans were generally humorless, undemocratic, and aggressive, and that they had already managed to tear Europe apart twice in the twentieth century; if given the chance, they would seek to do so again, he believed. "The German nation needs the most drastic cure in history," Vansittart argued. "If it is not applied, the world will die of the German disease."[5] Even Vansittart, however, acknowledged the existence of "good" Germans, while arguing that such people did not in any way alter the overall negative aspect of "Germanity."[6] In his book *Lessons of my Life* (1945), Vansittart was careful to note that "when I speak of Germans I do not mean 100 per cent. [*sic*] of Germans. I mean the majority."[7] In his view, "not all the German race lent itself to the conducted crescendo" of the Nazis. "On the contrary, many Germans disliked the whole performance."[8] Hence any assertion of 100 percent German complicity was, in his view, "mere silliness."[9] Morgenthau's primary target, meanwhile, was German heavy industry, which he believed, bore primary responsibility for Germany's prosecution of two world wars in less than half a century. Far from proclaiming undifferentiated German guilt, Morgenthau urged the prosecution of war criminals and Nazis, while arguing that Germans themselves should be responsible for their own reeducation, since "the most fertile soil for the seed of democracy would be those Germans who know it is useless to plot for dictatorships, war and conquest."[10] Morgenthau acknowledged that "there are German believers of democracy," people who "fought for human freedom, dignity and equality," and who died in large numbers resisting the Nazis.[11] Unfortunately, he wrote, such Germans had never been able to "sway the mass of the German people," with the result that "the present generation" of Germans "have become the most fanatical haters of democracy ever known in the world."[12] It was Morgenthau's hope that there were large numbers of Germans "free from the German war madness" outside Germany who could, in the postwar period, return to their native land and "become the nucleus for a regenerated Reich."[13]

It should be emphasized that Vansittart and Morgenthau represented specific, albeit influential viewpoints in the British Foreign Office and the U.S. government during the last years of the war, and that such negative views of Germany were by no means the only ones in currency during those years. On the opposite side of the spectrum of views, there were those within the U.S. government who, far from seeing Germans in a generally negative light, regarded them as potentially useful allies in future European struggles, particularly against the next potential enemy of the United States, the Soviet Union. In between these poles was a middle group which, although in favor of rigorous policies with respect to Germany during the first postwar years, nevertheless was willing to consider the possibility that Germans might be reeducated into productive, democratic members of the world community. At ground level during the American occupation of western Germany, proponents of a relatively lax stance predominated even at the beginning, as Morgenthau had predicted when he wrote that "no men in the armies of the United Nations are likely to be so susceptible as Americans to the danger of this people's bid for compassion."[14] American GIs, he feared, "just hadn't been trained to resist kindness from a good-looking fräulein or a motherly woman or a gentle old man or a wistful child."[15] In his 1946 book *Germany in Defeat* Percy Knauth, a reporter for *Time* and *Life* magazines who visited the humbled nation "behind the invading Allied armies," noted with disgust his impression "that the Germans, who six months ago were killing us with all their might, are now the people we like best on the whole continent of Europe," and that "the Germans, far from being the instigators of this war, are rapidly beginning to look like its victims" to gullible, kindhearted Americans.[16] As early as the fall of 1944, Saul K. Padover from the Psychological Warfare Division of the U.S. Army met a vehemently anti-Nazi American officer whom he designated "Ypsilon" in the town of Roetgen near Aachen. "If the regular MG (military government) stable contained even half a dozen Ypsilons, officers who disliked Nazis because of their Nazism, the outlook for a cleansing of fascism in Germany" would be good, Padover reflected a year later. "I had a suspicion, however, that Major Ypsilon was *sui generis* and that I would never meet another one like him. I never did."[17] Even allowing for anecdotal inaccuracy on the part of Padover, his account suggests that significant numbers of American military officials, far from being accusatory or even punitive in their dealings with Germans, were downright sympathetic to former Nazis. In November of 1945, barely half a year after the end of the war, survey results indicated that, in spite of Buchenwald and Auschwitz, eighty percent of American soldiers had a favorable attitude toward the citizens of the conquered nation.[18] Even Padover himself, a fierce critic of most Germans, explicitly opposed what he called a "hard policy" toward the conquered enemy, pointing out that "throughout Germany there are numerous Socialists and Christian Socialists and Liberals who hate the Hitler regime," and that "we must give them help and encouragement. It would be a mistake to spurn them."[19] Given the fact that not even Germany's fiercest critics explicitly subscribed to a theory of undifferentiated German guilt, the predominance of such concepts in the German popular imagination immediately after the end of the war — and even into the present — poses a puzzle.

There were two primary reasons why many Germans were reluctant to address the problem of guilt in the first postwar years; and there were three primary reasons why the larger problem of guilt was frequently reduced to the single bogeyman of collective guilt in the same period. The first reason why many Germans were reluctant to address the problem of guilt at all was the horrific nature and massive extent of German crimes. As the Protestant pastor Martin Niemöller declared in 1946, "no pen, no movie will suffice to show what happened."[20] The methodical murder of five to six million Jews was by no means the only crime committed by Germans, Niemöller acknowledged; however it alone beggared description and resisted comprehension. "It's no wonder," Niemöller declared, "that no one wants to accept guilt for these crimes," because if any German were willing to bear the burden of this guilt, "could the man live for even a minute longer, would he not have to walk out into the night like Judas and hang himself?" Previous generations, Niemöller wrote, had sneered at the idea of Hell and damnation as a superstitious fantasy and had treated sixteenth-century paintings of Hell by painters like Pieter Brueghel as caricatures. But the Hell depicted in these paintings, Niemöller wrote, was but "a kindergarten compared to the reality that has broken open in our midst. Hell has come to the surface of the earth."[21] Given the weight of this guilt, who could possibly be willing to bear it? Hence it was no wonder that Germans were treating the question of guilt like a hot potato, passing it as quickly as possible from hand to hand.

The second major reason for the avoidance of the question of guilt in the immediate aftermath of the Second World War was that many Germans saw themselves not as perpetrators but rather as victims. Therefore the whole question of guilt seemed to many of them an unfair imposition that turned the reality of their misery on its head. The German Wehrmacht had suffered horrendous losses by the end of the war, with millions of German men killed, wounded, missing in action, or taken prisoner by the various Allied forces. Most major German cities had been destroyed in air raids over the course of the war; cities like Berlin, Hamburg, and Dresden lay in ruins, and vast numbers of civilians had been killed or wounded. The lost war thus affected not just German soldiers but German civilians as well, bringing home the full horror of what Propaganda Minister Joseph Goebbels had enthusiastically called total war. Strict rationing during the last years of the war meant that ordinary Germans had little to eat; hunger and disease were widespread. As the Soviet Red Army closed in on Germany from the east, millions of Germans fled their homes in the provinces of East Prussia, Silesia, and Pomerania, and millions more were driven by Russians, Poles, and Czechs from their homes in the German East and from the ethnically German northwestern region of Czechoslovakia referred to by the Nazis and others as the "Sudetenland." In all, more than eleven million Germans fled willingly or unwillingly from their eastern homes in the period from 1944 to 1946, becoming homeless refugees seeking shelter and safety further west. In the precarious trek from east to west — carried out largely on foot and in bad weather — many of the old, the very young, and the infirm died. Even after a century of "ethnic cleansing," in which the Nazi German government itself was massively implicated, the expulsion of Germans from eastern territories in which many families had lived for centuries remains the single largest instance of such expulsions in modern European history. The millions of refugees from the east converged on remaining German territories further west in which, due to massive bombing, there were already severe housing shortages, as well as shortages of food and basic supplies. Families throughout Germany, and particularly in the areas invaded by the Red Army, feared that their women would be raped; in all too many instances this fear became reality. In addition to all these problems, the final months of the Second World War witnessed increasing lawlessness in Germany, including problems with youthful criminality. These and many more problems contributed to Germans' sense of victimization after the end of the war, leading them to focus more on their own problems than on the problems of other peoples. In his report on his experiences in Germany during 1944 and 1945, Padover noted an almost universal sense of self-pity and consequent attempts on the part of most Germans to elicit sympathy from their conquerors. "Investigation revealed that these complaints and expressions of self-pity are a more or less conscious technique of justifying an acceptance and toleration of Nazism,"

Padover wrote in a report to American military authorities.[22] In light of their own self-pity, the problem of guilt may have seemed a moot point to large numbers of Germans in 1945. As Karl Jaspers put it in the introduction to his book *Die Schuldfrage* (The Question of German Guilt, 1946),

> The temptation to evade this question is obvious; we live in distress — large parts of our population are in so great, such acute distress that they seem to have become insensitive to such discussions. Their interest is in anything that would relieve distress, that would give them work and bread, shelter and warmth. The horizon has shrunk.[23]

The historian Jürgen Kocka has echoed Jaspers's observation, suggesting that in the immediate postwar period "people tried to survive in the ruins. The horizon got narrower. You weren't making world history any more . . ., instead you were standing in line for rations and exchanging coffee for margarine."[24] The fundamental problem of survival was so overwhelming in the immediate postwar period that it tended to obscure any confrontation with moral and philosophical problems like the question of guilt.

As Vansittart had suspected, the first and most important reason why the question of guilt, if addressed at all, was frequently reduced to the problem of collective guilt, undoubtedly lay in Nazi propaganda itself, which always stressed the unity between Hitler and the German people. In Nazi ideology the *Führer* represented the concrete and yet mystical embodiment of the will of all healthy Germans. Far from being a dictator forced upon the Germans from outside or above, the Nazis argued, Hitler had emerged from within the German people, had been chosen by them, and was recognized by them not as the mechanically majoritarian representative of a democratic polity but as the organic, living incarnation of the German *Volk* itself. Germany was Hitler and Hitler was Germany. While the *Führer-Prinzip* seemed to delegate all responsibility to a godlike *Führer,* thus freeing ordinary Germans from responsibility, it simultaneously claimed that the *Führer* was in fact nothing more than the physical embodiment of the general will. Thomas Mann had already memorably described the psychopathology of this *Führer-Prinzip* in his 1930 novella *Mario und der Zauberer* (Mario and the Magician), in which the sinister Italian magician Cipolla, who dominates and brutalizes his audience — and who represents both Italian and German fascism — claims simply to be carrying out the audience's own will. He "acted in obedience to a voiceless common will which was in the air," relates the novella's narrator, noting that obedience and authority are intertwined with each other in the same way that *Volk* and *Führer* form a dialectical unity.[25]

For National Socialists, the purported mystical commutative property in existence between the German *Volk* and its *Führer* meant that any attempt by German emigrants or others to argue for the existence of an "Other Germany" and thus to drive a wedge between the German people and its Nazi leaders was false and doomed to failure. As Hannah Arendt argued in a 1945 article on the question of guilt published in the American journal *Jewish Frontier* — and in the German journal *Die Wandlung* (Transformation) slightly over a year later — the National Socialists' "central thesis . . . that there is no difference between Nazis and Germans" necessarily implied "that there is no distinction as to responsibility," i.e. that any attempt to differentiate between guilty and innocent Germans or between fascists and antifascists was virtually impossible.[26] If there was no distinction between Germans and their criminal government, then all Germans were equally guilty of German crimes. Even Germans who had not themselves committed specific misdeeds were, at the very least, accessories to and had knowledge of them, since they had probably known about the crimes of their government and done nothing to stop them. Arendt's argument here prefigured the role that knowledge or lack of knowledge about Nazi crimes would play in subsequent debates about German guilt. In the words of Eugen Kogon — who had himself been imprisoned in Buchenwald from 1939 to 1945 — there was "no German who did not know that there were concentration camps. No German who could have believed them to be sanatoriums."[27] In Arendt's view, "the total mobilization culminated in the total complicity of the German people."[28] Any distinction between guilty and innocent Germans had therefore become highly problematic, Arendt believed, not because of Allied intransigence but because of the propaganda and actions of the German government itself. Arendt asserted, moreover, that the Nazis' claims to be the embodiment of the German people were "not mere propaganda but are supported by very real and fearful facts."[29] Germans did indeed largely stand behind and support their criminal government, the philosopher believed. By the end of the war the Nazis had made no secret of their crimes, she claimed, and they had moved from an abstruse, perversely internationalist Aryan racism to older nationalist slogans, which included "the active identification of the whole German people with the Nazis."[30] Although some of these points — particularly the extent to which the Nazis did or did not seek to hide the exact nature of their crimes, and the degree to which ordinary Germans were specifically aware of those crimes — were eminently debatable, Arendt's arguments clearly suggested that the problem of collective guilt was already prefigured in Nazi propaganda and in the *Führer-Prinzip* itself.

The second reason for the widespread conflation of the larger problem of guilt with the more limited idea of collective guilt involved not so much Nazi propaganda as the popular response to the Nazis invoked by Arendt. The Nazi rise to power in 1933 had occurred in a more or less legal manner, since by July of 1932 a relative — albeit not absolute — majority of German voters had given the National Socialists the largest representation in the Reichstag, with over thirty-seven percent of the seats. In other words, by 1933 a plurality of the German electorate had chosen the Nazis in free elections. For the right-wing writer Ernst von Salomon this meant that Hitler had been supported by most Germans. In his 1951 book *Der Fragebogen* (The Questionnaire, translated into English as *The Answers*), written in response to postwar Allied efforts to ferret out individual Germans' specific complicity with the Nazi regime, von Salomon — one of the conspirators in the assassination of German Foreign Minister Walter Rathenau in 1922 — wrote that Hitler's dictatorship had been the result and reflection of democratic will:

> I fear that Hitler's assertion — that his ideological concept was the democratic concept — will prove a hard one to refute. . . . The winning of mass support through convincing arguments, the legitimate road to power by way of the ballot-box, the legitimisation by the people itself of power achieved — I fear it is hard to deny that these are democratic stigmata, revelatory perhaps of democracy in a decadent and feverish form, but democratic none the less.[31]

In other words, according to von Salomon, the Nazis came to power not through a putsch or by thwarting the will of the German people, but through the democratic support of ordinary Germans. Von Salomon's understanding of democracy is governed by an elitist disdain for the rule of the masses; it is clear that the writer would have preferred a traditional authoritarian regime that did not feel the need for "legitimisation by the people." His disdain for the Nazis is based not on their own scorn for democratic processes, but, on the contrary, on what he perceives as the Nazis' need to cater to the lowest interests of generalized mediocrity. Nevertheless von Salomon is clearly right in making a distinction between traditional authoritarian regimes and National Socialist totalitarianism, which certainly sought to legitimate itself as the will of the German people.

Even more problematic than the German people's decision for Hitler in 1933, however, was the failure of Germans to rid themselves of Hitler during the last years of the Second World War. If Germans were not generally in agreement with the Nazi government, then why had there been so few instances of open rebellion, even as it became clearer that the Nazis were committing unspeakable crimes against humanity? "How did the German people react to the injustice?" Kogon asked at the end of his book *Der SS-Staat* (The SS State, translated into English as *The Theory and Practice of Hell*), the first systematic analysis of the concentration camps to be published in the war's aftermath. "As a people not at all. That is a bitter truth."[32] In a November 1944 report to American military authorities Padover noted that even among self-described German anti-Nazis there was little concrete activity, and that the vast majority of Germans "were . . . passive and emotionally incapable even of contemplating the possibility of active resistance."[33] German resistance groups had recognized well before the end of the war the moral importance of overthrowing Hitler from within Germany. As the German leftist Karl Becker, a former member of the Reichstag living as a refugee in England, argued in a 1944 pamphlet, Germans could disprove the Nazis' commutative political identity thesis in only one way: by overthrowing the Hitler government and establishing a democratic Germany themselves without the help of the Allies. If they did not, according to Becker, Hitler's military defeat would become the moral defeat of the German nation itself, and "the German people will have lost all right to say that the German people is not Hitler."[34]

Such sentiments were by no means unique to German Communists and other leftists in exile. They were one of the motives for the attempt by conservative German army officers to assassinate Hitler on July 20, 1944, and they had been in evidence inside Germany itself as early as December, 1942, when an underground conference of the German resistance had urged "the overthrow of the Hitler government and the formation of a national democratic peace movement," insisting that "the longer the war lasts . . ., the heavier will be the weight of responsibility resting upon our people."[35] The failure of such resistance groups to overthrow the Hitler government weighed heavily on German anti-Nazis at war's end. As Friedrich Meinecke, the dean of German historians, noted in 1946, "it would have been a blessing if the German people had found in themselves the strength to throw off the Hitler yoke."[36]

The third reason for the conflation of the problem of guilt generally with collective guilt specifically is more speculative, albeit connected to the first two. Simply stated, the idea of collective guilt can be seen as a kind of paper tiger, a concept so outrageous in its undifferentiatedness that it was relatively easy to refute. Clearly, not all Germans could be held equally guilty of Nazi crimes, and it would have been an obscenity, for instance, to assert that Hitler's German opponents were as guilty as Hitler's German supporters. Of course, virtually no one — even Germany's most bitter opponents — did seriously make such an assertion, but in the Germany of the immediate postwar period there was a widespread perception not only that Vansittart's and Morgenthau's theses implied an undifferentiated guilt on the part of all Germans, but also that these theses represented the official policies of the Allied governments. The fact that both of these perceptions were inaccurate made little impact on popular discussions of the question of guilt itself. The historian Norbert Frei has suggested that the concept of collective guilt met with a "high level of psychological predisposition" in Germany in 1945, giving Germans a "welcome opportunity to feel themselves unjustly treated."[37] As the sociologist Helmut Dubiel has persuasively argued, "the most remarkable thing . . . about the rejection of the collective guilt thesis is that it was a reaction to an accusation which no one had made." Dubiel notes explicitly: "In no decree of the occupying powers, in no public statement of a

British, French, or American politician granted the power of definition was there ever mention of a collective guilt of all Germans."[38] To a large extent the belief that the Allies claimed all Germans to be collectively guilty at war's end, however false, is still current in Germany today; and its continued persistence shows that the concept of collective guilt became a national myth in Germany during the postwar years. In Dubiel's view, the Germans' "positively obsessive defense against an accusation made by no one can be explained only through the psychological interpretation of 'projection.'" In other words, according to Dubiel, the phantasmic persistence in Germany of the concept of collective guilt was itself an indirect admission of the "way that countless Germans were caught up in the historically unprecedented crimes of their state."[39] As Stefan Hermlin pointed out as early as 1946 in a review of Jaspers's book *Die Schuldfrage* — undoubtedly the most important philosophical reflection on the question of guilt published in Germany during the immediate postwar years — "this supposed collective guilt, which was to be borne equally by all Germans, [had] never been officially determined or asserted by the allies." Instead, the official standpoint of the Allied powers was that of the decisions made at Teheran, Yalta and Potsdam, which, in Hermlin's words, had spoken "of a differentiated guilt that affects the majority of all Germans, even if, in the final analysis, it extends beyond Germany."[40] In Hermlin's view — confirmed half a century later by Dubiel — Germans' almost hysterical negative reaction to the purported Allied charge of collective guilt — itself largely a figment of Germans' own imagination — might well have been the paradoxical "admission of a deeply felt guilt."[41] Hermlin's words suggested not only that Germans' vehement protests against the concept of collective guilt might themselves have been the product of a guilty conscience but also that Germans might intentionally or unintentionally have limited the problem of guilt to the blanket accusation of collective guilt precisely in order to avoid a careful, differentiated analysis of the problem of guilt in all its complexity. Precisely because so many Germans did indeed feel an overwhelming sense of guilt, they first limited the problem to its most easily refutable aspect — the largely fictive paper tiger of an undifferentiated national criminality — and then denied its validity. The seemingly empty and indefensible concept of collective guilt might thus have served as a rhetorically useful escape from the all-too-concrete problem of individual guilt. The attempt to escape from individual guilt could, in turn, have resulted in what Hermlin described as "the lack of any consciousness of guilt" on the part of individual Germans and what Arendt identified as the lack of "the consciousness of guilt."[42]

Viewed in this way the concept of "collective guilt," far from being an outside imposition on the German people, was in fact an original German creation based both on a deep German sense of complicity and, paradoxically, on Germans' conscious or unconscious wish to evade responsibility for that complicity. The concept of collective guilt was a fundamental part of both Protestant and Catholic thinking in Germany after the end of the Second World War, and it was entirely consistent with the Christian concept of original sin, a concept which informed the work of many German Christian writers, such as Elisabeth Langgässer and Ilse Aichinger. One chapter of Aichinger's novel *Die grössere Hoffnung* in fact begins with the sentence: "Adam and Eve are guilty!"[43] In particular for Protestants, as Marcus Holz has written, "the connectedness of all people in the common guilt was" a fundamental category.[44] Indeed, Holz suggests, almost without exception Protestant thinkers in the early CDU supported at least some notion of collective guilt.[45] Catholic thinkers also tended to support the notion of collective guilt, to the extent that individual guilt disappeared behind that of the collective.[46] Nor was it merely Christian thinkers who analyzed the situation in Germany in terms of collective guilt. Ernst Jünger confirmed the existence of a deeply felt sense of communal guilt in a journal entry he made during the summer of 1943:

> The greatest theft which Kniébolo (Hitler) perpetrated on the German people is the theft of justice — i.e., he deprived Germans of the possibility of being justified, of feeling themselves to be in the right with respect to the injustices committed against them in the past, and those which threaten them in the future. Of course the people as such made themselves complicit through acclamation — that was the terrible, the appalling undertone one sensed behind the storms of jubilation.[47]

Because of their fanatical support for Hitler, Jünger believed, the German people could no longer feel themselves to be unjustly treated, no matter what happened. Germans had been deprived of the right to consider themselves innocent and were forced to pass judgment on themselves as guilty. The warning that the German nation was plunging itself into guilt and would suffer horrendous consequences as a result had already been expressed by the Protestant pastor Julius von Jan in a sermon delivered to his Swabian congregation after the government-organized pogrom against German Jews that took place in November of 1938:

> Man reaps what he sows! Yes, these were terrible seeds of hatred that have now been sown once again. What a horrific harvest will grow from this if God does not grant our people and us the grace of sincere repentance.[48]

In a pamphlet distributed in Munich on February 18, 1943, the White Rose resistance group had declared that any German rebirth "must be preceded by the acceptance of the guilt which the German nation has heaped upon itself."[49] In the view of such Germans, the bombardment, destruction, and occupation of Germany could be viewed as God's righteous judgment on a guilty people; indeed, by 1942 the Protestant theologian Dietrich Bonhoeffer viewed the work of the German resistance as an "act of penitence."[50] In Aichinger's novel *Die grössere Hoffnung* the air war against Germany is depicted as something that Germans have essentially brought upon themselves:

> Don't be surprised about the clouds of smoke on your horizon! Your own lack of clarity is coming back. Your addiction to grabbing is grabbing back at you. . . . You yourselves have transformed matter into matériel. Don't be surprised![51]

For Ellen, the heroine of Aichinger's novel, the air war is a kind of revenge visited upon Germans by a material world that they have abused: "All things are angry. We held onto them too tightly, we hurt and humiliated them, and now they want their revenge!"[52]

In 1945 Wilhelm Röpke declared not only that "many German intellectuals have loaded themselves with an enormous guilt," but also, more importantly, "that probably some of them would actually contradict us if we had any idea of trying to find excuses for them."[53] In Padover's account of his travels through Germany in the wake of the victorious American army in 1944 and 1945, the concept of collective guilt is never once formulated by a representative of the American army; instead, it is Germans themselves who, from time to time, express their own sense of national guilt. "We are all innocent," declares one German in Aachen in the fall of 1944. "You must not punish the German nation."[54] But in the town of Eupen that same fall a devout Catholic woman goes down on her knees in front of Padover, "as if we were the judges who could grant her forgiveness," and she exclaims: "We are guilty, we are all guilty. May the Almighty God forgive us." In response to Padover's attempts to comfort her, she replies: "The Almighty has punished us and he will not forgive our sins. I myself have sinned against him by not raising my voice against the wicked."[55] The following March, in Krefeld, Padover encounters another devout German Catholic who, upon hearing his bishop pray for a "just peace," rises to his feet in front of the whole congregation and exclaims: "A just peace? How can we German Catholics ask for a just peace? If we were given a just peace, then we would all be hanged — that would be justice."[56]

Such sentiments were not limited to devout Catholics. In a declaration made in Stuttgart in October of 1945, a number of prominent German Protestant theologians asserted their unity with the rest of the German people not only in suffering but also in guilt. "Through us endless suffering has been visited upon many peoples and nations," they noted.[57] In an attempt to explain this declaration of guilt, Martin Niemöller argued that no German protestations of other nations' guilt could counter the weight of German guilt: "all of that is no more than a minuscule quantum compared to the heavy weight that we have taken upon our consciences, and I say this after having spent twelve days in Berlin, where there is hardly one woman who has not been scandalously mistreated, and where death stalks in a way that the world has never seen before."[58]

Nor were German Communists uniformly resistant to notions of German guilt. After the liberation of the Mauthausen concentration camp by American forces in May of 1945 the Communist Franz Dahlem, who had been interned at Mauthausen, stressed in a speech to the camp's former inmates that "the German people silently tolerated the extermination of millions of Jews from all over Europe by the Gestapo and the SS," and that large numbers of Germans had themselves succumbed to "the poison of anti-Semitism." Such misdeeds, Dahlem insisted, "simply could never be made good again . . . The German people will not escape this guilt."[59] Likewise, in February of 1946 the Communist historian Helmut Eschwege, in a note to his party comrade Paul Merker, stated: "The German people recognize their guilt toward the Jews, which stems from their active or passive participation by an overwhelming majority in the Hitler system."[60] Even the Social Democrat Kurt Schumacher, who fundamentally rejected notions of German collective guilt as reactionary, nevertheless claimed in an internal party memo of January 1947 that guilt was a reality that many Germans were still trying to repress.[61] As Jeffrey Herf has argued, such declarations of German guilt and the need for atonement tended to make politicians like Merker and Schumacher unpopular in both East and West during the postwar years; however they also clearly indicated that notions of collective guilt, far from being an originary creation of Germany's military opponents in the final years of the war, had fundamentally German roots that were subsequently repressed. As Norbert Frei has noted in an analysis of West German demands for amnesty in the early 1950s, the broad support for such demands implied an "indirect admission of the entire society's involvement in National Socialism."[62] Likewise Herf makes it clear that most of the major German politicians in both the East and the West proceeded from the assumption of widespread and deep-rooted German guilt.

At the end of the war the most famous living psychoanalyst in German-speaking Europe provided an analysis that confirmed the theory of Germans' psychological defensiveness with respect to the question of guilt. For Carl Gustav Jung — whose outraged German critics were quick to point out the eminent psychiatrist's own earlier flirtations with Nazi ideology, and who rather vaguely acknowledged that his own approach to the problem of collective guilt came "not with any feelings of cold-blooded superiority, but rather with an avowed sense of inferiority" — the problem of guilt went beyond questions of legality, politics, and morality and became above all a psychological phenomenon.[63] In an essay entitled "Nach der Katastrophe" ("After the Catastrophe") published in Switzerland in June of 1945, Jung compared the situation of ordinary Germans with that of the family members of a brutal murderer. While such family members may be morally and legally innocent of the crimes committed by their relative, they nevertheless feel subjectively guilty because of their direct family connection to the criminal; moreover, people outside the family will, all rational arguments to the contrary notwithstanding, hold them at least partly responsible for the murderer's awful behavior. In Jung's words, "guilt can be restricted to the lawbreaker only from the legal, moral, and intellectual point of view, but as a psychic phenomenon it spreads itself over the whole neighborhood." Thus, "a house, a family, even a village where a murder has been committed feels the psychological guilt and is made to feel it by the outside world."[64] Jung was careful to differentiate this psychological form of collective guilt — it could just as accurately, he argued, be called "contact guilt" (*Kontakschuld*) — from legal and moral forms of guilt. For him, psychological guilt "connotes the irrational presence of a subjective feeling (or conviction) of guilt, or an objective imputation of, or imputed share in, guilt."[65] Such guilt, in other words, is based primarily not on rational analysis but rather on the irrational, on feeling and emotion. "Contact guilt," Jung argued, is a tragic fate, because it "hits everybody, just and unjust alike, everybody who was anywhere near the place where the terrible thing happened."[66] Collective guilt in this psychological sense is, on the one hand, an objectively existent sense of subjective responsibility — the guilt by association felt by Germans for crimes committed by other Germans in the name of Germany — and, on the other hand, an objectively existent accusation — no matter how unfair — made by other European peoples against Germans in general for having besmirched European honor; "therefore it is not a condemnation of the German people to assert that it has a collective guilt but simply the acknowledgement of an accomplished fact."[67] No matter how unfairly, other Europeans see the German as a criminal, Jung argued:

> As a German, he has betrayed European civilization and all its values; he has brought shame and disgrace on his European family, so that one must blush to hear oneself called a European; he has fallen on his European brethren like a beast of prey, and tortured and murdered them. The German can hardly expect other Europeans to resort to such niceties as to inquire at every step whether the criminal's name was Müller or Meier.[68]

It is pointless, Jung suggested, to criticize the concept of collective guilt because of its irrationality; that irrationality is precisely what is at stake in the concept, and given the fact that irrationality is widespread throughout Europe and the rest of the world, one must address and not deny it. Contemporary Europeans like to see themselves as living in a rational, logical world in which the demons of the past and the forces of a brutal nature have been banished; but, as the Nazi dictatorship itself demonstrated, "the psychic conditions which breed demons are as actively at work as ever. The demons have not really disappeared but have merely taken on another form."[69] The demons that human beings once located in the forces of nature have now taken up residence in their psyche. Neither Germans themselves nor other Europeans can make the psychological fact of collective guilt disappear. While many Germans react defensively even to the slightest hint of collective guilt — the negative reaction to Jung's analysis proved him right on this point — the concept of collective guilt comes not so much from the outside as from "the judge who dwells in our own hearts."[70]

Jung went even further than this analysis of an objectively existent feeling of subjective guilt, however. There is, he claimed, an objective psychological correlation between the collective German psyche and National Socialist psychopathology. Jung suggested that Hitler himself could be chosen by Germans as their leader only because the psychopathology of his own psyche corresponded to the psychopathology in the collective German psyche. Germans suffer from a profound inferiority complex, Jung suggested, which leads them to ascribe all the negative characteristics that they fear and hate in themselves to other peoples; they therefore live in the illusion of being surrounded by hostile and inferior human beings. It cannot simply be a coincidence, the psychiatrist claimed, that Germans chose precisely the hysterical Hitler as their leader. They would not have chosen Hitler if he had not been "a reflected image of the collective German hysteria."[71] It may be a difficult thing, Jung admitted, to accuse an entire people of feelings of psychological inferiority and schizophrenia, but such an analysis is "the only explanation which could in any way account for the effect this scarecrow had on the masses."[72] For Jung, the legendary literary figure Faust is the epitome of the psychopathology of the German soul, with his split personality, limitless arrogance, satanic pact, and inability to come to terms with fundamental realities.

Unlike Jung, Karl Jaspers set out to establish an objective and differentiated approach to the problem; he was only secondarily interested in the psychological truth of accusations of collective guilt. His exploration of the question of guilt was the most systematic German analysis of the immediate postwar years. As Anson Rabinbach has argued, Jaspers's reflections "contributed to the removal of the remaining elements of National Socialist ideology and to the intellectual reconstruction of West Germany," making the philosopher the "'Praeceptor Germaniae' of a new postwar Germany."[73] Jaspers was careful to distinguish between four different kinds of guilt: criminal, political, moral, and metaphysical. The only kind of guilt that could actually be described as collective, he argued, was political guilt, because "everybody is co-responsible for the way he is governed."[74] Inasmuch as Germans permitted such a regime to rise among them, they bear political responsibility for the actions of that regime. "We are collectively liable," Jaspers argues.[75] In modern western states it is impossible for individuals to escape political responsibility by declaring themselves uninterested in politics, because even citizens who refrain from political action are responsible for the consequences of their inactivity. "Politically everyone acts in the modern state, at least by voting, or failing to vote, in elections. The sense of political liability lets no man dodge."[76] Political guilt is thus collective guilt, and the Allied victors are the ultimate judges of such political guilt — the final instance. "All Germans without exception share in the political liability," Jaspers declares.[77] "A criminal state is charged against its whole population."[78] Criminal guilt, on the other hand, is limited only to those persons who have actually committed clearly defined crimes, and who have been found guilty by a duly constituted court of law. In contrast to many ordinary Germans, who viewed the Nuremberg trials as an affront to the entire German people, Jaspers argues that because the Nuremberg tribunal clearly limits the concept of criminal guilt to a relatively small number of criminals, it actually relieves the German people of the accusation of criminal guilt — while simultaneously making their political guilt even clearer. Precisely because of the clarity with which the Nuremberg trials demonstrate such political guilt, they are perceived by the majority of Germans as an affront: "Thus the citizen feels the treatment of his leaders as his own, even if they are criminals. In their persons the people are also condemned. Thus the indignity and mortification experienced by the leaders of the state are felt by the people as their own indignity and mortification. Hence their instinctive, initially unthinking rejection of the trial."[79] The German people, Jaspers implies, have confused criminal with political guilt, in spite of the fact that the chief prosecuting attorney of the Allies at Nuremberg had clearly stated "that we do not intend to accuse the whole German people."[80]

Moral guilt, Jaspers argues, can be judged only by the individual human in communion with his own conscience and in dialog with friends and loved ones. It is the duty of every German to examine his or her own conscience with respect to moral guilt, and to understand that even a subjective feeling of innocence is no guarantee of guiltlessness. Even though many Germans may have believed themselves to be doing their duty in obeying the commands of the state and working for a German victory in the war, "this unconditionality of a blind national viewpoint . . . was, even if in good conscience, moral guilt."[81] The claim that one was deceived by the Nazis cannot serve as an exculpation: Germans must examine whether or not they are at least partially responsible for their own deception — "for we are responsible for our delusions — for every delusion to which we succumb."[82]

As Rabinbach has noted, Jaspers's concept of "metaphysical guilt is by far the most ambiguous and difficult to grasp of the four categories."[83] And yet it is also probably the most important, even more emphatically collective than the concept of political guilt. Metaphysical guilt, as Jaspers understands it, extends to all human beings and makes everyone in the world "co-responsible for every wrong and every injustice in the world."[84] Especially guilty in a metaphysical sense are those who stand by idly and watch while crimes are committed. However, ultimately everyone in the world is responsible for everyone else in the world, because there is a necessary metaphysical solidarity among all human beings. Metaphysical guilt can be judged only by God, not by legal or political institutions, and not even by the individual human conscience. In a metaphysical sense, almost every living human being is guilty: "I am guilty of being still alive."[85]

Particularly important in Jaspers's reflections on German guilt is his analysis of the way in which the concept of guilt impinges upon the problem of German identity itself. It is here that Jaspers's understanding of guilt begins to resemble that of Jung, although, unlike Jung, Jaspers is not concerned with the subjective perceptions of outside observers about Germany and Germans. Rather, he is interested in what Germans feel about themselves. Like Jung, Jaspers argues that "we feel something like a co-responsibility for the acts of members of our families," and he suggests that Germany itself can be compared to a family.[86] Just as the individual family member feels guilty "whenever wrong is done by someone in the family," so too the German "feels concerned by everything growing from German roots."[87] Again like Jung, Jaspers recognizes the irrationality of such identification, and, like Jung, he sees no way to escape such irrationality. "We feel ourselves not only as individuals but as Germans. Every one, in his real being, is the German people."[88] Hitler's rise to power suggests, according to Jaspers, that there must be something in "our national tradition . . ., mighty and threatening, which is our moral ruin."[89] To be German, therefore, means to accept a specific moral responsibility that comes from the consciousness of German guilt. There "can be no doubt that we Germans, every one of us, are guilty in some way."[90] German guilt is collective in the political sense and individual in all other senses, but to be German — i.e., to be part of a national collective — means to accept the ethical responsibility that comes from a consciousness of all forms of German guilt. To be German is therefore "not a condition but a task."[91] The only path to political freedom and moral rectitude comes through the consciousness of guilt, and there can be no genuine German identity without such consciousness. For all Germans, therefore, guilt and the consciousness that comes from it are inescapable.

Hannah Arendt's reflections on guilt largely prefigured her later, more famous conclusions in the 1963 report on the trial of Adolf Eichmann, *Eichmann In Jerusalem: A Report on the Banality of Evil.*[92] Arendt focused on the totalitarian nature of the German state, suggesting that the identification between state and people made any careful differentiation of guilt extremely difficult. The machinery of "administrative mass murder" in the Germany of the Third Reich was so complex and widespread, she argued, that it demanded, in one way or another, the participation of almost every

German.[93] "That everyone, whether or not he is directly active in a murder camp, is forced to take part in one way or another in the workings of this machine of mass murder — that is the horrible thing."[94] In the totalitarian German state neutrality had become impossible, and the Nazis had succeeded in "making the existence of each individual in Germany depend either upon committing crimes or on complicity in crimes."[95] The epitome of Nazi totalitarianism was not the bohemian propaganda minister Joseph Goebbels or the adventurer Hermann Göring but rather the ordinary, boring *pater familias* Heinrich Himmler. As Arendt saw it, Nazi totalitarianism had transformed the German bourgeois into an instrument of political murder, using the appearance of respectability for its own ends. Himmler had based "his newest terror organization, covering the whole country, on the assumption that most people are not Bohemians nor fanatics, nor adventurers, nor sex maniacs, nor sadists, but, first and foremost, job-holders, and good family-men."[96] The chief problem with Nazi totalitarianism was not what most people in the Allied countries thought it was: it was not that Germans were beasts or barbarians, but rather that the Nazis had created a political structure in which ordinary Germans, in order to carry out their jobs, became mass murderers or at the very least complicit in mass murder. It was precisely the ordinary German's belief that he had nothing to do with politics that was the problem: this belief allowed him to live in the illusion of guiltlessness even while committing the most brutal of crimes. After all, he was only doing his job. "The transformation of the family man from a responsible member of society, interested in all public affairs, to a 'bourgeois' concerned only with his private existence and knowing no civic virtue, is an international modern phenomenon," Arendt argues, and therefore not limited exclusively to Germany.[97] The ordinary Nazi was nothing more or less than a diligent worker, and "when his occupation forces him to murder people he does not regard himself as a murderer because he has not done it out of inclination but in his professional capacity."[98] It is true, Arendt acknowledges, that the traditional German virtues of inwardness and private life, as well as the traditional German scorn for politics and public life, may have made Germany and the German "bourgeois" particularly susceptible to this form of totalitarianism. But in principle the "bourgeois" could exist in any modern mass society where the separation between public and private has been carried to such an extreme that individual human beings no longer feel themselves responsible for or interested in public life or even in the content of their own job-related interactions with public life. Therefore German declarations of innocence have a perverse kind of credibility, Arendt believes, because they are founded on the very separation of public and private life that made possible the commission of German crimes in the first place. German Nazis were right when they claimed that they were only carrying out orders and doing their job; but their obtuse belief in the exculpatory power of such statements was part of the mindset that had made them into criminals.

Martin Niemöller's approach to German guilt was more personal than that of most other thinkers who deliberated on the problem of guilt in the immediate postwar years. Himself instrumental in formulating and ratifying the Protestant church's Stuttgart declaration on guilt in October of 1945, Niemöller returned to the problem repeatedly in speeches, sermons, essays, and letters in the following years. Even though he had been interned as a personal prisoner of Adolf Hitler in the Dachau concentration camp throughout most of the Third Reich, Niemöller pointedly refused to claim his own innocence or to separate himself from the problem of guilt. His own recognition of the problem of guilt, he wrote, had come during a visit that he and his wife made to Dachau shortly after the end of the war. At the crematorium there was a sign that read: "In the years 1933–1945 238,756 people were burned here." Niemöller recounted that his wife had fainted when she saw the sign, amazed at the enormity of the crimes committed in that place. But "it was something else that made me shiver with cold at that moment," the pastor admitted: not the number of people killed but the dates. "My alibi," Niemöller wrote, "spanned the period from 1 July 1937 to the middle of 1945. But the sign said: '1933–1945.' Adam, where are you? Man, where have you been?"[99] The sudden recognition that he had spent four years in freedom while other human beings were being tortured, murdered, and incinerated, Niemöller wrote, struck him with the force of a criminal indictment: "now the warrant for my arrest had been signed, and I could no longer escape."[100] It was as if, at Dachau, Niemöller had seen a wanted poster with his own face on it.

Niemöller's further reflections on the problem of guilt revolved around the notions of freedom and responsibility. Paradoxically, he wrote, it was during his four years outside the concentration camp, prior to his incarceration in 1937, that he had truly been unfree. "I was not a free man then. I had already evaded my true responsibility," he wrote.[101] True freedom, Niemöller claimed, came only with the recognition of responsibility. The unfree person seeks to escape responsibility, hiding under the shadow of a higher authority. But God grants human beings freedom, and that freedom entails a responsibility which they cannot evade by delegating it to others. Germans had been liberated from Hitler by the Allied armies, Niemöller declared, but the only true liberation is self-liberation; hence Germans would only truly be free once they had come to a recognition — each person in his own individual way — of their own responsibility. "Responsibility! For twelve years we were told about it . . ., as if our duties and responsibilities were being determined somewhere from above and from outside, and as if we ourselves need do nothing but obey."[102] But responsibility lies not in following the orders of an outside authority but in the inner voice of the conscience; and every fellow human being who is wronged and who suffers speaks with the voice of Christ crucified. Therefore if Germans now seek to evade their responsibility for other human beings, they are merely fleeing once again from the consciousness of freedom which they had so successfully avoided during the Third Reich. "We no longer knew about responsibility," Niemöller writes of the Third Reich itself. And of the present he declares: "We are being made responsible, but we do not want to be made responsible. And by refusing to be made responsible we are depriving ourselves of the possibility of becoming free again."[103] Hence for Niemöller the question of German guilt was really a question of German freedom: it was impossible to have the one without the other. And the German evasion of guilt was really an evasion of freedom.[104]

German writers addressed the problem of guilt from a variety of different viewpoints and with varying degrees of success in the years leading up to and following the end of the war. With respect to the question of whether the German nation as a whole was primarily a victim or a perpetrator, many writers were understandably ambivalent. The Communist writer Johannes R. Becher, later to be Minister of Culture in the German Democratic Republic, was a good example of that ambivalence. In an article entitled "Deutschland klagt an!" (Germany Accuses!) published in the journal *Aufbau* (Rebuilding) in the Soviet occupation zone in January of 1946, during the Nuremberg trials, Becher simultaneously accused prominent Nazis in Nuremberg of crimes against the German people — thus implicitly claiming that Germany was a victim of Hitler — and acknowledged that both Germany as a state and individual Germans had become at least partially guilty of Nazi crimes. "We bear witness to the monstrous crimes committed by the Nazi war criminals against us, the German people," declared Becher, suggesting that the primary guilt of the Nazis was a guilt with respect to Germany and Germans.[105] Invoking the millions of German soldiers who had become casualties of war, Becher implied that such soldiers were primarily victims of the Nazis, not perpetrators of a criminal war. "Millions of German men, fallen on the battlefields, bring their accusation," Becher wrote. Among these soldiers were "men in the bloom of manhood, youths, yes even children and old men," and they were all, Becher suggested, victims of the Nazis; even in silence they were, along with millions of other dead Germans, "screaming inside us."[106] Because Nazi leaders had appeared to Germans "in the mask of the virtuous citizen," many ordinary Germans had been unable to perceive them as the criminals that they were, Becher believed.[107] In addition to war and murder, therefore, the Nazis were guilty of a grotesque political deception. With respect to the attempted genocide of European Jewry, Becher mourned "the systematic eradication of our Jewish fellow citizens," which, he asserted, had covered Germans with such shame "that even after the dust of the Nazi criminals has long been scattered in the winds, we will still have to bear it." Therefore, he insisted, "what was done to the Jews was done to *us*."[108] This assertion of what Herf has called "solidarity with the Jews" was no doubt an attempt on Becher's part to increase ordinary Germans' understanding of and sense of anger at the crimes committed by the Nazi regime against German Jews, but it was nevertheless both an inadmissible cooptation of Jewish suffering and a misunderstanding of what was later to become known as the Holocaust, since what had been done to the Jews by the Nazis was done to them precisely as Jews and not to "us" as non-Jewish Germans. While Herf is no doubt correct in describing Becher's statement as an improvement on "the vagueness about anti-Semitism apparent in" much of Becher's previous writing, Becher was still remarkably imprecise in his formulations.[109] Moreover, Becher spoke only of "our Jewish fellow citizens," i.e. German Jews, and was silent about the Nazis' systematic murder of non-German Jews in Eastern Europe. In a ten-page article on Nazi crimes, Becher devoted only one ten-line paragraph to crimes committed outside Germany against non-Germans, admitting that "we would not be . . . on the way to transforming ourselves into new, freedom-loving German people if we did not include in our charges everything done by the Nazi war criminals to other peoples."[110] Once again, Becher's presentation of the German people as victims of the Nazis was probably an attempt to increase Germans' anti-Nazi fervor and thus to encourage a positive political and moral transformation. If Germans perceived themselves as victims of the Nazis, they would be less likely to identify themselves with the Nazis. Nevertheless, Becher's language obscured the nature of both German crimes and German complicity. The Nazis, Becher wrote, were guilty of high crimes against the German spirit and had "dishonored, shamed, and desecrated the name of Germany," so that today "the name of the German . . . has become . . . a curse and a calumny."[111] Finally, Becher acknowledged that every individual German must examine his or her own conscience and ask to what extent "he himself is affected by the devastating weight of our accusations." The public tribunal in Nuremberg must, Becher argued, be "accompanied by an *inner* judgment that every German must carry out upon himself."[112] If Germans were honest with themselves, they would probably find that no one was completely free of blame. Becher expressed his hope for the reappearance of "something like a conscience, like a national conscience."[113] Even more important than the judgments made by the Allied court at Nuremberg would be the judgments made in the future by conscientious Germans themselves.

Becher's colleague the playwright Friedrich Wolf was more explicit in his insistence on German guilt in an article published in the fall of 1945. All too many Germans, Wolf wrote, were seeking to exculpate themselves, claiming never to have committed any crimes nor to have been even partially responsible for injustice. "When one speaks today with many of our countrymen about the darkness of the past thirteen years," he noted sarcastically, "one could get the impression that there were no Nazis at all in Germany."[114] It was true,

Wolf acknowledged, that Hitler had misused and deceived the German people; but the German people were responsible for having allowed themselves to be so treated.[115] One of the least admirable character traits of the Germans, Wolf suggested, was their tendency to blame others for the problems they have created themselves. The German people's failure of self-recognition and self-criticism, Wolf implied, had helped to lead to the Nazi disaster in the first place, and now the same failure was interfering with any genuine understanding of the catastrophe. All too many Germans were turning away from the question of guilt and sticking their heads in the sand, Wolf argued. Instead of looking to others and blaming them for crimes, the playwright suggested, Germans ought to begin by examining their own consciences. In the course of such an examination they might come to realize that the ruined city of Berlin and many other ruined European cities were concrete reminders of German guilt. The vast army of the German dead gazed upon all Germans still living, Wolf wrote, wanting to know "whether we have learned something from this horrible lesson . . ., whether we have sat in judgment upon ourselves, whether we have gone through the decisive process inside our own hearts."[116] Ultimately Wolf agreed with Becher on the need to transform the outward trial taking place at Nuremberg into an inward trial carried out by the conscience of each individual German.

Bertolt Brecht was similarly ambivalent in his judgment of the German people. In most of his public statements, Brecht took the position that the German people were Hitler's first victim and therefore free of guilt. "Before Hitler and the people behind him in the army, the diplomatic corps, and in finance conquered Czechoslovakia, the Scandinavian countries, Holland, Belgium, France, the Balkans, and Belarus, they conquered the German people," he believed.[117] Brecht energetically sought to refute the Nazi thesis of complete identity between the German people and Hitler: "Hitler and the men behind him are not Germany, no matter what they may assert."[118] In such statements Brecht ignored the election victories of the Nazis during the early 1930s, the extent of popular support for the Nazis throughout most of the Third Reich, and the relative lack of resistance to the Nazis even during the final years of the war. And yet in private Brecht was far more critical and suspicious of ordinary Germans, acknowledging the existence of widespread popular support for the Nazis. One of the reasons for Brecht's willingness to live in a Communist dictatorship after the war was his fear that in a free democratic vote "the Nazis will be elected."[119] Much of Brecht's thinking about Germany during the 1940s and 1950s was governed by the concept of "deutsche misere" (German wretchedness) a specifically problematic German historical development which, Brecht believed, had led both to the self-destruction of German intellectuals and to particularly brutal forms of government, including ultimately the Nazi dictatorship. In Brecht's view the Nazi regime was anything but an inexplicable anomaly; it was rather the logical consequence of German history. As he wrote in a letter to the set designer Caspar Neher in December of 1946, "I never considered Nazism to be a deformity; I always considered it the result of normal development."[120] Ultimately, however, "deutsche misere" was the result of capitalist relations of production and could be overcome only by a socialist revolution. For Brecht, the road away from Hitler was "the road to social revolution."[121] The development of capitalism in Germany might have taken a particularly brutal path, but it was essentially capitalism, not Germany, that was at fault. It was not the German citizen as such but rather the German citizen as bourgeois who was a Nazi: "only when he is no longer a bourgeois is he no longer a Nazi."[122] National Socialism was, for Brecht, the "socialism of the petit-bourgeoisie,"[123] i.e. a desperate attempt on the part of German capitalists to avoid the advent of an actual socialist revolution — which would destroy their power — by creating a reassuring and counterrevolutionary "ersatz socialism."[124] Far more critical of the Nuremberg trials than Becher, Brecht described them as capitalism's attempt to disclaim its own responsibility for Nazi crimes: "Nuremberg: the counterrevolution eats its own children."[125] Ultimately, then, for Brecht questions of German guilt were moot points, obscuring the main problem, which was capitalist guilt and the continuing brutality and barbarity of class oppression.

Two important works dealing with the problem of German guilt in the immediate postwar period were Theodor Plievier's novel *Stalingrad* (1945) and Carl Zuckmayer's play *Des Teufels General* (The Devil's General, 1946), both of which featured as primary characters an aging German military officer who, over the course of many difficult wartime experiences, comes to understand the nature of guilt — not just German guilt generally but his own guilt specifically. At the beginning of Plievier's novel, Colonel Vilshofen is in charge of a tank regiment near Stalingrad, and his own views on the war are more or less in line with Nazi ideology. In the course of only one summer, Vilshofen's victorious tank regiment has worked its way southward from the Carpathian mountains over the Dniester River into Ukraine, then over the Mius and Don rivers, burning villages and flattening fields on its way to Stalingrad; Vilshofen's regiment is "one of the hundred fists that were to shatter and crush the independence and will of other nations."[126] The colonel is a highly competent military officer — and is therefore ultimately promoted to the rank of general — and a good leader of men who knows the names and geographic origins of the members of his tank crews. During the winter of 1942–3, as his regiment is decimated at Stalingrad, Vilshofen begins to question not only the leadership of the German high command but also the morality of the war itself. Recognizing the impossibility of breaking out of the trap into which the German Sixth Army has dug itself, Vilshofen asks: "What was our crime?"[127] As matters get even worse, he asks: "And who has lost his honor in this act and forfeited his life?"[128] Finally Vilshofen comes to understand that he has not simply been misled by Hitler and the military leadership; he has willingly, even eagerly participated in Nazi crimes himself, making himself just as guilty as all the rest. It is not the proud German eagle that should be the symbol of Nazi Germany, Vilshofen recognizes, but rather the crow, feeding on weakness, disease, and death. Far from simply feeling sorry for himself, Vilshofen comes to understand the role that he himself has played in his own destruction: "Now we must keep still and realize what we've done to not just one city and not just one country and not just one people."[129] What is happening to one German army at Stalingrad will happen to the entire German nation at home, Vilshofen realizes: it will be surrounded, trapped, and destroyed. The catastrophe is far more than simply military, "not only the wrong lines drawn on a strategic map, not only mistakes in columns of figures."[130] After the inevitable defeat of the Sixth Army, as he watches an endless procession of German prisoners of war being led away, Vilshofen asks himself:

> How heavy is the guilt?
> How does the dead Stalingrad army weigh in the balance, how much does this ghostly procession of prisoners weigh? What else must be laid upon the scales? Can guilt be weighed? How can it be weighed?
> Children shot, women shot, old men, helpless prisoners shot — according to orders, "as the law provides." What sort of law is that?[131]

In spite of all talk of military duty and honor, Vilshofen comes to understand that as a respected and conscientious officer he is, paradoxically, even more responsible for the defeat and dishonor of the men entrusted to his care than the many cowardly leaders who sought to escape from Stalingrad: "He had been even more catastrophic than the bad officers. It was not the bad officers . . . whom no one believed in who had led the troops into disaster. No, it was he, who had possessed credibility."[132]

But Plievier's novel shows that it is not just high military officers like Vilshofen who are guilty. Vilshofen's counterpart within the ranks of ordinary soldiers is noncommissioned officer August Gnotke, a former SA[133] man who — as Gnotke tells Vilshofen at the end of the novel — has also come to the gradual realization that he shares blame for his own fate and the fate of his comrades. As Vilshofen sees it, Gnotke:

> had retraced his steps to the source of the German disease. The generals were against the Führer because he was losing the war; this man was against the Führer because he had begun the war and because, ten years earlier, he had already begun a war against the German people and had misused the people for aims hostile to its own interests.[134]

Vilshofen's image of a "war against the German people" still makes it possible for Germans to view themselves as Hitler's first victims, not as perpetrators in their own right. But Gnotke's and Vilshofen's recognition of their own complicity in Hitler's war, and Vilshofen's ruminations on Russian civilian casualties make any declarations of innocence more difficult. Plievier's novel was one of the few works of the immediate postwar period explicitly to thematize the suffering of non-German civilians and hence the concrete guilt of the Wehrmacht — a topic still controversial over half a century later. At the end of the novel Gnotke and Vilshofen are seen marching through the frozen Volga landscape; their path toward each other is a path toward understanding and recognition of guilt.[135]

In Zuckmayer's *Des Teufels General*, the most popular German play of the immediate postwar period, it is the air force general Harras — like Plievier's Vilshofen, a fine military man with a keen understanding of his subordinates — who is transformed from a competent and efficient military technician into a bitter but ultimately helpless critic of the Nazi regime. At the beginning of the play Harras, although scornful of the most repulsive Nazi party functionaries, nevertheless takes pride in his status as "a technician, a soldier."[136] Just like his Nazi Party partners, Harras wants to get to the bottom of incidents of sabotage that have been causing some of his fighter planes to crash. By the end of the play it turns out that Harras's trusted subordinate Oderbruch, an engineer in the Reich Ministry for Air Travel, is himself responsible for the sabotage. Thus Oderbruch causes the death of the handsome and personable young officer Friedrich Eilers, who had earlier declared Oderbruch to be a man "to whom one can entrust one's fortune, without a receipt. Even one's wife and children."[137] The play thus revolves around the question of conflicting loyalties and responsibilities — to one's military comrades on the one hand and to humanity and moral principle on the other. In sabotaging German planes, Oderbruch is betraying the trust of his friends and comrades; but at the same time he is fighting against the larger evil of Nazi tyranny and making it more difficult for his Luftwaffe comrades to carry out Nazi military policy. Towards the end of the play Eilers's widow Anne visits Harras in the technical office of the airport where Harras is trying to get to the bottom of the sabotage and accuses him of being primarily responsible not simply for the death of her husband but for the death of her husband in the service of Nazi tyranny. It is not just that Harras must shoulder the "technical responsibility" for not yet having gotten to the bottom of the sabotage, but that, himself scornful of the Nazis and their ideology, he nevertheless served the Nazis and was willing to send others to their death in the Nazis' service. Anne Eilers accuses Harras of having let her husband die for the Nazis: "Die senselessly. You looked on and did nothing to save him. That is the guilt for which there can be no forgiveness."[138] Whereas Friedrich Eilers had believed in the Nazis and their war, thus having at least some subjective justification for his actions, Harras himself had served the Nazis without belief. "You kill without justification or belief, for a cause which you hate and despise," Anne Eilers declares.[139] In spite of the critic Dirk Niefanger's argument that because of his cynical superiority "the character Harras . . . is by no means put into question because of this accusation of guilt," the arguments of Anne Eilers contribute to Harras's despair and ultimate self-destruction.[140] Unable to get to the bottom of the sabotage and shocked by this forceful condemnation of him by the widow of his former subordinate, Harras decides — after some prodding by the Nazis — to commit suicide. In his last meeting with Oderbruch, the latter acknowledges to Harras his own role in the sabotage and explains his motivation. Asked by Harras what had happened to make him become an active opponent of the Nazis, Oderbruch replies that although he never lost "a brother in a concentration camp" or suffered persecution, "one day — I was ashamed of being a German."[141] If Hitler wins the war, Oderbruch believes, "then Germany is lost. Then the world is lost."[142] Germans like Harras are being made into Hitler's weapon, and their guilt will continue and carry on into future generations if individual Germans like Oderbruch do not take upon themselves the responsibility of resisting the Nazis. Oderbruch identifies his primary motivation as shame, and Harras ultimately accepts Oderbruch's argument, viewing his colleague's actions as a judgment of death upon himself (Harras) for his own complicity. What he sees as a "judgment of God" is, he declares, "signed with blood"; he is therefore strengthened in his determination to commit suicide, which he sees as the carrying out of the death penalty upon himself.[143] As he leaves to fly a plane that he knows is sabotaged, Harras acknowledges to Oderbruch the extent of his own guilt: "He who has been the devil's general on earth and bombed his way for him — must prepare a place for him in Hell, too. Don't give up, Oderbruch! You were right in everything."[144] Like Plievier's novel, Zuckmayer's play attacked the idea of the relatively innocent and good-hearted army officer, thus eroding exculpatory distinctions between the culpable Nazi Party and a supposedly blameless German Wehrmacht. As a human being and as a military officer, Harras is certainly more likeable and personable than the play's repulsive Nazi figures. But such superiority, far from exculpating Harras, actually makes him doubly guilty. Precisely because he is an effective, charismatic military leader, his failure to oppose the Nazis bears particular weight.[145]

The problem of German guilt was at the center of Ernst von Salomon's popular 1951 book *Der Fragebogen,* which clearly showed how the concept of collective guilt could be used in the postwar period for exculpatory purposes. A member of the so-called conservative revolution against the Weimar Republic during the 1920s and 1930s, von Salomon had been imprisoned for five years for conspiring to assassinate Walter Rathenau in 1922; his first novel *Die Geächteten* (The Ostracized, 1930) dealt with these events. As a revolutionary conservative brought up in the tradition of Prussian elitism, von Salomon despised the plebeian Nazis and kept his distance from them throughout the years of the Third Reich. He was nevertheless incarcerated by American authorities at the end of the war because of the role he had played in helping to destabilize the Weimar Republic. *Der Fragebogen* was based on the questionnaires distributed by American occupation authorities to German civilians in the immediate postwar years for the purpose of determining the extent of their complicity with the Nazi regime. In essence, the book was nothing more than von Salomon's completed questionnaire, expanded to monstrous size. By taking the questionnaire to such an absurd extreme, von Salomon sought to demonstrate the absurdity of the American questionnaires themselves. His book was essentially an autobiography covering the span of German history in the first half of the twentieth century, in which von Salomon had been born and lived most of his life. It would be impossible to understand his own individual life and actions, von Salomon seemed to be saying, without also understanding the entire complex history of the German nation. The individual, he believed, is caught up in a collective which he did not necessarily choose, but from which he cannot escape. Far from being a criminal, the helpless individual is in fact a victim.

At the center of *Der Fragebogen* is von Salomon's depiction of German history during the Third Reich. This chapter begins with a description of the so-called Night of Broken Glass (Reichskristallnacht), the officially organized pogrom against German Jews that occurred on November 9, 1938. Von Salomon and his female companion Ille experience the pogrom while strolling around their bourgeois neighborhood of Charlottenburg in Berlin, where they see SA thugs breaking the windows of stores owned by Jews. Horrified by such blatant disregard for law, order, and property rights, von Salomon and Ille quickly return to their apartment, where the youthful and somewhat naive woman asks her wiser male companion the crucial question: "Whose fault is it all?"[146]

Von Salomon's lengthy response to this question-within-the-questionnaire is initially a self-defensive "Do you mean it's mine?" immediately followed by the words "Yes, it's my fault too. We're all to blame." The words "we're all" serve to nullify the specific individual responsibility implied in the self-defensive question "Do you mean it's mine?" Confronted with Ille's denials that she is in any way responsible for what has happened, von Salomon declares:

> That's their trick, they make everybody guilty. All they've ever done is carry out the mandate of the people. The people means you, and me. But, God damn it all! I never gave them any mandate! When I thought a thing ought to be done I did it myself.[147]

In the first three sentences of this passage, von Salomon is a member of the German people in whose name crimes are committed; in the last three sentences, von Salomon is an individualist insisting on his own autonomy. Initially the writer seems to recognize his own participation in the larger collective entity "German people," and he understands that the Nazis are committing their crimes in the name of precisely this entity. In this way, he says, they are making "everybody guilty." But in the final sentences von Salomon dissociates himself both from the German collective and from the Nazis' crimes, implying that any Nazi claim to represent him as an individual is mendacious. A moment later the writer says to Ille: "And how many Party members do you imagine are doing and saying just this, just like you and I, honorable, decent Party members?"[148] It is not just non-Nazi Germans who are wondering how they have gotten into such a difficult moral and political predicament, von Salomon believes; throughout Germany there are "honest and upright" Nazi party members who would prefer to have nothing to do with the crimes now being committed in their name. What is important is not the way that von Salomon and many others may have contributed to the downfall of German democracy and helped the Nazis to power; the only thing that matters at the moment is these honest Germans' subjective feeling of horror when confronted with Hitler's crimes.

For von Salomon, the rise of the Nazis is the result not of specific political and moral failures but rather part of a much larger modern catastrophe involving the loss of religious faith and the rise of large-scale, impersonal collectives that render the individual powerless. As Richard Herzinger has put it, von Salomon views Hitler as "a kind of demonic figure of fate" and Nazi barbarity as "a trial that the German people must see through to the bitter end."[149] It is the task of the heroic, fatalistic individual to bear the burden of historical fate and maintain his personal integrity. "How could it come about that everyone was guilty, which means of course that no one was guilty?" Salomon asks, as if to emphasize the perverse attractiveness of the concept of collective guilt.[150] If everyone is equally guilty, then no individual can be blamed for specific misdeeds or failures; guilt becomes so diffuse and omnipresent as to become meaningless in any individual case. This is probably the primary reason for von Salomon's resentment of the American questionnaire, which, by its very existence, demands an individual confrontation with specific personal complicity; if all Germans were equally guilty, there would be no need for such a questionnaire. Seeking to head off any accusations of complicity because of his failure to protest Nazi atrocities, von Salomon asks Ille rhetorically why it is that he and his friends are "not standing in front of the synagogues with outstretched arms" to protect the life and property of German Jews during the pogrom. It is not so much that upright people are few in number. Rather, it is that individual action and even identity have themselves become meaningless:

> We can no longer live from within ourselves. Everything that is happening about us is not the product of the internal life of those who are doing it; it is the product of a collective. And a man who will not accept and believe in that collective is dead. The collective always acts unconditionally. It also demands our unconditional faith and acceptance. But this collective has not gathered us up into itself, it has atomised us. Atomised fragments cannot constitute a community, but only an explosive mass.[151]

Although von Salomon's self-justifications here are anything but clear and logical, at bottom is the vision of the National Socialists as representing a barbarous collective from which individualists like himself are excluded and therefore rendered socially and politically impotent. Such individualists have become mere atoms without a connection to the German whole, he believes. The all-powerful Nazi collective "gives no one the possibility of achieving solidarity by performing an individual act."[152] The Nazi thugs burning down synagogues are hence not acting of their own volition but rather as zombies imbued with the power of a brutal collective. Even individualist Germans who are excluded from the Nazi collective are incapable of resisting the onslaught of barbarism. They are, von Salomon argues, also zombies, because they do not participate in the life of the all-powerful collective. Since they are "dead," they cannot be held responsible for what they have — or have not — done. In their lifelessness and impotence, they are even more victimized than the actual victims. "The appalling thing is that we cannot help ourselves, and far more is happening to us than to the Jews," von Salomon declares.[153] Non-Jewish German individualists are far more to be pitied than Jews, he insists, blatantly minimizing the persecution of the Jews while maximizing the description of his own purported victimization.

In his efforts at self-justification von Salomon tells Ille the story of a nocturnal streetcar ride during which he had once become an unwilling witness to two SS men's torment of an elderly — and probably Jewish — woman. Von Salomon's efforts to help the woman by alarming the streetcar conductor are counterproductive. He must therefore endure the hatred of the very woman whom he has tried to help. In her eyes — he believes — he is simply drawing unwanted attention to her, therefore making her even more vulnerable to her tormentors. Von Salomon draws the conclusion — logical only if one accepts his premise of an all-powerful Nazi collective — that any demonstration of civil courage is necessarily counterproductive, resulting only in further degradation.[154] "If it is the case that we are all atomised, isolated, incompetent, sterile, without any direct connection with the now discredited collective," then no individual — least of all a skeptical individualist like von Salomon himself — can be considered guilty for the crimes of the collective.[155] In order to illustrate his point further, von Salomon cites the burning of the Reichstag building in 1933 — which he believes to have been an act of brave but futile resistance to Nazi tyranny — arguing that it led only to the strengthening of the Nazi Party and the further weakening of the German resistance. In "these circumstances," von Salomon believes, "all action is crime," and therefore the only reasonable response "is to do nothing. It is at any rate the only decent course. And it is also the most difficult thing in the world, a sort of Gandhi-ism without Gandhi."[156] Whether intentionally or not, von Salomon is here confusing Gandhi's nonviolent but certainly active resistance with a policy of fatalistic passivity. The helpless individual withdraws into heroic but impotent paralysis, observing with melancholy scorn the degradation of the world around him. After he has made these reflections and realized how the irresistible power of the collective helps to exculpate him as an individual, von Salomon finds: "To my surprise I suddenly felt in an excellent humour. There seemed to be something to the methods of the psychoanalysts after all."[157]

In response to item 110 of the questionnaire, which asks "Have you ever been a member of any anti-Nazi underground party or groups since 1933?" von Salomon responds "yes"; in response to question 111, which asks "Which one?" he replies "Master Group Imming." As it turns out in his subsequent explanations, "Frau Imming was my cleaning lady." Von Salomon claims that this woman was "the very personification of the resistance."[158] Frau Imming is a loquacious Social Democrat who speaks a folksy Berlin dialect; needless to say, she is highly critical of the Nazis. "I loved Frau Imming very much, and she loved me," von Salomon declares, as if the affection of a Social Democratic cleaning lady for her reactionary employer were sufficient evidence of the latter's anti-Nazi convictions. Moreover, von Salomon declares: "Approximately eighty per cent of the German nation belonged to Master Group Imming."[159] Thus even while von Salomon seems to accept the concept of collective guilt, he does so only for exculpatory purposes: in order to demonstrate that the vast majority of Germans, including himself, have nothing to do with Nazi tyranny. Like himself and Frau Imming, most Germans during the Third Reich were caught up in political developments which they were helpless to resist. Even though his *Fragebogen* is nothing but a massive demonstration of the perceived ridiculousness of the American questionnaires, von Salomon declares himself to be "the one person in all the world who has really taken . . . [the] Fragebogen seriously."[160]

In his novel *Das Beil von Wandsbek* (The Axe of Wandsbek, 1943; first German-language publication in 1947), the socialist Arnold Zweig took an entirely different approach to the problem of guilt. *Das Beil von Wandsbek* is the story of Albert Teetjen, a butcher in Hamburg who is facing severe competition from large department stores. Threatened by financial ruin because of his dwindling customer base, Teetjen agrees, in the autumn of 1937, to sell his skills to the Nazis, who are looking for the services of an amateur executioner to carry out death sentences on four left-wing inmates of the Fuhlsbüttel prison. For 2,000 marks, Teetjen — covered in a black mask to preserve his anonymity — chops off the heads of the condemned men. Initially, the butcher and his pretty wife Stine seem to have regained their financial stability as a result of this unconventional execution; but it is not long before word gets out in the neighborhood that their newfound prosperity is based on blood money. Some customers avoid Teetjen's butcher shop out of solidarity with the prisoners he killed; others, uncomfortable with the possibility that their meat is being cut with the same implement used in the execution — the axe of the novel's title — are worried about hygiene in the store; and Teetjen's SS buddies resent the fact that he did not share any of his sudden wealth with them. In the end, Teetjen loses almost all of his customers and is forced to give up his butcher shop; he and his wife commit suicide. They have betrayed their fellow working men and women and must therefore die. Their fate is that of Judas Iscariot in the Bible. But Teetjen's guilt, although inexcusable, is nevertheless understandable. Albert Teetjen is an ordinary man, a petit-bourgeois shopkeeper afraid of social decline. The guilt with which he covers himself has its origin in economic desperation.[161] The *Schuld* for which Teetjen is quite literally paid has a double meaning, connoting both moral guilt and monetary debt; in Albert Teetjen's case the latter precedes and ultimately leads to the former. Those with money can easily afford the luxury of being without *Schuld* — in both senses of the word — but the poor have a far more difficult time. Albert Teetjen is faced with financial ruin — a mountain of debt — and he therefore also takes upon himself moral ruin — a mountain of guilt. "Should he tell these people the tale of the debts that had . . . beset him, and explain that but for the pressure of debt and the prospect of disaster, he would never have deigned to act as executioner?" Teetjen asks himself in response to the accusations of his SS "comrades."[162]

In Zweig's novel guilt thus goes beyond the psychological, criminal, political, moral, and metaphysical categories developed by Jung and Jaspers; it acquires an economic component as well. In the social panorama of the book, a great many people are morally guilty, but it is Albert Teetjen who must "pay" for the guilt in public perception. The thoughtful prison warden Heinrich Koldewey, a traditional German conservative, detests Hitler and the Nazis, and he is convinced of the innocence of his four prisoners; but he does nothing to save the men in his care, and any efforts he makes against Hitler are too little, too late. Koldewey admits to himself that "everyone like him in the old Europe, or at least in Germany," is at the very least guilty of gross negligence and possibly even worse.[163] The capitalist Hans Peter Footh, owner of a small fleet of ships in Hamburg, is initially responsible for the offer made to his former army buddy Teetjen and therefore just as guilty for the four deaths as Teetjen is; moreover, Footh is eager to profit from the expropriation of a "Jewish-owned" shipping fleet and thus converts guilt into profit. Zweig's novel paints a complex portrait of class society in Nazi Germany; almost everyone in the novel except those actively resisting Nazi tyranny and those forced by the Nazis to leave Germany is in some way guilty of or at least connected to horrible misdeeds. But it is the socially weak and impecunious butcher Teetjen who becomes the embodiment of German guilt. Stine Teetjen's doctor Käte Neumeier — who marries Koldewey during the course of the novel, and who is initially responsible not only for the boycott against Teetjen's butcher shop but also for the renewed contact between Teetjen and Footh which had led to the executions in the first place — understands that the theory of collective guilt can be seen as an evasive maneuver on the part of her own bourgeois class. As she argues on her wedding night, at a moment when alcohol and excitement have brought back memories of her youthful radicalism, Karl Marx "would perhaps have said that the bourgeois mentality . . . always shelters behind the nation, when that class, which in fact cuts across all frontiers, gets into difficulties."[164] Whatever ordinary people think about their leaders, they must nevertheless suffer for what those leaders have done. Poor people have little or no influence over the course of political affairs; it is the wealthy members of the educated bourgeoisie who organize and profit from politics throughout most of the world; when things go wrong, however, they do not want to pay the price. If the social world can be thought of as a globe, then ordinary, uneducated people form the "more or less inarticulate core and filling" of that globe, while the privileged classes form the smooth, attractive surface.[165] "This same good society, to which we, too, belong, controls its own activities, and all the contents within the globe."[166] In the event of disaster, the privileged and powerful prefer to disappear beneath the surface of the sphere, placing the ordinary man on the street and his supposed collective responsibility between them and the consciousness of class guilt. If Marx had viewed the capitalist system as the organized expropriation of surplus value for the benefit of the wealthy, then Zweig views the discourse of collective guilt as the organized foisting-off of responsibility onto the poor and powerless. The ruling classes steal not only money but also innocence; the lower classes are not just poor but also — therefore — guilty. Hence Heinrich Vormweg's judgment that *Das Beil von Wandsbek* is only superficially a Marxist novel misses the mark; on the contrary, Zweig's novel adds a specifically Marxist dimension to discussions of German guilt.[167] In Zweig's novel it becomes clear that German capitalists bear the primary responsibility for Hitler's rise to power, but that they are all too happy to have a man like Albert Teetjen carry out their dirty work for them. If Teetjen is Judas, then Koldewey and his kind are Pontius Pilate, seeking to wash their hands of guilt by implicating the common people. Both Teetjen and Koldewey are guilty, and, as one character in the novel reflects, "men must answer for their deeds."[168] But Teetjen, like the vast majority of Hitler's minions, is both burdened with guilt and himself a victim, and he must pay not only for his own misdeeds but for those of others as well.

Wolfgang Koeppen's novel *Der Tod in Rom* (Death in Rome, 1954) deals with the problem of German guilt in a complex and sophisticated way. Strongly influenced by Thomas Mann's works *Der Tod in Venedig* (Death in Venice) and *Doktor Faustus, Der Tod in Rom* parallels the former work in telling the story of the death of a famous Northern European in an Italian city, and it parallels the latter work in following the career of a modernist German composer. At the center of the novel are two German men from different generations: the youthful composer Siegfried Pfaffrath — like Mann's Gustav von Aschenbach in *Der Tod in Venedig* an artist and a pederast — and his brutal uncle Gottlieb Judejahn, a former high Nazi official who has been condemned in absentia at Nuremberg for crimes against humanity. Now working for an Arab government, Judejahn is visiting Rome incognito to meet his wife and his brother-in-law Friedrich Wilhelm Pfaffrath, Siegfried's father. It is Judejahn who dies of a heart attack at the novel's end; prior to his heart attack, he shoots and kills a Jewish woman whose father had previously been victimized by the Nazis. Judejahn's son — given the appropriate name Adolf by his Nazi father — is now a young priest seeking to atone for the crimes of his family. Siegfried's father Friedrich Wilhelm is described in the novel as a German *Bildungsbürger* and *Spießer*, "the pedant and owner of the leather-bound edition of Goethe."[169] Friedrich Wilhelm sees himself as a fine, upstanding German citizen who has nothing to do with the crimes of the Nazis — "My father could tell himself that he was innocent of murder and arson. All he'd done was watch." — but in fact it is precisely ordinary citizens like him who made it possible for Nazis like his criminal brother-in-law, the murderer Judejahn, to come to power and remain in power.[170] As Judejahn himself reflects on seeing a group of such bourgeois and petit-bourgeois German conformists during his peregrinations through Rome:

> He had gone further than the burghers in the hall, but it was they who had made it possible for him to go so far. They had underwritten his wanderings with their lives. They had invoked blood, they had summoned him, exhorted him, the world will be won by the sword, they had made speeches, there was no death to compare with death in battle, they had given him his first uniform, and had cowered before the new uniform he had made for himself, they had praised his every action, they had held him up as an example to their children, they had summoned the 'Reich' into being, and endured death and injury and the smoke from burning bodies all for the sake of Germany.[171]

For Friedrich Wilhelm and his wife Anna, music and the other arts serve the purpose of giving life a noble, uplifting flair, "an optimistic sky, a rosy dome over the grey globe."[172] The more problematic and horrible life becomes, "the more loftily the pink superstructure had to float over the all too human." Pfaffrath and his wife believe "in the confectioner's temple of art, a sweet substance formed into ideal allegory," and therefore they are deeply disturbed by Siegfried's relentlessly modern, severe music.[173] Of course Siegfried has chosen his profession and his approach to music precisely in order to create as much spiritual distance as possible between himself and the family of which he is so deeply ashamed. Because art for the Philistine Friedrich Wilhelm had always been a compensation and cosmetic disguise for an inadequate social reality — in other words: a lie — Siegfried subjects his art to the most severe of aesthetic and moral criteria. His music is dedicated to truth: "The legend says that when we behold the truth, we turn to stone. I'd like to see the unveiled picture, even if I turn into a pillar."[174] For Siegfried music becomes a vehicle in the search for a truth that had been denied by the Nazis; art is Siegfried's substitute for a missing God. Tormented by the enormity of German crimes and his family's own complicity in those crimes — "it happened happened happened it can't be changed can't be changed it's damned damned damned damned" — Siegfried views himself as guilty — and therefore damned — by association, what Jung had called "contact guilt."[175] His family is nothing but a trap that he wants to escape: "the family, the prison they wanted to lock me up in for life."[176] Because of his self-disgust at his own relationship to his family, Siegfried has a horror of sex; his pederasty can be understood as a refusal to engage in sexual reproduction: "the uncanny lust for life to which we are condemned revolted him, the urge to procreate which made fools of even the poorest people, this appearance of eternity which is no eternity . . ."[177] For Siegfried sexual reproduction means the continuation of the very force that led to Nazi tyranny in the first place; it is therefore a crime:

> Siegfried did not want to reproduce himself. The thought of causing a life that could be subjected to unforeseeable encounters, coincidences, actions, and reactions and which through deed, thought, or further reproduction of its own could once again have consequences throughout the future, the idea of being the father of a child, this provocation to the world, truly appalled him and spoiled any contact with girls for him, even if they were using contraceptives, which were in and of themselves already humiliating and disgusting, and which humiliatingly and disgustingly pointed out the very thing which was to be prevented. Physical procreation seemed to Siegfried a crime. . . .[178]

Siegfried's life is dedicated to atonement for the crimes of his family. His refusal of sexual intercourse is a logical refusal to propagate the family itself. As Ernestine Schlant has written in a cogent analysis of this novel, Siegfried's "break with the parent generation" leads not to "renewal through mourning, but to extinction."[179]

Siegfried's cousin Adolf Judejahn has become a priest for similar reasons. Adolf's most profound life experience had come at the end of the Second

World War, shortly after his training as a school boy at a Nazi citadel, where he had been taught to defend the fatherland against foreign invaders. As the Nazi regime collapsed, Adolf and his comrades were packed into a train and shipped off; but the train was stopped by enemy bombers. As Adolf and his fellow schoolboys make their way by foot along the railroad tracks after leaving the train, they suddenly encounter a group of inmates from a concentration camp who have themselves escaped from a train. "The children found themselves eyed by skeletons, by corpses. The children trembled in their Party school uniforms."[180] Confronted with these starving former prisoners, the children suddenly realize that they are all alone, without adult protection; as they look at the emaciated inmates of the concentration camp, they suddenly feel as if "they had no bones, no skeletons, as if they were nothing but brown Party jackets, which some evil charm had suspended in the spring air."[181] Ultimately Adolf finds himself face-to-face with a Jewish boy "exactly the same age as Adolf, but only half his weight." After the Jewish boy has eaten some of the food that Adolf has brought with him, Adolf feels "as if everything that he had thought and learned until now had been sucked away." His head is empty, "an empty air balloon." The Jewish boy begins to ask him questions:

> "Are you a Nazi?" asked the Jewish boy. "My father," said Adolf. "My family is dead," said the Jewish boy. And Adolf thought that his father was probably dead, that he must be dead; but the fact that his father was dead said nothing to him. If he was crying, then he was crying for himself, or maybe not even for himself, he did not know why he was crying, maybe he was crying for the world, but he was not crying because of his father. Had he not loved him? He didn't know. Had he hated him? He didn't think so.[182]

While Adolf feels a profound sense of guilt when confronted with the Jewish boy — it is this sense of guilt that makes him and the other boys afraid of punishment — he is simultaneously unable to separate himself from his father, a Nazi criminal. Adolf is therefore pulled in conflicting directions. Perhaps his father, like the father of the Jewish boy, is dead; perhaps he even deserved to die. But Adolf's tears cannot be shed for a father whom he is no longer allowed to love. "He even wanted to be friendly and loving to his parents," the novel's readers are told, but the hardest thing in the world for him is to love his own father.[183] In search of a better father, Adolf becomes a priest. Whereas the atheist Siegfried has dedicated himself to music as a substitute father-figure and superego, Adolf dedicates himself to God. The greater power of God protects Adolf from his seemingly omnipotent biological father, but at the same time Adolf fears revenge from that real father, a human god of death and destruction.

Guilt and punishment take different forms throughout the novel. Gottlieb Judejahn's fanatical Nazi wife Eva is described as "a Nordic ghost," the Germanic equivalent of one of the Greek Eumenides.[184] For her, true German guilt is the failure to have fought hard enough for the fallen *Führer*. Eva mourns for the lost and betrayed German Reich and for the dead Hitler, and she feels guilty for having survived the death of her beloved hero. To have survived Hitler is to have made oneself guilty, as if one had contributed to his death. Eva Judejahn is thus a fury seeking revenge. She is, as her son Adolf reflects, "a devil unto herself, tormenting herself body and soul."[185] In his eyes, both his mother and his father are being caught up and devoured by snakes like Laocoön in the famous Hellenic statue: "the hate-spewing, venom-tongued, giant serpents of their madness were swallowing his parents whole."[186]

The war criminal Judejahn himself is a primitive and uneducated man who is able to feel greatness and power only when he kills other people. "Even little Gottlieb had always guessed that there was only this one power, the power of death, and only one clear way of exercising power, which was killing."[187] Judejahn's guilt is for having failed to carry out the orders of his *Führer* with sufficient diligence. "Judejahn had no regrets about having killed, he hadn't killed enough, that was his fault."[188] Throughout his life Judejahn tries to escape the power of a petit-bourgeois schoolteacher-father and the small, pathetic, ignorant little boy that he once used to be. "Little Gottlieb wanted to be a man; he wanted to defy God the father and his own school teacher father."[189] All of Gottlieb's crimes are thus an attempt to escape what he sees as his own powerlessness. His worship of the all-powerful *Führer* had been an attempt to escape his own insignificance, to invoke a power even greater than the internalized voice of his paternal superego:

> Judejahn heard a voice, not the voice of God nor the voice of conscience, it was the thin, hungry, self-improving voice of his father, the primary schoolteacher, whispering to him: You're a fool, you didn't do your homework, you're a bad pupil, a zero, an inflated zero.[190]

In the service of Hitler, Judejahn imagines himself magnificent and powerful, lord over life and death. The murder that he commits at the end of the novel comes at the very moment when he feels his own mortality, shortly before the heart attack that ends his life. Powerless to defend himself, Judejahn then receives extreme unction from none other than his son the priest, the representative of the very God whom he has spent his entire life trying to escape. "There was Hell there was Hell there was Hell," Adolf thinks feverishly as he tries to save his father from eternal damnation.[191]

Gottlieb Judejahn's wife's name is Eva, and one of the epigraphs at the beginning of the novel, from Dante's *Inferno*, refers to "il mal seme d'Adamo," i.e., "the evil seed of Adam." In the context of the novel, "Adam" is clearly the Nazi murderer Judejahn, and it is the two young men

Adolf and Siegfried who must seek to live with their original sin and refuse to pass it on by passing on their seed. In the German language the word for original sin is *Erbsünde,* which means literally inherited sin. Because of the guilt that they have inherited, Adolf and Siegfried seek in their own different ways to atone for the sins of their fathers, but in the end they are unable to escape from the hell that the Nazis have created. Far from being the gate to paradise, Rome is the gateway to a hell-on-earth, filled with the "dirty, buzzing flies" that symbolize the underworld and its avengers.[192] Adolf and Siegfried cannot escape from guilt and punishment, or from the hell into which they have been born. They have become the executors of their own damnation. Ultimately this novel describes an inferno in which all of its major figures live in varying degrees of torment. As Schlant has pointed out, this is a world in which "the Germans are already dead and inhabitants of hell."[193] Koeppen seems to be suggesting that, for Germans, any escape from this torment has become forever impossible. Germans know the horrors from which they are trying to escape, but they have no idea where to find a possible refuge. The furies they carry with them wherever they go will quickly seek them out and punish them. Like Adolf and Siegfried, Germans are "always on the run, always on a path which . . . comes from somewhere but which leads nowhere."[194]

Notes

[1] "ist vielleicht das schwerste Problem, vor dem wir alle ohne jede Ausnahme stehen . . ." Rudolf Pechel, "Fragen um die deutsche Schuld," in *Deutsche Gegenwart: Aufsätze und Vorträge 1945–1952,* 39–46; here, 39 (Stuttgart: no publisher, 1952 [private printing on the occasion of Pechel's seventieth birthday]). Originally in the *Deutsche Rundschau,* August 1946. Unless otherwise specified, all translations from German in this book are my own; the German appears in the notes, followed by sources. I have added the notation "my translation" in a limited number of cases where confusion might otherwise occur.

[2] "ein Spiegel des deutschen Selbstverständnisses." Barbro Eberan, *Luther? Friedrich "der Große"? Wagner? Nietzsche?. . .?. . .? Wer war an Hitler schuld? Die Debatte um die Schuldfrage 1945–1949* (Munich: Minerva, 1983), 210.

[3] "ist sie die eigentliche Frage, die hinter all unserer Unruhe, unserem Hin und Her, unserer innersten Unzufriedenheit steht." Martin Niemöller, "Die Erneuerung unserer Kirche," in *Reden 1945–1954,* 19–22; here, 19 (Darmstadt: Stimme, 1958).

[4] "Wo geht sie zu Ende, die Straße dieser Schuld, wo hört sie auf?" Aichinger, *Die grössere Hoffnung* (Amsterdam: Bermann-Fischer/Querido, 1948), 70.

[5] Lord Vansittart, *Lessons of My Life* (New York: Alfred A. Knopf, 1945), 241.

[6] Vansittart, *Lessons of My Life,* 279, 277.

[7] Vansittart, *Lessons of My Life,* 240.

[8] Vansittart, *Lessons of My Life,* 245.

[9] Vansittart, *Lessons of My Life,* 241.

[10] Henry Morgenthau, Jr., *Germany is Our Problem* (New York: Harper & Brothers, 1945), 145.

[11] Morgenthau, *Germany is Our Problem,* 136.

[12] Morgenthau, *Germany is Our Problem,* 136, 140.

[13] Morgenthau, *Germany is Our Problem,* 149. On persistent misinterpretations and misrepresentations of Morgenthau in Germany, see Bernd Greiner, "Mit Sigmund Freud im Apfelhain oder Was Deutsche in 45 Jahren über Henry Morgenthau gelernt haben," *Mittelweg* 36 (August/September 1992), 44–58.

[14] Morgenthau, *Germany is Our Problem,* 191.

[15] Morgenthau, *Germany is Our Problem,* 190.

[16] Percy Knauth, *Germany in Defeat* (New York: Knopf, 1946), ix, 224.

[17] Saul K. Padover, *Experiment in Germany: The Story of an American Intelligence Officer* (New York: Duell, Sloan, and Pearce, 1946), 122.

[18] Dagmar Barnouw, *Germany 1945: Views of War and Violence* (Bloomington: Indiana UP, 1997), 61. In the subsequent pages Barnouw also explores some of the ambiguities and complexities of official U.S. Army anti-fraternization policies in Germany.

[19] Padover, *Experiment in Germany,* 216. Barnouw, who calls Padover "an extreme and quite troubling case of psychological denseness and moral-political self-righteousness" with respect to the conquered nation (*Germany 1945,* 63), does not seem to recognize that even Padover's position cannot be equated with a blanket accusation of collective guilt against all Germans.

[20] "Keine Feder, kein Film reicht aus, um das zu schildern." Niemöller, "Die Erneuerung unserer Kirche," 19.

[21] "Es ist kein Wunder . . . daß an dieser Schuld kein Mensch schuldig sein will." "könnte der Mensch noch einen Augenblick leben, könnte der Mensch noch eine Stunde Schlaf finden, muß der Mensch nicht hingehen wie Judas und in die Nacht hinausschreiten und sich erhängen?" "ein Kindergarten gegenüber der Wirklichkeit, die in unserer Mitte aufgebrochen ist. Die Hölle ist auf die Erdoberfläche gekommen." Niemöller, "Die Erneuerung unserer Kirche," 20.

[22] Padover, *Experiment in Germany,* 116.

[23] Karl Jaspers, *The Question of German Guilt,* trans. E. B. Ashton (New York: Dial Press, 1947), 27. In German: "Es liegt nahe, der Frage sich zu entziehen. Wir leben in Not, ein großer Teil unserer Bevölkerung in so großer, so unmittelbarer Not, daß er unempfindlich geworden zu sein scheint für solche Erörterungen. Ihn interessiert, was der Not steuert, was Arbeit und Brot, Wohnung und Wärme bringt. Der Horizont ist eng geworden." Karl Jaspers, *Die Schuldfrage: Von der politischen Haftung Deutschlands* (Munich: Piper, 1996), 15.

[24] "Man versuchte, in den Trümmern zu überleben. Der Horizont verengte sich. Man machte nicht mehr Weltgeschichte . . ., sondern man stand für Lebensmittel an, tauschte Kaffee gegen Margarine . . ." Jürgen Kocka, "Zerstörung und Befreiung: Das Jahr 1945 als Wendepunkt deutscher Geschichte," in *Geschichte und Aufklärung,* 120–39; here 127 (Göttingen: Vandenhoeck und Ruprecht, 1989).

[25] Thomas Mann, *Mario and the Magician,* trans. H. T. Lowe-Porter (London: Martin Secker, 1930), 90. In German: ". . . einen stummen in der Luft liegenden Gemeinschaftswillen vollführte." Mann, "Mario und der Zauberer," in *Die Erzählungen,* 2:502–42; here, 527 (Frankfurt: Fischer, 1967).

[26] Hannah Arendt, "Organized Guilt and Universal Responsibility," in Arendt, *The Jew as Pariah: Jewish Identity and Politics in the Modern Age,* ed. Ron H. Feldman, 225–36; here, 225 (New York: Grove Press, 1978). Originally published in *Jewish Frontier,* January 1945. In German: "zentrale These . . ., daß es einen Unterschied zwischen Nazis und Deutschen nicht gibt," "daß es eine Teilung der Verantwortung nicht gebe"; "Organisierte Schuld," *Die Wandlung,* 1, no. 4 (April 1946), 333–44; here, 333–34.

[27] "Kein Deutscher, der nicht gewußt hätte, daß es Konzentrationslager gab. Kein Deutscher, der sie für Sanatorien gehalten hätte." Eugen Kogon, *Der SS-Staat: Das System der deutschen Konzentrationslager* (Munich: Kindler, 1974), 394. Originally published in 1946. Abridged English translation: *The Theory and Practice of Hell,* trans. Heinz Norden (New York: Farrar, Straus & Cudahy, 1950). The chapter from which this sentence is taken does not appear in the published English-language translation.

[28] "Die totale Mobilmachung hat in der totalen Komplizität des deutschen Volkes geendet." Arendt, "Organisierte Schuld," 334. This sentence does not appear in the English-language version.

[29] Arendt, "Organized Guilt and Universal Responsibility," 225. In German: "Daß diese Behauptungen nicht bloße Propaganda sind, sondern sich auf eine sehr reale Unterlage, auf eine furchtbare Wirklichkeit berufen können. . . ." Arendt, "Organisierte Schuld," 334.

[30] Arendt, "Organized Guilt and Universal Responsibility," 226, 227. In German: "die aktive Identifikation des gesamten Volkes mit den Nazis." Arendt, "Organisierte Schuld," 335.

[31] Ernst von Salomon, *The Answers,* trans. Constantine Fitzgibbon (London: Putnam, 1954), 243–44. In German: "Aber ich fürchte, Hitlers Behauptung, seine ideologische Konzeption sei die Konzeption der Demokratie, wird schwer zu widerlegen sein . . . das Gewinnen der Massen durch Überreden, die Legitimation des Weges zur Macht durch Wahlen, die Legitimation der Macht selbst durch das Volk, — ich fürchte, es wird schwer zu widerlegen sein, daß dies demokratische Stigmen sind, vielleicht sehr späte und überhitzte Formen der Demokratie anzeigend, aber Formen der Demokratie." Ernst von Salomon, *Der Fragebogen* (Reinbek: Rowohlt, 1997), 345.

[32] "Als Volk überhaupt nicht. Das ist eine bittere Wahrheit." Kogon, *Der SS-Staat,* 395.

[33] Padover, *Experiment in Germany,* 115.

[34] Karl Becker, *Zero Hour for Germany* (London: I.N.G. Publications, 1944), 72. "I.N.G." stands for "Inside Nazi Germany."

[35] *The Signs of Awakening: German Underground Speaks: The Peace Manifesto of the Rhineland Conference* (New York: German American, 1943), 25, 19.

[36] Friedrich Meinecke, *The German Catastrophe: Reflections and Recollections,* trans. Sidney B. Fay (Cambridge, MA: Harvard UP, 1950), 97. Original German: "Es wäre ein Segen gewesen, wenn das deutsche Volk in sich selbst die Kraft gefunden hätte,

das Hitlerjoch abzuschütteln." Meinecke, *Die deutsche Katastrophe: Betrachtungen und Erinnerungen* (Brockhaus: Wiesbaden, 1946), 143.

[37] "hohe psychische Disponiertheit," "willkommener Anlaß . . ., sich ungerecht behandelt zu fühlen." Norbert Frei, *Vergangenheitspolitik: Die Anfänge der Bundesrepublik und die NS-Vergangenheit* (Munich: C. H. Beck, 1996), 399.

[38] "In keinem Dekret der Besatzungsmächte, in keiner öffentlichen Äußerung eines mit Definitionsmacht ausgestatteten britischen, französischen oder amerikanischen Politikers war jemals von einer kollektiven Schuld aller Deutschen die Rede." Helmut Dubiel, *Niemand ist frei von der Geschichte: Die nationalsozialistische Herrschaft in den Debatten des Deutschen Bundestages* (Munich: Carl Hanser, 1999), 71.

[39] "Die geradezu obsessive Abwehr eines Vorwurfs, den niemand erhoben hatte, erlaubt einzig die psychoanalytische Deutung als 'Projektion.'" "Verstrickung zahlloser Deutscher in die historisch beispiellosen Verbrechen ihres Staates." Dubiel, *Niemand ist frei von der Geschichte,* 71.

[40] "diese angebliche kollektive, von allen Deutschen gleichmäßig zu tragende Schuld [war] niemals von den Alliierten offiziell festgestellt oder behauptet worden." "von einer differenzierten Schuld, die zum überwiegenden Teil alle Deutschen betrifft, wenn sie auch letztlich über Deutschland hinausgeht." Stefan Hermlin, "Karl Jaspers 'Die Schuldfrage,'" in Hermlin, *Äußerungen 1944–1982* (Berlin: Aufbau, 1983), 34–39; here, 34.

[41] "Eingeständnis einer tiefempfundenen Schuld." Stefan Hermlin, "Aus dem Lande der Großen Schuld," in *Äußerungen 1944–1982,* 15–19; here, 15.

[42] "Mangels jeglichen Schuldbewußtseins." Hermlin, "Aus dem Lande der Großen Schuld," in *Äußerungen 1944–1982,* 15. Arendt, "Organized Guilt and Universal Responsibility," 230.

[43] "Adam und Eva sind schuld!" Aichinger, *Die grössere Hoffnung,* 318. In subsequent editions of the novel, this passage does not begin the chapter.

[44] "die Verbundenheit aller Menschen in der gemeinsamen Schuld." Marcus Holz, *Christliche Weltanschauung als Grundlage von Parteipolitik: Eine Analyse des genuin Christlichen in der frühen CDU/CSU (1945–50) aus der Betrachtung des christlichen Menschenbildes und seiner ideengeschichtlichen Hintergründe* (doctoral dissertation, Universität der Bundeswehr, Munich, 1992), 219.

[45] Holz, *Christliche Weltanschauung,* 225.

[46] Holz, *Christliche Weltanschauung,* 206.

[47] "Der größte Raub, den Kniébolo [Hitler] dem deutschen Volke zufügt, ist der Rechtsraub — das heißt, er hat den Deutschen der Möglichkeit beraubt, Recht zu haben und sich im Recht zu fühlen gegenüber den Unbilden, die ihm zugefügt werden und die ihm drohen. Freilich hat sich das Volk als solches mitschuldig gemacht durch Akklamation — das war der furchtbare, bestürzende Unterton, den man unter den Jubelstürmen, den Jubelorgien vernahm." Ernst Jünger, *Strahlungen* (Tübingen: Heliopolis, 1949), 401.

[48] "Was der Mensch sät, das wird er auch ernten! Ja, es ist eine entsetzliche Saat des Hasses, die jetzt wieder ausgesät worden ist. Welche entsetzliche Ernte wird daraus erwachsen, wenn Gott unserm Volk und uns nicht Gnade schenkt zu aufrichtiger Buße." "O Land, Land, höre des Herrn Wort!" *Die Zeit,* 4 November 1999, 55.

[49] Cited in Karl Dietrich Bracher, *The German Dictatorship: The Origins, Structure, and Effects of National Socialism,* trans. Jean Steinberg (New York: Praeger, 1970), 444.

[50] Cited in Bracher, *The German Dictatorship,* 442.

[51] "Wundert euch nicht über die Rauchwolken an eurem Horizont! Eure eigene Unklarheit kommt zurück. Eure Sucht, zu greifen, greift nun nach euch. . . . Ihr selbst habt die Materie zum Material gemacht. Wundert euch nicht!" Aichinger, *Die grössere Hoffnung,* 322.

[52] "Alle Dinge sind zornig. Wir haben uns zu fest an sie geklammert, wir haben ihnen weh getan und sie erniedrigt und sie wollen sich rächen!" Aichinger, *Die grössere Hoffnung,* 325–26.

[53] Wilhelm Röpke, *The German Question,* trans. E. W. Dickes (London: George Allen & Unwin, 1946), 79. German original: "daß viele deutsche Intellektuelle eine gewaltige Schuld auf sich geladen haben," "daß wahrscheinlich einige unter ihnen uns geradezu widersprechen würden, wenn wir es uns einfallen lassen wollten, sie zu entschuldigen." Wilhelm Röpke, *Die deutsche Frage* (Erlenbach-Zurich: Eugen Rentsch, 1945), 89. I have modified the translation slightly, rendering "Schuld" as "guilt" rather than "responsibility."

[54] Padover, *Experiment in Germany,* 58.

[55] Padover, *Experiment in Germany,* 145.

[56] Padover, *Experiment in Germany,* 320.

[57] "Durch uns ist unendliches Leid über viele Völker und Länder gebracht worden." Martin Greschat, ed., *Die Schuld der Kirche: Dokumente und Reflexionen zur Stuttgarter Schulderklärung vom 18./19. Oktober 1945* (Munich: Kaiser, 1982), 102.

[58] "alles das ist ja nur ein Quäntchen gegenüber dem Zentnergewicht dessen, was wir auf unsere Gewissen geladen haben, und das sage ich, nachdem ich zwölf Tage in Berlin gewesen bin, wo es kaum noch eine Frau gibt, die nicht schmählich behandelt worden wäre, und wo ein Sterben umgeht, wie es die Welt noch nicht gesehen hat." Niemöller, "Zum Schuldbekenntnis," in *Reden 1945–1954,* 16–18; here, 16.

[59] Cited in Jeffrey Herf, *Divided Memory: The Nazi Past in the Two Germanys* (Cambridge, MA: Harvard UP, 1997), 76.

[60] Cited in Herf, *Divided Memory,* 85.

[61] Cited in Herf, *Divided Memory,* 251.

[62] Cited in Herf, *Divided Memory,* 400, note 8.

[63] Carl Gustav Jung, "After the Catastrophe," in *Civilization in Transition,* trans. R. F. C. Hull, 194–217; here, 195 (New York: Pantheon, 1964). Original German: "nicht von der Seite der kaltblütigen Ueberlegenheit . . ., sondern der eingestandenen Unterlegenheit." Carl Gustav Jung, "Nach der Katastrophe," *Neue Schweizer Rundschau,* 13, no. 6 (1945/1946), 67–88; here, 68. For a critique of Jung, see Dr. W. Schellworth, "Ein Tiefenpsychologe blickt in die deutsche Seele," *Aufbau,* 2, no. 7 (1946), 766–67.

[64] Jung, "After the Catastrophe," 195. Original German: "Die Schuld kann nur juristisch, moralisch und intellektuell auf den Rechtsbrecher engeschränkt werden; als psychisches Phänomen dagegen dehnt sie sich über die örtliche und menschliche Umgebung aus." "Ein Wald, ein Haus, eine Familie, ein Dorf sogar, wo ein Mord

geschehen ist, fühlt die psychische Schuld und bekommt sie auch von außen zu fühlen." Jung, "Nach der Katastrophe," 68.

[65] Jung, "After the Catastrophe," 195. Original German: "das irrationale Vorhandensein eines subjektiven Schuldgefühls . . . oder einer objektiv zugemuteten Schuld." Jung, "Nach der Katastrophe," 68.

[66] Jung, "After the Catastrophe," 197. Original German: "Kontaktschuld," "trifft alle, Gerechte und Ungerechte, alle, die irgendwie in der Nähe jenes Ortes waren, wo das Furchtbare geschah." Jung, "Nach der Katastrophe," 69. Translation slightly altered in order to render the term "Kontaktschuld" more accurately.

[67] "darum ist es keine Verurteilung des deutschen Volkes, wenn man behauptet, es habe eine Kollektivschuld, sondern bloß die Feststellung eines vorgefundenen Tatbestandes." Jung, "Nach der Katastrophe," 70.

[68] Jung, "After the Catastrophe," 197. Original German: "Er hat als Deutscher die europäische Kultur und ihre Güter verraten, er hat seiner europäischen Familie Schande angetan, so daß man erröten muß, wenn man als Europäer bezeichnet wird; er hat seine europäischen Brüder räuberisch angefallen, gefoltert und ermordet. Der Deutsche kann nicht erwarten, daß Europa sich zu jener "finesse" aufschwingt, jeweils zuerst in Erfahrung zu bringen, ob der Verbrecher Müller oder Meier heißt." Jung, "Nach der Katastrophe," 70.

[69] Jung, "After the Catastrophe," 211. Original German: "die psychischen Bedingungen, welche Dämonen erzeugen, [sind] so aktiv wie nur je am Werke. Die Dämonen sind eben nicht wirklich verschwunden, sondern haben nur die Gestalt geändert": Jung, "Nach der Katastrophe," 83.

[70] Jung, "After the Catastrophe," 202. Original German: "weniger von außen als vom Richter im eigenen Herzen." Jung, "Nach der Katastrophe," 74.

[71] Jung, "After the Catastrophe," 204. Original German: "ein Spiegelbild der allgemeinen deutschen Hysterie." Jung, "Nach der Katastrophe," 76.

[72] Jung, "After the Catastrophe," 204. Original German: "die einzige Möglichkeit, sich die Massenwirkung dieses Popanzes einigermaßen zu erklären." Jung, "Nach der Katastrophe," 76.

[73] Anson Rabinbach, *In the Shadow of Catastrophe: German Intellectuals between Apocalypse and Enlightenment* (Berkeley: U of California P, 1997), 131.

[74] Jaspers, *The Question of German Guilt*, 31. In German: "Es ist jedes Menschen Mitverantwortung, wie er regiert wird." Jaspers, *Die Schuldfrage*, 17.

[75] Jaspers, *The Question of German Guilt*, 61. Translation slightly altered. In German: "Wir 'haften' kollektiv." Jaspers, *Die Schuldfrage*, 40.

[76] Jaspers, *The Question of German Guilt*, 62. In German: "Politisch handelt im modernen Staat jeder, zum mindesten durch seine Stimmabgabe bei Wahlen oder durch Unterlassung des Wählens. Der Sinn politischer Haftung erlaubt es niemandem auszuweichen." Jaspers, *Die Schuldfrage*, 41.

[77] Jaspers, *The Question of German Guilt*, 73. In German: "Jeder Deutsche, ausnahmslos, hat teil an der politischen Haftung." Jaspers, *Die Schuldfrage*, 49.

[78] Jaspers, *The Question of German Guilt*, 52. In German: "Ein Verbrecherstaat fällt dem ganzen Volk zur Last." Jaspers, *Die Schuldfrage*, 33.

[79] Jaspers, *The Question of German Guilt*, 52. In German: "In der Behandlung der eigenen Staatsführer, selbst wenn sie Verbrecher sind, fühlt sich daher der Staatsbürger mit behandelt. In ihnen wird das Volk mit verurteilt. Daher wird die Kränkung und Würdelosigkeit in dem, was die Staatsführer erfahren, vom Volke als eigene Kränkung und Würdelosigkeit empfunden. Und daher die instinktive, zunächst noch gedankenlose Ablehnung des Prozesses." Jaspers, *Die Schuldfrage*, 33.

[80] Jaspers, *The Question of German Guilt*, 52. In German: "daß wir nicht beabsichtigen, das ganze deutsche Volk zu beschuldigen." Jaspers, *Die Schuldfrage*, 32.

[81] Jaspers, *The Question of German Guilt*, 65; translation modified. In German: "Denn diese Unbedingtheit einer blinden nationalen Anschauung . . . war in gutem Gewissen zugleich moralische Schuld." Jaspers, *Die Schuldfrage*, 44.

[82] Jaspers, *The Question of German Guilt*, 66. In German: "wie ich für meine Täuschung, für jede Täuschung, der ich verfalle, verantwortlich bin." Jaspers, *Die Schuldfrage*, 45.

[83] Rabinbach, *In the Shadow of Catastrophe*, 144.

[84] Jaspers, *The Question of German Guilt*, 32. In German: "mitverantwortlich . . . für alles Unrecht und alle Ungerechtigkeit in der Welt." Jaspers, *Die Schuldfrage*, 17.

[85] Jaspers, *The Question of German Guilt*, 71. In German: "daß ich noch lebe, ist meine Schuld." Jaspers, *Die Schuldfrage*, 48.

[86] Jaspers, *The Question of German Guilt*, 79. In German: "Wir fühlen etwas wie Mitschuld für das Tun unserer Familienangehörigen." Jaspers, *Die Schuldfrage*, 53.

[87] Jaspers, *The Question of German Guilt*, 79. "wenn einer aus unserer Familie unrecht tut," "So fühlt der Deutsche . . . sich mitbetroffen von allem, was aus dem Deutschen erwächst." In German: Jaspers, *Die Schuldfrage*, 53.

[88] Jaspers, *The Question of German Guilt*, 80. In German: "Wir wissen uns nicht nur als Einzelne, sondern als Deutsche. Jeder ist, wenn er eigentlich ist, das deutsche Volk." Jaspers, *Die Schuldfrage*, 54.

[89] Jaspers, *The Question of German Guilt*, 80. In German: "daß in unserer Überlieferung etwas steckt, mächtig und drohend, das unser sittliches Verderben ist." Jaspers, *Die Schuldfrage*, 53.

[90] Jaspers, *The Question of German Guilt*, 73. In German: "Daß wir Deutschen, daß jeder Deutsche in irgendeiner Weise schuldig ist, daran kann . . . kein Zweifel sein." Jaspers, *Die Schuldfrage*, 49.

[91] Jaspers, *The Question of German Guilt*, 80. In German: "das Deutschsein nicht Bestand, sondern Aufgabe." Jaspers, *Die Schuldfrage*, 54.

[92] Hannah Arendt, *Eichmann in Jerusalem: A Report on the Banality of Evil* (New York: Viking, 1963).

[93] Arendt, "Organized Guilt and Universal Responsibility," 229. In German: "Verwaltungsmassenmordes." Arendt, "Organisierte Schuld," 338.

[94] Arendt, "Organized Guilt and Universal Responsibility," 230. In German: "Daß in dieser Mordmaschine jeder auf diese oder jene Weise an einen Platz gezwungen ist, auch wenn er nicht direkt in den Vernichtungslagern tätig ist, macht das Grauen aus." Arendt, "Organisierte Schuld," 338.

[95] Arendt, "Organized Guilt and Universal Responsibility," 228. In German: "die private Existenz jedes Individuums auf deutschem Boden davon abhängig zu machen, daß es Verbrechen entweder begeht oder ihr Komplize ist." Arendt, "Organisierte Schuld," 336.

[96] Arendt, "Organized Guilt and Universal Responsibility," 232. In German: "Und er hat seine neueste, das gesamte Land umfassende Terror-Organisation bewußt auf der Annahme aufgebaut, daß die meisten Menschen nicht Bohemiens, nicht Fanatiker, nicht Abenteurer, nicht Sexualverbrecher und nicht Sadisten sind, sondern in erster Linie jobholders und gute Familienväter." Arendt, "Organisierte Schuld," 340.

[97] Arendt, "Organized Guilt and Universal Responsibility," 233. In German: "Die Verwandlung des Familienvaters aus einem an den öffentlichen Angelegenheiten interessierten, verantwortlichen Mitglied der Gesellschaft in den Spießer, der nur an seiner privaten Existenz hängt und öffentliche Tugend nicht kennt, ist eine moderne internationale Erscheinung." Arendt, "Organisierte Schuld," 342.

[98] Arendt, "Organized Guilt and Universal Responsibility," 234. In German: "Wenn sein Beruf ihn zwingt, Menschen zu morden, so hält er sich nicht für einen Mörder, gerade weil er es nicht aus Neigung, sondern beruflich getan hat." Arendt, "Organisierte Schuld," 343.

[99] "'Hier wurden in den Jahren 1933–1945 238 756 Menschen verbrannt.'" "Was mich in diesem Augenblick in einen kalten Fieberschauer jagte, das war etwas anderes." "Mein Alibi reichte vom 1. Juli 1937 bis Mitte 1945. Da stand: '1933–1945.' Adam, wo bist du? Mensch, wo bist du gewesen?" Niemöller, "Der Weg ins Freie," in *Reden 1945–1954*, 23–42; here, 31.

[100] "Und jetzt war der Steckbrief da, und diesem Steckbrief konnte ich nicht mehr ausweichen." Niemöller, "Der Weg ins Freie," 32.

[101] "Ich war damals kein freier Mensch. Ich hatte mich damals bereits meiner wahren Verantwortung begeben." Niemöller, "Der Weg ins Freie," 32.

[102] "Verantwortung! Man hat es uns zwölf Jahre vorerzählt . . ., als würden irgendwo von oben und außen her unsere Pflichten und Verantwortungen gültig geregelt und wir selber brauchten nichts zu tun, als zu gehorchen." Niemöller, "Der Weg ins Freie," 29.

[103] "Wir haben um keine Verantwortung mehr gewußt. Wir werden heute verantwortlich gemacht und wollen doch nicht verantwortlich gemacht werden. Und damit, daß wir uns weigern, uns verantwortlich machen zu lassen, begeben wir uns der Möglichkeit, wieder frei zu werden." Niemöller, "Der Weg ins Freie," 30.

[104] Erich Fromm had developed a similar viewpoint — albeit not from a Christian perspective — in his book *Escape from Freedom* (New York: Farrar & Rinehart, 1941).

[105] "Wir legen Zeugnis ab von den ungeheuerlichen Verbrechen, wie sie von seiten der Nazikriegsverbrecher gegen uns, das deutsche Volk, begangen wurden." Johannes R. Becher, "Deutschland klagt an!," *Der Aufbau*, 2, no. 1 (January 1946), 9–18; here, 9.

[106] "Millionen deutscher Männer, auf den Schlachtfeldern gefallen, klagen an," "Männer im blühenden Mannesalter, Jünglinge, ja auch Kinder und Greise," "schreien in uns." Becher, "Deutschland klagt an!," 9.

[107] "in der Maske des Biedermanns." Becher, "Deutschland klagt an!" 11.

[108] "die systematische Ausrottung unserer jüdischen Mitbürger," "daß wir daran noch zu tragen haben werden, wenn der Staub der Naziverbrecher längst in alle Winde

verweht sein wird." "Was den Juden angetan wurde, wurde u n s angetan." Becher, "Deutschland klagt an!," 12.

[109] Herf, *Divided Memory*, 78.

[110] "wir wären . . . . nicht auf dem Wege, uns zu neuen freiheitlichen deutschen Menschen zu wandeln, würden wir nicht in unserer Anklage miteinbeziehen alles das, was die Nazikriegsverbrecher andern Völkern angetan haben." Becher, "Deutschland klagt an!" 15–16.

[111] "[haben] den Namen Deutschland entehrt, geschändet und entheiligt," "der Name eines Deutschen . . . zu einem Schmäh- und Fluchwort . . . geworden ist." Becher, "Deutschland klagt an!" 15.

[112] "von einem i n n e r e n Gericht begleitet sein, das ein jeder Deutsche über sich selbst abhält." Becher, "Deutschland klagt an!" 16.

[113] "so etwas wie ein Gewissen, wie ein nationales Gewissen." Becher, "Deutschland klagt an!" 16–17.

[114] "Wenn man heute mit vielen unserer Landsleute über die vergangenen finsteren 13 Jahre spricht," "so könnte man den Eindruck gewinnen, als ob es in Deutschland überhaupt keine Nazis gegeben habe." Friedrich Wolf, "Auch wir können nicht schweigen," *Aufbau*, 1, no. 3 (November 1945), 201–05; here, 201.

[115] Wolf, "Auch wir können nicht schweigen," 201.

[116] "ob wir etwas von dieser furchtbaren Lehre begriffen haben . . ., ob wir in uns selbst zu Gerichte saßen, ob wir in uns selbst den entscheidenden Prozeß vollzogen." Wolf, "Auch wir können nicht schweigen," 204.

[117] "Bevor Hitler und seine Hintermänner in Armee, Dilopmatie und Finanz die Tschechoslowakei, die skandinavischen Länder, Holland, Belgien, Frankreich, den Balkan und Weißrußland unterworfen haben, haben sie das deutsche Volk unterworfen." Bertolt Brecht, "Bericht über die Stellung der Deutschen im Exil," in Brecht, *Werke*, ed. Werner Hecht et al., vol. 23, *Schriften 3*, 32–33; here, 32 (Berlin, Weimar, and Frankfurt: Aufbau and Suhrkamp, 1993).

[118] "Wir sagen, daß Hitler und seine Hintermänner nicht Deutschland sind, was immer sie behaupten mögen." Brecht, "Bericht über die Stellung der Deutschen im Exil," 33.

[119] "Dann werden die Nazis gewählt." Journal notice from 12.9.53, in Bertolt Brecht, *Werke*, vol. 27, *Journale 2*, 347.

[120] "Ich habe den Nazismus nie für einen Auswuchs gehalten, immer für ein Ergebnis normalen Wachstums." Bertolt Brecht, *Werke*, vol. 29, *Briefe 2*, 401.

[121] Bertolt Brecht, "The *Other* Germany 1943," trans. Eric Bentley, in Brecht, *Werke*, vol. 23, 24–30; here, 28.

[122] "nur wenn er kein Bürger mehr ist, ist er kein Nazi mehr." Journal entry from 1.1.48, in Brecht, *Werke*, vol. 27, *Journale 2*, 259.

[123] "der Sozialismus der Kleinbürger" Journal entry from 24.12.47, in Brecht, *Werke*, vol. 27, *Journale 2*, 258.

[124] "Sozialismusersatz." Bertolt Brecht, "Von der Jugend," in Brecht, *Werke*, vol. 23, *Schriften 3*, 130–31; here, 131. Victor Klemperer takes a fundamentally similar position when he declares that socialism was a "Tarnkappe" [magic cap] used by the Na-

zis for the purpose of camouflage. See Victor Klemperer, *Kultur: Erwägungen nach dem Zusammenbruch des Nazismus* (Berlin: Neues Leben, 1946), 53.

[125] "Nürnberg: Die Konterrevolution frißt ihre eigenen Kinder." Journal entry from 5.1.46, in Bertolt Brecht, *Werke*, vol. 27, *Journale 2* (1995), 239.

[126] Theodor Plievier, *Stalingrad*, trans. Richard and Clara Winston (New York: Appleton-Century-Crofts, 1948), 8. Translation modified. German original: "eine der hundert Fäuste, die Selbstständigkeit und Willen anderen Volkes zermürben und zerschlagen sollten." Theodor Plievier, *Stalingrad* (Berlin: Aufbau, 1984), 14.

[127] Plievier, *Stalingrad*, trans. Richard and Clara Winston, 82. Translation modified. In German: "was haben wir denn verbrochen . . .?" Plievier, *Stalingrad*, 123.

[128] Plievier, *Stalingrad*, trans. Richard and Clara Winston, 117. Translation modified. In German: "und wer hat bei diesem Akt seine Ehre verloren und sein Leben verwirkt?" Plievier, *Stalingrad*, 174.

[129] Plievier, *Stalingrad*, trans. Richard and Clara Winston, 123. Translation modified. German original: "Jetzt heißt es stillhalten und spüren, was wir nicht nur einer Stadt und nicht nur einem Land und nicht nur einem Volk angetan haben." Plievier, *Stalingrad*, 182.

[130] My own translation. German original: "nicht nur falsche Zirkelbogen auf Generalstabkarten, nicht nur fehlerhafte Zahlenkolonnen . . ." Plievier, *Stalingrad*, 520.

[131] Plievier, *Stalingrad*, trans. Richard and Clara Winston, 347. German original: "Wie schwer wiegt die Schuld? Wieviel wiegt die tote Stalingradarmee, wieviel wiegt dieser gespenstische Gefangenenzug, und was ist noch auf die Schale zu legen? Ist die Schuld aufzuwiegen, wie ist sie aufzuwiegen? Kinder erschossen, Frauen, Greise, hilflose Gefangene erschossen, wie der Befehl es verlangt, 'wie das Gesetz es befahl!' Was ist das für ein Gesetz . . .?" Plievier, *Stalingrad*, 520.

[132] My own translation. German original: "daß er als guter Offizier . . . verhängnisvoller als der schlechte Offizier gewesen wäre, und nicht der Unkameradschaftliche . . . dem niemand Glauben schenkte, sondern er, der das Vertrauen besessen hat, hätte die Truppe in den Untergang geführt." Plievier, *Stalingrad*, 522. For an alternative English-language translation: Plievier, *Stalingrad*, trans. Richard and Clara Winston, 348.

[133] *Sturmabteilungen*, or storm troopers, the paramilitary fighting group of the Nazi party.

[134] Plievier, *Stalingrad*, trans. Richard and Clara Winston, 350. German original: "Er ist den Weg zurückgegangen bis zum Grunde der deutschen Krankheit. Generale sind gegen die Sache des 'Führers,' weil er den Krieg verliert — der ist dagegen, weil er den Krieg begonnen hat und weil er, und vor zehn jahren schon, den Krieg gegen das deutsche Volk angefangen und das Volk für volksfeindliche Interessen mißbraucht hat." Plievier, *Stalingrad*, 524.

[135] Hence I take issue with Michael Rohrwasser's contention that Plievier evades the problem of guilt in *Stalingrad*. See Michael Rohrwasser, "Theodor Plieviers Kriegsbilder," in *Schuld und Sühne: Kriegserlebnis und Kriegsdeutung in deutschen Medien der Nachkriegszeit (1945–1961)*, ed. Ursula Heukenkamp, vol. 1, 139–53, especially 149–50 (Amsterdam: Rodopi, 2001).

[136] "ein Techniker, ein Soldat." Carl Zuckmayer, *Des Teufels General* (Stockholm and Vienna: Bermann-Fischer and Schönbrunn, 1947), 76.

[137] "dem man sein Vermögen anvertrauen [kann], ohne Quittung. Sogar Weib und Kinder." Zuckmayer, *Des Teufels General,* 49.

[138] "technisch die Verantwortung," "Sinnlos sterben. Sie haben zugeschaut und ihn nicht gerettet. Das ist die Schuld, für die es kein Verzeihen gibt." Zuckmayer, *Des Teufels General,* 160.

[139] "Sie töten ohne Recht und Glauben, für eine Sache, die Sie hassen und verachten." Zuckmayer, *Des Teufels General,* 161.

[140] "die Figur Harras wird durch diesen Schuldvorwurf . . . keineswegs in Frage gestellt." Dirk Niefanger, "Die Dramatisierung der 'Stunde Null,'" in Erhart and Niefanger, *Zwei Wendezeiten,* 47–70; here, 68.

[141] "Mir starb kein Bruder im KZ." "Doch eines Tages — da habe ich mich geschämt, daß ich ein Deutscher bin." Zuckmayer, *Des Teufels General,* 168.

[142] "dann ist Deutschland verloren. Dann ist die Welt verloren." Zuckmayer, *Des Teufels General,* 166.

[143] "Gottesurteil," "mit Blut geschrieben." Zuckmayer, *Des Teufels General,* 171.

[144] "Wer auf Erden des Teufels General wurde und ihm die Bahn gebombt hat — der muß ihm auch Quartier in der Hölle machen. Fallen Sie nicht um, Oderbruch. Sie hatten recht, mit allem." Zuckmayer, *Des Teufels General,* 172.

[145] Even in the immediate postwar period Zuckmayer was criticized by some reviewers for having drawn Harras too positively, thus potentially reinforcing German militarism. Influenced by the Eichmann and Auschwitz trials in the early 1960s, and after further criticisms that the figure of Harras was not presented in a sufficiently negative light — and, conversely, that the figure of Oderbruch had failed to appear in a sufficiently positive light — Zuckmayer published a slightly revised version of *Des Teufels General* in 1966; in this version Zuckmayer made it even clearer that Harras ultimately accepts his own guilt. However, even the 1946 version of the play makes it clear that Harras's suicide is motivated at least in part by feelings of guilt. For Zuckmayer's revisions, see Gunther Nickel and Ulrike Weiß, eds., *Carl Zuckmayer 1896–1977: "Ich wollte nur Theater machen"* (Marbach: Deutsches Literaturarchiv, 1996), 350–53; on early criticisms of the play, see Nickel and Weiß, *Carl Zuckmayer,* 337–42. On the figure of Harras, see Anthony Waine, "Carl Zuckmayer's *Des Teufels General* as a Critique of the Cult of Masculinity," *Forum for Modern Language Studies,* xxix, no. 3 (July 1993), 257–70. For a critique of Zuckmayer's approach to the problem of guilt in the play, see Jochen Vogt, *"Erinnerung ist unsere Aufgabe" — Über Literatur, Moral und Politik 1945–1900* (Opladen: Westdeutscher Verlag, 1991), 13–16. See also Volker Wehdeking, "Mythologisches Ungewitter: Carl Zuckmayers problematisches Exildrama 'Des Teufels General,'" in *Die deutsche Exilliteratur 1933–1945,* ed. Manfred Durzak (Stuttgart: Reclam, 1973), 509–19.

[146] Von Salomon, *The Answers,* 220. In German: "'Wer hat schuld an alledem?'" Von Salomon, *Der Fragebogen,* 324.

[147] Von Salomon, *The Answers,* 220. In German: "Etwa ich? Doch, ich auch! Wir alle!" "Das ist es ja, das ist ihre Kunst, sie machen jeden schuldig. Sie haben immer nur einen Auftrag des Volkes vollstreckt. Volk, das bist auch du und bin auch ich. Aber ich habe, verdammt nochmal, keinen Auftrag gegeben. Was ich geglaubt hatte, es müßte getan werden, habe ich selber getan." Von Salomon, *Der Fragebogen,* 324.

[148] Von Salomon, *The Answers,* 221. In German: "Und was meinst du, wieviel Parteimitglieder sind dabei, das gleiche zu tun und zu reden wie du und ich, ehrliche, anständige Parteimitglieder?" Von Salomon, *Der Fragebogen,* 325.

[149] "eine Art dämonische Schicksalsgestalt," "eine Prüfung, die das deutsche Volk bis zum bitteren Ende durchstehen müsse." Richard Herzinger, "Ein extremistischer Zuschauer — Ernst von Salomon: Konservativ-revolutionäre Literatur zwischen Tatrhetorik und Resignation," *Zeitschrift für Germanistik* (Neue Folge), 8, no. 1 (1998), 83–96; here, 90. For information on von Salomon's account of his involvement in the conservative revolution against the Weimar Republic, see Martin Sabrow, *Die verdrängte Verschwörung: Der Rathenau-Mord und die deutsche Gegenrevolution* (Frankfurt: Fischer, 1999).

[150] Von Salomon, *The Answers,* 280. In German: "Wie konnte es kommen, daß alle schuld hatten, daß also niemand schuld hatte?" Von Salomon, *Der Fragebogen,* 378.

[151] Von Salomon, *The Answers,* 280–81. In German: "warum stehen wir nicht mit ausgebreiteten Händen vor den brennenden Synagogen . . .?" "Wir können gar nicht mehr aus uns heraus leben. Alles, was um uns herum geschieht, lebt nicht aus denen heraus, die es tun; es lebt aus einem Kollektiv heraus. Wer sich zu diesem Kollektiv nicht bekennen kann, der ist tot. Das Kollektiv handelt immer unbedingt. Es verlangt auch das unbedingte Bekenntnis. Aber dieses Kollektiv, es hat uns nicht aufgenommen, sondern atomisiert. Atomisierte Teilchen bilden keine Gemeinschaft, sondern eine Sprengmasse." Von Salomon, *Der Fragebogen,* 378–79.

[152] "Es gibt keinem eine Möglichkeit, durch einen Einzelakt zu Solidarität zu gelangen." Von Salomon, *Der Fragebogen,* 379. My translation. For an alternative English translation, see von Salomon, *The Answers,* 281.

[153] Von Salomon, *The Answers,* 281. In German: "Das Entsetzliche ist, da wir uns selber nicht helfen können, daß viel mehr noch als den Juden uns geschieht." Von Salomon, *Der Fragebogen,* 379.

[154] Von Salomon, *The Answers,* 281–82. In German: von Salomon, *Der Fragebogen,* 379–80.

[155] Von Salomon, *The Answers,* 283. In German: "wenn es so ist, daß wir gleichzeitig alle atomisiert sind, vereinzelt, unfähig, steril, ohne jeden direkten Zusammenhang mit dem also diskreditierten Kollektiv." Von Salomon, *Der Fragebogen,* 380.

[156] Von Salomon, *The Answers,* 283. In German: "Nun, da unter diesen Umständen jedes Tun ein Verbrechen ist, so ist das einzige, was bleibt, nichts zu tun. Es ist jedenfalls das einzig Anständige. Und es ist zugleich das Schwerste, was es gibt, eine Art Gandhismus ohne Gandhi." Von Salomon, *Der Fragebogen,* 380.

[157] Von Salomon, *The Answers,* 283. In German: "Ich war zu meiner Überraschung plötzlich guter Laune. An den Methoden der Psychoanalyse schien doch etwas dran zu sein." Von Salomon, *Der Fragebogen,* 381.

[158] Von Salomon, *The Answers,* 293, 294. In German: "Waren Sie seit 1933 Mitglied einer verbotenen Oppositionspartei oder Gruppe?" "ja," "Welcher?" "Obergruppe Imming," "Frau Imming war meine Putzfrau." "das eigentliche Sinnbild des Widerstandes." Von Salomon, *Der Fragebogen,* 390, 391.

[159] Von Salomon, *The Answers,* 298. Translation modified. In German: "Ich liebte Frau Imming sehr, und sie liebte mich." "Der Obergruppe Imming gehörten etwa achtzig Prozent des deutschen Volkes an." Von Salomon, *Der Fragebogen,* 395, 392.

[160] Von Salomon, *The Answers,* 290. In German: "den einzigen Menschen in der ganzen Welt, der ihren Fragebogen wirklich ernst nimmt." Von Salomon, *Der Fragebogen,* 388.

[161] On the economic aspects of Zweig's novel, see Monika Melchert, "Die Zeitgeschichtsprosa nach 1945 im Kontext der Schuldfrage," in Heukenkamp, *Deutsche Erinnerung,* 101–66; here, 110–14.

[162] Arnold Zweig, *The Axe of Wandsbek,* trans. Eric Sutton (London: Hutchinson International Authors, 1948), 296. In German: "Sollte er diesen Leuten vorrechnen, in welchen Schulden er schon damals gesteckt, begreiflich machen, daß er sich ohne den Zwang von Schulden und Niedergang niemals dazu bereit gefunden hätte, sich zum Henker zu erniedrigen?" Arnold Zweig, *Das Beil von Wandsbek* (Berlin: Aufbau, 1959), 414. Original German-language edition: Zweig, *Das Beil von Wandsbek* (Stockholm: Neuer Verlag, 1947).

[163] "alle seinesgleichen im alten Europa, zumindest aber in Deutschland." Zweig, *Das Beil von Wandsbek,* 267. My translation. For an alternative English-language translation, see Zweig, *The Axe of Wandsbek,* 190.

[164] Zweig, *The Axe of Wandsbek,* 276. German original: "Er hätte vielleicht gesagt, der bürgerliche Geist . . . schiebt immer dann das Volk vor, wenn es seiner eigenen, quer über alle Grenzen geschichteten Klasse schiefgegangen ist." Zweig, *Das Beil von Wandsbek,* 388–89.

[165] Zweig, *The Axe of Wandsbek,* 276. German original: "mehr oder minder stumme Mitte und Substanz einer Kugel." Zweig, *Das Beil von Wandsbek,* 389.

[166] Zweig, *The Axe of Wandsbek,* 277. German original: "Diese gute Gesellschaft, zu der auch wir gehören, regiert sich selbst und die ganze Materie der Kugel." Zweig, *Das Beil von Wandsbek,* 389.

[167] Heinrich Vormweg, "Gerechtigkeit über sich fühlend: Arnold Zweigs Roman 'Das Beil von Wandsbek,'" in Durzak, *Die deutsche Exilliteratur 1933–1945,* 326–34; here, 332.

[168] "Der Mensch muß schon geradestehen für das, was er tut." Zweig, *Das Beil von Wandsbek,* 314. My translation. For an alternative English-language translation, see Zweig, *The Axe of Wandsbek,* 225.

[169] Wolfgang Koeppen, *Death in Rome,* trans. Michael Hofmann (London: Penguin, 1994), 29. "der Korrekte und Besitzer der in Leder gebundenen Goetheausgabe." German original: Wolfgang Koeppen, *Der Tod in Rom* (Frankfurt: Suhrkamp, 1975), 29. Alternative translation, also published as *Death in Rome,* by Mervyn Savill (New York: Vanguard, 1961), 28. I cite the Hofmann translation unless otherwise noted.

[170] Koeppen, *Death in Rome,* 150. In German: "Mein Vater konnte sich einbilden, zu Mord und Brand nicht beigetragen zu haben. Er hatte nur zugesehen." Koeppen, *Der Tod in Rom,* 140.

[171] Koeppen, *Death in Rome,* 55–56. Original German: "Er war weiter gegangen als die Bürger in der Halle, aber sie waren es, die ihm erlaubt hatten, so weit zu gehen. Sie hatten sein Wandern mit dem Tod gebilligt. Sie hatten das Blut beschworen, sie

hatten ihn gerufen, sie hatten ihn angefeuert, dem Schwert gehört die Welt, sie hatten Reden geschwungen, kein schönerer Tod als in der Schlacht, sie hatten ihm die erste Uniform gegeben und hatten sich vor der neuen Uniform, die er sich schuf, geduckt, sie hatten all sein Tun gepriesen, sie hatten ihn den Kindern als Vorbild gezeigt, sie hatten 'das Reich' gerufen und Mord und Schlag und Leichenrauch für Deutschland hingenommen. . . ." Koeppen, *Der Tod in Rom*, 53–54.

[172] Koeppen, *Death in Rome*, 155. Original German: "einen optimistischen Himmel, eine rosa Kuppel über dem grauen Erdkreis." Koeppen, *Der Tod in Rom, 145.*

[173] Koeppen, *Death in Rome*, 156. Original German: "doch umso erhabener hatte der rosa Überbau über dem Menschlich-Allzumenschlichen zu schweben," "an den Konditortempel der Kunst aus süßer Masse allegorisch ideal geformt." Koeppen, *Der Tod in Rom*, 145.

[174] Koeppen, *Death in Rome*, 166. Original German: "Ich möchte das entschleierte Bild sehen, selbst wenn ich zur Säule erstarre." Koeppen, *Der Tod in Rom*, 155.

[175] "das ist geschehen geschehen geschehen das ist nicht zu ändern nicht zu ändern das ist verdammt verdammt verdammt verdammt." Koeppen, *Der Tod in Rom*, 47. My translation. For alternative translations, see 49 in the Hofmann version and 50 in the Savill version.

[176] Koeppen, *Death in Rome*, 84. Original German: "die Sippe, dieses Gefängnis, in das sie mich sperren wollten, lebenslänglich." Koeppen, *Der Tod in Rom*, 80.

[177] Koeppen, *Death in Rome* (Savill translation), 117–18; translation modified. Original German: "eklig dünkte ihm die Lebensgier zu der wir verdammt sind, die Fortpflanzungssucht, die noch die Ärmsten betört, dieser Schein von Ewigkeit, der keine Ewigkeit ist." Koeppen, *Der Tod in Rom*, 104. For an alternative translation, see 110 in the Hofmann version.

[178] "Siegfried wollte sich nicht fortpflanzen. Der Gedanke, ein Leben zu verursachen, das unabsehbaren Begegnungen, Zufällen, Aktionen und Reaktionen ausgesetzt sein und durch Tat, Gedanke oder weitere Vermehrung seinserseits wieder noch in alle Zukunft wirken konnte, die Vorstellung Vater eines Kindes zu sein, diese Herausforderung der Welt, entsetzte ihn wahrhaft und verdarb ihm den Umgang mit Mädchen, selbst dann, wenn sie Verhütungsmittel anwandten, die an sich schon peinlich eklig waren und peinlich eklig auf das zu Verhütende hinwiesen. Körperliche Zeugung schien Siegfried ein Verbrechen zu sein. . . ." Koeppen, *Der Tod in Rom*, 160. My translation. For alternatives, see 172 in the Hofmann translation and 185 in the Savill translation.

[179] Ernestine Schlant, *The Language of Silence: West German Literature and the Holocaust* (New York: Routledge, 1999), 41.

[180] Koeppen, *Death in Rome*, 74. Original German: "Gerippe guckten die Kinder an. Tote guckten sie an. Die Kinder in der Uniform der Parteischule fürchteten sich." Koeppen, *Der Tod in Rom*, 71.

[181] Koeppen, *Death in Rome*, 74–75. Original German: "als ob sie selbst keine Skelette mehr hätten, kein Knochengerüst, als ob sie nur noch eine braune Parteijacke seien, die durch bösen Zauber in der Frühlingsluft hing." Koeppen, *Der Tod in Rom*, 71.

[182] "genau so alt wie Adolf, aber es hatte nur die Hälfte von Adolfs Gewicht." "als ob alles, was er bisher gedacht und gelernt hatte, nun ausgeräumt war," "ein leerer Luftballon," "'Bist du Nazi?' fragte der jüdische Junge. 'Mein Vater,' sagte Adolf.

'Meine Leute sind tot,' sagte der jüdische Junge. Und da dachte Adolf, daß auch sein Vater tot sein würde, er mußte tot sein; aber es sagte ihm nichts, daß sein Vater tot war. Wenn er weinte, dann weinte er um sich, oder nicht einmal um sich, er wußte nicht, warum er weinte, vielleicht weinte er um die Welt, aber er weinte nicht um seinen Vater. Hatte er ihn nicht geliebt? Er wußte es nicht. Hatte er ihn gehaßt? Er glaubte es nicht." Koeppen, *Der Tod in Rom*, 72–73. My translation. For alternative translations, see 75–76 in the Hofmann version and 79–80 in the Savill version.

[183] Koeppen, *Death in Rome*, 118. Translation modified. Original German: "selbst den Eltern wollte er freundlich und liebend begegnen." Koeppen, *Der Tod in Rom*, 111.

[184] Koeppen, *Death in Rome* (Savill translation), 27. Original German: "ein nordisches Gespenst." Koeppen, *Der Tod in Rom*, 29.

[185] Koeppen, *Death in Rome*, 143. Original German: "sie war ihr eigener Teufel, sie quälte Seele und Leib." Koeppen, *Der Tod in Rom*, 134.

[186] Koeppen, *Death in Rome* (Savill translation), 155; 144 in the Hofmann translation. Translation modified. Original German: "die haßgeifernden giftzüngelnden Riesenschlangen ihres Wahnsinns verschlangen die Eltern ganz." Koeppen, *Der Tod in Rom*, 135.

[187] *Koeppen, Death in Rome*, 56; translation modified. Original German: Koeppen, *Der Tod in Rom*, 54. "der kleine Gottlieb hatte es immer schon geahnt, daß es nur diese eine Macht gab, den Tod, und nur eine wirkliche Machtausübung: das Töten." For an alternative translation, see 58 in the Savill version.

[188] Koeppen, *Death in Rome*, 168. Original German: "Judejahn bedauerte nicht, getötet zu haben, er hatte zu wenig getötet, das blieb seine Schuld." Koeppen, *Der Tod in Rom*, 157.

[189] Koeppen, *Death in Rome*, 81. Original German: "er wollte dem Schullehrer-Vater und Gott-Vater trotzen." Koeppen, *Der Tod in Rom*, 77–78. Savill's translation (86) of "Gott-Vater" as "his godfather" is incorrect.

[190] Koeppen, *Death in Rome*, 42. Original German: "Judejahn hörte insgeheim eine Stimme, nicht die Stimme Gottes, und er vernahm sie nicht als Gewissensruf, es war die dünne, die hungrige und fortschrittsgläubige Stimme des Vaters Volksschullehrer, die flüsterte: du bist dumm, du hast deine Aufgaben nicht gelernt, du bist ein schlechter Schüler, eine Null, die aufgeblasen wurde." Koeppen, *Der Tod in Rom*, 41.

[191] Koeppen, *Death in Rome*, 201. Original German: "es gab die Hölle es gab die Hölle es gab die Hölle." Koeppen, *Der Tod in Rom*, 186.

[192] Koeppen, *Death in Rome* (Savill translation), 71. Original German: "Fliegen summten hier. Schmutzige Fliegen." Koeppen, *Der Tod in Rom*, 65. For an alternative translation, see 68 in the Hofmann version.

[193] Schlant, *The Language of Silence*, 41.

[194] Koeppen, *Death in Rome* (Savill translation), 128. Translation modified. Original German: "ewig auf der Flucht zu sein, ewig auf einem Weg, von dem man wußte, daß er woher kam, aber nirgends wohin führte." Koeppen, *Der Tod in Rom*, 112. For an alternative translation, see 119 in the Hofmann version. In both the original and the two published English-language translations, this phrase is part of a rhetorical question.

2: The Writer, the Conscience, and Absolute Presence

KOEPPEN'S DER TOD IN ROM is one indication that postwar German culture generally and literature specifically were fundamentally implicated
in and cognizant of a nexus of knowledge, guilt, and catastrophe. However
Der Tod in Rom was not published until 1954, well after the zero hour itself.
It shows one postwar German writer's response to the situation that had led
Johannes R. Becher, in January of 1946, to express a desire for the development of "something like a . . . national conscience" in and around the zero
hour,[1] but as a work that appeared almost a decade after the zero hour, it is a
mediated response, reflecting not just the zero hour but the German restoration and rebuilding that was already well underway in the middle of the
1950s.

In order to explore the mechanisms by which literature comes to imagine itself as "something like a . . . national conscience" at the zero hour itself, it is necessary to return to the mid-1940s and analyze two works that
show the way in which the consciousness of the writer can become synony-
mous with a more generalized conscience as the agent of an absolute power
associated with the divine — much in the way that Koeppen's Siegfried is
associated with the divine judgment of art and Koeppen's Adolf with the
Christian God. Although the two works I will explore — Hans Erich Nossack's *Der Untergang* (Destruction, 1948) and *Nekyia: Bericht eines Überlebenden* (Nekyia: The Account of a Survivor, 1947) — do not, for the
most part, make explicit the relationship between the writer's consciousness
and the consciousness of German guilt, they do demonstrate the way in
which writers could, in the wake of the national catastrophe, imagine themselves as allied with a destructive divinity visiting punishment on their fellow
citizens. Walter Jens's *Nein: Die Welt der Angeklagten* (No: The World of
the Accused, 1950), which appeared several years after the two works by
Nossack, is connected to them in its insistence on the writer's alliance with
an absolute consciousness/conscience. Finally, a brief look at two works
written by German-language authors outside Germany in the 1940s —
Hermann Broch's celebrated exile novel *Der Tod des Vergil* (The Death of
Vergil, 1945) and Max Frisch's play *Als der Krieg zu Ende war* (When the
War Was Over, 1949) — shows that Nossack and Jens, far from inventing a
unique discourse of literature as conscience, were transforming possibilities

inherent in German literary idealism and making use of them in the zero-hour situation. In other words their response to what appeared to be an unprecedented event was in fact predetermined by tradition.

As an autobiographical account of Nossack's own zero hour, the destruction of Hamburg in 1943, *Der Untergang* (written shortly after the event but not published until 1948) is, like so many other works of the zero hour, faced toward a past which is irrevocably lost. In Nossack's account, the future is little more than a fairy tale for children. A radical break with the past and the imagination of a future with infinite possibility might be comforting, Nossack's narrator imagines, but it would be a lie. Any story beginning with the words "Tomorrow, when it's all over . . ." would, in the context of Hamburg's present, be a fairy tale.[2] The ellipsis that follows the invocation of a possible tomorrow suggests the narrator's inability even to imagine a future extending beyond the horrific present. All access to the past may have been broken off, but the inability to connect with the past does not yet imply the compensatory turn toward the future that was later to become part of the zero hour myth. In fact it is precisely because the connection to the past has been broken off that the future appears inaccessible: in Nossack's imagery, there is no rainbow bridge leading over the abyss of the present to the future. The word "Abgrund" (abyss) appears again and again in the text, so often that the narrator expresses the fear that his readers may believe he is exaggerating. But the word is no exaggeration, he insists, and anyone who doubts him has no comprehension of the enormity and finality of Hamburg's destruction. In this context both survival and death seem little more than coincidences, without fundamental meaning.

And yet personal survival is also, paradoxically, based on the narrator's ability to negate his own person, thus earning the pardon of an ill-defined providence. "The abyss was very close to us, perhaps even under us, and we were floating over it only because of some unidentified grace. The only thing we could do was not to be loud and not to have too much weight. All it would have taken would have been for someone to start shouting, and we would all have been lost."[3] Faced with previously unimaginable horrors, the individual personality must shrink in order to decrease its vulnerability. The abyss over which the narrator floats is his present, and the present is all he has. Only small size and light weight offer the possibility of a grace that might blow him over the danger zone. Powerlessness is the fundamental fact of a zero hour in which human agency has been reduced to nothingness.

In this world of nullity, human response can take two possible routes. On the one hand people can acknowledge the fact of their powerlessness; on the other, they can seek, through frenetic activity, to hide their impotence from themselves and others. Those following the first route understand that they are trapped in a present where access to both the past and the future is cut off; those choosing the second option neurotically deny the enormity of their loss. For those in the first group, the destruction of their world means the end of ordinary life; while the second group clings desperately to ordinary life in order to obscure a more profound reality. The second group proceeds about its business as if nothing has happened, saying "through their actions: See, life goes on!"[4] As the narrator puts it, the two kinds of people "lived together in the same house and sat next to each other at the same table," but nevertheless "breathed the air of utterly different worlds." Indeed, "they spoke the same language but meant with their words entirely different realities."[5] For the narrator himself the continuation of ordinary life seems impossible. Again and again he describes his alienation from the routine activities of life. As he and his wife are walking through their devastated neighborhood, they see one house "alone and undestroyed in the wilderness of rubble," and in that house a woman is cleaning windows. This ordinary activity appears bizarre and unaccountable to the narrator: "We gave each other a nudge and stood as if hypnotized, we thought we were looking at a crazy woman." And when the narrator sees a group of children doing garden work in a front yard somewhere, he finds their actions "so incomprehensible that we told other people about it as if it were something extraordinary." When he sees people on their balconies drinking coffee, it seems to him "like a movie, it was actually impossible." And when he and his wife finally understand "that it was only we who were looking at others' actions with eyes askew," they are shocked by their own alienation. As the narrator puts it, "the world is divided into two groups, and between them lies an invisible abyss which both groups know about. The people on this side and on the other side have begun to hate each other."[6] If the future has become a fairy tale that cannot be told, the past can perhaps be understood only in the narrative form of a parable with which the narrator can make his own history more comprehensible to those who have not experienced it:

> Once upon a time there was a man who had no mother. A fist thrust him naked into the world, and a voice called out: You're on your own! Then he opened his eyes and didn't know what to make of the world around him. And he dared not look behind, for behind him was nothing but fire.[7]

This parable — whose pessimistic tone resembles a passage from Georg Büchner's play *Woyzeck* — is an invocation of a radical, inescapable present. The subject of the parable has no mother and therefore no connection to a reassuring past or to tradition. Nor has he willed his own coming into the world. Far from being a hero of the zero hour, the narrator of this parable is at an utter loss.

Beyond the world of daily necessity and the hoped-for end of the war the narrator perceives nothing, and he believes that no one else can see beyond the present either: "At that time no one thought any further ahead."[8]

Death seems a foregone conclusion not only for the narrator but also for his fellow citizens. "Perhaps we have received the fatal wound, and whatever comes next will be nothing but dying."[9]

This sense of finality is entirely characteristic of the culture of the zero hour. No visions of a grand rebuilding or of a newer, better Germany make the loss of the past more bearable; instead, the narrator suggests that the destruction of Hamburg heralds the end of European history. The city and the continent are both gone for good. What remain are the living dead and those who are already ghosts. Even those who have busied themselves with the ordinary tasks of daily life are not necessarily thinking up grand schemes for the future: like their counterparts, they are lost in a present from which there is no release. In the midst of their frenetic activity they suddenly stop, forgetting any projects they may have, and gather together with other people to listen to the news.

> To an outsider it must have seemed as if we had a lot of time, and yet we were people without rest. We didn't have a lot of time, we no longer had any time at all, we were outside time. Everything we did became instantly meaningless in our own eyes.[10]

The dissociation from time renders meaning impossible. For those outside time, any action taking place within time makes no sense. Hence ordinary life has become radically alienating for the narrator. It is only in the context of the disappearance of the past and the absence of the future that the narrator is able to find himself in a present that, precisely through the terrible alienation of everyday life, bears the seeds of transformation and transcendence. Civil and political authority have disappeared, along with all those aspects of life that bind human beings to routine. With the shattering of "the cold, greedily dividing window pane" that normally separates human beings from awareness of the sublime, "the infinity behind man blew unchecked into the infinity in front of him, sanctifying his countenance for the transmission of the eternal."[11] In this timeless moment of access to the eternal, the eyes of human beings become large and transparent, like the eyes of Russian icons. Already the narrator is aware that this hour of a nothingness that gives access to the infinite will soon come to an end. Therefore he wishes to fix the image of this moment of absolute presence in his mind and in the minds of his readers: "Before everything loses its history in a nebulous mass, let us fling this countenance as a constellation into the heavens, a reminder of our final possibility."[12] In the face of eternity, the narrator has lost all fear; the present is "a moment when man showed himself to be no longer the slave of his institutions."[13]

In the final pages of *Der Untergang,* time is personified as a scolding mother calling her lost children back to everyday life and work. She "watches over us, she commands us to work and calls us to lunch, and we obey her."[14] But even as the narrator and the other citizens of Hamburg return to their daily lives, they are aware that everyday life is nothing but an illusion: "They don't believe in it. The stage-set is missing, the appearance of reality."[15] In ordinary life human beings live "wedged in between yesterday and tomorrow without a moment of today."[16] Everyday life, in other words, is a trap, a prison, which robs human beings of their own presence. But now everyday life has become permanently alienated, and human beings know that it is nothing but a game, without deeper reality. "What we have gained and what has changed is this: we have arrived in the present. We have released ourselves from time," the narrator insists.[17] The destruction of Hamburg thus makes possible the awareness of a divine presence that exists outside time, in an eternal present. The fate of the man-made city has made the narrator aware of the fragility and illusory nature of all human institutions, rending the veil which separates him from a deeper reality and giving him access at least to an inkling of the divine, what he had previously referred to as "some unidentified grace." That moment is one of horror, devastation, impotence, and despair; but at the same time it liberates the narrator from the chains of illusion that had bound him to a routine, mundane existence. The narrator now finds himself in an alliance with the divine — even if the divinity is death itself. Rather than playing with the attributes of an existence now recognized to be unreal, the narrator plays with his divine friend and ally. "We've run out into the street again and are playing with death. And time sits sadly in a corner, feeling useless."[18]

By forming an alliance with the very power that has destroyed his own life and the life of his city, the narrator seeks to overcome his powerlessness. It is this alliance with the divine — in the form of death personified — that is the narrator's last chance. Now on the other side of the abyss, he looks back at the other human beings still caught in a veil of illusion and declares their desire to continue with everyday life to be "almost cynical."[19] The destruction of Hamburg is a kind of judgment, the narrator believes, and he feels no anger against the Allied bomber pilots who have carried out that destruction; they are, for him, merely the instruments of a higher power with which he is in collusion.

Because of his alliance with a divine presence outside of time, the narrator-writer is able to preserve an element of eternity in the midst of destruction. The physical destruction of the narrator's home has not rendered the imaginary habitation of the writer inaccessible; even the destruction of the drafts and notes in his apartment can not prevent him from telling his story. Although the narrator asks himself why he is writing, he leaves his question unanswered, as if it were purely rhetorical, since a narrator can do nothing but narrate.

Far from being a radical beginning ex nihilo, the narrator's invocation of daily life as an illusion, and of a divine power rendered palpable by Hamburg's destruction are part of an aesthetic and philosophical tradition that reaches back to Schopenhauer's *Die Welt als Wille und Vorstellung* (The World as Will and Representation, 1819–1840) and, beyond the pessimism of German Romantic philosophy, to Plato's distinction between absolute reality and the illusions of the senses. In spite of Plato's argument that art is even further removed from absolute reality than the world of the senses, the alliance between Nossack's narrator and an absolute reality is by no means unprecedented. The framework of an idealistic aesthetics in which art allows access to essential reality provides Nossack's narrator with the support he needs to make his way over the physical and psychological abyss that has opened up with the destruction of Hamburg. Although the narrator claims to make himself infinitesimally small, his alliance with a divinity greater than himself enlarges him and makes possible precisely that rainbow bridge over the abyss that he had previously claimed was illusory. The narrator may have rejected the maternal power of time, of clocks, and of everyday life, but he has become an ally of an even greater masculine power in the face of which everything else seems negligible. "He lives over there, where there aren't any more houses. Every afternoon he comes through the old gateway. He's our friend. We always ask him to take us home with him."[20] Like Robert Lindhoff, the chronicler-hero of Kasack's *Die Stadt hinter dem Strom,* who sojourns as a living man in the city of the dead, the narrator of *Der Untergang* is in an alliance with death that renders him immortal and unassailable. In the face of the catastrophe now lying behind him, he finds that the cares and troubles of everyday life are unimportant: "The worst is behind us, and compared to that the bad doesn't count. It's not so terrible."[21] Narration, allied with the greater power that has destroyed the narrator's city, enables survival in a spiritual world now transformed by the encounter with absolute presence.

In Nossack's novella *Nekyia: Bericht eines Überlebenden,* the direct narration of the concrete destruction of a real city that prevails in *Der Untergang* recedes behind a dreamlike account of disappearance, catastrophe, and aloneness. Whereas the narrator of *Der Untergang* begins his story with the concrete information "I experienced the destruction of Hamburg as a witness,"[22] the narrator of *Nekyia* never identifies the name of the empty city through which he roams, or of the sleeping companions with whom he finds himself at the beginning of the story, people who lie around "like lumps of clay" and snore restlessly.[23] Indeed, the novella's narrator seems to be the only conscious human being left in the world after an unidentified catastrophe. Why and for whom is the narrator telling his story? "One can hardly assume that books will ever be printed again as was our wont," the narrator acknowledges; nor would there be readers interested in such books, even if, at some unspecified time in the future, they were to be printed again. As senseless as his narration may seem, however, the narrator is haunted throughout the events that he relates by "a completely unreasonable verse that I must have heard somewhere." The verse goes like this:

Why were we given a voice
if we don't also sing at the abyss? When
was a voice ever lost?

Although he acknowledges that this verse is irrational and incomplete, the narrator declares that it was "a kind of aid" to him in a time of danger, and he even suspects

> that I would have been doomed without this verse. In a sense it made me immune to events, so that I never participated in them completely and they found no point of attack. Yes, it must have functioned as a kind of magic cap.[24]

If the narrator of *Der Untergang* had declared that the only possibility for survival lies in not being loud and not having too much weight, then the narrator of *Nekyia* has found precisely the means by which he can make himself disappear, thus eliminating all vulnerability to the outside world. His verse and his singing voice are his talisman.

The narrator of *Nekyia* seems to have survived the unspecified catastrophe as a kind of ghost. When he returns to the unnamed city, which seems to have been emptied of all its inhabitants, he enters a house and looks into a mirror in which he cannot see himself or any of the objects that lie before his eyes, even though he can see all of the objects that lie behind him. Nor does the narrator have a name. Prior to the catastrophe he had a name, but he has now become separated from that name. He indulges in the Romantic fantasy that his name — like the mirror image bartered away by Erasmus Spikher in E. T. A. Hoffmann's tale "Die Abenteuer der Silvester-Nacht" (The Adventures of New Year's Eve, 1815) — may now enjoy an existence independent of him: "What if my name and my image were still alive somewhere?"[25] Is it possible, the narrator wonders, that his name is now somewhere else — "on the edge of the bed of some woman, and she is allowing herself to be deceived by it?"[26] When he sees the mirror without his image in it, the narrator believes that he is alive, and that the mirror itself is somehow faulty. "The other possibility didn't occur to me: that my image had been destroyed." How could he have possibly thought otherwise, asks the narrator, because "we cannot imagine any human being without his mirror image; and one can ask whether a living organism without such an image can even be called a human being."[27] But the narrator ultimately comes to an important realization. "I owe my life," he believes, "solely to this: I had been so loosely connected to my name and my image that they were unable to pull me with them when they were destroyed."[28] The ability to separate oneself from one's name and one's past like a lizard losing its tail is an attribute of survival. Like the narrator of *Der Untergang*, the narrator of *Nekyia* appears to have survived the catastrophe only by a process of shrinkage: he has separated a central core of his self from some other part of him that was destined for destruction. His survival is based on the division of the self into a nameless core that functions like a ghost, moving around a dead city, reflecting on the past, and singing a song that guarantees its survival; and an empty shell, designated by the words "image" and "name" and associated with inauthenticity. The loss of this negative mirror image seems not to trouble the narrator: "It was like paper money that falls unnoticed out of one's wallet, nothing more. The wind blows it away — perhaps someone finds it and can do something with it; but perhaps it falls into a puddle and dissolves."[29]

In many ways the narrator seems to be dead; and yet, he wonders, if he is dead, where are all the other dead people? Why is the world empty of other ghosts? "No, I couldn't be dead. Because only a living person could be as lonely as I was."[30] Indeed, the narrator reflects, his existence as a ghost seems to have come to an end with the catastrophe; it is only now that he is truly alive. Previously, the narrator remembers, people had treated him as if he had been a ghost, bumping into him on the street as if they did not even see him. It was his previous life, hence, that was inauthentic, unreal. Now, after the catastrophe that has eliminated all other human beings or transformed them into "lumps of clay," the narrator is truly alive. And ultimately, he declares to the future listeners with whom he imagines himself to be in conversation, it does not particularly matter whether one is alive or dead; "all that is important is that we are speaking to each other."[31] As in *Der Untergang*, life prior to the great catastrophe seems to have been inauthentic; because of the catastrophe the narrator has awakened to a more authentic life in which, even if he is separated from his name and his image and from other human beings, he is more truly alive than ever before.

As in *Der Untergang*, time seems to have ceased functioning. Time is a function of the world that has come to an end with the catastrophe. The narrator lives in an absolute present in which only mutual communication guarantees existence, and in which lack of communication, and lack of recognition, mean annihilation.

> In the past there was nothing more reliable than the counting of time. Everything was precisely divided and could be expressed in numbers. Someone was thirty years old and someone else had lived a thousand years ago. These calculations were probably correct, but the preconditions are no longer the same. Time has been shattered.[32]

In this postcatastrophic world of the zero hour, designations of time no longer have a meaning. If the narrator turns his face to those who lived a thousand years ago, then they are there, and he can speak to them. But "if I don't turn to face them, then they are not there at all, and no number can change that."[33] Existence, whether in the past or in the future, is a function of mutual contact with the narrator. To his future listener he declares: "And with you, my friend, it's the same; you are there because you're listening to me."[34] If existence is based on contact with the narrator, then future and past no longer have a meaning. Both are part of an immeasurable present. Should there ever again be a need to use numbers and measurements for time, the narrator declares, then the beginning of time will not be any specific action but rather speech itself — "I will have to say: such-and-such many hours or days or years from the moment when I was able to speak about it."[35]

For the narrator, strength lies not just in the ability to sing but also in the power to create. Towards the end of the story the narrator finds himself, together with a friend-enemy who functions as his alter ego, in a nebulous crater full of wet clay.[36] As his alter ego looks on, the narrator begins to create the image of a woman. While speaking with his alter ego, he watches in amazement as his creation comes to life:

> Soon I thought I discerned a twitching of her legs, as if she were trying to raise her foot from the ground. Then again it was as if breast and stomach were rising and she were breathing. One would only have had to call her by a name, and she would have walked towards us.[37]

When the narrator's alter ego notices that this new creation has no navel and is therefore imperfect, he rushes to repair the mistake. "How can she have a navel if she was not born by a mother," yells the narrator at him, warning him to keep away.[38] Nevertheless the narrator's heedless alter ego sticks his index finger into the claylike belly of the new creature, which immediately disintegrates into mud, burying him beneath it. At the same time, the destruction of his alter ego buries the narrator himself, who sinks into nothingness, separated from his past and from everything else that is familiar. As he tells this story to a woman he sees in the mirror of the empty house he had explored earlier, he imagines himself kneeling before her and burying his face in her womb, as if doing penance for having arrogated to himself the power of creation that belongs to mothers.

During another dream sequence the narrator imagines himself in the presence of a number of male authority figures, including his father, his teacher, and a mysterious judge referred to as the "original ancestor." This primogenitor has banished the narrator's mother from human contact, including contact with her son, because of an Aeschylean crime against patriarchal power which, the narrator believes, threatened not only the peace but also the existence of the world. The fundamental task that the narrator must accomplish is a reconciliation between the stern, eternal law of the father-judge and the softer, evanescent matriarchal power of the creator-mother. When he has accomplished this reconciliation, the past will once again be restored to the world's inhabitants, and daily life will be able to resume, now in accordance with "the voice of the great ancestor," which will be "clear and infallible."[39] At that moment the inchoate human beings lying around unconscious near the narrator will wake up and be able to wash their faces and give each other names. "And when the names ring forth, the earth will awaken and think: Now I must let trees and flowers grow."[40] At the end of *Nekyia* the narrator knows that his task is to stand guard and prevent the human clumps of clay around him from seeking to return to the city too soon — from prematurely seeking the moment of human birth. The narrator's moment is the "span of life . . . which stretches from death to birth," a span, the narrator assures us, "which we know can stretch out over far greater spaces; we tend to be silent about it, I suspect, because it does not allow itself to be limited by numbers."[41] If human beings seek to return too soon to quotidian life, then they will drive the mystical "words of this other life" to distraction, forcing them deep into the silence of the ocean, "where their home is, which was also our home."[42] The narrator's alter ego, he knows, will one day try to brush him aside and go into the city, return to everyday life. But as in the previous dream, in which the alter ego's efforts had brought catastrophe, the narrator knows, that "if curiosity drives him there too early, he will be doomed. And how much new damage would be caused by this: everything would have been in vain."[43]

And yet the narrator also recognizes that there is an inner integrity to his alter ego's desire for a return to the clarity and security of everyday life. It is possible, he believes, that instead of causing a catastrophe, this return to everyday life, however premature, might ultimately bring about precisely the universal reconciliation which he desires. Just as the narrator of *Der Untergang* had suspected that he himself, through his alliance with the power of destruction, was to blame for the destruction of the city, so too the narrator of *Nekyia* believes that "I may be to blame for everything."[44] The female forces of creation, preservation, and continuation represented by his mother are in a constant struggle with the male forces of destruction and renewal. But even though the narrator of *Nekyia* knows that he is partially to blame for the catastrophe, he is also aware that a return to everyday life would make him equally guilty. He must, hence, remain as a witness and a warning; if he succeeds, he will, in later years, achieve "an undying name" and be acknowledged by others as a shepherd of men.[45] His job, he believes, is to speak with the voice of his father.[46]

These two works by Nossack articulate a vision of the zero hour as a moment of transcendence defined by the nullification of quotidian existence and the revelation of an absolute presence that had previously been hidden. The narrators of both works feel the pangs of a guilty conscience, for they are both allied with the destructive power of righteous judgment. For both, narration and song are talismans enabling survival in the midst of destruction. And in both works the distinction between the quotidian world prior to the catastrophe and the world of transcendence made possible by the catastrophe is crucial. In *Nekyia* that split runs through the narrator himself, dividing his self into an all-too-eager alter ego that wishes to return immediately to everyday life and to begin the cycle of creation and destruction again, even at the cost of meaninglessness, and a judgmental, paternal super-ego that seeks to prevent the return to quotidian existence pending some future reconciliation between the maternal power of preservation and the paternal power of destruction and renewal.

One further work of fiction, Walter Jens's novel *Nein: Die Welt der Angeklagten,* makes the postwar writer's imaginary alliance with the judgmental conscience in the wake of the zero hour even more explicit. In the totalitarian world of Jens's novel, humanity is divided into three kinds of people: those who have been accused of a crime; those who bear witness against the accused; and the judges whose job it is to pass sentence on the guilty. Even though it eschews actual historical references, Jens's novel is the ultimate literary invocation of collective guilt: it is not just one character who is guilty, but virtually the entire world. The action of the novel takes place at an unspecified time in a nightmarish future when religion, university study, and most forms of art have been banned:

> Five years after the last war, which had left only one world power, now omnipotent, they destroyed the churches. Seven years after the war they began to close the first universities. Nine years after the war they issued the law on art that damned writers, painters, and musicians to silence.[47]

What has been destroyed in this world is culture and all of its institutions — everything that, by dividing man from himself, makes it possible for him to achieve self-awareness. The novel's hero, Walter Sturm, is the last writer left in the world, and Jens's novel tells the story of Sturm's inquisition and judgment, and particularly his confrontation with the supreme judge, himself an intellectual who is growing older, and who has selected Sturm as his successor. The supreme judge wears a mask in order to hide his individuality even from himself; he has become pure function. His philosophy is fundamentally similar to that of the Grand Inquisitor in Dostoyevsky's *The Brothers Karamazov:* that human beings are happiest when they are deprived of freedom and the pain of knowledge and thought.[48] "We closed the churches and the universities," the supreme judge declares. "And we burned the books, and they became happy. They should have nothing else in their heads but working and being happy."[49] Except for Sturm and the other writers who have already been condemned and executed, the hominids in this story live precisely the quotidian, thoughtless existence so despised by the narrators of Nossack's stories. The only two people left in the world who understand the functioning of the totalitarian system depicted in *Nein* are the supreme judge and Sturm himself. The supreme judge has chosen Sturm as his successor because, as a writer, he is capable of memory and thought; as the last representative of a dying culture, he is able to separate himself from the quotidian world of other hominids, thus giving their lives, and the social system itself, meaning. The writer's consciousness is hence even more global than the quotidian totalitarianism that he rejects. Sturm's partner and opponent, the supreme judge, tells him that the system which controls the world has become virtually automatic; it would therefore be possible for almost anyone to become the supreme judge, watching over but not understanding the absurd movements of the accused and the condemned. "But it would be good," the supreme judge adds, "if there were always someone there who is not just being driven along but who is capable of watching the movement of the waves carefully and who could take pleasure in the observation of the bodies dancing up and down on the waves."[50] Walter Sturm's designated task is to be the witness and interpreter of a world that would have no meaning whatsoever without him. The judge explains:

> People have become happy. . . . But they don't know it. They are accused, they become witnesses, and they become judges. But they don't know it. They don't think of God, they don't love, they all make the same movements, and they have all learned what they are to do during the hours when they're not working. But they don't know about it. They all have the same thoughts, make the same gestures. But they don't know it. All they do now is talk to themselves. But they don't know it.[51]

In this world the process of civilization has been reversed, and human beings have returned to a second, nightmarish state of nature. Like the human subject imagined in Kleist's famous essay "Über das Marionettentheater" (On the Puppet Theater) they have lost all self-consciousness; however their lack of self-consciousness signals not the entry into a superhuman paradise as envisioned by Kleist but rather the entry into a subhuman hell.[52] The only people with true consciousness, the judge insists, are Walter and himself; hence it is only they who can, as supreme judges, represent the consciousness and conscience of a community without knowledge of itself. Walter must, hence, choose between two equally unpalatable options: a life in which he negates his own existence by putting on a mask and becoming the supreme judge over his fellow citizens in a world that has no meaning outside his own comprehension of it; and a death that is nevertheless still a judgment, since it condemns both the existing world and all of human history to meaninglessness. As the novel's title suggests, Sturm chooses the latter course. But because of his decision, human history in the sense of meaningful continuity comes to an abrupt end. Sturm and his counterpart the supreme judge are literally the last men left on earth: "You are the last," the supreme judge says to him before he dies.[53] What comes after Sturm's death is a world in which the hominids who people the earth are no longer homo sapiens in the sense of knowledge and ratiocination. In the final words of the novel: "Sun and moon looked down on a not very large planet. Figures lived on it. Formerly they were called: human beings."[54]

Like George Orwell's *1984* (1949) and Aldous Huxley's *Brave New World* (1932), Jens's novel *Nein* is a dystopia about a totalitarian world. Published in West Germany shortly after the catastrophe of Nazism and shortly after the beginning of the cold war, it is filled with the foreboding of a possible world totalitarianism. However the dystopia depicted in Jens's novel is precisely the dumb continuation of a meaningless existence in the face of catastrophe decried by Nossack and other writers. In declining the offer of supreme power, the chief character of Jens's novel is a hero of renunciation and abnegation of the quotidian world. His crime is the refusal to condone or to participate in totalitarianism. But in spite of his ultimate refusal to accept the position of supreme judge, Walter Sturm is nevertheless the last person in the world to make this sort of conscious choice. In the totalitarian world of *Nein,* it is the writer and his ratiocination that provide the last link to a world of meaning and continuity with a transcendent tradition. Everyone else in Jens's world lives completely enclosed in a smooth, pleasant, but inescapable quotidian trap.

A brief look at two works by German-language writers living outside Germany will confirm that similar themes occupied many writers in and around the end of the Third Reich. In a context dominated by harsh debates between emigrant writers and writers who had remained in Germany during the Nazi dictatorship, such convergences demonstrate at least one area of common agreement: the belief in the writer's almost divine mission as an agent of absolute conscience.

Hermann Broch's *Der Tod des Vergil* narrates the famous Roman poet's passage from life to death as an almost ecstatic mystical journey from the quotidian to the absolute. Following the Dantean tradition, which viewed Vergil as a proto-Christian pointing the way to the coming of Christ, Broch fills his novel with references to the advent of the divine, to absolute presence, and to a consequent break with all previous history. In imagery much like that of Nossack, Broch's Vergil imagines his soul in an alliance with the divine principle in the universe, floating over an abyss of nothingness.[55] Like Nossack's characters, Broch's Vergil understands that human beings need to understand the insignificance of their quotidian existence. The goal of all writing, Vergil believes, is the simultaneity of eternity, a simultaneity that can be achieved only by the recognition and acknowledgment of death.[56] Hence the artistic muses stand in the service of death.[57] For Vergil, too, literature is in communication with the "original ancestor."[58] The words of the poet form an alliance with and are ultimately subsumed by the Word of God, and it is this absolute Word that Vergil hears at the moment of his death and transfiguration. Out of the emptiness of nothingness, the Word creates an absolute universe, and it is the Word that carries Vergil's soul over the abyss and into a new, higher existence.

Max Frisch's play *Als der Krieg zu Ende war* offers little hope of trans-figuration through death, but it too features a main character, Agnes Anders, who willingly chooses death in order to reject a mendacious, inauthentic life. Like the main character in Nossack's *Nekyia,* Agnes ultimately splits in two, becoming, at the moment of her death, both a woman committing suicide and a narrator commenting to the audience on the woman's actions. Since the reason for Agnes's suicide is her unwillingness to live together with a husband who is an unrepentant war criminal, her rejection of the quotidian and her ethical decision for death are directly related to the problem of German guilt. The enjoyment of everyday life is acceptable only if it is compatible with humanity and dignity:

> Because it won't work for us to live in the same house as a criminal, and we won't turn against him. It won't work, or we will share his guilt, which is destroying us.[59]

For Agnes, too, everyday life must be questioned, for under it lies an abyss.

The works by Nossack and Jens, as well as those by Broch, Frisch, Kasack, and others, suggest that many postwar German-language writers viewed themselves as a last link to western traditions. They saw themselves as the representatives and remnants of meaning in a world that had been rendered radically senseless by a break with those traditions. For most of these writers, the world of everyday reality and postwar reconstruction had become fundamentally immoral or amoral. Those simply going through the motions of quotidian life in the face of catastrophe and guilt, they believed, were not only refusing to recognize and acknowledge the extent of the catastrophe but also failing to seize the transformative opportunities offered by an epiphany in which a *metanoia* — a radically new life — had become possible. Postwar German writers at the zero hour and afterward saw their stance as radically nonconformist in its confrontation with the everyday world. Theirs was a world of alienation from an immoral and fundamentally flawed existence. Hence the primary figures in many of these writers' works have a tendency to set themselves up as judges not only over themselves and their own pasts but also over their fellow citizens. It is not just for exile writers like Thomas Mann and Johannes R. Becher that literature becomes the conscience of the German nation. The place reserved for the writer in the literary world of Jens's novel can be understood as a metaphor for his place in postwar German society. He was to be the supreme judge, the last embodiment of critical consciousness in an otherwise absurd world. Allied with the power of a higher spirit unknown to his fellow citizens, he was there to observe and judge them. He took on all the attributes that Freud had designated as functions of the superego: observation, judgment, and ego ideal.

While these works bear witness to sternness and punishment, they also suggest the disintegration and division of the literary self. The literary figures in these novels are not simply the impregnable judges of their fellow men: they too belong among the convicted in Jens's "world of the accused." Walter Sturm and Agnes Anders sentence themselves to death, and the figures in many other works of the immediate postwar period suggest a profound split in identity: everywhere there are mirrors and doubles, names and images that have become separated from essences. These literary representatives of disintegration aptly reflect the political reality of a Germany that was itself undergoing a political split, transforming itself into what the writer Kurt Drawert was later to call "Spiegelland" ("mirror land").[60] But the split was not just between west and east, exiles and inner emigrants, past and present; in addition, it ran right through the world of German literary identity. A literary world later deemed to have been one of the creators of postwar West German identity was, at the same time, established as the most persistent, fundamental critic of that identity.

Notes

[1] "so etwas wie ein Gewissen, wie ein nationales Gewissen." Becher, "Deutschland klagt an!" *Der Aufbau*, 2, no. 1 (January 1946), 16–17. Unless otherwise specified, all translations from German in this book are my own; the German appears in the notes, followed by sources. I have added the notation "my translation" in a limited number of cases where confusion might otherwise occur.

[2] "Morgen, wenn alles vorbei ist, dann. . . ." Hans Erich Nossack, *Der Untergang* (New York: Harcourt, Brace & World, 1962 [originally 1948]), 20. All translations of this work are my own unless otherwise noted. For an alternative English-language translation, see Nossack, *The Fall,* translation and introduction by Ronald Dale Tullius (University of Texas at Austin M.A. Thesis, 1975), 33.

[3] "Der Abgrund war ganz nah neben uns, ja, vielleicht unter uns, und wir schwebten nur durch irgendeine Gnade darüberhin. Das einzige, was wir tun konnten, war, nicht laut zu sein und nicht zu viel Gewicht zu haben. Es hätte nur einer von uns zu schreien brauchen, und wir wären alle verloren gewesen." Nossack, *Der Untergang,* 34. Alternative English translation: Nossack, *The Fall,* 46–47.

[4] "Die einen sagen durch ihr Tun: Seht, das Leben geht weiter!" Nossack, *Der Untergang,* 28–29. Alternative English translation: Nossack, *The Fall,* 41.

[5] "in demselben Hause zusammenlebten und am gleichen Tische beieinandersaßen," "die Luft ganz verschiedener Welten einatmeten." "Sie redeten dieselbe Sprache, aber sie meinten mit ihren Worten ganz andere Wirklichkeiten." Nossack, *Der Untergang,* 28. Alternative English translation: Nossack, *The Fall,* 41.

[6] "einsam und unzerstört in der Trümmerwüste," "Wir stießen uns an, wir blieben gebannt stehen, wir glaubten eine Verrückte zu sehen." "so unbegreiflich, daß wir anderen davon erzählten, als wäre es wunder was." "wie ein Film, es war eigentlich unmöglich." "daß nur wir mit verkehrten Augen auf das andere Tun blickten," "die Welt [ist] in zwei Teile geteilt, dazwischen liegt ein unsichtbarer Abgrund, um den beide wissen. Die Menschen diesseits und jenseits haben einander zu hassen

begonnen." Nossack, *Der Untergang*, 30. Alternative English translation: Nossack, *The Fall*, 43, 42.

[7] Nossack, *The Fall*, 42. Translation slightly modified. In German: "Es war einmal ein Mensch, den hatte keine Mutter geboren. Eine Faust stieß ihn nackt in die Welt hinein, und eine Stimme rief: Sieh zu, wie du weiterkommst. Da öffnete er die Augen und wußte nichts anzufangen mit dem, was ihn umgab. Und er wagte nicht, hinter sich zu blicken, denn hinter ihm war nichts als Feuer." Nossack, *Der Untergang*, 29.

[8] Nossack, *The Fall*, 50. In German: "Weiter dachte damals kein Mensch." Nossack, *Der Untergang*, 39.

[9] Nossack, *The Fall*, 51. In German: "Wir empfingen vielleicht die tödliche Wunde, und was noch folgt, ist nur ein Verenden." Nossack, *Der Untergang*, 39.

[10] Nossack, *The Fall*, 48. Translation altered. In German: "Für ein außenstehendes Wesen muß es so ausgesehen haben, als ob wir viel Zeit gehabt hätten, und dennoch waren wir Gehetzte. Wir hatten nicht viel Zeit, wir hatten überhaupt keine Zeit mehr, wir waren aus der Zeit heraus. Alles, was wir taten, wurde uns sofort sinnlos." Nossack, *Der Untergang*, 35–36.

[11] "die Unendlichkeit hinter dem Menschen [wehte ungehemmt] ins Unendliche vor ihm und heiligte sein Antlitz zum Durchgang für Ewiges." Nossack, *Der Untergang*, 36. Alternative English translation: Nossack, *The Fall*, 48.

[12] "Laßt uns dieses Antlitz, ehe alles zur gesichtslosen Masse wird, als Sternbild an den Himmel werfen, zur Erinnerung an unsere letzte Möglichkeit." Nossack, *Der Untergang*, 36. Alternative English translation: Nossack, *The Fall*, 48.

[13] Nossack, *The Fall*, 52. Translation modified. In German: "ein Augenblick, wo sich der Mensch nicht mehr als der Sklave seiner Einrichtungen zeigte." Nossack, *Der Untergang*, 41.

[14] Nossack, *The Fall*, 80. Translation modified. In German: "Sie wacht noch über uns, sie befiehlt uns zu arbeiten und ruft uns zum Mittagessen, und wir gehorchen ihr." Nossack, *Der Untergang*, 70.

[15] "Sie glauben nicht daran. Die Kulisse fehlt, die Illusion der Wirklichkeit." Nossack, *Der Untergang*, 69. Alternative English translation: Nossack, *The Fall*, 78–79.

[16] Nossack, *The Fall*, 79. In German: "eingezwängt zwischen dem Gestern und Morgen, ohne eine Sekunde Gegenwart." Nossack, *Der Untergang*, 70.

[17] "was wir gewonnen haben und was anders wurde, das ist: Wir sind gegenwärtig geworden. Wir haben uns aus der Zeit gelöst" Nossack, *Der Untergang*, 70. Alternative English translation: Nossack, *The Fall*, 80.

[18] "Wir sind wieder auf die Straße gelaufen und spielen mit dem Tode. Da setzt sich die Zeit traurig in einen Winkel und kommt sich nutzlos vor." Nossack, *Der Untergang*, 71. Alternative English translation: Nossack, *The Fall*, 81.

[19] "der beinah zynische Wunsch" Nossack, *Der Untergang*, 57. Alternative English translation: Nossack, *The Fall*, 67.

[20] Nossack, *The Fall*, 80. In German: "Er wohnt dort drüben, wo keine Häuser mehr sind. Er kommt jeden Nachmittag durch den alten Torbogen. Er ist unser Freund. Wir bitten ihn immer, uns dorthin mitzunehmen, wo er wohnt." Nossack, *Der Untergang*, 71.

[21] "Wir haben das Schwerste hinter uns, das Schwerere zählt dagegen nicht. Es ist nicht so schlimm." Nossack, *Der Untergang*, 71. Alternative English translation: Nossack, *The Fall*, 81.

[22] "Ich habe den Untergang Hamburgs als Zuschauer erlebt." Nossack, *Der Untergang*, 7.

[23] "wie Lehmklumpen." Nossack, *Nekyia: Bericht eines Überlebenden* (Frankfurt: Suhrkamp, 1961 [originally 1947]), 7.

[24] "Es ist kaum anzunehmen, daß je wieder Bücher gedruckt werden, wie wir es gewohnt waren," "ein ganz unvernünftiger Vers, den ich irgendwo einmal gehört haben muß." "Wozu ward eine Stimme uns verliehn,/wenn wir nicht auch am Abgrund singen? Wann/ging eine Stimme je verloren dann?" "eine Art Hilfe," "daß ich ohne diesen Vers zugrunde gegangen wäre. Er hat mich gleichsam immun gegen die Geschehnisse gemacht, so daß ich niemals völlig an ihnen teilnahm und sie keinen Angriffspunkt fanden. Ja, er muß wie eine Art Tarnkappe gewirkt haben." Nossack, *Nekyia*, 8–9.

[25] "Wie nun, wenn mein Name und mein Bild auch noch irgendwo lebten?" Nossack, *Nekyia*, 56. See E. T. A. Hoffmann, "Die Abenteuer der Silvester-Nacht," in *Werke*, 1:205–32 (Frankfurt: Insel, 1967); in English, Hoffmann, "A New Year's Eve Adventure," trans. Alfred Packer, in *The Best Tales of Hoffmann*, ed. E. F. Bleiler, 104–29 (New York: Dover, 1967).

[26] "auf dem Rande des Bettes einer Frau und sie läßt sich durch ihn täuschen?" Nossack, *Nekyia*, 56–57.

[27] "Auf die andere Möglichkeit kam ich nicht, ich meine, daß mein Bild zugrunde gegangen wäre." "Wir können uns keinen Menschen ohne sein Spiegelbild denken, und es ist die Frage, ob einem Lebewesen ohne ein solches überhaupt die Bezeichnung Mensch gegeben werden darf." Nossack, *Nekyia*, 28.

[28] "daß ich einzig der Tatsache mein Leben verdankte, so locker mit meinem Namen und meinem Bilde verbunden gewesen zu sein, daß sie mich nicht nachzuziehen vermochten, als sie zugrunde gingen." Nossack, *Nekyia*, 28–29.

[29] "Es war nur wie ein Geldschein, den man unbemerkt aus der Tasche verliert, nicht mehr. Der Wind weht ihn fort, vielleicht findet ihn jemand und weiß damit etwas anzufangen; vielleicht fällt er auch in einen Tümpel und löst sich auf." Nossack, *Nekyia*, 29.

[30] "Nein, ich konnte nicht tot sein. Denn so einsam, wie ich war, konnte nur ein Lebender sein." Nossack, *Nekyia*, 26.

[31] "einzig, daß wir zusammen sprechen, ist wichtig." Nossack, *Nekyia*, 25.

[32] "Früher gab es nichts Zuverlässigeres als die Zeitrechnung. Es war alles genau eingeteilt und ließ sich in Zahlen ausdrücken. Einer war dreißig Jahr alt und ein andrer hatte vor tausend Jahren gelebt. Die Rechnung stimmte wohl auch, aber die Voraussetzung ist nicht mehr die gleiche. Die Zeit ist zerbrochen." Nossack, *Nekyia*, 35.

[33] "wenn ich mich nicht zu ihnen hinwende, dann sind sie gar nicht da, und keine Zahl ändert etwas daran." Nossack, *Nekyia*, 35–36.

[34] "Und mit dir, mein Freund, ist es dasselbe; du bist da, weil du mir zuhörst." Nossack, *Nekyia*, 36.

[35] "es wird heißen müssen: Soundsoviel Stunden oder Tage oder Jahre von dem Augenblick an, da ich darüber zu sprechen vermochte." Nossack, *Nekyia*, 36.

[36] Nossack, *Nekyia*, 50.

[37] "Bald glaubte ich ein Zucken ihrer Beine wahrzunehmen, als versuchte sie, den Fuß vom Boden zu heben. Dann wieder war es, als höben sich Brust und Bauch und sie atmete. Man hätte sie nur noch mit einem Namen zu rufen brauchen, und sie wäre auf uns zugeschritten." Nossack, *Nekyia*, 108.

[38] "Wie kann sie denn einen Nabel haben, wenn sie von keiner Mutter geboren ist," Nossack, *Nekyia*, 109.

[39] "die Stimme des Urahn," "deutlich und unfehlbar." Nossack, *Nekyia*, 153.

[40] "Und wenn die Namen erschallen, wird die Erde davon erwachen und denken: Nun muß ich Blumen und Bäume wachsen lassen." Nossack, *Nekyia*, 152.

[41] "Spanne Leben . . ., die sich vom Tode bis zur Geburt erstreckt," "von der wir wissen, daß sie sich über sehr viel weitere Räume erstrickt, und von der wir wohl nur deshalb zu schweigen pflegen, weil sie sich nicht durch Zahlen begrenzen läßt." Nossack, *Nekyia*, 128–29.

[42] "*Worte dieses anderen Lebens*," "wo ihre Heimat ist, die auch die unsrige war." Nossack, *Nekyia*, 129.

[43] "wenn ihn die Neugier zu früh dorthin treibt, richtet er sich zugrunde. Doch wieviel neuer Schaden würde dadurch entstehen, und alles wäre umsonst gewesen." Nossack, *Nekyia*, 153.

[44] "ich habe vielleicht die Schuld an allem." Nossack, *Nekyia*, 129.

[45] "ein unsterblicher Name." Nossack, *Nekyia*, 152.

[46] Nossack, *Nekyia*, 59.

[47] "Fünf Jahre nach dem letzten Kriege, den eine einzige, nun allgewaltige Macht überlebt hatte, zerstörten sie die Kirchen. Sieben Jahre nach dem Kriege begannen sie die ersten Universitäten zu schließen. Neun Jahre nach dem Kriege erließen sie das Gesetz über die Kunst, das die Dichter, Maler und Musiker zum Schweigen verdammte." Walter Jens, *Nein: Die Welt der Angeklagten* (Munich: Piper, 1968), 7. Originally published in 1950; the later version was slightly altered by Jens.

[48] Fyodor Dostoyevsky, *The Brothers Karamazov*, trans. David McDuff (London: Penguin, 1993), 283–304.

[49] "Wir haben die Kirchen geschlossen und die Hochschulen," "Und wir haben die Bücher verbrannt, und sie sind glücklich geworden. Sie sollen keinen anderen Gedanken haben, als zu arbeiten und glücklich zu sein." Jens, *Nein*, 274.

[50] "Aber es wäre gut . . . wenn immer einer da wäre, der nicht nur mittreibt, sondern der das Wellenspiel genau zu beobachten vermag und seine Freude an der Beobachtung der auf den Wellen auf- und abtanzenden Körper hätte." Jens, *Nein*, 275.

[51] "Die Menschen sind glücklich geworden . . . Aber sie wissen es nicht. Sie werden angeklagt, sie werden Zeuge, und sie werden Richter. Aber sie wissen es nicht. Sie

denken nicht an Gott, sie lieben nicht, sie machen alle die gleichen Bewegungen, und sie haben alle gelernt, was sie in den Stunden zu tun haben, in denen sie nicht arbeiten. Aber sie wissen nicht darum. Sie haben alle die gleichen Gedanken, gebrauchen die gleichen Gesten. Aber sie wissen es nicht. Sie führen alle nur noch Selbstgespräche. Doch sie wissen es nicht." Jens, *Nein*, 276.

[52] Heinrich von Kleist, "On the Puppet Theater," in Kleist, *An Abyss Deep Enough*, ed. and trans. Philip B. Miller, 211–16 (New York: E. P. Dutton, 1982).

[53] "Du bist der letzte." Jens, *Nein*, 292.

[54] "Sonne und Mond blickten auf einen nicht sehr großen Planeten. Gestalten lebten auf ihm. Früher nannte man sie: die Menschen." Jens, *Nein*, 295.

[55] Hermann Broch, *Der Tod des Vergil* (Zurich: Rhein, 1958), 108.

[56] Broch, *Der Tod des Vergil*, 91–92.

[57] Broch, *Der Tod des Vergil*, 294.

[58] "Ur-Ahn." Broch, *Der Tod des Vergil*, 206.

[59] "Denn es geht nicht, daß wir im gleichen Hause wohnen mit einem Verbrecher, und wir wenden uns nicht gegen ihn. Es geht nicht, oder wir teilen seine Schuld, die uns zerbricht." Max Frisch, *Als der Krieg zu Ende war* (New York: Dodd, Mead, 1967 [original copyright 1949]), 119.

[60] Kurt Drawert, *Spiegelland: Ein deutscher Monolog* (Frankfurt: Suhrkamp, 1992).

3: Two Kinds of Emigration

THE PHYSICAL AND POLITICAL devastation of Germany in 1945 was compounded by a moral, spiritual, intellectual, and cultural devastation that, while particularly evident at war's end, had begun long before 1945. Germany's intellectual ruin was intensified by the loss of many of its major talents, who had left the country during the 1930s. The National Socialists' persecution of independent artists, writers, and scientists precipitated an intellectual exile that was unprecedented in human history. Germany lost thousands of its most talented and educated citizens, from writers like Bertolt Brecht and Anna Seghers to scientists like Albert Einstein. Peter Gay has rightly called the German exile "the greatest collection of transplanted intellect, talent, and scholarship the world has ever seen."[1]

How would Germans who had remained in Germany during the years of the Hitler dictatorship come to terms with the legacy and experiences of those who, unlike them, had fled Germany during the Nazi years — emigrants despised and vilified by the National Socialists, deprived of their German citizenship, and cut off from the linguistic and popular roots of their national culture? In the aftermath of the Nazi dictatorship, this was surely one of the most important questions facing the citizens of the defeated nation. Moreover, how was Germany to recover from such a tremendous loss of talent and intellect? Perhaps even more troubling, what was the real meaning of a much-used — and abused — phrase like "German culture" in a context defined by the absence of so many of Germany's most famous cultural figures from Germany itself? Was "German culture" still to be located physically inside Germany, or did "German culture" now primarily mean the culture of German exiles living outside Germany? Was the *Kulturnation* located inside the territory of the no-longer-existing *Staatsnation* after 1945, or had German emigrants taken it with them?

Germany's best known living writer, the ailing Thomas Mann, who had left his homeland in 1933 and was living in exile in Santa Monica, California at the end of the Second World War while working on his last major novel, *Doktor Faustus,* suggested in 1945 that it was not just German culture but Germany itself that had become difficult to locate. Reflecting on a possible return to his native land, he asked what precisely it meant to "return to Germany" in a situation as confused as that prevailing in Central Europe after the end of the war: "And where is Germany? Where can one locate it, even if only geographically? How does one return home to one's fatherland, which no longer exists as a unity?"[2] Mann's questions were far from rhetorical. In the context of 1945 it was no longer clear precisely what the word "Germany" meant or where "Germany," if indeed it existed, was located. The debate that emerged in 1945 about Mann specifically and German emigrants more generally represented the first major literary-cultural battle of the postwar period, an early attempt to locate the *Kulturnation* on the map of the defeated nation.

As the man widely acknowledged to be the nation's preeminent *homme de lettres,* Mann had tremendous prestige both at home and abroad; moreover, as an exile he represented those Germans who had chosen to openly reject the Nazi regime by leaving their homeland. Ludwig Marcuse described Mann in his memoirs as the "Kaiser of all the German emigrants, and particularly the overlord of the tribe of writers," declaring that "everything was expected of him, he was credited with everything, he was made responsible for everything."[3] The debate about Mann that arose in Germany in the aftermath of the lost war was a clear indication of the profound difficulties faced by both exiles and non-exiles in integrating into one unified national *Kultur* the German cultures that had been torn asunder from 1933 to 1945, cultures that were still separated at war's end. Kurt Sontheimer has suggested that much of the "emigrant baiting" that was to persist in West German politics throughout the 1950s and 1960s "was already clearly prefigured in many of the attacks against Thomas Mann."[4] The debate that emerged in 1945 was to prove constitutive for the state of postwar West German literary — and perhaps also political — culture more generally. As Mann himself noted, the debate that revolved around him concerned the entirety of the German emigration, for which Mann, whether willingly or not, became the representative embodiment. With perhaps disingenuous modesty, the writer admitted later that "the significance of the debate raging in Germany about my work and my person, which I have gazed upon in amazement, far exceeds this unimportant person."[5]

Whereas many other German emigrants separated Germany into a pure culture represented by the emigrants themselves and an evil, imposter state usurped by the Nazis, Mann was less convinced of the purity of German culture, and he stressed the unity of the nation on all levels. Although he played an important role as an elder cultural statesman for the "other" Germany while in exile, he believed that the very core of German culture was itself implicated in Hitler's crimes, and therefore he refused to reject the notion of German collective guilt outright. As he put it in a speech delivered at the Library of Congress in Washington in 1943 and published in the *Atlantic Monthly* during the following year, Mann believed that the very aspects that were best in German culture, and that had won for Germany the admiration of other nations, had also helped to make possible that which was worst in German culture. In other words, for Mann, the often-asked question "How could a country that produced Beethoven and Bach also have produced Hitler?" was based on an undialectical and false premise. He believed that Germany's evil and Germany's good were intertwined and not so easily separated. Mann declared that "the case of Germany is confusing and complicated because good and evil, the beautiful and the calamitous, are mixed up in it in the most peculiar way."[6] Two years later, also at the Library of Congress, Mann carried his thoughts further in an address entitled "Germany and the Germans," given at the end of May, 1945, on the occasion of his seventieth birthday. Characterizing his remarks as a brief mental history of Germany, Mann declared:

> This story should convince us of one thing: that there are *not* two Germanys, a good one and a bad one, but only one, whose best turned into evil through devilish cunning. Wicked Germany is merely good Germany gone astray, good Germany in misfortune, in guilt, and in ruin.[7]

In the novel *Doktor Faustus*, on which he was working at the time, Mann was to express this idea as the "mystery of identity" between good and evil that is inherent in the novel's hero, the composer Adrian Leverkühn, of his music, and of Germany itself.[8]

Throughout most of the Second World War, Mann had been making radio speeches from the United States that were broadcast into Germany to German listeners.[9] In those speeches he had urged Germans to defend the honor of the German nation by resisting the Nazi dictatorship and working for the defeat of Hitler's armies. In a speech about the Nazi concentration camps broadcast over the radio to Germany on May 8, 1945, the day of German surrender, Mann made his belief in German culpability explicit to a German audience. Specifically including himself in this culpability by using the first person plural, he declared that "our shame lies open to the eyes of the world," and that "everything German, everyone who speaks German, writes German, has lived in German, is affected by this shameful revelation." Although Mann was referring primarily to the death camps, the shame of which he spoke included all the crimes of the Nazi regime. "Humanity shudders in horror at Germany!" said the man celebrated by others, but not by himself, as a representative of a "better" Germany.[10] Two years later, in *Doktor Faustus*, Mann used the novel's narrator Serenus Zeitblom to express similar opinions. According to Zeitblom, Nazi tyranny has made "Germanness, everything German in the world intolerable," because "it is, after all, German people, tens of thousands, hundreds of thousands, who have perpetrated things at which humanity shudders, and everything that has lived in German stands exposed as an object of loathing and example of evil" — including, of course, himself and other "good" Germans.[11]

Such forceful sentiments were not particularly comforting for Germans living in Germany at war's end, because they suggested that ordinary German citizens, even non- or anti-Nazis, were in some way responsible for Hitler's crimes and therefore for their own desperate and miserable situation. Although Mann had gone so far as to include himself explicitly in collective responsibility for German crimes, and although he made no moral distinction between emigrants and nonemigrants in his radio broadcasts and speeches, many German nonemigrants perceived Mann's views as a direct attack on them for not having dissociated themselves from Hitler's regime by leaving Germany. This perception, although false, helped to precipitate a debate about the relative virtue of emigration versus nonemigration and clearly revealed that there was powerful resentment inside Germany against those Germans who had left their country and in many cases — including that of Thomas Mann — actively contributed to other countries' efforts to defeat Germany.

Given both Nazi vilifications of emigrants and ongoing resentment by nonemigrants, exiles were not, for the most part, warmly welcomed home in postwar Germany, particularly in the west. Although invitations to return to Germany after the end of the Second World War were made by various people and institutions to a number of individual exile writers, from Brecht to Fritz von Unruh, there were few general calls for all exiles to return home. As a rule, the need for the emigrants' return was recognized more readily in the Soviet occupation zone — where Communist emigrants were working with the Soviets to create a new, Communist Germany — than in the western occupation zones, where conservative hostility to the emigrants, many of them left-wingers, was more open and virulent. The German leaders of the Soviet zone were themselves former emigrants, while for the most part the German leaders in the western zones emerged from the ranks of those who had remained in Germany during the Third Reich. Hence the first major call for the emigrants' return came, in November 1945, from Johannes R. Becher's Cultural Federation for the Democratic Renewal of Germany (Kulturbund zur demokratischen Erneuerung Deutschlands, founded in the Soviet zone in 1945), whose very name spoke volumes about the intended role of *Kultur* in postwar German national identity formation not just for traditional elites but for the Communist Party as well. It was not until almost two years later, in June of 1947, that the conference of West German state governors issued a similar resolution, declaring: "A genuine new beginning is . . . unthinkable . . . without the Germans currently living beyond our borders. For this reason we call upon them to build a better Germany with us."[12] That two years passed between the end of the war and the issuing of this statement showed how reluctant authorities in the western zones were to welcome home their exiled fellow nationals.

The question that hung in the air after May of 1945 was whether exiles like Mann, who had left Germany in the wake of Hitler's rise to power, would now return to Germany after Hitler's defeat. The debate surrounding Mann's possible return to Germany started harmlessly enough. Three months after the war's end, in the first half of August, 1945, Walter von Molo, one of the founders of the German PEN Club and the author of numerous historical novels about subjects like Frederick the Great of Prussia, published an open letter to Mann in a number of newspapers put out by the American army for the German population, including the *Münchner Zeitung,* the *Stuttgarter Stimme,* and the *Hessische Post.*[13] Von Molo's letter also appeared in newspapers in the United States, England, Sweden, and South America.[14] In this letter von Molo, who had largely withdrawn from political life during the years of the Nazi dictatorship, begged Mann to return to Germany and help in the reconstruction of his homeland, assuring Mann that most Germans had remained in Germany during the years of the Third Reich not because they agreed with or even supported Hitler but because they had nowhere else to go. Indeed, by describing the physical Germany as a "huge concentration camp," von Molo insinuated that the vast majority of ordinary Germans, far from being criminals, had themselves been victims of the Nazis.[15]

Von Molo's wording seemed to suggest that exile from the German "concentration camp," far from being a difficult burden, had been a privilege of the particularly fortunate. Implying that Mann had no reason either to hate or to fear his own people and therefore no reason not to return to Germany, von Molo declared that, in spite of insidious Nazi hate propaganda, the German people were not guilty of the hatred and evil represented by the Third Reich. Von Molo also invoked Germany's "greats and its masters" — whom he declared the Germans had truly earned and deserved — as a reminder that the *Kulturnation* was not identical with the *Staatsnation* and a plea for Mann to understand that the supposedly unblemished *Kulturnation* still represented the "real" Germany. Stressing the suffering and victimization of the German people, von Molo insisted on an absolute separation between the evil of the Nazis and the essential goodness of their fellow countrymen, whom von Molo specifically identified with Mann by using the second person possessive pronoun: "In its innermost core, your people, which has now been starving and suffering for a third of a century, has nothing in common with the misdeeds and crimes, the shameful horrors and lies, the fearsome aberrations of the diseased, who for this very reason trumpeted so much about their health and perfection."[16]

Given Mann's contrary conviction that there were not two Germanys but only one Germany, in which evil and good were intertwined, such sentiments were destined to elicit the writer's ire. In many respects, however, von Molo's sentiments were not foreign to Mann, even though the latter wrote privately that von Molo's invitation was "stale and bad."[17] In his May 8 radio speech — which von Molo had read, and which was probably the immediate reason for the latter's decision to address an open letter to Mann[18] — Mann had also spoken of the German people as a "basically good people that loves civilization and law,"[19] and two years earlier he had asserted "that the Hitler Party came to absolute power only through terror and in-trigue, through a *coup d'état*," implying that the German people bore little or no responsibility for Hitler's rise to power.[20] Nevertheless, von Molo's seemingly harmless letter already contained several exculpatory assertions and one glaring omission with which Mann was bound to take issue. What von Molo had neglected to take into account in his letter to Mann was the physical, psychological, and spiritual suffering of German exiles. The only people about whom von Molo wrote as victims were the citizens of Germany who had remained in Germany — as if Germans who had left Germany, far from suffering, had somehow escaped the suffering reserved for their father-land. Von Molo's positive assertions were three-fold: 1) that the German people had in their vast majority remained virtuous during the years of the Third Reich; 2) that they were therefore absolutely separated from the Nazi regime that had claimed not only to represent them but to be the institu-tional embodiment of their innermost desires; and 3) that the German peo-ple were therefore themselves Hitler's first innocent victim. Mann himself was not completely immune to these ideas, but his position was far more critical than that of von Molo, whose letter contained a clear rejection of the concept of German "collective guilt," to which Mann himself was attracted. As Mann had written earlier, the very concept of Germany as a unified na-tion implied at least a certain collective responsibility, if not a collective guilt: "if Germany exists as a historical structure, as a collective personality, then there is also this: responsibility." Mann had stressed that criminals like Hitler and Himmler would have been complete nonentities "if manly German power and blind knightly faithfulness were not, with unholy, leonine cour-age, fighting and dying to the present date for these villains."[21] The problem of collective responsibility, if not collective guilt, was thus at the core of the debate that subsequently emerged between Mann and intellectuals who had, like von Molo, remained in Germany during the years of the Third Reich.

Before Mann's response to von Molo was published in Germany, the lat-ter's statement was followed by yet another from Frank Thiess, a respected au-thor of historical and erotic novels who had, like von Molo, for the most part kept his distance from the Nazis during the years of the Third Reich. In his re-sponse to von Molo's invitation to Mann, Thiess used the term "inner emigra-tion" to refer to writers who had remained in Germany but distanced themselves from the Nazi regime. Since the first year of Nazi rule, this term, and terms similar to it, had been used by Germans both at home and abroad to refer to Germans who remained in their homeland but nevertheless felt them-selves alienated from the Nazi regime. As a result of Thiess's prominent use of the term in his 1945 debate with Mann, some subsequent scholars made the mistake of assuming that the idea of separating out two emigrations, an "inner" emigration and an "outer" emigration, had originated with Thiess.[22]

Mann himself had used the term "inner emigration" as early as 1933, when he had considered himself to be one of the German writers so described; and ten years later Mann had invoked an "inner emigration" in his 1943 speech in Washington.[23] Describing the uprooted situation of emigrants like himself, the exiled literary statesman had compared his own alienation from Germany to a similar alienation faced by anti-Nazi Germans who had remained in Germany: "Believe me: for many there Germany has become just as foreign as it is for us; an 'inner emigration' with numbers in the millions there is waiting for the end, just as we are waiting."[24]

The concept of "inner emigration" brings together two elements that directly contradict each other: "emigration," which specifically means departure from a country, in this case German writers' homeland Germany; and "inner," which implies precisely the opposite: staying "inside" Germany. The term implies that it is possible to "leave" Germany while nevertheless staying "inside" Germany. This apparent contradiction is resolved by the idealistic concept of *Kultur:* Mann in 1943 and Thiess in 1945 were both suggesting that it was possible to "emigrate" from the evil, Nazi Germany spiritually while remaining inside it physically. The concept suggested that there were two kinds of intellectual "emigrants" from Nazi Germany: the "outer" or physical emigrants, who had physically removed themselves from the geographical entity Germany; and the "inner" or spiritual emigrants, who had removed themselves on the level of ideals and *Geist* from the morally repugnant Germany while remaining physically inside German borders. Mann's 1943 use of the term had made no attempt to distinguish the moral worth of the two "emigrations." But in his 1945 response to von Molo's invitation, Thiess went so far as to imply that the second, idealistic "emigration" was more honest and patriotic than the first, purely physical kind. Thiess's self-justifying preference for "inner emigration" was to prove typical of many writers like himself who sought to justify their actions or inaction during the Third Reich. His arguments corresponded to a widespread vituperation against not only Mann himself but also the entire German exile community.

The vituperation against exiles that emerged in 1945 can at least in part be explained psychologically by two factors, one of which the literary scholar Hans Mayer, himself an "outer emigrant" during the years of the Third Reich, identified as the simple fact of Germany's military defeat. Whether the German Wehrmacht was or was not the "aristocratic form of emigration" — as Gottfried Benn snobbishly referred to it[25] — it was decisively defeated in 1945, and with it Germany itself as a nation-state was defeated. Conversely all German emigrants, since they had spent the years of the war outside the country and had frequently supported other nations' war efforts against the Nazis, could be viewed as victors. As Mayer put it, "all emigrants seemed suddenly to have triumphed together with the victors," whereas anyone who had remained inside Germany, conformist or not, "had been defeated along with the other losers."[26]

Connected to the sense of having been defeated was the strong psychological sense of collective guilt or responsibility for Nazi atrocities. Describing how after the liberation of the Buchenwald concentration camp the citizens of Weimar had been declared participants in guilt "for the horrors now revealed"[27] and forced by American occupation authorities to observe the horrors of the camp, Mann's Serenus Zeitblom acknowledges:

> The thick-walled torture cell into which a worthless regime, dedicated from the beginning to nothingness, had transformed Germany is now thrown open, and our disgrace lies open to the eyes of the world, of the foreign commissions, to whom these unbelievable pictures are now being shown everywhere, and who report on them at home: what they have seen in all its hideousness goes beyond anything that the human imagination is capable of picturing to itself. I say: our disgrace.[28]

Zeitblom's insistence on the pronoun "our" is an open acknowledgement that he is including himself in the condemnation of what is German. At the same time his description of Germany as a thick-walled torture cell recalls von Molo's description of Germany as a concentration camp; but in Zeitblom's description it is clear that most Germans are on the side of the torturers, not on the side of the victims — hence the term "our disgrace."

The concept of "inner emigration" was an important way for postwar Germans to fend off both outward and inner accusations of collective guilt, because a German who had spiritually "emigrated" from Germany could dissociate himself from guilt for what had happened there. As Karl Paetel put it explicitly in the first collection of documents on the "inner emigration" published after the war:

> Now National Socialism is defeated. Germany is to become democratic. But even today most of the "German experts" in the great democracies cling to the conception that all Germans share responsibility for Hitler's predatory war, and that in essence all Germans are National Socialists.[29]

The existence of an "inner emigration" was therefore supposed to disprove the concept of "collective guilt." As Paetel pointed out in discussing the role of Frank Thiess, his essay on the "inner emigration" was "typical for the position and thinking of thousands of German intellectuals who did not leave the Reich."[30] Criticizing what they see as Germans' reluctance to identify themselves with emigrants — "we recognize our past better in the bearer of the Iron Cross than in the German emigrant" — Alexander and Margarete Mitscherlich subsequently sought to explain Germans' postwar vituperation against exiles like Mann and Willy Brandt by suggesting that such exiles excited the "envy of greater guiltlessness" by proving that there "was an alternative to the force of the dictatorship." In order to repress this guilt, the Mitscherlichs wrote, Germans claimed that "emigration was cowardice; desertion is inexcusable, etc."[31] Such arguments tend to overlook the fact that Mann in particular was perfectly willing to include himself in the concept of collective guilt and thus made no absolute distinction in this regard between "inner" and "outer" emigration. At the same time, however, it was precisely Mann's willingness to entertain notions of German collective guilt that made him so controversial in postwar Germany.

In his provocative essay, Frank Thiess made a distinction between two kinds of writers who had remained in Germany: those who supported or conformed to the Nazi regime and those who did not support or even opposed it. Making an implied parallel between the asserted freedom and goodness of "inner emigrants" and the essential goodness of the German people that von Molo had previously claimed, Thiess insisted that "the world on which we inner-German emigrants supported ourselves was an interior space that Hitler was unable to conquer, in spite of all his efforts."[32] This claim was essentially similar to that made by Thomas Mann's children Klaus and Erika Mann for the spiritual existence of an "other" Germany; but for Thiess that "other" Germany had been fully capable of existing physically within Hitler's evil and false Germany.[33]

It is possible that if Thiess had contented himself simply with asserting the existence of an intellectual "inner emigration" that remained essentially uninfected by Hitler's barbarity, Mann would not have felt directly attacked. After all, in spite of Thiess's claim that "even such a keen and intelligent observer of German affairs as Thomas Mann" had not understood the "inner emigration,"[34] Mann himself had indeed previously acknowledged and shown sympathy for the problems of an "inner emigration." But Thiess did not stop at such a seemingly harmless assertion. Instead, he went on to vent what Kurt Sontheimer has called "a series of nasty remarks that were above all especially tailored for Thomas Mann himself as the representative spokesman for the outer emigration."[35] Directly contradicting Mann's convictions about the portability of German *Kultur,* Thiess declared that a German writer needed "German space, German earth, and the echo of German people" — an assertion which came uncomfortably close to National Socialist *Blut und Boden* (blood and soil) rhetoric and condemnations of rootless cosmopolitanism and as such directly contradicted the idealistic separation between *Kulturnation* and *Staatsnation* implicit not only in the self-understanding of "outer" emigrants like Mann but also in the concept of an "inner emigration."[36] Moreover, Thiess implied that it was the "inner emigrants" who had been the true German patriots because they had shared in the suffering of the German people, while the "outer" emigrants had conveniently managed to escape an endangered Germany. In making this assertion, Thiess transformed von Molo's sin of omission into a sin of commission. Where von Molo had simply failed to take into account the suffering of German emigrants, Thiess actually denied it. Indeed, he went so far as to imply that German emigrants had been able to enjoy the suffering of their native country as uninvolved consumers of a theatrical spectacle. In a Nietzschean assertion of the dignity and essential worth of suffering, Thiess claimed that remaining in Germany had been a difficult and painful task that nevertheless strengthened and improved the individual. Those who had remained in a suffering Germany knew and felt more than those who had escaped in time. Thiess's words drew a firm line between the inner and the outer emigration, directly valuing the former over the latter:

> I too have frequently been asked why I did not emigrate, and I could always answer only in the following way: if I were to succeed in surviving . . . this horrible epoch, I would have won so much for my spiritual and human development that I would emerge richer in knowledge and experience than if I had observed the German tragedy from the balcony and orchestra seats of foreign countries. It makes a difference whether I experience the burning of my home myself or watch it in the weekly newsreel, whether I am hungry myself or simply read about starvation in the newspapers, whether I survive the hail of bombs on German cities myself or have people give me reports about it, whether I diagnose the unprecedented decline of a people directly in a hundred individual cases or simply register it as a historical fact.[37]

Schlant justifiably calls Thiess's language "a shocking example of the recalcitrance and obtuseness of those who described their passive attitude toward the Nazi regime as 'inner emigration.'"[38] Thiess's images carry von Molo's invocation of German emigrants as a privileged elite to a vindictive extreme, insisting in a self-pitying way on the recognition of German victimization. The writer's words betray a refusal to understand the real suffering of German emigrants: loss of family, property, prestige, homeland, and all too frequently life itself; financial danger; homesickness; difficulties with foreign languages, foreign customs, and foreign state authorities. Anyone who could speak of "the balcony and orchestra seats of foreign countries" obviously knew nothing of the suicides of Walter Benjamin, Stefan Zweig, and Ernst Toller, for instance, and clearly had not read Brecht's moving poem "An die Nachgeborenen" (To Those Born Later), in which German exiles are said to change countries more often than they change their shoes.[39]

Referring implicitly to Thomas Mann's radio messages to German listeners, Thiess declared: "I believe it was more difficult to keep one's personality here than to send messages to the German people from over there."[40] Thiess compared inner emigrants to soldiers remaining at their post in the thick of battle, thus implying that physical emigrants like Mann were guilty of dereliction of duty. Inner emigrants, he suggested, were filled with "the certainty that as German writers we belonged in Germany and should hold out at our posts, no matter what happened" — as if a writer like Mann had not been certain about his own belonging to Germany and had at any rate chosen to desert his country in its time of need.[41] But, Thiess declared in a gesture of extraordinarily arrogant magnanimity, "We do not expect any reward for not having deserted Germany."[42]

Three years after the exchange between Mann and Thiess, Hans-Joachim Lang suggested that Thiess had cleverly played upon ordinary Germans' "most secret desires for self-justification," thus creating the so-called "case of Thomas Mann." Lang called this "an unparalleled trick."[43] In hindsight it is possible to read into Thiess's arrogance and lack of self-awareness a simultaneous defensiveness and aggression that might imply at least a repressed consciousness of personal guilt or responsibility.

Whatever Thiess's conscious or unconscious motivation, however, the ideas he had expressed and the implied accusations against Mann infuriated the exiled writer, who nevertheless refrained from responding to the article directly. When he read Thiess's thoughts on September 18, 1945, Mann wrote in his journal that the article was "distorted and provocative," and added: "Here as there — une race maudite (an accursed race)."[44] In a letter written during the middle of October, Mann declared: "If Frank Thiess had intended to widen the gap between inside and outside irreparably, he could not have written in any other way."[45]

Meanwhile, at the beginning of September, even before he had read Thiess's article, Mann had written a reply to von Molo for New York's German-language exile newspaper *Aufbau* entitled "Warum ich nicht nach Deutschland zurückgehe" ("Why I Am Not Returning to Germany"). Published on September 28 in New York, the reply later found its way into many German newspapers and, because of the delay in its publication, created the impression that it was also a response to Thiess's article on the "inner emigration." In this open letter to von Molo, Mann explicitly focused on the suffering of German exiles, making a clear distinction between it and the problems experienced by Germans in Germany. Emigrants had experienced "the life of a wanderer from country to country, passport difficulties, hotel existence," but such experiences were not shared by the "inner emigration," Mann insisted: "You never went through that, all of you who . . . swore allegiance to the 'charismatic *Führer*' and pursued cultural activities under Goebbels."[46]

Mann's suggestion that any writer who had stayed in Germany during the Third Reich had sworn allegiance to Hitler was without doubt unfair. He went on to deny explicitly the very possibility of a pristine "inner emigration" that he had celebrated only two years earlier. Declaring that Nazi totalitarianism had affected all cultural production in the Third Reich, and that even supposedly independent culture had helped to stabilize and legitimate the Nazi regime, Mann wrote: "It was not permissible, it was impossible to create 'culture' in Germany while all around we know what was happening: its effect was to beautify depravity, to prettify crime."[47] Mann illustrated his point that artistic innocence had been impossible during the Third Reich by suggesting that even a seemingly harmless production of Beethoven's opera *Fidelio* played into the hands of the Nazis by creating the impression that culture in Germany was as it should be and that nothing fundamental had changed. Mann's argument suggested that producers of culture have a specific political responsibility that cannot be evaded by taking recourse to a realm of cultural freedom independent of the political realm. This meant that the concept of "inner emigration" was bankrupt. Mann made this point explicit by condemning all literature produced in Germany between 1933 and 1945: "It may be superstition, but in my eyes books that could be printed at all in Germany from 1933 to 1945 are less than worthless and ought not to be touched. They are impregnated with the smell of blood and disgrace. They ought all to be pulped."[48]

In making such a blanket condemnation of all literature published in Germany during the Third Reich, Mann was clearly allowing his anger and bitterness to get the better of him. He was overlooking not only his own previous invocation of a German "inner emigration" but also numerous instances of genuinely anti-Nazi literature published in Germany during the years of the Third Reich, from Ernst Niekisch's magazine *Der Widerstand* (Resistance) to Ernst Jünger's novel *Auf den Marmorklippen* (On the Marble Cliffs, 1939). And yet even his bitterness did not induce Mann to separate himself spiritually from the concept of Germany or to deny his own participation in that concept: "I will never cease to think of myself as a German writer," he declared.[49] Mann even asserted that there was a comparison between German "inner emigrants" and the most famous German literary hero, Faust, the man who makes a pact with the devil: "The pact with the devil is a temptation deeply rooted in the old Germany, and a German novel about recent years, about suffering because of Germany, would no doubt have to have as its topic precisely this horrible promise."[50] Since the soul of Goethe's Faust — if not of the legendary German subject on whom Goethe's play was based — is ultimately saved from the devil, Mann's Faust metaphor implied that the German soul was perhaps not irredeemably lost. And indeed, in the novel that was to appear two years later, Adrian Leverkühn's final musical masterpiece, *The Lamentation of Dr. Faustus,* ends with a "hope beyond hopelessness, the transcendence of despair," which "abides as a light in the night."[51]

In using the Faust metaphor in his response to von Molo, Mann was not only suggesting the possibility of an ultimate German redemption but also giving German newspaper readers a hint about the novel he was then working on, which had precisely such an artistic pact with the devil as its theme. Serenus Zeitblom, the narrator of *Doktor Faustus,* is precisely an inner emigrant. He begins his composition on May 23, 1943 and ends it when the war itself has come to an end. In this sense *Doktor Faustus* is the majestic attempt of Germany's most famous "outer" emigrant to imagine the situation of a humanist "inner emigrant." Mann's sympathies are clearly with his narrator Zeitblom, who is presented as loving his homeland painfully but also welcoming the defeat of its tyrannical rulers. However *Doktor Faustus* was not to be published until two years after the public discussion involving von Molo and Thiess; Mann's German audience did not pick up on this hint in 1945. Even in his reply to von Molo, Mann referred explicitly to the dialectical image of Germany he had presented in his two Washington speeches: "The evil Germany . . . is the good that has lost its way, the good in unhappiness, in guilt, and in decline."[52] In the novel *Doktor Faustus* and in the Washington speeches, however, Mann presented a picture of German culture that was far more complex and nuanced than the blanket condemnation of September 1945.

After the publication of Mann's letter to von Molo in Germany in October of 1945, the literary debate initiated by von Molo and Thiess and then carried further by the publication of Mann's open letter in German newspapers continued to dominate German cultural discussion until well into the following year. Indeed, the repercussions of the debate continued to be felt four years later, when two new German states were to emerge out of the postwar chaos. Most of the German participants sided with Thiess and condemned Mann for betraying his fatherland; the postwar West German tendency to reject the experiences of emigrants and to embrace the "inner emigration" was to make a powerful mark on German cultural politics in the coming decades, weakening Mann's emigrant invocation of the German *Kulturnation* at precisely the time when a divided Germany desperately needed such antipolitical confirmation.

Thiess's belittling of Mann's suffering as an emigrant and simultaneous invocation of the suffering of Germany became a particularly popular motif in the debate. On October 23, 1945, for instance, Edwin Redslob used the pages of Berlin's *Tagesspiegel* to compare German suffering during and after the war to the suffering of Christ upon the cross, suggesting that the exiled writer all too closely resembled his skeptical namesake, the doubting Thomas: "But just as the doubting Thomas of the Bible first had to feel the wounds of the Savior in order to believe in the miracle of the resurrection, so too we would like — through knowledge of the suffering and the miracles that have not just punished Germany but also saved it — to give Thomas Mann an inkling of what has transpired here."[53] This comparison raised what had happened in Germany during the years of the Hitler dictatorship to the level of a religious miracle, placing Germany rather vaguely into the position of both the suffering savior and the justly punished sinner — both redeemer and redeemed.

In the summer of 1945 the "inner emigrant" poet Werner Bergengruen put such sentiments into poetic form in a work addressed "to the peoples of the world":

Peoples of the world, who slipped out of God's hands,
Peoples, we suffered for your sins and your lands.
Suffered, housed on Europe's age-old stage of fate,
Suffered for all the atonement of late.[54]

The image of a suffering, persecuted Germany taking upon itself the sins of the world cannot help but be offensive to the many who viewed Germany not as a victim but as a victimizer. The ease with which Bergengruen was nevertheless able to put such a questionable parallel into verse form suggests that he and a great many other German intellectuals had not yet even begun the difficult task of recognizing, let alone trying to atone for, German crimes against humanity. Mann's sympathetic portrayal of a German "inner emigrant" in *Doktor Faustus* was thus, alas, not representative.

In an unusual twist on the theme of suffering, Otto Flake, author of numerous society novels set in the posh resort town of Baden-Baden, wrote in the *Badener Tageblatt* of December 8, 1945 that by living through and carrying out the evils of the Third Reich, Germany had performed a heroic and beneficent task, demonstrating to the peoples of the world the tremendous danger of nihilism in the contemporary world:

> Germans were foolish enough to live out for the modern world the danger that in fact threatens it: specifically, the megalomania that appears as soon as the old bonds are destroyed. In their blindness, the Germans were ready to welcome a satanic division of labor — the same division that allows those who are all too hard-working to take over the servicing of the sewers while others, their hands in their pockets, look on in disdain.[55]

Like Thiess's own original contribution to the debate, Flake's was characterized by an extraordinary insensitivity to the extent of German crimes against humanity. In reality, of course, the Nazi government, far from asking Germans to take over "the servicing of the sewers" for other nations, had declared Germans to be a master race, forcing other nations to take on the role of slaves, and sometimes literally to perform the most demeaning tasks. Flake seemed blissfully unaware of this fact, declaring: "so that humanity could come to the most horrible of all lessons, to a lesson that will hopefully remain unforgotten, the Germans pulled the chestnuts from the fire."[56] Flake's use of the saying "to pull the chestnuts out of the fire for someone," which means the same thing in German as in English, was singularly banal and inappropriate. Once again it implied that in fighting the Second World War and committing all the crimes that accompanied it Germans had somehow been doing other nations a favor. Exactly what chestnuts had been pulled out of what fire Flake did not make clear; but it was evident that for him Germans were the redeemers of humanity. If this was how German intellectuals defended the concept and value of "inner emigration," then it was clear that the conquered nation had a long way to go before it could begin to grasp what had happened during the years of the Nazi dictatorship.

In *Die Schuldfrage,* Jaspers suggested that one of the most common ways of evading the problem of German guilt was to resort to precisely the kind of vague and pompous historico-philosophical ponderings embodied in the declarations of Flake, Thiess, and Bergengruen. As Jaspers wrote,

> Interpreting our own disaster as due to the guilt of all, we give it a metaphysical weight by the development of a new interpretation, in which Germany is the sacrificial substitute in the catastrophe of the age. It suffers for all. It erupts in the universal guilt, and atones for all.[57]

Jaspers suggested that such evasions of guilt are a "digression into 'aestheticism,'" ignoring the specificity of German crimes and allowing a new kind of "false collective feeling of our own value."[58] Out of the concrete nature of German evil they abstract a "false magnificence . . . that fogs up the mind."[59] In general, most of the categories of evasiveness listed by Jaspers — from mutual accusations through proud denial to aestheticization — were present in the Mann-Thiess debate, once again confirming the strong connection between the debate about inner emigration and the problem of collective guilt.

The extent of the anger expressed by many German intellectuals against Mann in the immediate postwar years suggests that the debate surrounding him had touched a raw nerve. The young Hamburg journalist Herbert Lestiboudois reached the height of vituperation against Mann when, claiming to speak for his entire generation, he grandly declared: "we can achieve reconciliation with the entire world, but not with Thomas Mann."[60] Such hostility was echoed in a political rally held four years after the end of the war by German right-wingers, one of them a former major general of the Wehrmacht who rejected "emigrants sent in from outside like Thomas Mann."[61] Such a formulation implied that Mann was essentially a foreign agent, no longer a "real" German. In the same year, 1949, the city council of Marktredwitz, ascribing to Mann a "lack of education of the heart and of friendship for Germany," officially decided to change a street name from Thomas-Mann to Goethe-Straße.[62] If German citizens could not get moral absolution from the most famous living representative of the *Kulturnation,* they would seek it from the long-since safely departed.

Not all German intellectuals agreed in attacking Mann, and the fact that there were a few inside Germany who defended him is perhaps much more telling than the attacks themselves; such defenses pointed toward that "way of purification" through self-criticism, which, Jaspers argued, was necessary for true German spiritual freedom.[63] Three years after the Mann-Thiess debate, for instance, the left-wing Cologne daily *Die Volksstimme* noted that Mann's response to von Molo's original invitation had been "a declaration of belonging to Germany. He remained our own true son, and not a prodigal."[64] After the publication of *Doktor Faustus* in 1947, Bruno E. Werner accurately wrote in Munich's *Neue Zeitung* that much of the controversy surrounding Mann had been based on simple misunderstanding by critics "without exact knowledge" of the writer's actual opinions.[65] That it was not just Mann's critics but also some of his supporters who failed to understand the complexity of the author's position was revealed when Berlin's *Tägliche Rundschau* asserted, as late as 1949, that the very Mann who, in his 1945 Washington speech and in the open letter to von Molo, had explicitly rejected "the theory of the two Germanys, a good one and a bad one,"[66] had always "claimed allegiance to the 'other Germany.'"[67]

Dolf Sternberger, the editor of *Die Wandlung,* one of the most influential journals of the immediate postwar period, was an articulate and thoughtful defender of Mann. In the sixth issue of his journal, published in June of 1946, Sternberger wrote to celebrate Mann's greatness and humanity as a writer and to express his embarrassment at the thoughtless attacks on such a figure. Sternberger chose the writer's 1939 novel *Lotte in Weimar* as the centerpiece of his defense, for he believed that its respectful treatment of Goethe, whom Sternberger defined as "the most significant, the most valuable person to be found in the German tradition," definitively proved Mann's fundamental participation in and love for the highest achievements of German culture.[68] At the same time, he argued, the novel also demonstrated to contemporary Germans the importance of a similar respect for the country's greatest twentieth-century writer, whom Sternberger called "the most significant, the most famous, and the most respected writer in the German language."[69] Writing that "the so-called case of Thomas Mann" had exposed a shocking "lack of respect and blindness for distinctions of rank," Sternberger reminded his German readers that, in view of the writer's poor health, the time allowed them to show Mann the respect he deserved was inevitably limited.[70]

Sternberger's — and also Mann's — use of the Goethe novel as literary proof of Mann's adherence to the *Kulturnation* pointed the way to the future and to a possible cooling of the rhetoric in postwar Germany's first great literary debate. As much as Mann and his German opponents may have disagreed on difficult contemporary problems like collective guilt and the relative value of the "two emigrations," there was one thing that all the protagonists in the debate agreed on: the value of the *Kulturnation* itself as represented by its greatest writers and poets, especially Johann Wolfgang von Goethe. In his end-of-the-year reply to Mann, Thiess had explicitly invoked this allegiance to Goethe:

> Previously, Thomas Mann, you used to speak of Goethe's Germany, to which you were devoted with deep and never-changing love. Be assured, now that the seducer (*Verführer*) has been destroyed, that we too are

conscious of having no other leader (*Führer*) than Goethe, that star of German authority in the world which now shines brighter than ever.[71]

In Thiess's play on words, Hitler the *Führer* (leader) is turned into Hitler the *Verführer* (seducer), and Goethe becomes the true *Führer* of the German people. Such a transposition allows National Socialism as a political philosophy to be negated while leaving unquestioned a problematic word — and concept — like *Führer*.

As it happened, the two hundredth anniversary of Goethe's birth occurred at the end of the immediate postwar period, on August 28, 1949, during the year in which first the three western occupation zones and then the Soviet occupation zone declared themselves to be the separate political states named the Federal Republic of Germany (on May 23) and the German Democratic Republic (on October 7). In honor of the Goethe anniversary, which happened to fall between those two dates, the cities of Frankfurt, where Goethe was born, and Weimar, where Goethe lived most of his life and died, once again invited Germany's greatest living representative of the *Kulturnation* to visit his homeland and give speeches in the two cities now separated by the Iron Curtain. Many critics noted that four years after the war's end it was more difficult for Germans to travel inside Germany than it had been for Goethe two centuries earlier, when Germany had been divided into a far greater number of principalities. In view of the cold war tensions causing the German division, Friedrich Sieburg, literary critic and co-editor of the journal *Die Gegenwart* (The Present), suggested that the *Kulturnation* itself was being eroded. Referring to Mann's conspicuous disrespect for the meaning of the inner-German border, Sieburg lamented the fact that the great writer was once again at the center of a cultural-political controversy. The split within German culture between an outer and an inner German emigration had now been replaced by a split in cultural sensibilities between the west and the east, with each part claiming to represent the true tradition of German *Kultur*, while conveniently forgetting the traditional role of the *Kulturnation* as the guarantor of a national unity that transcended political division:

> Four years after the collapse we have reached the point where it is no longer considered normal for a great German-language writer to be celebrated simultaneously in the city of Goethe's birth and in the place of his world-spanning work. From Frankfurt to Weimar — in the minute space that covers the greatest of German life paths — the world is so changed that whoever is of value to us over there can hardly be valuable here. . . . Thus the Iron Curtain runs through the middle of the fragile world of our spiritual values. Is our Goethe no longer *their* Goethe?[72]

Sieburg's invocation of "the fragile world of our spiritual values" suggested that in the cold war then beginning the *Kulturnation* might not provide as stable and unquestioned a location for an undivided Germany as it had for Mann and others during the Third Reich. But Mann himself refused to acknowledge the immanent division of his homeland. In spite of the fact that Frankfurt was located in the German West and Weimar in the German East, and that the cold war between the United States and the Soviet Union had reached a feverish intensity with the Soviet blockade of all land routes into West Berlin from June 24, 1948 until May 12, 1949, Germany's best-known living representative of the *Kulturnation* did not reject the invitations he received from East and West to return home in honor of the Goethe anniversary. In the 1945 letter to von Molo, Mann had written that he still entertained the "dream of feeling the ground of the old continent beneath my feet once again," and that "when the hour comes, if I am alive and the transportation situation as well as a laudable state authority allows it, then I will go."[73] In honor of Goethe, Mann made the arduous trip to his homeland in the summer of 1949, returning to Germany sixteen years after he had become an exile in the spring of 1933. The writer demonstrated his adherence to the concept of the *Kulturnation* by ignoring the new political boundaries between East and West and visiting both Frankfurt and Weimar. As Mann declared in the two cities, "Who should represent and guarantee the unity of Germany if not an independent writer, whose real home . . . is the free German language, untouched by zones of occupation?"[74] Mann could make such a declaration only as an "outer" emigrant who had both willed and experienced the continuity of German culture abroad, and whose concept of German identity allowed no unbridgeable distinctions between good and bad or West and East. As Mann saw it, Goethe's greatness was restricted to neither the East nor the West; and his belief that German cultural unity continued even in the face of the nascent cold war suggested that, after so many years of exile in which the concept of the *Kulturnation* had played an important role for German emigrants, the same concept might play a similar role in sustaining the idea of German unity during the difficult years of political division that lay ahead. Unfortunately, however, such a sovereign idea of the German *Kulturnation* remained for the most part a prerogative of "outer" emigrants; Germany's "inner emigrants," many of whom had rudely rejected the experience of emigrants like Mann, were thus deprived of a powerful concept that could have helped them preserve the dream of German cultural unity in the years ahead. The rejection of the emigrant experience was part and parcel both of National Socialist propaganda and of postwar West German culture, and it helped set the tone for the literary cold war between East and West, in which the idea of a greater German *Kulturnation* was weakened.

Notes

[1] Peter Gay, *Weimar Culture: The Outsider as Insider* (New York: Harper & Row, 1970), xiv.

[2] "Und wo ist Deutschland? Wo ist es aufzufinden, auch nur geographisch? Wie kehrt man heim in sein Vaterland, das als Einheit nicht existiert?" J. F. G. Grosser, ed., *Die grosse Kontroverse: Ein Briefwechsel um Deutschland* (Hamburg: Nagel, 1963), 79. Unless otherwise specified, all translations from German in this book are my own; the German appears in the notes, followed by sources. I have added the notation "my translation" in a limited number of cases where confusion might otherwise occur.

[3] "Kaiser aller deutscher Emigranten, ganz besonders Schutzherr des Stamms der Schriftsteller," "Von ihm wurde alles erwartet, ihm wurde alles verdankt, er wurde für alles verantwortlich gemacht." Ludwig Marcuse, *Mein zwanzigstes Jahrundert: Auf dem Weg zu einer Autobiographie* (Munich: Paul List, 1960), 288.

[4] "war damals in vielen Stellungnahmen gegen Thomas Mann schon bestens vorgebildet." Kurt Sontheimer, *Thomas Mann und die Deutschen* (Munich: Nymphenburger Verlagshandlung, 1961), 153.

[5] "der Streit, der in Deutschland geht um mein Werk und meine Person und dem ich mit Staunen zugesehen habe, an Bedeutung weit hinausreicht über diese gleichgültige Person." Thomas Mann, "Ansprache im Goethejahr 1949," in *Gesammelte Werke in Zwölf Bänden,* vol. 11, *Reden und Aufsätze 3,* 481–97; here, 486–87 (Frankfurt: S. Fischer, 1960).

[6] "Der Fall Deutschland ist darum so verwirrend und kompliziert, weil Gutes und Böses, das Schöne und das Verhängnisvolle sich darin in der eigentümlichsten Weise vermischen." Thomas Mann, "Schicksal und Aufgabe," in Mann, *Gesammelte Werke in Zwölf Bänden,* vol. 12, *Reden und Aufsätze 4,* 918–39; here, 924 (Frankfurt: S. Fischer, 1960).

[7] Thomas Mann, "Germany and the Germans," in *Thomas Mann's Addresses Delivered at the Library of Congress 1942–1949,* 45–66; here, 64 (Washington: Library of Congress, 1963). Translator not identified. In German: "Eines mag diese Geschichte uns zu Gemüte führen: daß es nicht zwei Deutschland gibt, ein böses und ein gutes, sondern nur eines, dem sein Bestes durch Teufelslist zum Bösen ausschlug. Das böse Deutschland, das ist das fehlgegangene gute, das gute im Unglück, in Schuld und Untergang." Thomas Mann, "Deutschland und die Deutschen," in *Gesammelte Werke in Zwölf Bänden,* 11:1126–48; here, 1146.

[8] Thomas Mann, *Doctor Faustus: The Life of the German Composer Adrian Leverkühn As Told by a Friend,* trans. H. T. Lowe-Porter (New York: Alfred Knopf, 1948), 378. In German: "Geheimnis der Identität." Thomas Mann, *Doktor Faustus: Das Leben des deutschen Tonsetzers Adrian Leverkühn, erzählt von einem Freunde* (Frankfurt: Fischer, 1998), 502.

[9] Originally published in Thomas Mann, *Deutsche Hörer! 25 Radiosendungen nach Deutschland* (Stockholm: Berman-Fischer, 1942) and subsequently expanded to include Mann's later speeches. Republished in Mann, *An die gesittete Welt: Politische Schriften und Reden im Exil* (Frankfurt: S. Fischer, 1986), 473–622.

[10] "offen liegt unsere Schmach vor den Augen der Welt," "alles Deutsche, alles was deutsch spricht, deutsch schreibt, auf deutsch gelebt hat, is von dieser entehrenden Bloßstellung mitbetroffen." "Die Menschheit schaudert sich vor Deutschland!" Thomas Mann, "Die Lager," in *Gesammelte Werke in Zwölf Bänden,* 12:951–53; here, 951.

[11] "das Deutschtum, alles Deutsche der Welt unerträglich," "deutsche Menschen, Zehntausende, Hunderttausende, sind es nun einmal, die verübt haben, wovor die Menschheit schaudert, und was nur immer auf deutsch gelebt hat, steht da als ein Abscheu und als Beispiel des Bösen." My translation. Mann, *Doktor Faustus,* 450, 635. For the corresponding passages in the Lowe-Porter translation, see 338, 481.

[12] "An einen wirklichen Neubeginn unseres Lebens ist . . . nicht zu denken ohne die Hilfe der übrigen Welt, ganz besonders nicht ohne die Deutschen, die heute außerhalb unserer Grenzen weilen. Deshalb rufen wir sie auf, mit uns ein besseres Deutschland aufzubauen." Cited in Gerhard Roloff, *Exil und Exilliteratur in der deutschen Presse 1945–1949* (Worms: Georg Heintz, 1976), 131. Dieter Sattler, State Secretary in the Bavarian Ministry of Education, was probably the spiritual father of such calls for so-called "remigration." See Jost Hermand and Wigand Lange, eds., *"Wollt ihr Thomas Mann wiederhaben?" Deutschland und die Emigranten* (Hamburg: Europäische Verlagsanstalt, 1999), 63, note 5.

[13] On the timing of the letter, see Leonore Krenzlin, "Große Kontroverse oder kleiner Dialog? Gesprächsbemühungen und Kontaktbruchstellen zwischen 'inneren' und 'äußeren' literarischen Emigranten," *Galerie: Revue culturelle et pedagogique,* 15, no. 1 (1997), 7–25, especially 12 and 23, note 22.

[14] Jost Hermand, "Zum Vorverständnis," in Hermand and Lange, *"Wollt ihr Thomas Mann wiederhaben?"* 7–55; here, 23

[15] "in dem allmählich gewordenen großen Konzentrationslager." Walter von Molo, "Offener Brief an Thomas Mann," in *Thomas Mann im Urteil seiner Zeit: Dokumente 1891–1955,* ed. Klaus Schröter, 334–36; here, 334 (Hamburg: Christian Wegner, 1969).

[16] "Ihr Volk, das nunmehr seit einem Dritteljahrhundert hungert und leidet, hat im innersten Kern nichts gemein mit den Missetaten und Verbrechen, den schmachvollen Greueln und Lügen, den furchtbaren Verirrungen Kranker, die daher wohl so viel von ihrer Gesundheit und Vollkommenheit posaunten." Von Molo, "Offener Brief an Thomas Mann," 335.

[17] "flau und schlecht." Thomas Mann, *Tagebücher 1944–1.4.1946,* ed. Inge Jens (Frankfurt: S. Fischer, 1986), 244.

[18] Von Molo had already written privately to Mann some time earlier; the subsequent decision for an open letter was evidently also spurred on by Johannes Franz Gottlieb Grosser, who later edited an anthology that continues to be the standard documentation of the controversy. See Krenzlin, "Große Kontroverse oder kleiner Dialog?" 13–14; and Leonore Schiller-Krenzlin, "Hinter den Offenen Briefen: Initialzündung und Motivationsgeflecht des Streits zwischen innerer und äußerer Emigration," in *Literatur im politischen Spannungsfeld der Nachkriegszeit: Protokoll der internationalen Konferenz anläßlich des 50. Jubiläums des 1. Deutschen Schriftstellerkongresses vom Oktober 1947,* ed. Ursula Heukenkamp and Ursula Reinhold, 169–86; especially 174–75 (Berlin: Institut für deutsche Literatur, 1998 [unpublished conference proceedings]).

[19] "von Hause aus guten, Recht und Gesittung liebenden Volk." Thomas Mann, "Die Lager," 952.

[20] "daß die Hitler-Partei nur durch Intrige und Terror, durch einen Staatsstreich zur absoluten Macht gekommen ist." Thomas Mann, "Schicksal und Aufgabe," 928.

[21] "gibt es Deutschland als geschichtliche Gestalt, als kollektive Persönlichkeit, dann gibt es auch dies: Verantwortung." "wenn nicht deutsche Manneskraft und blinde Mannentreue bis zum heutigen Tage mit unseligem Löwenmut für diese Schurken stritte und fiele." Thomas Mann, "Das Ende," in *Gesammelte Werke in Zwölf Bänden,* 12:944–51; here, 946.

[22] For an overview of the term and a critique of its attribution to Thiess, see Reinhold Grimm, "Innere Emigration als Lebensform," in *Exil und Innere Emigration,* ed. Reinhold Grimm and Jost Hermand, 31–73, especially 42 (Frankfurt: Athenäum, 1972). On more recent attributions to Thiess, see Volker Wehdeking, "Zwischen Exil und 'vorgeschobenem Posten' der Kulturnation: Thomas Mann als Projektionsfigur für die im Land gebliebenen Nichtfaschisten," in Rüther, *Literatur in der Diktatur,* 145–62, especially 149.

[23] For Mann's 1933 usage of the term, see Mann, *Tagebücher 1933–1934,* ed. Peter de Mendelssohn (Frankfurt: Fischer, 1977), 243, entry for 7 November 1933. See also Wehdeking, "Zwischen Exil und 'vorgeschobenem Posten,'" 149.

[24] "Glauben Sie mir: für viele dort ist das Vaterland ebenso zur Fremde geworden wie für uns, eine nach Millionen zählende 'innere Emigration' dort wartet auf das Ende, wie wir es tun." Thomas Mann, "Schicksal und Aufgabe," 922–23.

[25] "aristokratische Form der Emigration." Cited in Grimm, "Innere Emigration als Lebensform," 37.

[26] "schienen alle Emigranten plötzlich mitgesiegt zu haben mit den Siegern." "war mitbesiegt mit den Besiegten." Hans Mayer, "Konfrontation der inneren und äußeren Emigration: Erinnerung und Deutung," in Grimm and Hermand, *Exil und innere Emigration,* 75–87; here, 83.

[27] "den nun bloßgelegten Greueln," from Mann, *Doktor Faustus,* 634.

[28] "Der dickwandige Folterkeller, zu dem eine nichtswürdige, von Anbeginn dem Nichts verschworene Herrschaft Deutschland gemacht hatte, ist aufgebrochen, und offen liegt unsere Schmach vor den Augen der Welt, der fremden Kommissionen, denen diese unglaubwürdigen Bilder nun allerorts vorgeführt werden, und die zu Hause berichten: was sie gesehen, übertreffe an Scheußlichkeit alles, was menschliche Vorstellungskraft sich ausmalen könne. Ich sage: unsere Schmach." My translation. Mann, *Doktor Faustus,* 634–35. For the corresponding passage in the Lowe-Porter translation, see Mann, *Doctor Faustus,* 481.

[29] "Jetzt ist der Nationalsozialismus geschlagen. Deutschland soll demokratisch werden. Aber auch heute noch hält der größte Teil der 'Deutschland-Experten' in den großen Demokratien an der Auffassung fest, daß allen Deutschen die Mitschuld am Hitlerschen Raubkrieg zukommt, und daß im Grunde alle Deutschen Nationalsozialisten sind." Karl O. Paetel, "Das Gesicht des innerdeutschen Widerstandes," in *Deutsche innere Emigration: Anti-Nationalsozialistische Zeugnisse aus Deutschland,* ed. Karl O. Paetel, 32–38; here, 33 (New York: Friedrich Krause, 1946).

[30] "typisch für Haltung und Denken von tausenden von deutschen Intellektuellen, die das Reich nicht verließen." Paetel, ed., *Deutsche innere Emigration*, 93.

[31] "Emigration war Feigheit; Fahnenflucht ist unentschuldbar etc." Alexander Mitscherlich and Margarete Mitscherlich, *Die Unfähigkeit zu trauern: Grundlagen kollektiven Verhaltens* (Munich: Piper, 1991 [originally 1967]), 68.

[32] "die Welt, auf die wir innerdeutschen Emigranten uns stützten, war ein innerer Raum, dessen Eroberung Hitler trotz aller Bemühungen nicht gelungen ist." Frank Thiess, "Die innere Emigration," in Klaus Schröter, *Thomas Mann im Urteil seiner Zeit: Dokumente 1891–1955*, 336–38; here, 337 (Hamburg: Christian Wegner, 1969).

[33] Erika Mann and Klaus Mann, *The Other Germany* (New York: Modern Age, 1940).

[34] "auch ein so scharfer und kluger Beobachter der deutschen Verhältnisse wie Thomas Mann." Thiess, "Die innere Emigration," 336.

[35] "eine Reihe von Bosheiten, die vor allem auf Thomas Mann selbst gemünzt waren, zumal er der repräsentative Sprecher der äußeren Emigration war." Sontheimer, *Thomas Mann und die Deutschen*, 146.

[36] "des deutschen Raums, der deutschen Erde und des Widerhalls deutscher Menschen." Thiess, "Die innere Emigration," 337. Thiess is approvingly citing a statement reportedly made by the writer Erich Ebermayer to Mann in 1934.

[37] "Auch ich bin oft gefragt worden, warum ich nicht emigriert sei, und konnte immer nur dasselbe antworten: falls es mir gelänge, diese schauerliche Epoche . . . lebendig zu überstehen, würde ich dadurch derart viel für meine geistige und menschliche Entwicklung gewonnen haben, daß ich reicher an Wissen und Erleben daraus hervorginge, als wenn ich aus den Logen und Parterreplätzen des Auslands der deutschen Tragödie zuschaute. Es ist nun einmal zweierlei, ob ich den Brand meines Hauses selbst erlebe oder ihn in der Wochenschau sehe, ob ich selber hungere oder vom Hunger in den Zeitungen lese, ob ich den Bombenhagel auf deutsche Städte lebend überstehe oder mir davon berichten lasse, ob ich den beispiellosen Absturz eines Volkes unmittelbar an hundert Einzelfällen feststellen oder nur als historische Tatsache registrieren kann." Thiess, "Die innere Emigration," 337.

[38] Ernestine Schlant, *The Language of Silence: West German Literature and the Holocaust* (New York: Routledge, 1999), 22.

[39] "An die Nachgeborenen," in Bertolt Brecht, *Die Gedichte von Bertolt Brecht in einem Band*, 723–25; here, 725 (Frankfurt: Suhrkamp, 1981). In English: "To Those Born Later," in Bertolt Brecht, *Poems 1913–1956*, ed. John Willett and Ralph Manheim (London: Methuen, 1987), 318–20; here, 320.

[40] "Ich glaube, es war schwerer sich hier seine Persönlichkeit zu bewahren, als von drüben Botschaften an das deutsche Volk zu senden." Thiess, "Die innere Emigration," 338.

[41] "die Gewissheit, daß wir als deutsche Schriftsteller nach Deutschland gehörten und, was auch käme, auf unseren Posten ausharren sollten." Thiess, "Die innere Emigration," 337.

[42] "Wir erwarten dafür keine Belohnung, daß wir Deutschland nicht verließen . . ." Thiess, "Die innere Emigration," 338.

[43] "geheimsten Wünsche nach Selbstrechtfertigung," "Fall Thomas Mann," "ein Streich ohnegleichen." Hans-Joachim Lang, "Der letzte Deutsche," in Schröter, *Thomas Mann im Urteil seiner Zeit*, 365–74; here, 367.

[44] "schiefen und aufreizenden." "Hier wie dort — une race maudite." Mann, *Tagebücher 1944–1.4.1946,* 254.

[45] "Wenn Frank Thieß die Absicht gehabt hätte, die Kluft zwischen innen und außen unheilbar zu erweitern, hätte er nicht anders schreiben können, als er getan hat." Cited in Mann, *Tagebücher 1944–1.4.1946,* 704–05.

[46] "das Wanderleben von Land zu Land, die Paßsorgen, das Hoteldasein." "Das haben Sie alle, die Sie dem 'charismatischen Führer' . . . Treue schworen und unter Goebbels Kultur betrieben, nicht durchgemacht." Thomas Mann, "Warum ich nicht nach Deutschland zurückgehe," in *Gesammelte Werke in Zwölf Bänden,* vol. 12, *Reden und Aufsätze 4,* 953–62; here, 954–55.

[47] "Es war nicht erlaubt, es war unmöglich, 'Kultur' zu machen in Deutschland, während rings um einen herum das geschah, wovon wir wissen: es hieß die Verkommenheit beschönigen, das Verbrechen schmücken." Mann, "Warum ich nicht nach Deutschland zurückgehe," 957.

[48] "Es mag Aberglaube sein, aber in meinen Augen sind Bücher, die von 1933 bis 1945 in Deutschland überhaupt gedruckt werden konnten, weniger als wertlos und nicht gut in die Hand zu nehmen. Ein Geruch von Blut und Schande haftet ihnen an. Sie sollten alle eingestampft werden." Mann, "Warum ich nicht nach Deutschland zurückgehe," 957.

[49] "Nie werde ich aufhören, mich als deutscher Schriftsteller zu fühlen." Mann, "Warum ich nicht nach Deutschland zurückgehe," 959.

[50] "Der Teufelspakt ist eine tief-altdeutsche Versuchung, und ein deutscher Roman, der eingegeben wäre von den Leiden der letzten Jahre, vom Leiden an Deutschland, müßte wohl eben dies grause Versprechen zum Gegenstand haben." Mann, "Warum ich nicht nach Deutschland zurückgehe," 960–61.

[51] Mann, *Doctor Faustus,* 491. Original German: "Hoffnung jenseits der Hoffnungslosigkeit, die Transzendenz der Verzweiflung," "steht als ein Licht in der Nacht." Mann, *Doktor Faustus,* 648.

[52] "Das böse Deutschland . . . ist das fehlgegangene gute, das gute im Unglück, in Schuld und Untergang." Mann, "Warum ich nicht nach Deutschland zurückgehe," 960.

[53] "Aber wie der ungläubige Thomas der Bibel erst die Wundmale des Heilands fühlen mußte, um an das Wunder der Wiederauferstehung zu glauben, so möchten wir Thomas Mann durch Kenntnis des Leidens und der Wunder, durch die Deutschland nicht nur gestraft, sondern auch geheilt wurde, ein Ahnen von dem geben, was sich bei uns vollzog." Grosser, ed., *Die grosse Kontroverse,* 39.

[54] "Völker der Welt, die der Ordnung des Schöpfers entglitt/Völker, wir litten für Euch und für Eure Verschuldungen mit./Litten, behaust auf Europas uralter Schicksalsbühne,/Litten stellvertretend für Alle ein Leider der Sühne." Loosely translated. Werner Bergengruen, "An die Völker der Erde," in Paetel, *Deutsche innere Emigration,* 101–2; here, 102.

[55] "Der Deutsche war töricht genug, der modernen Welt die Gefahr vorzuleben, die ihr tatsächlich droht, die Maßlosigkeit nämlich, die auftritt, sobald man die Bindungen zerstört, in ihrer Verblendung waren die Deutschen bereit, eine Art satanischer Arbeitsteilung zu bejahen — dieselbe, die den allzu Beflissenen den

Kloakendienst übernehmen läßt, während die anderen, die Hände in den Hosen, verächtlich zuschauen." Grosser, ed., *Die grosse Kontroverse*, 56.

[56] "Damit die Menschheit zur schrecklichsten der Erfahrungen kommen konnte, zu einer Lehre, die hoffentlich unvergessen bleibt, haben die Deutschen die Kastanien aus dem Feuer geholt." Grosser, ed., *Die grosse Kontroverse*, 56.

[57] Karl Jaspers, *The Question of German Guilt*, trans. E. B. Ashton (New York: Dial Press, 1947), 116–17. Translation modified. Original German: "Man gibt dem eigenen Unheil, das man als Folge der Schuld aller deutet, ein metaphysisches Gewicht durch die Auslegung zu einer neuen Einzigkeit: In der Katastrophe des Zeitalters ist Deutschland das stellvertretende Opfer. Es leidet für alle. An ihm kommt die Schuld aller zum Ausbruch und die Sühne für alle." Jaspers, *Die Schuldfrage: Von der politischen Haftung Deutschlands* (Munich: Piper, 1996), 79.

[58] Jaspers, *The Question of German Guilt*, 117. In German: "Entgleiten ins 'Ästhetische,'" "falsches kollektives Selbstwertgefühl." Jaspers, *Die Schuldfrage*, 79, 80.

[59] "falsche Großartigkeit . . ., welche das Gemüt vernebelt." My translation, from Jaspers, *Die Schuldfrage*, 75. For an alternative English-language translation, see Jaspers, *The Question of German Guilt*, 111.

[60] "Wir können uns mit einer ganzen Welt versöhnen aber nicht mit Thomas Mann. . . ." Grosser, ed., *Die grosse Kontroverse*, 92.

[61] "von außen geschickte Emigranten vom Schlage eines Thomas Mann." Cited in Roloff, *Exil und Exilliteratur in der deutschen Presse 1945–1949*, 128.

[62] "Mangel an Herzensbildung und Deutschfreundlichkeit." Cited in Roloff, *Exil und Exilliteratur in der deutschen Presse 1945–1949*, 128.

[63] Jaspers, *The Question of German Guilt*, 118. In German: "Weg der Reinigung." Jaspers, *Die Schuldfrage*, 80.

[64] "Thomas Mann sagte ab, jedoch sein Antwortbrief war ein Bekenntnis zu Deutschland. Er blieb unser aller unverlorener Sohn." Cited in Roloff, *Exil und Exilliteratur in der deutschen Presse 1945–1949*, 127.

[65] "ohne exakte Kenntnis." Cited in Roloff, *Exil und Exilliteratur in der deutschen Presse 1945–1949*, 126.

[66] "die Theorie von den beiden Deutschland, einem guten und einem bösen." Mann, "Warum ich nicht nach Deutschland zurückgehe," 960.

[67] "Immer hat sich der Dichter zum 'anderen Deutschland' bekannt. . . ." Cited in Roloff, *Exil und Exilliteratur in der deutschen Presse 1945–1949*, 127.

[68] "der bedeutendste, der teuerste, der in der deutschen Überlieferung gefunden werden kann." Dolf Sternberger, "Thomas Mann und der Respekt," *Die Wandlung*, 1, no. 6 (June 1946), 451–59; here, 454.

[69] "bedeutendsten, berühmtesten, angesehensten Schriftsteller deutscher Sprache." Sternberger, "Thomas Mann und der Respekt," 458.

[70] "der sogenannte Fall Thomas Mann gerade hat bei uns zulande so viel Respektlosigkeit, Rangblindheit an den Tag gebracht, daß es zum Erschrecken ist." Sternberger, "Thomas Mann und der Respekt," 454.

[71] "Sie haben, Thomas Mann, früher einmal von dem Deutschland Goethes gesprochen, an dem Sie mit tiefer und immer gleicher Liebe hingen. Seien Sie versichert, daß auch wir, nachdem der Verführer vernichtet wurde, uns dessen bewußt sind, keinen anderen Führer mehr zu haben als den heller als je strahlenden Stern deutscher Weltgeltung, Goethe." Frank Thiess, "Der Weltdeutsche und die 'Innere Emigration,'" in Klaus Schröter, ed., *Thomas Mann im Urteil seiner Zeit: Dokumente 1891–1955* (Hamburg: Christian Wegner, 1969), 338–43; here, 342.

[72] "Vier Jahre nach dem Zusammenbruch ist es soweit mit uns gekommen, daß es nicht mehr mit rechten Dingen zugehen kann, wenn ein großer Schriftsteller deutscher Sprache gleichzeitig in Goethes Geburtsstadt und am Ort seines weltumspannenden Wirkens gefeiert wird. Von Frankfurt bis Weimar, also auf der winzigen Spanne, die den größten deutschen Lebensweg umfaßt, verändert sich die Welt so, daß, wer uns dort etwas gilt, kaum auch hier etwas gelten darf. . . . So geht der Eiserne Vorhang mitten durch die gebrechliche Welt unserer geistigen Werte. Ist unser Goethe nicht mehr *ihr* Goethe?" Friedrich Sieburg, "Frieden mit Thomas Mann," in Schröter, *Thomas Mann im Urteil seiner Zeit,* 375–78; here, 375. Emphasis in the original.

[73] "Traum, den Boden des alten Kontinents noch einmal unter meinen Füßen zu fühlen," "wenn die Stunde kommt, wenn ich lebe und die Transportverhältnisse sowohl wie eine löbliche Behörde es erlauben, so will ich hinüberfahren." Mann, "Warum ich nicht nach Deutschland zurückgehe," 962.

[74] "Wer sollte die Einheit Deutschlands gewährleisten und darstellen, wenn nicht ein unabhängiger Schriftsteller, dessen wahre Heimat . . . die freie, von Besatzungen unberührte deutsche Sprache ist?" Thomas Mann, "Ansprache im Goethejahr 1949," 488.

4: The Property of the Nation

> *The pencils have been sharpened like knives. The fountain pens have been freshly tanked up. The new color ribbons are trembling with impatience. The typewriters are scraping their hooves nervously. German culture and the surrounding villages are holding their breaths. It can only be a matter of seconds now. There! Finally the starting gun has sounded! The pens are whizzing over the paper. The fingers are racing over the keys. . . . The race of the year has begun: the Goethe Derby on the classic 200-year stretch!*
>
> — Erich Kästner[1]

> *I would have preferred it if Goethe had been born ten years later.*
> — a Frankfurt politician in 1949[2]

IN A 1949 MANIFESTO proclaiming the importance of Goethe for postwar Germans, the Socialist Unity Party (Sozialistische Einheitspartei or SED) of Germany — soon to become the ruling party of the German Democratic Republic — expressed thoughts that directly echoed those of Thomas Mann, and which helped to explain why authorities in the Soviet zone believed it was so important for them to secure Mann's visit to Weimar that year. Goethe, declared the SED's manifesto, "embodied German spiritual and linguistic unity in a torn and splintered Germany. He had a decisive role in the formation of German national consciousness."[3] Otto Grotewohl, a leading SED politician soon to be the first Prime Minister of the GDR, declared in a speech to German youth held in the spring of 1949 that Goethe had been the "symbol of our unified national culture," and had, through his works, raised "our nation from the twilight of historical emptiness to the rank of a world nation."[4] Grotewohl believed that "in Goethe the German nation can achieve the highest expression of modern national self-awareness."[5] If Goethe had played such an important role in guaranteeing German linguistic and cultural unity in the past, then surely, the ideologues of the East German ruling party believed, the great man could be invoked to guarantee national unity in a divided and uncertain political present characterized by the now virulent cold war. "For us there is only one Goethe, and he belongs to the entire German people," declared Grotewohl.[6] Both the SED manifesto on Goethe and Grotewohl's speech showed that the Communist authorities about to proclaim a separate state in their zone were just as aware of the traditional importance of *Kultur* as were bourgeois conservatives, and that they were eager and willing to claim that cultural heritage for themselves.

Over the course of the nineteenth century, Goethe had come to be viewed as the greatest representative of the German *Kulturnation*. He was, as the distinguished scholar Ernst Robert Curtius argued, the one great German classicist, and moreover the last undisputed literary genius to be produced by the postclassical western world after Dante and Shakespeare, figures who, as Curtius declared, had achieved a creative totalization of western traditions. In the scholar's view, Goethe was "the last distillation of the European spiritual world in a great individual," and as such he was "more and other than a German poet."[7] Nevertheless, Goethe's universal achievement had important implications for the German nation. As Anton Kaes has written, "Goethe and Weimar classicism" came to form "the imaginary center of Germany's national existence."[8] But in addition, according to Karl Robert Mandelkow, one of the characteristics of post-1945 Goethe reception "was the elevation of the poet to be the representative not just of a humanist Germany, but of Christian Europe itself."[9] Through their reaffirmation of Goethe, Germans could experience both national greatness and a profound connection to the European traditions of the past. The *Kultur* embodied by Goethe and other less exalted figures was a realm outside history and beyond economics, a quiet realm of noble contemplation and greatness. As Curtius argued, this *Kultur* connected its admirers in a golden chain of truth "that winds its way through the millennia. The noblest pass it on to each other."[10] Through Goethe and the *Kultur* that he represented Germans could have direct access to unquestioned, timeless greatness.

Theodor W. Adorno has written that cultural conservatives in Germany during the first half of the twentieth century were driven by a fundamentally static understanding of culture as a lasting value impervious to the vagaries of economic downturns. Precisely because of the rapid economic changes associated with the onset of modernity, *Kultur* became, Adorno believed, both a refuge and a form of self-justification. It represented an ideal never achieved in reality, but the fact that one adhered to the ideal helped to excuse one's failure to achieve it. In a world of instability and change, *Kultur* remained an unchanging, reliable quantity. In the view of Wilhelm Röpke in 1945, German intellectuals had "saved this pan-German culture through the inferno and preserved it as a valuable reserve." Indeed, Röpke argued, German *Kultur* was "one of the few assets that will belong to Germany after the war and with which it can make a new beginning."[11] As one German scholar put it in 1946: "As individuals and as a nation we have lost more than we can say; but our intellectual-spiritual property and our greatest possession therein, the mighty heritage of Goethe, can never be taken away from us if we do not give it up ourselves."[12] Unlike factories, apartment houses, and government buildings, *Kultur* was impervious to physical destruction and could not be dismantled and appropriated by occupying armies. Simultaneously, because the Goethean heritage "belongs not just to Germany, but to the world," it created a bridge between an isolated Germany and the rest of the world.[13] As Friedrich Meinecke saw it, Goethe and the tradition he represented would play a vital role in "the winning back of a spiritual contact with the other Occidental countries."[14] At the same time, the connection between Goethe and the pan-European cultural heritage was a way to restore international links that had been destroyed during the years of the "Third Reich." It was no coincidence that one of the most important cultural institutions created by the West German government in the postwar period to propagate German culture abroad was called the "Goethe Institute" (1951).

Kultur had always provided idealistic shelter from the risks of a changing social situation; paradoxically, however, in providing such a shelter it also helped to stabilize and perpetuate the very forces that had made shelter necessary. Herbert Marcuse has referred to this paradox as the "affirmative" aspect of culture, which helps to reconcile its admirers with an unjust society.[15] According to Adorno, *Kultur* insisted on its removal from the sphere of capitalist relations of production "in order, as it were, to offer universal security in the middle of a universal dynamic."[16] Because it offered a refuge from an insecure society, *Kultur* could not be separated completely from that society. It functioned as a kind of pressure valve, allowing for the escape of pent-up tensions. But the security provided by *Kultur* helped to preserve the insecurity of modern economic and social relations.

In 1945, however, it was unclear just how secure German *Kultur* actually was. The war had destroyed not just factories and government buildings but also major cultural centers. Ernst Beutler, the head of the Freies Deutsches Hochstift, an organization dedicated to preserving Goethe's heritage, suggested after the Allied air raid that destroyed much of Frankfurt, including Goethe's childhood home, on March 22, 1944 that the physical destruction of Frankfurt had created a cultural gap as well. Now that Goethe's Frankfurt no longer existed, he believed, "a gap has opened up, unbridgeable. It is as if Goethe had only now truly died."[17] Beutler was not the only German shaken by the destruction of Goethe's home. In a moving elegy entitled "Rückkehr nach Frankfurt" (Return to Frankfurt) published in *Die Wandlung* in October of 1946, the poet Marie Luise Kaschnitz described wandering through the ruined city after the war and encountering the destruction of one of Germany's most famous cultural monuments:

> And the house was a hole, it was empty air,
> Jeering rubbish, a senseless sensation;
> And signs had been posted here and there.
> They declared: Property of the nation.[18]

Surrounded by the city in which Goethe spent his childhood, the citizens of Frankfurt had felt a living connection to the great poet; now that connection was gone.

It was more than just Allied bombs that threatened the continuity of German culture at the end of the war. German cultural values were threatened from inside the nation as well. *Kultur* and the *Bildung* (education and development of the individual) associated with it in German tradition were supposed to cultivate the senses, the imagination, and aesthetic and moral judgment, thus helping to create better human beings. As Schiller had written in his *Briefe über die ästhetische Erziehung des Menschen* (Letters on the Aesthetic Education of Man), "there is no other way to make the sensuous man rational than by first making him aesthetic."[19] The person who had learned to appreciate and understand music, art, and poetry was not only more knowledgeable but also more complete and more moral than the person who had not undergone an aesthetic education. In the playful realm of aesthetics — Schiller called it a "Reich der Freiheit" (empire of freedom) — sensuality and moral principle could be reconciled with each other. For ordinary human beings, aesthetic sensibility provided a route toward truth and moral goodness that might otherwise be closed to them. What was aesthetically good and what was morally good were supposed to form a unity; beauty and morality went hand-in-hand.

The Second World War and the many German crimes against humanity associated with it, however, presented the achievements of German *Kultur* and *Bildung* in a less than favorable light. After all, this supposedly superior nation had embroiled Europe in a murderous war and imprisoned, tortured, and killed millions of people, including vast numbers of women and children, in concentration camps. In what way did these crimes square with the notion of German *Kultur* as uniquely beneficent? Friedrich Wolf wrote in 1945 that he was often asked in other countries how it was possible that "of all places it was in Germany, which counted such sublime spirits as Johann Sebastian Bach, Beethoven, and Goethe . . . as its own," that a man like "Hitler and this whole bestial band of Nazi thugs" had gained absolute power.[20]

One of the people asking the same question was Plievier's fictional German officer Vilshofen from the novel *Stalingrad,* who reflects on the many crimes committed by German soldiers in the Volga region, only to wonder how these crimes fit in with the magnificent achievements of German culture:

> Is it the law of the German people, the same people who brought forth a Gutenberg, a Matthias Grünewald, a Martin Luther, a Beethoven, an Immanuel Kant? Is it the law of a creative people living by the fruits of its own creations?[21]

The same basic question was to be asked again and again in different ways during the postwar period. It was clear after 1945 that the German *Staats-*

nation had ceased to exist; but given the nature of German crimes against humanity, it was also not clear whether the *Kulturnation* was still intact.

There were several possible answers to the question posed by Plievier's Vilshofen as to the relationship between German *Kultur* and German military and political barbarity. The most widespread and comforting explanation was that Hitler and his minions had represented a radical break from the German cultural tradition — what the literary scholar Victor Klemperer called "the most extreme opposite of the basic views of the German classical era."[22] In the view of Klemperer and others, the Nazis had sought to completely destroy the tradition of German *Kultur*. Such an argument also provided a seemingly reasonable explanation for German crimes against humanity: these crimes had been possible precisely because Germans under the Nazis had broken with a previously intact and praiseworthy humanist tradition. If this was true, then the most important task facing postwar Germans in the cultural realm was to reforge the link with a broken tradition — not a zero hour at all but rather a conservative restoration in the wake of Nazi barbarism. The true answer to the barbarity of Nazism, Klemperer argued, was: "Keep going down the path of culture!"[23] Curtius, too, argued that "the remedy can only lie in taking up tradition anew."[24] Most Germans with political and cultural authority in the four occupation zones seemed to agree with Klemperer and Curtius. As Klemperer approvingly noted, the major postwar German political parties "are very much in agreement that Nazi inhumanity, which passed itself off as German humanity, should be countered with the pure humanity of the Herder-Goethe era."[25]

This was the position taken by Hans-Egon Holthusen, an influential poet and literary intellectual who was later to write one of the first histories of postwar literature. In November of 1945 Holthusen published a poem entitled "Tabula Rasa" in the first issue of the newly founded *Die Wandlung*. The poet's vision of a radically clean slate onto which the intellectual history of postwar Germany would subsequently be written later became a powerful factor in the creation of the myth of 1945 as a cultural zero hour. Invoking 1945 as both a beginning and an end — "To make an end. To set a beginning" — Holthusen spoke of the zero hour as a negative situation in which Germans, severed from the past, were therefore also cut off from the core of their identity: "We are no longer ourselves." For Holthusen, the radical break with tradition implied by the "tabula rasa," far from being positive, was in fact part of the reason for the German catastrophe and could lead only to further catastrophes:

> We tore down all the bridges, razed
> What was given to our care.
> Fire from all the roofs! We praise
> The future, and with it comes despair.[26]

Now that the comforts of tradition were lost, Germany was a "tabula rasa" without a past. Its future was associated only with "despair," and any access to the truth of eternity was doubtful. Holthusen's poem shows that the first major literary invocation of radical discontinuity after the German defeat was entirely negative, suggesting that the break would only perpetuate suffering and horror.

The most important element in a revitalization of German culture, many intellectuals believed, would be Goethe, who acquired a profound national significance in the wake of the "Tabula Rasa" of 1945. As Johannes R. Becher argued, "if Goethe had been alive among the German people, then his living strength would have engendered such an overpowering hatred of Nazi barbarism that the movement would have failed at the very beginning."[27] As Hans-Dietrich Dahnke has suggested, the most prevalent postwar diagnosis was that "the abandonment of Goethe was a direct expression of . . . the decline that ultimately reached its nadir in the insanity of fascism."[28] In the context of an increasingly contentious cold war, such questions about *Kultur* and barbarity acquired additional importance; and as the primary representative of traditional German culture Goethe became an object of dispute. As Germans' room for political maneuvering narrowed, they fought their battles instead in the cultural sphere. At the end of 1948 Brecht referred to this process of displacement as a "battle of the spirits" in which political "struggle withdraws into the landscapes of culture."[29] Kaes has suggested that "in the period between the collapse and the currency reform, discourse about Goethe gained in significance just as, in a Germany deprived of political authority, the sphere of culture became the only remaining sphere in which German identity could be articulated."[30]

In addition to its traditional function as a fill-in for unavailable political power, German *Kultur* now also served an exculpatory function: for many Germans, the *Kulturnation* as represented by its highest achievements was to provide a cultural counterweight to the nation's heavy moral and political sins. This exculpatory function was outlined by the exiled Austrian writer Franz Werfel in a May, 1945 address "To the German People," in which Werfel declared that the German classical tradition represented the only possible salvation for Germans from their collective guilt. Werfel enjoined Germans to "think back with humility and gratefulness to your great and holy masters, who will be your witnesses in eternity. Only they can take the shame away from you."[31] For Werfel and many other representatives of postwar literary life, Germany's "great and holy masters" would build a bridge back to that tradition that Holthusen declared to be the source of comfort and eternity. The most prominent bridge-builder would be "the wonderful person born into the world two hundred years ago by a young German woman," as Mann described Goethe in Weimar and Frankfurt during the summer of 1949.[32]

On August 28, 1945, seventeen months after the destruction of Goethe's house in Frankfurt, Ernst Beutler gave a speech to commemorate the one hundred and ninety-sixth anniversary of Goethe's birth. He argued that the great humanist was capable of providing Germans with important assistance in establishing a postwar national identity. Given that Germany had lost its *Reich*, its *Kaiser*, its President, and its flag — most of the symbols of national-political identity, although Beutler did not mention the *Führer* in this context — what was left now and always for Germans to claim was "the freedom of the German spirit," represented above all by Goethe, in whose every word, "even in his most bitter, lives a healing strength." Goethe's birthday, Beutler argued, showed Germans "that we are still ourselves."[33] Because of Goethe's literary creations, the rest of the world still had reason to love and respect Germany, and — perhaps more important — Germany still had reason to love and respect itself.

The extent to which conservatives and leftists agreed on Goethe's importance is indicated by the fact that both the Communist Johannes R. Becher and the conservative Swabian poet Otto Heuschele — himself at the very least a political conformist during the "Third Reich" — offered fundamentally comforting pictures of Goethe's influence. For Becher, "Goethe's omnipresence was a light in our darkness,"[34] while for Heuschele "the greatest spirits of our people are just good enough to be leaders and teachers."[35] For both, German *Kultur* had remained immune to the depredations of the Nazis.

Far from envisioning 1945 as teaching a lesson of radical discontinuity, many Germans on both the right and the left and in both the West and the East believed that the German catastrophe called for a renewed commitment to forgotten values, particularly the classical idealism represented by Goethe. In their view, Germany had already witnessed more than enough radical breaks in the twentieth century, and it was time now for a reestablishment and restoration of lost traditions — as Hans Paeschke suggested in the first issue of *Merkur*, one of the most important intellectual journals to emerge in the postwar period.[36] For Curtius, the radical destructiveness of the twentieth century was part of a much longer history of self-destruction in western civilization. Goethe's respect for the European cultural tradition, he believed, had been a response to this problem; in the context of the massive destruction experienced by Germany in the last few years of the Second World War, therefore, respect for Goethe and his approach to tradition was all the more important.

Marie Luise Kaschnitz's view of cultural destruction is representative of an idealistic approach that, while aware of pervasive physical collapse, nevertheless ultimately insists on the permanence of cultural values. As the poetic narrator in Kaschnitz's "Rückkehr nach Frankfurt" stands in front of the no-longer-existing house in the city of Goethe's birth, "Where the world first excited him/And he pleased the world," the poem's narrator suddenly sees

Goethe himself "in flesh and blood," and she is horrified that the great master will notice the destruction of his home: "I was terrified as at the Last Judgment/For he was observing his house."[37] These words put Goethe into the position of God on Judgment Day, and they imply that the narrator feels a sense of shame, possibly even guilt for the destruction of the house. But she is reassured to observe that:

> He did not gaze into the grave,
> He was counting the rows of windows,
> He was spying into rooms of purest air
> As if candlelight were shining there.[38]

The narrator thus realizes that the immortal Goethe does not see the destruction of his own home; what he sees is an intact building untouched by bombs. The narrator interprets her vision as a sign that although buildings may be destroyed, the cultural tradition for which they stood remains untouched and untouchable:

> Then I knew him to be untouched
> By the bloody crime,
> Because those who are themselves complete
> Can only see completion.
> And I heard, before he disappeared,
> A tone of bright elation
> And read on the sign over refuse and sand
> The words: property of the nation.[39]

The intact house that Goethe saw in Kaschnitz's poem was soon to be recreated in reality. In view of the upcoming two hundredth anniversary of Goethe's birth, Beutler's Freies Deutsches Hochstift, which owned the property, together with the city of Frankfurt, decided in 1947 to rebuild the Goethe House and make it resemble as nearly as possible the destroyed original, thus bringing an all-too vulnerable physical reality into alignment with the presumably incorruptible spiritual ideal. If the Goethe in Kaschnitz's poem had failed to recognize the destruction of his birthplace because it was a merely physical blemish on an intellectual tradition that remained pristine, then the owners of the Goethe House decided that what had been destroyed by the war must be rebuilt to conform to that higher spiritual reality. In order to make a home for the genuine furniture and mementos that had been removed from the house prior to its destruction, the context in which those items had been placed on display for visitors would be faithfully recreated.

The decision to rebuild the Goethe House was not without controversy. Some critics saw it as a falsification, indeed a counterfeiting. They argued that the house in which Goethe had grown up was gone for good, and that any attempt at a historically accurate reconstruction was an insult to the truth and to the real house which no longer existed. For the journalist Walter Dirks, soon to become an important critic of what he saw as a thoughtless postwar West German cultural and political restoration of older values, the reconstruction of the Goethe House was one of the first and most crucial symbolic acts of that restoration, built on a "central lie."[40]

The debate about the reconstruction of the Goethe house suggested that postwar Germans were not as confident about the invulnerability of their cultural traditions as many of them claimed to be. If indeed the tradition was as impervious to physical destruction as Kaschnitz's poem suggested, then there was no obvious need for a recreation of the Goethe House; that recreation became necessary only if, as supporters of reconstruction believed, the tradition was physically linked to certain sacred objects and places. Moreover, not all Germans were as convinced as Kaschnitz that their cultural traditions were unsullied and unproblematic. For a tradition devoted to the unity of "the good, the true, and the beautiful," Hitler's concentration camps were a radical challenge. Not all SS officers were the uncultivated barbarians invoked by Adorno when he described Nazi cultural policy as "the incursion of the savage hordes into the enclosures of spirit." In Adorno's view, the typical Nazi was filled with "envy of *Kultur,* against which he sullenly rebels, because it excludes him."[41] In fact, however, more than a few Nazi leaders had been avid devotees of German music and poetry. Mann's Serenus Zeitblom declares that he would consider it irresponsible to label the Nazi dictatorship "something quite foreign to the nature of our people, forced upon us."[42] On the contrary, according to Zeitblom, even the greatest figures of the German tradition already bore traces of the horrors to come.

Four years after the end of the war, the young Swiss playwright Max Frisch expressed his skepticism about the value of *Kultur* in fending off barbarism by reminding his readers that Reinhard Heydrich, one of the most brutal of Nazi leaders, had been a man of cultural refinement:

> In my opinion one of the decisive lessons . . . that our generation has had to learn is the frequently revealed fact that — to express it with a concrete example — a man like Heydrich, the murderer of Bohemia, was a distinguished and very sensitive musician, who could hold forth with spirit and true connoisseurship, even with love, on Bach, Händel, Beethoven, Bruckner.[43]

The fact that some Nazi criminals had been relatively cultivated men, educated in the tradition of the German *Bildungsbürgertum,* challenged conventional German notions of progress and civilization. What troubled Germans and other Europeans so much about Nazi crimes was not just their brutality and amorality but also the fact that they had been committed in the name of

a nation previously celebrated as one of the pinnacles of western civilization — committed, as Frisch put it, not by "a people from whom we expect
the worst, because they don't have running water and can't read; but by a
nation that possesses and creates at a high level what we have, until now,
understood as *Kultur*."[44]

The writer Ernst Wiechert, imprisoned by the Nazis in Buchenwald for
several months during the summer of 1938, wrote a report entitled *Der
Totenwald* (Forest of the Dead) about his experiences in the concentration
camp; this became one of the first literary documents about Buchenwald published after the war's end. Wiechert's report is particularly moving as the reflection of a German conservative and member of the *Bildungsbürgertum* who is
absolutely shocked at the extreme barbarity his supposedly cultivated fellow
countrymen are capable of. Johannes — as Wiechert's alter ego is called in the
book — cannot understand how it is possible for the perpetrators and victims
in Buchenwald to speak the same language and worship the same God. Particularly shocking for Johannes is the fact that one of the concentration camp
commanders is the son of a Protestant minister and thus a representative of
German literary and moral *Bildung*. The sheer horror of his experiences in
Buchenwald makes Johannes begin to doubt the cultural mission of his nation.
"Greater shame was never heaped upon the heads of any people than upon
this one as it now furnished its own hangmen," Johannes reflects.[45]

Over half a century after the liberation of the concentration camps, the
image of the camp commander who listens rapturously to classical music one
minute and remorselessly kills his helpless victims the next has become so
familiar as to become a cliché. It has lost the power to elicit surprise, even
though it still offends. However, in the immediate aftermath of the Second
World War the thought that men like Wiechert's "minister's son," educated
in the highest of European cultural traditions and beneficiaries of Schiller's
"aesthetic education of man" could be capable of murderous barbarism was
still profoundly shocking. One of the interconnected stories that form
Heinrich Böll's novel *Wo warst du, Adam?* (Where Were You, Adam? 1951)
concerns precisely such a concentration camp commander, a lover of choral
music, who soon discovers the "enormous latent fund of musical talent
among" his Jewish prisoners, and who therefore gives each prisoner a voice
test upon his or her arrival at the concentration camp; the outcome of this
test determines whether the prisoner will live or die.[46] Paul Celan's 1946
poem "Todesfuge" (Fugue of Death) probably the most beautiful and dis-
turbing poetic depiction of the death camps, personifies death in the form of
a concentration camp commander who is a music-loving "Meister aus
Deutschland" ("master from Germany") ordering his inmates to play music
for him. Celan's use of the word "Meister" suggests not a slave driver but
rather an artistic master or "maestro," an artist of prodigious and widely acknowledged skill:

He shouts stab deeper in earth you there you others you sing and
   you play
he grabs at the iron in his belt and swings it and blue are his eyes
stab deeper your spades you there and you others play on for
   the dancing[47]

Celan's poem gives voice to the recognition that culture and barbarism, far
from being diametrically opposed to each other, can go hand in hand in the
modern world — indeed, that Germans' image of themselves as a superior
Kulturnation may have made it easier for the Nazis to perpetrate brutal
crimes against members of other — supposedly inferior — nations and races.
In the postwar years this recognition fundamentally shook Germans' and
other Europeans' self-image of themselves as civilized. As Jung put it shortly
after the war's end, "we used to be able to relegate such things to 'Asia!'"
Now, however, it was clear that barbarism could be equally at home in
Europe. Thus Nazi crimes were, in Jung's words, "a blow aimed at all Europeans."[48] It was no longer clear how to distinguish barbarity from civilization. Max Horkheimer and Theodor W. Adorno expressed the coincidence
of barbarity and civilization in the modern European world at the beginning
of *Dialektik der Aufklärung* (Dialectic of Enlightenment, 1947): "the fully
enlightened earth radiates disaster triumphant."[49]

Perhaps the starkest indication of the proximity between civilization and
barbarism is the fact the city of Weimar, where the tradition of German classicism had reached fruition in the late eighteenth and early nineteenth centuries, was located only five miles away from what would later be the
Buchenwald concentration camp, where thousands of people died during the
last five years of Nazi rule.[50] According to German tradition, the very oak
tree under whose branches Goethe had once communed with nature was located on the site of the concentration camp. In his August, 1945 speech in
commemoration of Goethe's birthday, Ernst Beutler wondered publicly how
it was possible for history to have gone so horribly wrong that Germans
could now think of this place, "to which so many happy and earnest Weimar
memories are attached . . ., only with shame and terror."[51] The proximity between Goethe's Weimar and the Nazi concentration camp became for postwar Germans a metaphor for the way in which it was possible to combine
absolute evil with the highest achievements of German *Kultur*. Wiechert
mentions the Goethe oak in *Der Totenwald;* it affords his alter ego Johannes
spiritual comfort. By the time he leaves Buchenwald several months later,
however, Johannes has ceased to find consolation in Goethe:

Once more Johannes went up to the oak, beneath which he had stood
so often. The stars filled the dark sky as distant and cold as ever. This
was a place to which no comfort flowed from those far-distant worlds.
The hand of man cast the lots here, indifferent to life or death.[52]

Just as for Ernst Beutler the destruction of Frankfurt had meant that now Goethe seemed truly dead, for Johannes his experiences in the Buchenwald concentration camp have removed him from the world of the great German who once wandered through this forest.

In 1948 the Dutch socialist Nico Rost published a German translation of the diary that he had kept while imprisoned in the Dachau concentration camp during the final year of the war. He called the diary *Goethe in Dachau: Literatur und Wirklichkeit* (Goethe in Dachau: Literature and Reality). Rost's literary experiences and disappointments in Dachau were not entirely dissimilar to those of the German conservative Wiechert in Buchenwald — a man whose work Rost respected. Rost's intention in keeping a literary diary was to remove himself as far as possible from the horrific reality of the concentration camp: to become a kind of spiritual inner emigrant inside Dachau, thus demonstrating the absolute nature of his freedom. Rost's diary is above all a way for him "to concentrate my thoughts and energies on literature . . ., in order, thereby, not constantly . . . [to think] of food, vermin, the roll call, and so on." The literature that he eagerly reads, as well as his own diary entries about that literature, are therefore "a kind of self-protection" intended to help him overcome "all the material of this place, i.e. the matter of the SS, a crust of bread, watery soup, lice, and fleas."[53] Increasingly, however, Rost finds Goethe's Olympian superiority intolerable: "No! — No! — No! — I can't read such remarks, even if they come from a genius like Goethe, without rising up in arms against them inwardly."[54] Nevertheless, Rost suspects that Goethe's genius may have ultimately been a "permanent, heroic struggle against the tragic, a struggle against drowning in it himself."[55] As such, Goethe's struggle against the tragic principle helps Rost to survive the horrors of Dachau.

In a novella published in 1951, Stefan Hermlin addressed in fiction the very problem faced by the real-life Nico Rost in Dachau. Hermlin's story-within-a-story deals with the experiences of a Jewish partisan during the Warsaw ghetto uprising of 1943. This partisan, who is also the narrator of the framed story, is an enthusiastic reader of Friedrich Hölderlin, and he acknowledges that his devotion to reading is "an attempt to reconcile myself to the present, to create for myself a private normality, of which . . . reading is a part."[56] Even more than Rost, Hermlin's character is filled with doubt as to the appropriateness of his activities. In a world of torture and depravity, does it make sense to devote oneself to Romantic poetry? The partisan admits that it would be pointless to ascribe to his literary activities "a militant, an active moral significance . . . There are situations in which art, any art, is opposed to life, and in which art ought actually to have nothing more to say to life." And yet even in this self-criticism Hermlin's partisan is unsure: is it not possible that his very self-doubt is a result of the enemy's unceasing physical and psychological attacks, "the clearest indication that the enemy has succeeded in getting me to where he wants me to be?"[57]

In view of the horrific experiences of Europeans like Wiechert and Rost, some Germans in the postwar period believed that it was impossible to preserve the Goethe cult and the *Kulturnation* in their prewar form. For them, as for one dejected character in Walter Kolbenhoff's *Heimkehr in die Fremde* (Coming Home to a Foreign Country, 1949), "Hofmannsthal and the ovens of Auschwitz don't go together."[58] An important critic of any unreflective continuation of the Goethe cult was Jaspers, who, agreed that the unprecedented situation faced by Germans after the war had caused them to doubt the roots of their own identity, and argued that it was impossible to return to the comforts of a previous tradition as if nothing had happened. The philosopher took this position with respect not only to Goethe but to all of the German cultural heritage. In his introduction to the first issue of *Die Wandlung*, Jaspers declared: "We have lost almost everything: the state, the economy, the secure conditions of our physical existence, and, even worse than that: valid and binding norms, moral dignity, the unifying self-consciousness of a people."[59] The threefold spiritual loss of ethical norms, moral value, and a unifying consciousness of self means in essence the loss of collective identity, and it is precisely this collective identity that had previously been guaranteed by the Goethe cult and the entire panoply of German cultural heroes venerated by the *Bildungsbürgertum*. Jaspers argued that it was impossible to return to this tradition, because "we ourselves have become different people since 1933." Hence, any "simple hooking up with the situation before 1933" was impossible.[60]

The city of Frankfurt awarded Jaspers its Goethe prize in 1947, two years before celebrating the two hundredth anniversary of Goethe's birth by awarding the same prize to Thomas Mann. In his acceptance speech, delivered on August 28, 1947, the one hundred and ninety-eighth anniversary of Goethe's birth, Jaspers carefully laid out his reasons for believing that the cult of Goethe could no longer be continued. Acknowledging that it was precisely ancestors like Goethe under whose auspices Germans achieve identity, Jaspers nevertheless declared that postwar Germany was permanently separated from all previous traditions. Given the enormity of the German catastrophe even the past was no longer as certain as it had previously seemed, the philosopher argued. Jaspers admitted that it was in living "with Goethe" that Germans became Germans — "to live with Goethe, perhaps that is the only thing that really turns us into Germans" — but he argued that in the postwar situation living "with Goethe" had become extremely difficult.[61]

Jaspers suggested that the thousands of years of western history that had resulted in Goethe were now over, and that what faced Germans after 1945 was a kind of posthistory. Such words were a radical invocation of a new beginning, neither positively nor negatively inflected, but rather presented as an unavoidable fact. Precisely because Goethe and his reception were so important in the constitution of German identity, Jaspers argued, it was important to redefine the meaning of Goethe in the postwar situation. Just as the Germany of 1947 was no longer the Germany of 1933, so too the postwar Goethe must become different from the prewar Goethe. Although he acknowledged the scholarly achievement of prewar Goethe specialists, Jaspers suggested that Germans' "*Bildung* through Goethe" had ultimately become "a calamity," and that prewar Goethe worship had become a slavish cult depriving Germans of intellectual independence and contributing to a failure to understand the problems of a modern world that Goethe had never known.[62] "We are not permitted to deify anyone. The epoch of the *Goethe cult is over*," declared Jaspers, predicting that "if we wish to be alive spiritually, a revolution in the understanding of Goethe lies ahead of us."[63]

Jaspers's attempt to redefine the contours of postwar German Goethe reception did not cause an immediate controversy in 1947. But two years later, as Germany was celebrating the two hundredth anniversary of the great man's birth, his views precipitated a literary debate about the meaning of Goethe in the postwar world. In the spring of 1949, Curtius, who had published his scholarly opus *Europäische Literatur und lateinisches Mittelalter* (European Literature and the Latin Middle Ages) a year earlier, chastised Jaspers for what he saw as an impertinent attack on one of the greatest representatives of western *Kultur*. The focus of Curtius's work since the late 1920s had been the unity and continuity of the European cultural tradition from the middle ages until the present, and therefore the scholar was understandably upset at Jaspers's insistence on radical discontinuity, seeing it as "a shameful and impotent attempt to lay hands on the noblest legacy of German spirit."[64] Writing in *Die Zeit*, Curtius suggested that Jaspers was striving to become a new *praeceptor germaniae*. Criticizing Jaspers's book *Die Schuldfrage*, Curtius wrote: "He has demonstrated our collective guilt with such clarity that it is only with a guilty conscience that we can continue to live."[65] At any rate, Curtius declared, Goethe himself was free of any supposed collective guilt. Moreover, Jaspers's insistence on discontinuity and change was itself outdated, Curtius argued, a relic "from the junk room of faith in progress, whose last paltry hour struck in 1848." Given the horrors of the recent past, contemporary Europeans could no longer believe in progress as during the first half of the nineteenth century. Reminding his readers of Sternberger's earlier insistence — in the pages of Jaspers's journal *Die Wandlung* — on respect for Thomas Mann, Curtius asked: "Is it immodest of us to request respect for Goethe?"[66]

In spite of the vehement difference of opinion between them, both Jaspers and Curtius agreed on the national and international significance of Goethe; in addition, both recognized that the current situation was characterized by a profound break in cultural continuity. Like the debate about the reconstruction of the Goethe House, the Curtius-Jaspers controversy clearly showed both the uncertainty Germans felt in trying to integrate their cultural traditions into a postwar world and the tremendous importance that this effort, however difficult, had for them. For many Germans, Curtius stood on the side of a reassuring cultural continuity. He defended a heritage too important to be lost. His message to Germans was to reassert their connection to cultural traditions that had been tossed aside during the Nazi years. Jaspers, on the other hand, was perceived as the representative of a disrespect for tradition that could ultimately lead to the very nihilistic denial of values that was perceived as having led to the Nazi catastrophe in the first place. On the fourth anniversary of the end of the Second World War, the critic and writer Gustav René Hocke, who had been a student of Curtius's, and who was one of the early theorists of the youthful postwar literature embodied by the recently-formed Gruppe 47, declared in *Die Welt am Sonntag* that Goethe was "a gigantic mirror of continuous being" who was being attacked by the champion of "a wishy-washy ideology of the 'discontinuous'" that could ultimately lead to a nihilistic rejection of all cultural values.[67] Hocke's attack on Jaspers showed that in many ways the younger authors then in the process of proclaiming their innovativeness were just as invested in the ideology of German classicism, and in the specific concept of a *Kultur* untouched by politics and history, as their elders.

Jaspers was attacked not just in the West but also in the East. Alexander Dymschitz, the chief cultural officer in the Soviet military administration in Germany, labeled Jaspers a reactionary philosopher whose thinking contributed to the denigration of "high and noble concepts." Like Grotewohl, Dymschitz saw Goethe as "the herald of Germany's national unity"; anything that seemed to interfere with Goethe's ability to play that role needed to be combated.[68] In his own commemoration speech on August 28, 1949, Johannes R. Becher spoke out against "the existentialist blather about" Goethe's "inability to grasp the whole problematic of the human being," arguing that, in contrast to the misery "of existentialism, we find in Goethe that fear has been overcome," so that human beings can raise themselves "in triumph even over death."[69]

While Becher agreed with Curtius in venerating Goethe, his ultimate goal was quite different: the appropriation of Goethe as a figurehead for Communist cultural politics. In an almost ludicrous attempt to connect the Goethe who had disapproved of the French Revolution with contemporary Communist politics and ideology, Becher insisted that "the light in the west which dawned in Goethe's time has been followed in our time by the bright rays which the Russian Revolution shined on us."[70] In Becher's words, the purportedly democratic-socialist transformation of the Soviet zone had rendered East Germans "capable of understanding a figure like Goethe more profoundly and more comprehensively than was possible for the generations that preceded us."[71] For the Communist functionary Alexander Abusch, "Goethe's work stands with Hegel's as the high point of dialectical thinking in the period before Marx and Engels."[72]

As these words suggested, the supposedly indivisible cultural heritage represented by Goethe and celebrated by Mann had, by 1949, become one of the victims of the cold war. Within this context, both of the nascent German states sought to claim for themselves the authentic heritage of the *Kulturnation,* thus substantially weakening the ability of *Kultur* to serve as a bridge over politically troubled waters. Erich Kleinschmidt has diagnosed the situation thus: "Both camps co-opted Goethe as an effective ideological standard-bearer," even if the contents of this appropriation differed in West and East.[73] In both Germanys a revived Goethe cult was presented as an adequate response to the German crimes of the immediate past and as an insurance policy against potential relapses in the future. In the West Goethe was presented in the largely apolitical and idealistic terms of the inner emigration, while in the East Goethe was depicted as the optimistic precursor of a future — and now present — socialist Germany.

Given the heated rhetoric in East and West, it was left to exiles to remind Germans of the unity of their cultural traditions and to criticize the dishonest appropriation of Goethe's legacy. One of Jaspers's defenders was the Austrian exile, scholar Leo Spitzer, who wrote from the United States to complain about the way that Goethe was being used in the late 1940s as an object for national cultural browbeating — what Spitzer called "the collective We, which suggests a kind of national mobilization."[74] The activities in Germany during the Goethe anniversary, Spitzer claimed, were "combat engagements in the service of national prestige," and Germans were working "on the erection of unavoidable, eternal marble statues or Lenin masks." Any attempt to change the monumental image of Goethe immediately seemed to impinge on "the power-political interests of the nation." Ultimately, what Germans were trying to say by putting Goethe on a pedestal and declaring him to be untouchable was: "We [are] the untouchable nation of this untouchable poet."[75] Germans' worship of Goethe, in other words, had become little more than a self-protective mechanism.

The debates about cultural tradition that occurred in Germany during the first five years after the end of the Second World War demonstrated the profound uncertainty Germans felt as a supposed *Kulturnation* that had nevertheless shown itself capable of the worst barbarity. The fact that the cultural tradition represented by Goethe had been incapable of preventing the Nazi disaster challenged the traditional belief that *Bildung* and *Kultur* invariably lead to the moral improvement of both the individual and the nation. The most widespread reaction to this challenge was simply to deny it. Most German intellectuals who voiced an opinion on the matter after 1945 insisted on the unchanging value of their cultural traditions, arguing that the

German catastrophe had become possible only because Germans had strayed from the tradition represented by Goethe. Hence Meinecke — who had, prior to the First World War, become the most important scholarly proponent of the concept of a *Kulturnation* in his book *Weltbürgertum und Nationalstaat* (Cosmopolitanism and the National State) — proposed dealing with the moral catastrophe by establishing cells of Goethe admirers throughout the country, believing that such cells might strengthen the power of a neglected tradition. As Meinecke wrote, Goethe's poems, along with those of Schiller and Mörike, were "perhaps the most essentially German parts of our literature. He who steeps himself in them will detect something indestructible — a German *character indeliblis* — in the midst of all the destruction and misfortune of our Fatherland."[76] Meinecke's words strongly echoed the traditional German belief in *Kultur* as a provider of security in a world of impermanence.

Shortly after the end of the war Jung had already expressed the basis of Jaspers's critique by suggesting that "old forms which once had their value cannot be left unexamined and simply used again, for the eternal verities cannot be passed on mechanically; rather, they must, in every era, be born anew in the human soul."[77] Jung's countryman Max Frisch was even more critical, recognizing the potential for a supposedly unchanging culture to be used apologetically. In view of the fact that the Nazis themselves had made use of the ideology of the German *Kulturnation,* Frisch argued in 1949 against using *Kultur* as a kind of apolitical and reassuring alibi for the crimes that Germans had committed — the kind of alibi already attacked by the fictional Colonel Vilshofen in Plievier's *Stalingrad.* Criticizing a *Kultur* perceived as separated from social and political life, Frisch insisted that culture "understood as a noble idol . . . will [not] save us."[78] Goethe and the other masters of German *Kultur* should not be misused to explain away or diminish the enormity of German crimes, Frisch argued. If Mann had insisted that it was too easy for Germans to separate their "good" cultural traditions from their "bad" political traditions and label the former genuinely German and the latter imposters, Frisch was suggesting in a similar way that cultural achievements, no matter how brilliant, can never be an excuse for political barbarity.

The Germanist Richard Alewyn, a former emigrant who had recently returned to Germany, made a substantially similar argument in an important speech given at the University of Cologne in 1949 that was to influence profoundly the course of postwar German understanding of Goethe specifically and the cultural tradition more generally. Although Germany and the rest of the world were celebrating the two hundredth anniversary of Goethe's birth, Alewyn declared, "it was not so very long ago that all the loudspeakers in Germany were spewing forth another name that is still ringing in their ears. Yesterday Hitler, today Goethe, and tomorrow?" Goethe could not erase

Hitler, Alewyn argued; the Nazi dictatorship had created a massive gap between the contemporary world and the world of German classicism. Like Holthusen, Alewyn suggested that Germans themselves had destroyed the bridges connecting them to their own traditions: "Did we not with our own hands explode the last bridges over which we used to come and go? And does not Goethe's house lie in ruins as an irrevocable sign of this fact?"[79] Acknowledging Germans' desperate need to seek in Goethe the source of a cultural tradition that would protect them in the midst of postwar destruction, Alewyn nevertheless insisted that what Germans had done during the years of the Third Reich could not be undone: "Between us and Weimar lies Buchenwald." One could try in various ways to dissociate oneself from Germany, Alewyn argued, but "what will not work . . . is to boast about Goethe while denying Hitler. There are only Goethe *and* Hitler, humanity *and* bestiality." In words that sounded very much like Thomas Mann's own earlier thoughts, the scholar declared: "At least for the generation living today, there cannot be two Germanys. There is only one or none at all." If Germans wanted to enjoy the best parts of their national cultural traditions, they also had to acknowledge what was worst and most painful: "If we concern ourselves with Goethe, then we are permitted to do so only on the condition that we must not avoid confrontation with ourselves."[80]

In a postscript to the various debates about Goethe and the German cultural tradition, Adorno, now back in Germany, declared in 1950: "The word has not yet gotten out that culture in the traditional sense of the word is dead."[81] In accordance with Jaspers, Adorno contended that "the German situation unequivocally demands a spiritual reorientation."[82] Arguing against what he called postwar Germans' attempt to seek "shelter in the conventional and in the past," Adorno declared that "traditional aesthetic forms" had lost their power, since "they are all given the lie by the catastrophe of the society out of which they grew."[83] Referring explicitly to Frisch's concept of "culture as alibi," Adorno noted that "today not the least important function of *Bildung* is to make it possible to forget and repress the horrors experienced and one's own responsibility."[84]

In an essay written during the Goethe year 1949, Adorno declared not only that "culture takes part in society's connectedness with guilt,"[85] but also that "the entirety of traditional culture [is today becoming] null and void: through an irrevocable process, its . . . legacy has become dispensable, unnecessary, trash."[86] In words that were to have a profound impact on the course of postwar German aesthetic thinking, Adorno described the situation of cultural criticism after the end of the Second World War:

Cultural criticism finds itself confronted with the last step in the dialectic of culture and barbarism: to write a poem after Auschwitz is barbaric, and this eats away even at the knowledge that proclaims why it has become impossible to write poems today.[87]

Although Adorno's criticism is sometimes misunderstood as a blanket prohibition on poetry, it is more properly conceived of as an insistence that in the postwar situation, after the supposedly civilized world has learned painfully to recognize the barbarity of which it is capable, culture can no longer stand on its own as an independent, autonomous sphere but must, rather, be accompanied by the self-criticism which Adorno calls *Kulturkritik* (cultural criticism).[88] But the necessity of criticizing *Kultur* does not make *Kulturkritik* morally superior to *Kultur* or immune to the contradictions inherent in modern society. On the contrary, in Adorno's view neither culture nor cultural criticism should be allowed to conceive of themselves as separate from the social context of which they are a part. No longer can *Kultur* be a sphere of spirit which remains, as Adorno puts it, "in self-satisfied contemplation."[89] And yet, paradoxically, in a world of totalitarianism and the increasing uniformity of consumerism, Adorno sees in the autonomous sphere of *Kultur* something akin to Schiller's "Reich der Freiheit," the possibility of freedom from total domination. Adorno's dialectical philosophy is driven by the insistence on acknowledging and probing the contradictions inherent in the interplay between culture, cultural criticism, and society.

Notes

[1] "Die Bleistifte sind messerscharf gespitzt. Die Federhalter haben frisch getankt. Die neuen Farbbänder zittern vor Ungeduld. Die Schreibmaschinen scharren nervös mit den Hufen. Die deutsche Kultur und die umliegenden Dörfer halten den Atem an. Es kann sich nur noch um Sekunden handeln. Da! Endlich ertönt der Startschuß! Die Federn sausen übers Papier. Die Finger jagen über die Tasten. . . . Das Rennen des Jahres hat begonnen: das Goethe-Derby über die klassische 200-Jahr-Strecke!" Erich Kästner, "Das Goethe-Derby," cited in Bettina Meier, *Goethe in Trümmern: Zur Rezeption eines Klassikers in der Nachkriegszeit* (Wiesbaden: Deutscher Universitäts-Verlag, 1989), 86. Unless otherwise specified, all translations from German in this book are my own; the German appears in the notes, followed by sources. I have added the notation "my translation" in a limited number of cases where confusion might otherwise occur.

[2] "Es wäre mir lieber, Goethe wäre zehn Jahre später geboren worden." Joachim G. Leithäuser, "Das Goethejahr ist überstanden . . .: Rückblick und Bilanz," *Der Monat*, 2, no. 15 (1949/1950), 286–96; here, 292.

[3] "verkörperte in einem zersplitterten und zerrissenen Deutschland die deutsche Einheit im Geistigen und Sprachlichen. Er hat einen entscheidenden Anteil an der

Bildung eines deutschen Nationalbewußtseins." Cited in Wolfram Schlenker, *Das "Kulturelle Erbe" in der DDR: Gesellschaftliche Entwicklung und Kulturpolitik 1945– 1965* (Stuttgart: Metzler, 1977), 84.

[4] "unsere Nation aus dem Dämmerlicht der Geschichtslosigkeit in den Rang einer Weltnation." Otto Grotewohl, "Amboss oder Hammer: Rede an die deutsche Jugend zum Todestag von Goethe," in *Deutsche Kulturpolitik*, 57–79; here, 78 (Dresden: Verlag der Kunst, 1952).

[5] "In Goethe kann die deutsche Nation den höchsten ihr gemäßen Ausdruck des modernen nationalen Selbstbewußtseins erreichen." Grotewohl, "Amboss oder Hammer," 79.

[6] "Für uns gibt es nur einen Goethe, und der gehört dem ganzen deutschen Volke." Grotewohl, "Amboss oder Hammer," 79.

[7] "die letzte Selbstkonzentration der abendländischen Geisteswelt in einem großen Individuum," "mehr und anderes als ein deutscher Dichter." Ernst Robert Curtius, "Aus: Goethe — Grundzüge seiner Welt," in *Goethe im Urteil seiner Kritiker: Dokumente zur Wirkungsgeschichte Goethes in Deutschland Teil IV 1918–1982*, ed. Karl Robert Mandelkow, 308–13; here, 312 (Munich: C. H. Beck, 1984).

[8] "Goethe und die Weimarer Klassik bildeten das imaginäre Zentrum der nationalen Existenz Deutschlands." Anton Kaes, "Literatur und nationale Identität: Kontroversen um Goethe 1945–49," in *Kontroversen, alte und neue [Akten des VII. Internationalen Germanisten-Kongresses Göttingen 1985*, vol. 10], ed. Albrecht Schöne, 199–206; here, 201 (Göttingen: Niemeyer, 1986).

[9] "war die Überhöhung des Dichters nicht nur zum Repräsentanten eines humanistischen Deutschland, sondern des christlichen Abendlandes schlechthin." Karl Robert Mandelkow, *Goethe in Deutschland: Rezeptionsgeschichte eines Klassikers,* vol. 2 (Munich: Beck, 1989), 137.

[10] "die sich durch die Jahrtausende schlingt. Die Edlen reichen sie einander weiter." Curtius, "Aus: Goethe — Grundzüge seiner Welt," 308.

[11] "Diese Gesamtkultur haben sie durch das Inferno gerettet und als eine kostbare Reserve bewahrt, die zu den wenigen Aktiven gehört, die Deutschland nach dem Kriege übriggeblieben sein werden und mit denen es einen neuen Anfang machen kann." Wilhelm Röpke, *Die deutsche Frage* (Erlenbach-Zurich: Eugen Rentsch, 1945), 89. My translation. Alternative English translation: Röpke, *The German Question,* trans. E. W. Dickes (London: George Allen & Unwin, 1946), 79.

[12] "So unsagbar viel wir als einzelne und als Volk verloren haben: Unser geistig-seelisches Eigentum und unser höchster Besitz darin, das gewaltige Erbe Goethes, kann uns nie entrissen werden, wenn wir es nicht selbst aufgeben." August Kippenberg, president of the Bremen branch of the Goethe society, on August 31, 1946, in *Goethe in Deutschland 1945–1982,* ed. Brita Eckert (Frankfurt: Buchhändler-Vereinigung, 1982), 11.

[13] "gehört nicht nur Deutschland, sondern der Welt." Kippenberg, in Eckert, *Goethe in Deutschland 1945–1982,* 11.

[14] Friedrich Meinecke, *The German Catastrophe: Reflections and Recollections,* trans. Sidney B. Fay (Cambridge, MA: Harvard UP, 1950), 117. In German: "die Wiedergewinnung eines geistigen Kontaktes mit den übrigen abendländischen

Völkern." Meinecke, *Die deutsche Katastrophe: Betrachtungen und Erinnerungen* (Brockhaus: Wiesbaden, 1946), 171.

[15] Herbert Marcuse, "Über den affirmativen Charakter der Kultur," in *Kultur und Gesellschaft*, 56–101 (Frankfurt: Suhrkamp, 1965). English translation: "The Affirmative Character of Culture," in Herbert Marcuse, *Negations: Essays in Critical Theory*, trans. Jeremy J. Shapiro (Boston: Beacon Press, 1968).

[16] Theodor W. Adorno, "Cultural Criticism and Society," in *Prisms*, trans. Samuel and Shierry Weber, 17–34; here, 22 (Cambridge, MA: MIT Press, 1981). In German: "gleichsam um inmitten universaler Dynamik universale Sekurität zu gewähren." Adorno, "Kulturkritik und Gesellschaft," in *Prismen: Kulturkritik und Gesellschaft*, 7–31; here, 12 (Frankfurt: Suhrkamp, 1976). This essay was written in 1949 and first published in *Soziologische Forschung in unserer Zeit*, ed. Karl Gustav Specht (Cologne: Westdeutscher Verlag, 1951), 228–40.

[17] "Nun das alles nicht mehr ist, hat sich eine Kluft aufgetan, unüberbrückbar. Es ist, als sei er [Goethe] nun erst wirklich gestorben." Ernst Beutler, "An Goethes hundertundzwölftem Todestage, dem 22. März 1944, starb auch das Haus seiner Kindheit, starb die Stadt seiner Jugend," in Mandelkow, *Goethe im Urteil seiner Kritiker*, 4:258–60; here, 258.

[18] "Und das Haus war ein Loch, ein Kellerschacht,/Ein Haufen Dreck zum Hohn/Und Schilder waren dort angebracht/Darauf stand: Besitz der Nation." Loosely translated. Marie Luise Kaschnitz, "Rückkehr nach Frankfurt," *Die Wandlung*, 1, no. 10 (October 1946), 847–57; here, 854.

[19] Friedrich Schiller, *On the Aesthetic Education of Man in a Series of Letters*, trans. Reginald Snell (Bristol: Thoemmes Press, 1994), 108. Original German: "Es gibt keinen andern Weg, den sinnlichen Menschen vernünftig zu machen, als daß man denselben zuvor ästhetisch macht." Friedrich Schiller, *Ueber die ästhetische Erziehung des Menschen in einer Reihe von Briefen*, in *Schillers Werke* (Nationalausgabe), vol. 20, part 1, *Philosophische Schriften*, ed. Benno von Wiese, 309–412; here, 383 (Weimar: Hermann Böhlaus Nachfolger, 1962).

[20] "gerade bei euch Deutschen — die solch erhabene Geister wie einen Sebastian Bach, einen Beethoven, einen Goethe . . . zu den Ihren zählten," "Hitler und dieses ganze bestialische Naziotentum." Friedrich Wolf, "Auch wir können nicht schweigen," *Aufbau*, 1: 3 (November 1945), 201–5; here 202.

[21] Theodor Plievier, *Stalingrad*, trans. Richard and Clara Winston (New York: Appleton-Century-Crofts, 1948), 346. Spelling corrected and punctuation altered. German original: "Ist es das Gesetz des deutschen Volkes, desselben Volkes, das einen Gutenberg, einen Matthias Grünewald, einen Martin Luther, einen Beethoven, einen Immanuel Kant hervorgebracht hat, eines schaffenden und von den Früchten seines Schaffens lebenden Volkes?" Plievier, *Stalingrad*, (Berlin: Aufbau, 1984), 520.

[22] "den äußersten Gegensatz zu den Grundanschauungen der deutschen klassischen Zeit." Victor Klemperer, *Kultur: Erwägungen nach dem Zusammenbruch des Nazismus* (Berlin: Neues Leben, 1946), 6.

[23] "Weiter auf dem Wege der Kultur!" Klemperer, *Kultur*, 12.

[24] "Das Heilmittel könnte nur in einem neuen Ergreifen der Überlieferung liegen." Curtius, "Aus: Goethe — Grundzüge seiner Welt," 309.

[25] "sind durchaus einig darin, daß der nazistischen Unmenschlichkeit, die als deutsche Menschlichkeit ausgegeben wurde, die reine Humanität der Herder-Goethe-Zeit entgegenzustellen sei." Klemperer, *Kultur*, 55.

[26] "Ein Ende machen. Einen Anfang setzen." "Wir sind nicht mehr wir selbst." "Wir brachen alle Brücken ab, zerstörten/Sehr rasch und unbeirrbar, was uns frommt./Aus allen Dächern Feuer! Wir beschwören/Die Zukunft, die mit der Verzweiflung kommt." Hans-Egon Holthusen, "Tabula Rasa," *Die Wandlung*, 1, no. 1 (November 1945), 65.

[27] "Wäre Goethe im deutschen Volke lebendig gewesen, so hätte diese seine lebendige Kraft solch einen überwältigenden Haß gegenüber der Nazibarbarei erzeugt, daß deren Bewegung hätte schon in den Ansätzen scheitern müssen." Johannes R. Becher, "Aus: Der Befreier," in *Goethe im Urteil seiner Kritiker*, 318–32; here, 321

[28] "In der Abkehr von Goethe . . . habe der Niedergang, der im Wüten des Faschismus seinen Tiefpunkt erreichte, unmittelbaren Ausdruck gefunden." Hans-Dietrich Dahnke, "Humanität und Geschichtsperspektive: Zu den Goethe-Ehrungen 1932, 1949, 1982," *Weimarer Beiträge*, 28, no. 10 (1982), 66–89; here, 77.

[29] "katalaunische Geisterschlacht," "weicht wieder der Kampf aus in die kulturellen Gefilde." Bertolt Brecht, *Werke*, ed. Werner Hecht et al., vol. 27, *Journale* 2 (Berlin, Weimar, and Frankfurt: Aufbau and Suhrkamp, 1995), 286.

[30] "In der Zeit zwischen Zusammenbruch und Währungsreform gewann der Diskurs über Goethe an Bedeutung in dem Maße, wie in dem politisch entmündigten Deutschland die Sphäre der Kultur zur einzig verbleibenden Sphäre wurde, in der sich deutsche Identität artikulieren konnte." Kaes, "Literatur und nationale Identität," 199.

[31] "Gedenket mit Demut und Dankbarkeit eurer heiligen und großen Meister, die in der Ewigkeit für euch zeugen. Sie allein können die Schmach von euch nehmen. . . ." Franz Werfel, "An das deutsche Volk," *Bayerische Landeszeitung*, 25 May 1945, reprinted in *"Als der Krieg zu Ende war": Literarisch-politische Publizistik 1945–1950*, ed. Gerhard Hay, Hartmut Rambaldo, and Joachim W. Storck (Marbach: Deutsche Schillergesellschaft, 1995), 23–24; here, 24.

[32] "der wunderbare Mensch, den vor zweihundert Jahren ein junges deutsches Weib zur Welt gebar." Thomas Mann, "Ansprache im Goethejahr 1949," in *Gesammelte Werke in Zwölf Bänden*, vol. 11, *Reden und Aufsätze 3*, 490 (Frankfurt: S. Fischer, 1960).

[33] "die Freiheit des deutschen Geistes," "auch seinem bittersten, eine heilende Kraft lebt." "das wir noch wir selbst sind." Ernst Beutler, *Besinnung: Ansprache zur Feier von Goethes Geburtstag* (Wiesbaden: Dieterich'sche Verlagsbuchhandlung, 1946), 30.

[34] "Goethes Allgegenwart war Licht in unserer Finsternis." Becher, "Aus: Der Befreier," 328.

[35] "Die größten Geister unseres Volkes sind zu Führern und Lehrern gerade gut genug." Otto Heuschele, "Sommer 1945," in *Betrachtungen und Deutungen: Neue Essays*, 79–89; here, 87 (Stuttgart: Hans E. Günther, 1948).

[36] Hans Paeschke, "Verantwortlichkeit des Geistes," *Merkur*, 1, no. 1 (1947), 100–110; here, 109–10.

[37] "Wo ihn zuerst die Welt erregt/Und er der Welt gefiel," "in Fleisch und Blut," "ich erschrak wie vorm jüngsten Gericht,/Weil er sein Haus ansah." Kaschnitz, "Rückkehr nach Frankfurt." Bettina Meier intriguingly suggests that the line "ich erschrak wie vorm jüngsten Gericht" ("I was terrified as at the Last Judgment") implies a consciousness of personal and collective guilt on the part of the poetic voice. Because Goethe's house has been destroyed "by the nation charged with administering his legacy," Meier writes, the viewer "feels . . . guilt in view of the squandering of this legacy," a guilt that Meier expressly describes as "on behalf of the entire nation." The problem with this interpretation is that there is no textual evidence inside (or outside) the poem that it was Germans who destroyed Goethe's house. The shock of the narrator could much more plausibly be the natural result of a confrontation between the mortal viewer and the divine Goethe, a confrontation that has ample tradition in German poetic literature. I suspect that Meier has attributed to Kaschnitz a more sophisticated political consciousness of guilt than is warranted by the idealistic text. See Meier, *Goethe in Trümmern*, 46.

[38] "Doch schaute er gar nicht hinab in die Gruft,/Er zählte die Fensterreihen,/Er spähte in Räume aus lauter Luft/Als strahle dort Kerzenschein." Kaschnitz, "Rückkehr nach Frankfurt," 854.

[39] "Da wußte ich ihn unerreicht/Vom blutigen Vergehen,/Weil die Vollendeten vielleicht/Nur die Vollendung sehen./Und hörte selbst, eh alles schwand/Den letzten hellen Ton/Und las auf dem Schild über Schutt und Sand/Die Worte: Besitz der Nation." Kaschnitz, "Rückkehr nach Frankfurt," 855.

[40] "zentrale Lüge." Cited in Bettina Meier, "Goethe in Trümmern: Der Streit um den Wiederaufbau des Goethehauses in Frankfurt," in Jochen Vogt, *"Erinnerung ist unsere Aufgabe,"* — *Über Literatur, Moral und Politik 1945–1900*, 28–40; here, 30, 36 (Opladen: Westdeutscher Verlag, 1991).

[41] "der Einbruch der wüsten Horde ins Gehege des Geistes." "Neid auf die Kultur, gegen die er dumpf aufbegehrt, weil sie ihn ausschließt." Theodor W. Adorno, "Kulturkritik und Gesellschaft," 11. My translation. For an alternative translation, see Adorno, "Cultural Criticism and Society," 22.

[42] "etwas unserer Volksnatur durchaus Fremdes, Aufgezwungenes." Thomas Mann, *Doktor Faustus: Das Leben des deutschen Tonsetzers Adrian Leverkühn, erzählt von einem Freunde* (Frankfurt: Fischer, 1998), 636. My translation. Alternative English-language translation: Mann, *Doctor Faustus: The Life of the German Composer Adrian Leverkühn as Told by a Friend*, trans. H. T. Lowe-Porter (New York: Alfred Knopf, 1948), 482.

[43] "Zu den entscheidenden Erfahrungen . . ., die unsere Generation hat machen müssen, gehört meines Erachtens die vielfach offenbarte Tatsache, daß, um es mit einem namentlichen Beispiel anzudeuten, ein Mann wie Heydrich, der Mörder von Böhmen, ein hervorragender und sehr empfindsamer Musiker gewesen ist, der sich mit Geist und echter Kennerschaft, sogar mit Liebe hat unterhalten können über Bach, Händel, Mozart, Beethoven, Bruckner." Max Frisch, "Kultur als Alibi," *Der Monat*, 1, no. 7 (April 1949), 83–85; here, 84.

[44] "einem Volk, dem wir alles zutrauen, weil es keine Wasserspülung hat und nicht lesen kann; sondern bei einem Volk, das alles besitzt und in hohem Grade leistet, was wir bisher unter Kultur verstanden." Frisch, "Kultur als Alibi," 84.

[45] Ernst Wiechert, *Forest of the Dead,* trans. Ursula Stechow (London: Victor Gollancz, 1947), 77–78. Original German: "Und mehr Schande war niemals auf die Stirn eines Volkes gefallen als auf jenes, das nun ihre Henker stellte." Ernst Wiechert, *Der Totenwald: Ein Bericht* (Berlin: Union, 1977), 81.

[46] Heinrich Böll, *And Where Were You, Adam?* trans. Leila Vennewitz (London: Secker & Warburg, 1970), 105. In German: "ungeheure musikalische Kapazität in." Heinrich Böll, *Wo warst du, Adam?* (Leipzig: Reclam, 1985), 106. For an alternative English-language translation, see Böll, *Adam, Where Art Thou?* trans. Mervyn Savill (London: Arco, 1955), 117. Schlant refers to this commander as something of a cliché; however it should be pointed out that such figures had not yet become clichés by the beginning of the 1950s. By definition, a cliché is something that has been talked about a great deal, and if this figure had indeed been a cliché in the early 1950s, then Schlant's point about "silence" with respect to the Holocaust would not make sense. See Ernestine Schlant, *The Language of Silence: West German Literature and the Holocaust* (New York: Routledge, 1999), 35.

[47] Paul Celan, "Todesfuge," trans. Christopher Middleton, in *Modern German Poetry 1910–1960,* ed. Michael Hamburger and Christopher Middleton (London: Macgibbon & Lee, 1966), 318–21. (Dual-language edition.) "Er ruft stecht tiefer ins Erdenreich ihr einen ihr andern singet und spielt/er greift nach dem Eisen im Gurt er schwingts seine Augen sind blau/stecht tiefer die Spaten ihr einen ihr andern spielt weiter zum Tanz auf."

[48] Karl Gustav Jung, "After the Catastrophe," in *Civilization in Transition,* trans. R. F. C. Hull, 194–217 (New York: Pantheon, 1964). Original German: "Früher durfte man ja solche Dinge noch nach 'Asien' relegieren!" "bedeuten einen Schlag gegen den Europäer überhaupt." Jung, "After the Catastrophe," 200. Carl Gustav Jung, "Nach der Katastrophe," *Neue Schweizer Rundschau,* 13: 6 (1945/1946), 67–88; here, 73.

[49] Max Horkheimer and Theodor W. Adorno, *Dialectic of Enlightenment,* trans. John Cumming (New York: Continuum, 1995), 3. Original German: "die vollends aufgeklärte Welt strahlt im Zeichen triumphalen Unheils." Max Horkheimer and Theodor W. Adorno, *Dialektik der Aufklärung: Philosophische Fragmente* (Frankfurt: S. Fischer, 1969), 9. Originally published in Amsterdam in 1947.

[50] On this proximity and the cultural discourse about it in the postwar and postreunification period, see Klaus Neumann, "Goethe, Buchenwald, and the New Germany," *German Politics and Society,* 17, no. 1 (Spring 1999), 55–83.

[51] "an den sich so viele frohe und ernste Weimarer Erinnerungen knüpfen, . . . nur noch mit Scham und Grauen." Beutler, *Besinnung,* 9.

[52] Wiechert, *Forest of the Dead,* 121. In German: "Johannes ging noch einmal bis zu der Eiche, unter der er so oft gestanden hatte. Die Sterne hingen schon am dunklen Himmel, fern und kalt wie immer. Hier floß kein Trost aus jenen fernen Welten herab. Menschenhände warfen die Lose, gleichmütig, ob sie zum Leben oder zum Tode fielen." Wiechert, *Der Totenwald,* 129.

[53] "um meine Gedanken und meine Energien auf die Literatur zu konzentrieren . . ., um gerade dadurch nicht immer an . . . Essen, Ungeziefer, Appell und so weiter [zu

denken]." "eine Art Selbstschütz," "die gesamte hiesige Materie, das heißt die Materie der SS, einer Brotkruste und der Wassersuppe, der Läuse und der Flöhe. . . ." Nico Rost, *Goethe in Dachau: Literatur und Wirklichkeit* (Berlin: Volk und Welt, 1948), 108.

[54] "Nein! — nein! — nein! — ich kann hier in Dachau solche Äußerungen, selbst wenn sie von einem Genie wie Goethe stammen, nicht lesen, ohne innerlich dagegen in Aufruhr zu geraten." Rost, *Goethe in Dachau,* 248.

[55] "beständiger heroischer Kampf gegen das Tragische, um nicht selbst darin zu versinken." Rost, *Goethe in Dachau,* 221.

[56] "der Versuch, mich mit der Gegenwart auszusöhnen, mir eine private Normalität zu schaffen, zu der . . . die Lektüre gehört." Stefan Hermlin, "Die Zeit der Gemeinsamkeit," in *Erzählungen,* 135–204; here, 149 (Berlin: Aufbau, 1974).

[57] "eine militante, eine aktiv-moralische Bedeutung. . . . Es gibt Situationen, in denen die Kunst, jede Kunst dem Leben entgegensteht, in denen sie ihm eigentlich nichts mehr zu sagen haben dürfte." "der deutlichste Ausdruck dafür, daß es dem Feind gelungen ist, uns dahin zu bringen, wohin er will?" Hermlin, "Die Zeit der Gemeinsamkeit," 149.

[58] "Hofmannsthal und die Öfen von Auschwitz vertragen sich nicht." Walter Kolbenhoff, *Heimkehr in die Fremde* (Frankfurt: Suhrkamp, 1988 [originally 1949]), 137.

[59] "Wir haben fast alles verloren: Staat, Wirtschaft, die gesicherten Bedingungen unseres physischen Daseins und, schlimmer noch als das: die gültigen uns alle verbindenden Normen, die moralische Würde, das einigende Selbstbewußtsein als Volk." Karl Jaspers, "Geleitwort für die Zeitschrift 'Die Wandlung,'" in *Philosophische Aufsätze* (Frankfurt: Fischer, 1967), 18–20; here, 18.

[60] "wir selbst sind andere geworden seit 1933." "einfaches Anknüpfen an den Zustand vor 1933." Jaspers, "Erneuerung der Universität," in *Philosophische Aufsätze,* 9–17; here, 10, 9.

[61] "Mit Goethe zu leben, vielleicht macht uns das erst eigentlich zum Deutschen." Karl Jaspers, "Unsere Zukunft und Goethe," *Die Wandlung,* 2, no. 7 (October 1947), 559–78; here, 563.

[62] "ein Verhängnis." Jaspers, "Unsere Zukunft und Goethe," 561.

[63] "Wir dürfen keinen Menschen vergöttern. Die Zeit des *Goethe-Kultus ist vorbei,*" "vor uns steht, wenn wir geistig leben werden, eine Revolution der Goethe-Aneignung." Jaspers, "Unsere Zukunft und Goethe," 573, 575. Emphasis in the original.

[64] "einen beschämenden und ohnmächtigen Versuch, das edelste Erbe deutschen Geistes anzutasten." Cited in Hay, Rambaldo, and Storck, *"Als der Krieg zu Ende war,"* 499, from the *Rhein-Neckarzeitung,* 17 May 1949.

[65] "Er hat unsere Kollektivschuld so sonnenklar erwiesen, daß wir nur noch mit schlechtem Gewissen weiterleben." Curtius, "Goethe oder Jaspers," in Mandelkow, *Goethe im Urteil seiner Kritiker,* 4:304–7; here, 304; originally in *Die Zeit,* 28 April 1949.

[66] "aus der Rumpelkammer eines Fortschrittsglaubens, dessen letztes Stündlein 1848 gekommen war." "Ist es unbescheiden, wenn wir um Respekt vor Goethe bitten?" Curtius, "Goethe oder Jaspers," 307.

[67] "ein riesiger Spiegel kontinuierlichen Seins" "eine verschwommene Ideologie des 'Diskontinuierlichen.'" Cited in Hay, Rambaldo, and Storck, *"Als der Krieg zu Ende war,"* 498, from *Die Welt am Sonntag,* 8 May 1949.

[68] "den Künder der nationalen Einheit Deutschlands." Cited in Eckert, *Goethe in Deutschland 1945–1982,* 85, 86.

[69] "das existenzialistische Geschwätz von," "Unfähigkeit, die ganze Problematik des Menschen zu erfassen," "des Existenzialismus finden wir bei Goethe die Angst überwunden." Becher, "Aus: Der Befreier," 326, 327.

[70] "Dem Licht im Westen, das zur Zeit Goethes aufging, ist in unserem Zeitalter der Glanz gefolgt, den die russische Revolution über uns ausstrahlte." Becher, "Aus: Der Befreier," 328–29.

[71] "imstande, eine Gestalt wie Goethe tiefer und umfassender zu erkennen, als es den Generationen vor uns möglich gewesen ist." Becher, "Aus: Der Befreier," 319.

[72] "Goethes Werk ist neben Hegel der Höhepunkt dialektischen Denkens in der Zeit vor Marx und Engels." Cited in Leithäuser, "Das Goethejahr ist überstanden . . .," 295.

[73] "Beide Lager vereinnahmten Goethe für sich als wirksamen ideologischen Bannerträger." Erich Kleinschmid, "Der vereinnahmte Goethe: Irrwege im Umgang mit einem Klassiker 1932–1949," *Jahrbuch der Deutschen Schillergesellschaft,* 28 (1984), 461–82; here, 462.

[74] "das Kollektive Wir, das eine Art nationale Mobilisierung nahelegt." Leo Spitzer, "Zum Goethekult," *Die Wandlung,* 4 (Summer 1949), 581–92; here, 584.

[75] "Kampfhandlungen im Dienste des Nationalprestiges." "an der Erichtung impassibler, ewiger Marmorstandbilder oder Lenin-Masken." "'Wir [sind] das unantastbare Volk dieses unantastbaren Dichters. . . .'" Spitzer, "Zum Goethekult," 590.

[76] Meinecke, *The German Catastrophe,* 120–21. In German: "vielleicht das Deutscheste vom Deutschen in unserem gesamten Schrifttum. Wer sich ganz in sie versenkt, wird in allem Unglück unseres Vaterlandes und inmitten der Zerstörung etwas Unzerstörbares, einen deutschen *character indelebilis* spüren." Meinecke, *Die deutsche Katastrophe,* 176.

[77] "auch können nicht alte Formen, die einmal ihren Wert hatten, unbesehen wieder angewendet werden; denn die ewigen Wahrheiten wollen nicht mechanisch überliefert, sondern in jeder Epoche neu aus der menschlichen Seele geboren werden." Jung, "Nach der Katastrophe," 88.

[78] "Kultur in diesem Sinn, begriffen als ein nobler Götze . . . ist sicher nicht das, was uns retten kann." Max Frisch, "Kultur als Alibi," 84.

[79] "Aber es ist ja noch nicht so lange her, daß alle Lautsprecher Deutschlands einen anderen Namen ausspien, von dem Ihnen noch die Ohren gellen. Gestern Hitler, heute Goethe, und morgen?" "Haben wir nicht selbst die letzten Brücken gesprengt, auf denen wir hinüber- und herüberzugehen pflegten? Und liegt nicht zum unwiderruflichen Zeichen dessen Goethes Haus in Trümmern?" Richard Alewyn, "Goethe als Alibi?" in Mandelkow, *Goethe im Urteil seiner Kritiker Teil IV,* 333–35; here, 334.

[80] "Zwischen uns und Weimar liegt Buchenwald." "Was aber nicht geht, ist, sich Goethes zu rühmen und Hitler zu leugnen. Es gibt nur Goethe *und* Hitler, die Humanität *und* die Bestialität." "Es kann zum mindesten für die heute lebende Generation, nicht zwei Deutschlands geben. Es gibt nur eines oder keines." "Wenn wir uns mit Goethe beschäftigen, dann darf es nur unter der Bedingung geschehen, daß wir vor uns selbst nicht ausweichen." Alewyn, "Goethe als Alibi?" 335.

[81] "Es hat sich noch nicht herumgesprochen, daß Kultur in traditionellem Sinn tot ist. . . ." Theodor W. Adorno, "Auferstehung der Kultur in Deutschland?" in *Kritik: Kleine Schriften zur Gesellschaft*, 20–33; here, 23 (Frankfurt: Suhrkamp, 1971). Originally published in *Frankfurter Hefte*, 5, no. 5 (May 1950), 469–77.

[82] "die deutsche Situation gebietet nun einmal unabweislich eine geistige Neu-Orientierung." Adorno, "Auferstehung der Kultur in Deutschland?" 24.

[83] "Schutz beim Herkömmlichen und Gewesenen," "Den überlieferten ästhetischen Formen," "Sie alle werden Lügen gestraft von der Katastrophe jener Gesellschaft, aus der sie hervorgingen." Adorno, "Auferstehung der Kultur in Deutschland?" 27.

[84] "Bildung heute hat nicht zum geringsten die Funktion, das geschehene Grauen und die eigene Verantwortung vergessen zu machen und zu verdrängen." Adorno, "Auferstehung der Kultur in Deutschland?" 28.

[85] "Kultur am Schuldzusammenhang der Gesellschaft teilhat." Adorno, "Kulturkritik und Gesellschaft," 17. My translation. For an alternative translation: Adorno, "Cultural Criticism and Society," 26.

[86] "die gesamte traditionelle Kultur [wird heute] null und nichtig: durch einen irrevokablen Prozeß ist ihre . . . Erbschaft in weitestem Maße entbehrlich, überflüssig, Schund geworden." Adorno, "Kulturkritik und Gesellschaft," 30. My translation. For an alternative translation: Adorno, "Cultural Criticism and Society," 34.

[87] "Kulturkritik findet sich der letzten Stufe der Dialektik von Kultur und Barbarei gegenüber: nach Auschwitz ein Gedicht zu schreiben, ist barbarisch, und das frißt auch die Erkenntnis an, die ausspricht, warum es unmöglich ward, heute Gedichte zu schreiben." Adorno, "Kulturkritik und Gesellschaft," 31. My translation. For an alternative translation: Adorno, "Cultural Criticism and Society," 34.

[88] For a lucid explication of Adorno's ideas (and a slightly divergent translation of the essay's most famous passage), see Neil H. Donahue, *Voice and Void: The Poetry of Gerhard Falkner* (Heidelberg: Universitätsverlag C. Winter, 1998), 19–34.

[89] "in selbstgenügsamer Kontemplation." Adorno, "Cultural Criticism and Society," 34.

5: Yogis and Commissars

WITH INCREASING INSISTENCE after 1945, German writers asked: what is the political role of literature? This question went beyond the ethical question of the writer's relationship to political authority in a totalitarian state; implicitly and explicitly, men and women of letters asked not just what they should have been doing during the Nazi dictatorship but also what they should do in the future, during the postwar period then beginning. As Ernst Wiechert put it in an impassioned article published in January of 1946, "What we must ask ourselves is no longer or not yet the question how it could have happened but rather the question: what is happening now, and what is to be done?"[1] Hermann Brill phrased the same fundamental question somewhat differently a year after Wiechert: "What can the writers, what can the poets do to help the German people on the way to a real, genuine, internalized democracy?"[2] The question about writers' responsibility to society necessarily raised the question about writers and politics. As the journalist Gert H. Theunissen suggested in June of 1946, "The question about the German intellectuals and their relationship to politics is more than just a literary or academic affair; never before has this been such a question of conscience in Germany as it is today."[3] After the political failures of so many intellectuals during the Nazi years — ranging from passive acceptance to active complicity with the regime — many believed, with Wiechert, that there were ethical lessons to be learned for the present and future. They were convinced that writers had political and moral responsibilities even in a nontotalitarian state, as well as an important role to play in helping to secure a just, democratic society during the postwar period.

To explicate the question in the manner of Theunissen or even to pose it in the way that Brill did, however, was already to assume that writers play a particularly important role in the development of national culture. Why, one might ask, should one ascribe to writers any more responsibility in securing a democratic future for Germany than to any other group of educated professionals: to doctors, lawyers, or teachers, for instance? Most of these groups had submitted more or less willingly to National Socialist *Gleichschaltung* (enforced coordination and uniformity) during the years of the Third Reich, and they too had their own Nazi-dominated professional organizations, just as German writers had gathered together in the Reichsschrifttumskammer.[4] Were writers to be held more accountable than others in the postwar period?

Such questions were rarely asked during the immediate postwar period. Few writers in occupied Germany were willing to question the vital importance of their work in helping to shape the contours of a future national culture. From the left to the right, from young to old, from inner to outer emigrants, there was virtual unanimity on this point. Most were convinced that in a time of trouble and uncertainty writers and their supposedly eternal truths held the key to a better German future. Dissenting voices like that of Kurt W. Marek, a writer and editor living in Hamburg — who argued that literature, founded so exclusively on the imagination, was becoming increasingly powerless in the face of the "conquest by reality of cognition and understanding" — were rare.[5] In a sonnet published in 1946 and dedicated "To German Poetry," Dorothea Taeger expressed the view that the kindly voice of poetry had helped Germans to survive and make sense of the dark years of Nazi tyranny:

Through many hells her voice still glides,
Cloaked in a silken, whispery veil;
On a breath of air she lightly guides
The good that does not end or fail. . . .

Though Satan lurks inside his pit,
He hears only the song he sings,
His eye sees but what seeks his bit; —
Untouched by him her pure tone rings.

Praise to you, who speak of God and time;
In bitter trouble you could lead.
You helped the desperate ones to see,

Who still sought comfort, remedy in rhyme.
You aided brothers in their need,
And the breathing of your spirit set us free.[6]

The conviction that literature and poetry would play a privileged role in healing the nation extended even beyond Germany to prisoners-of-war being held abroad, some of whom — most notably Hans Werner Richter and Alfred Andersch — were to play a crucial role in the early development of postwar literature. Werner Jahn, one of the contributors to *PW,* a journal put out by German prisoners of war in Fort Devens, Massachusetts, described in 1945 what he thought would be the role of writers in establishing a new and better Germany:

> No one is more called upon than the poet to furnish us with an inter-
> pretation of human existence. Through the medium of the word, the
> poet thickens being and becoming into an experience with general va-
> lidity. In the chaos and noise of events, it is the poet alone who can
> capture that which remains and lift it up through his work to a stable
> being that stands above the times.[7]

Such sentiments formed a relative constant during the years of postwar occupation, transcending geographical and ideological differences. Three years
after war's end the leftist literary critic Hans Mayer, who had spent the Nazi
years in France and Switzerland, declared:

> In terms of the history of ideas and the development of human moral-
> ity, all the higher development of mankind is linked to the activities of
> writers. Philosophers have rarely ruled, and this was probably no disad-
> vantage; but there has hardly been a social and life form built on rea-
> sonable principles that did not call upon the dreams of the poets and
> interpreters.[8]

As Alfred Kantorowicz declared in 1947, "it is the spiritual Germany that
still enjoys credit in the world, and our hopes rest on it, if there is still
hope."[9] In a poem written in 1941 and published after the war's end,
Gottfried Benn, like Dorothea Taeger, invoked poetry as a force "beyond
the rubble of the World's cadaver," providing "just one refuge free from
blood and hate." For Benn, "there is but one — the poem's — confronta-
tion/that bans reality with mystic word."[10] In this and in other poems Benn
invoked the power of poetry as an almost divine source of eternal consolation in a world of politics and vanity. Benn's celebration of poetry coincided
with many other German intellectuals' sense of writers' unique calling as
"heralds of the true and valid," as Klaus R. Scherpe has put it.[11] The widespread belief among German writers and intellectuals that their work was in-
dispensable for the future health of the nation was no doubt reassuring in
the uncertainty of the postwar years; at the same time it also corresponded to
the traditional belief that Germany's "Dichter und Denker" ("writers and
thinkers") were privileged articulators of the *Kulturnation*.

In his novel *Die Stadt hinter dem Strom*, one of the most respected literary works of the immediate postwar period, the inner emigrant Hermann
Kasack gave allegorical representation to the widespread belief in writers'
higher calling. Toward the end of the novel, its hero Robert Lindhoff, himself a writer who, although still living, has become the chronicler of the city
of the dead, is granted a mystical vision. As his stay in the city nears its end,
Robert Lindhoff sees an image that symbolizes the past and future history of
the world and the role played in that history by the most important
representatives of the human spirit: "a gathering of men" wearing "dignified

robes" and revolving "in a measured ceremonial dance."[12] These mysterious figures are "the thirty-three guardians of the world, the keepers of the golden scale" who oversee "the course of humanity."[13] The burden placed on these writers and spiritual figures is no less than the future of the world, for it is they who, by the mere fact of their existence, increase the spiritual and intellectual strength of humanity. Their watchful eyes always focused on the cosmic scale in which true spirit and its nefarious opposite are weighed; they contribute to the development of goodness, keeping "the game of creation going."[14] Whenever evil begins to triumph over good, the representatives of spirit exercise their power to bring about change: "They did not intervene actively, but they also did not let the matter rest in contemplative observation; through their mere existence they helped."[15]

For Kasack the word *Geist* (spirit or intellect) is coterminous with goodness, while *Ungeist* (anti-spirit) is identical to evil. The possibility of an evil *Geist* does not seem to exist; if it is evil, it becomes the opposite of *Geist*. Thus the Enlightenment unity between knowledge and morality is reaffirmed. Left to its own devices, the great scale of creation seems weighted toward evil; but with the help of the "guardians of the world" it can be coaxed toward the good. The seeming contradiction between the statements "through their mere existence they helped" and "they also did not let the matter rest in contemplative observation" underlines the problem of identifying precisely how writers and other intellectual leaders are supposed to give concrete assistance to society.

Kasack's novel is at once an allegorical interpretation of human life and world history and a commentary on the state of German affairs at that time. In a period in which the powers of darkness and hatred (*Ungeist*) have triumphed in Germany, it is now time for reconciliation and peace, positive forces that are above all represented by those spiritual figures such as writers and religious leaders entrusted with reinforcing what is good in the world. The chronicler Robert Lindhoff is an allegorical embodiment of the sensitive contemporary writer, presumed to have communion with the greatest spirits of the past and thus to exist as a living human being in a realm occupied primarily by the dead. The writer's job of preserving the connection to the past history of the human spirit necessarily isolates him from the world of the living. In agreement with many other members of the inner emigration, Kasack takes the contemplative position that a writer should not actively engage in politics. When Robert Lindhoff does ultimately return from the city of the dead to the real-life world of postwar Germany, with its "people huddling, staring, loitering, gathering things in rubbish-filled streets," his attempts to intervene positively in human affairs contrast with his own disorientation in the world of the living, and he must ultimately return to the city beyond the river.[16] "He had been banished far too deeply into timelessness, he felt, to find satisfaction in the temporary nature of fleeting moments."[17] Lindhoff is an Odysseus who can never really return from the land of the dead. "I no longer belong among you," he imagines saying to his wife, whom he will not see until the moment of his death.[18] Representatives of the contemplative spirit are out of place in the world of public affairs. They occupy a "Zwischenreich" (an in-between empire) and hold communion with both the living and the dead. As "guardians of the world" they are good-willed observers, not active agents in human affairs.

The question in Germany at the end of the Second World War was not whether or not the writer has an ethical responsibility, but rather precisely what the nature of this responsibility was, and in particular what political form it was to take. There were two extreme positions with respect to the political role of writers, and both of them could be made to seem justified as a response to the situation of German writers during the Nazi period. The first position was that writers did indeed have a fundamental political responsibility, and that they should exercise that responsibility in both their writing and their lives. This political position seemed to many writers a necessary response to the failures of writers during the Nazi period, particularly the perceived ethical shortcomings of those writers of the inner emigration who had sought to occupy a position above politics. The second position was that writers had the responsibility to liberate themselves from particular political positions, and perhaps even from politics as a whole. Literature and the arts were, for those holding this position, a realm in which human beings could exercise their freedom independent of the constraints of mundane reality, and any political engagement on the part of the writer risked destroying this freedom, transforming art from a self-sufficient end into a mere political tool. For its adherents, the anti-political position was the only reasonable response of ethical writers to efforts by the Nazis or by any other totalitarian government to dominate literature.

The debates among German writers about political literature were by no means unique in the world after the end of the Second World War. The late 1940s were characterized by an international debate on this issue whose most famous representatives were Jean-Paul Sartre, who took the position that literature should be "engaged," i.e. take a political stance, and T. S. Eliot, who believed that writers should avoid direct political commitments in their work. Both Sartre and Eliot had adherents in Germany and exercised a significant influence. For Sartre, writers were in a double bind. As he explained in a lecture on "The Responsibility of the Writer" delivered at the Sorbonne in November of 1946 to commemorate the foundation of the United Nations Educational, Scientific, and Cultural Organization (UNESCO), the very nature of the writer's profession is freedom, and therefore he must refuse to be bound by political dogmas and ideologies; but as a representative of freedom he is simultaneously forced to be on the side of those oppressed groups who are struggling to be free, such as workers and blacks.[19] The primacy of freedom hence forces the writer in two mutually conflicting directions, creating a tension between his own individual freedom on the one hand and the freedom of the oppressed groups with whom he is in solidarity on the other. Himself a member of the privileged classes, the writer is nevertheless driven by his ideal of freedom to support the cause of the powerless; but the latter will inevitably mistrust him as long as he insists upon the purity of his writerly freedom.

Although he was far from denying the ethical importance of literature, Eliot represented the other side of the international literary-political debate of the late 1940s. In a series of lectures given in Germany in 1946 on "The Unity of European Culture" — lectures that later became a part of the poet's *Notes towards the Definition of Culture* — Eliot argued that inasmuch as politics belongs to a realm of more or less mechanistic tinkering, it is necessarily alien to the primarily organic nature of culture. Culture, Eliot argued, cannot be constructed deliberately in the way that a machine is constructed: like a tree, it "is something that must grow; you cannot build a tree, you can only plant it, and care for it, and wait for it to mature in its due time; and when it is grown you must not complain if you find that from an acorn has come an oak, and not an elm-tree."[20] Whereas culture belongs entirely to the realm of the organic, political structures occupy a mid-point between the organic and the mechanistic. Writers who dedicate themselves primarily to politics are therefore, Eliot believes, in danger of alienating themselves from the organic growth of culture and thus rendering their works mechanical. Politicized literature also polarizes cultural figures, Eliot argues, creating alliances and enmities where none existed before. An obsession with politics ultimately erodes the unity of European culture. It is, therefore, vitally important for European writers to rise above politics and to recognize that their responsibility lies in the preservation of European culture.

Eliot was making the same point about European culture as a whole that Thomas Mann was to make in 1949 with respect to German culture as a whole. If, for Mann, German culture was indivisible and should not take account of the cold war tensions that threatened a division of the fatherland, for Eliot European culture represented a common tie binding together the citizens of different European countries in spite of political and ideological disagreements. The overarching sense of a European unity preserved by culture could disappear, however, if politics became the exclusive focus of intellectuals' attention.

Two factors aggravated the debates about political literature that occurred in Germany between 1945 and 1949. The first and most obvious factor was the increasingly virulent cold war between the United States and the Soviet Union, in which the victorious former Allies of the Second World War were pitted against each other in a battle for political and military power in Europe generally and Germany specifically. The cold war was fought on a great many levels and in many arenas, from the military to the diplomatic to the scientific to the psychological to the cultural. Just as it was important for the two major antagonists to achieve superiority or at least equality in the military realm, so too it became important to demonstrate superiority in the cultural realm. The debates and diplomatic maneuvering around such Soviet cultural figures as the writer Alexander Solzhenitsyn in the 1960s and 1970s became important milestones in the larger history of the cold war. In the period immediately following the end of the Second World War, the Soviet Union under Stalin was governed by a cultural-political policy that demanded a high degree of ideological conformity from writers under the rubric of socialist realism.[21] The major political champion of this policy was Stalin's chief ideologist Andrei Zhdanov, who, after the end of the war, initiated a campaign against "the inferior modern bourgeois literature of the west" and against "crawling and scraping to *petit-bourgeois* foreign literature."[22] Zhdanov believed that writers in the Soviet Union should present a realistic but positive picture of society — avoiding excursions into the fantastic or the avant-garde — and that they should do so as partisan supporters of socialism. Good socialist-realist literature was to concern itself particularly with the problems and triumphs of the victorious working class, not with the decadent and irrelevant problems of classes doomed to extinction, such as the aristocracy or the bourgeoisie. With the Second World War alliance between the Soviet Union and the capitalist states of the west at an end, Zhdanov believed, there was growing resentment in the west against socialism's successes both inside and outside the Soviet Union. Imperialists throughout the world "are afraid of socialism, they are afraid of our socialist country, which is a role model for all of humanity."[23] Writers must help the Communist Party of the Soviet Union and the Soviet state itself in fulfilling the correct ideological mission; those unwilling to conform ideologically to the demands of the Communist Party — particularly the poet Anna Akhmatova and the novelist Mikhail Zoschenko — were, Zhdanov charged, "literary scum," their works marred by "melancholy, pessimism, and disappointment in life," characteristics incompatible with the optimistic triumphalism of developed socialist society.[24]

After Zhdanov declared in September of 1947 that the Second World War cooperation between the Soviet Union and the United States had come to an end, and that the world was now divided into two political camps in irreconcilable opposition to each other, many Soviet writers obediently toed the party line, even going so far as to compare the United States under President Harry Truman with Germany under Hitler.[25] In a 1947 open letter to their American colleagues, Soviet writers proclaimed that the United States represented the next bastion of a fascist threat to humanity.[26] Although Zhdanov's arguments against bourgeois literary tendencies were directed primarily toward Soviet writers, they were not without effect in the Soviet-occupied zone of Germany, where the Socialist Unity Party followed the lead of the Soviet Communists, and where Alexander Dymschitz, the Soviet officer in charge of cultural policy in the eastern zone, interpreted and promulgated the directives of the Soviet Communists' Central Committee for East German Communists.

The United States did not seek to exercise ideological control over its writers and other cultural figures in the same way. However the immediate postwar period did witness a severe worsening of the political situation for writers and other creative artists in the United States, many of whom were called in front of the House Un-American Activities Committee (HUAC) and forced to answer questions about possible involvement with the Soviets or with the Communist Party. After testifying in front of HUAC at the end of October, 1947 and attempting to warn Congress that "the great American people would lose much and risk much" if they "allowed anyone to restrict the free competition of ideas in the realm of culture," Bertolt Brecht left the United States to return to Europe; writers who refused to testify before HUAC risked imprisonment or unemployment.[27] By the early 1950s Richard Rovere, associate editor of *The New Yorker* magazine, was warning that in the United States "politics are beginning to determine culture."[28]

In addition to the increasing postwar anti-Communist hysteria in the United States — a hysteria commemorated in Arthur Miller's famous play *The Crucible* (1953), in which Miller implicitly compared the postwar Red Scare to the seventeenth-century witch hunts in Salem, Massachusetts — there were foreign-policy consequences in the cultural cold war between the United States and the Soviet Union. U.S. intelligence services helped to fund anti-Communist forums and journals of opinion — such as the Congress for Cultural Freedom, with its associated journals, including *Der Monat* (The Month) in Germany and *Encounter* in the United Kingdom — and the United States government created various channels through which to broadcast its own point of view in the ideological struggles: the United States Information Agency, Voice of America, Radio Free Europe, the various *Amerika-Häuser* set up throughout West Germany in the 1940s and 1950s, and, in the powderkeg capital of Germany, divided Berlin, Radio im amerikanischen Sektor (RIAS). Thus the United States, which, at the end of the Second World War had, in Frances Stonor Saunders's words, still been a "virgin in the practice of international *Kulturkampf*," had, by the 1950s, learned to engage in cold war "as a psychological contest" whose primary weapon, as Saunders sees it, "was to be culture."[29] Among other things, Koeppen's novel *Tauben im Gras* (Pigeons on the Grass, 1951) is a satire of this cultural cold war. It features the visit to a bombed-out Munich by an esteemed Anglo-American writer named Mr. Edwin. This character bears more than a passing resemblance to T. S. Eliot when, at a public lecture in Munich's *Amerika-Haus*, he invokes the western Christian tradition, whose brightness — however weakened — is, Edwin insists, "the only warming light in the world."[30]

In the postwar debates about politicized literature, left-wing and/or pro-Soviet writers tended to support the position that literature should be politicized, while pro-western writers and critics opposed politicized literature, claiming it was an expression of totalitarian domination. The primary literary-critical methodologies in the United States and West Germany during the first two decades after the end of the Second World War — the so-called New Criticism and *werkimmanente Kritik* respectively — went so far as to demand that works of literature should be understood primarily without reference to social, political, historical, or even personal circumstances. In the realm of the visual arts, abstract expressionism dominated western art during the late 1940s and 1950s, and its artistic and critical proponents explicitly resisted any references pointing beyond the artwork to nonaesthetic, let alone political factors. While it would surely be mistaken to identify either abstract expressionism or New Criticism solely as expressions of the cold war — on the contrary, both movements need to be understood within the context of the internal history of criticism and art as reactions to previous movements as well — it would be equally misguided to seek to understand such movements without the overarching historical-political context provided by the tensions between the two superpowers.[31]

The second major factor aggravating debates about literature and politics in Germany during the immediate postwar period had more to do with the German past than with the German present, and it was directly related to the previous debate about inner emigration. The distinguishing literary-social characteristic of the literature of inner emigration had been its political indeterminacy. Such literature could rarely be nailed down to a direct political statement against the Nazis; it was only for this reason that such works could be published at all in the period between 1933 and 1945. Probably the most prestigious form of literary production during the Nazi period was poetry, not prose; inner emigrants tended to write nature poems that avoided concrete references to social or political conditions. Hence, as Röpke noted in 1945, the camouflaged protests of the inner emigration "were only recognizable by a trained eye, and even then it was not always possible to be sure that it was not a case of optical illusion or of the sprouting of some mere weed."[32] In order to avoid being co-opted by the Nazi regime, the novelists of inner emigration frequently chose to write not about the present but about the past, and they often set their plots outside Germany. The most famous novel of inner emigration was Jünger's *Auf den Marmorklippen* (1939), which was interpreted by many readers and almost certainly intended by Jünger himself as an attack on Nazi barbarity.[33] However, Jünger did not use the words National Socialist or Nazi even once in the book, which is set in an indeterminate magical land at an unspecified time. The figure of the *Oberförster* (chief forester), who represents vulgar brutality in the novel, could have been but did not have be read as an allegory for Hitler or Göring. Likewise the poets in the novel who resist the demands of barbarians to compose odes for them could have been but did not have to be interpreted as members of the inner emigration refusing to conform to Nazi demands; while the poets in the novel who corrupt their craft in order to produce the kind of material that the barbarians want could have been but did not have to be interpreted as Nazi writers willing to furnish the Party with whatever literary support it demanded. Jünger's readers were left to choose for themselves whether to opt for a political or a nonpolitical interpretation of the novel.[34] Political indeterminacy characterized most of the output of such writers, even works considered, like *Auf den Marmorklippen*, to be genuinely anti-Nazi.

This indeterminacy cut both ways: it could be interpreted either as resistance to or as conformism with the Nazi regime, depending on the interpreter. In a typically polemical attack on inner emigration and its aesthetics of indeterminacy, the young Communist critic Wolfgang Harich declared: "if I had been forced to rely on this literature alone, I could easily have become a sturdy SS man." The inner emigrants, he insisted, "could not create a single antidote against fascism within us or make us immune to these times."[35] Arrayed against Harich and critics like him were most of the inner emigrants and their supporters, who, in criticism and literature, argued for the integrity of aesthetic withdrawal from the world. Not only Kasack's *Die Stadt hinter dem Strom* but also key postwar texts such as Ernst Kreuder's two novels *Die Gesellschaft vom Dachboden* (The Society of the Attic, 1946, translated into English as *The Attic Pretenders*), and *Die Unauffindbaren* (The Ones Who Can't Be Located, 1948) celebrated the withdrawal of the writer from the world as a declaration of independence and freedom. True writers were, in the words of Kreuder's title, precisely the ones who refused to let themselves be found or pinned down to any one-sided political meaning. Such works and ideas from nonemigrants received powerful support from one of the most famous German-language novels of the 1940s, Hermann Hesse's *Das Glasperlenspiel* (The Glass Bead Game), for which its author won the Nobel Prize for Literature in 1946. Hesse's novel was a celebration of pure, apolitical intellectualism, of monkish withdrawal from the world.

The ongoing debate among German writers about politicized literature came to a head in the second half of 1947 and the first half of 1948, a one-year period that marked a turning-point in the transformation from the relatively open-ended situation of occupied Germany in May of 1945 to the divided and politicized cold war German states founded in 1949. During this period German writers came together in two conferences at which the political role of literature formed the central object of debate. The first postwar German writers' conference took place in early October of 1947 — shortly after Zhdanov had promulgated his two-camps doctrine of international struggle — in the Soviet sector of Berlin, with writers from all over Germany in attendance. The second conference took place in the third week of May, 1948 in Frankfurt, in the

American occupation zone. Because writers from the Soviet zone had been denied travel privileges to Frankfurt, only writers from the western zones of occupation were able to attend the second conference. In the varying positions
taken by writers at the two conferences one can clearly see the emerging fault-
lines of cold war literary criticism, in which political literature came to be associated with the Soviet bloc and an avowedly nonpolitical literature with the west.
In addition, the impending division of Germany itself can already be read between the lines of the literary debates at the two conferences.

The first writers' conference was organized by the Schutzverband
Deutscher Autoren (Protective League of German Authors, SDA) —
founded in November 1945 as a successor organization to the previous
Schutzverband Deutscher Schriftsteller (Protective League of German Writers, SDS, which had been swallowed up by the Nazis) — in cooperation with
Becher's Kulturbund. Membership in both organizations extended well beyond the Soviet zone: the SDA sought to represent German authors in general, while the Kulturbund, calling on the best of the German humanist
tradition, sought to integrate Germans in the effort to create a democratic,
antifascist future and to avoid the political division of the nation.[36] The efforts of the two organizations to ensure a representative presence at the Berlin conference of authors from all four occupation zones, as well as
representatives of the inner and outer emigration, were largely successful.
Although the Berlin conference was strongly dominated by writers favoring a
politicized literature, it also featured several writers who argued against politicized literature, and a number of the most important literary figures from
the western zones and West Berlin, including the Catholic writer Elisabeth
Langgässer and Ernst Rowohlt, one of the major publishers in the western
zones. Although one of the primary goals of the conference organizers was
to overcome the postwar tensions between inner and outer emigrants, this
goal was not achieved, and in spite of the intentions of its organizers, the
conference ultimately demonstrated not the unity but the division of German culture.

Among those demanding a politicized literature at the Berlin writers'
conference were the authors Erich Weinert and Stephan Hermlin and the
critics Hans Mayer and Axel Eggebrecht, all of whom argued for a literature
of political engagement. As Hermlin put it, the aesthetics of political indeterminacy favored by the inner emigrants was "beginning to bar the way
back to reality."[37] In agreement, Mayer insisted that "we live in a society in
which social conflicts have grown so heated that writers have no choice but
to become clearly conscious of their position within these conflicts, whether
they wish to or not."[38]

Ironically, the most famous intervention in favor of political writing at
the 1947 Berlin writer's conference came not from a Communist but from
an anti-Communist and not from a German but from an American: the

young journalist Melvin Lasky, correspondent for the American journals *Partisan Review* and *New Leader*. Lasky's anti-Soviet intervention at the Berlin writers' conference was provoked by a speech given by the leader of the Soviet delegation at the conference, playwright Wsewolod Witalyevich Wishnevsky, who one year earlier had reported for the Soviet party organ *Pravda* on the Nuremberg Trials, and who was a veteran of both the Russian Revolution and the Second World War. In Berlin Wishnevsky attacked the United States in words reminiscent of the appeal by Soviet writers to their American colleagues published in Germany only two days before the Berlin conference began. In keeping with the current Soviet Party line that the United States now represented the chief bastion of reactionary power in the world, Wishnevsky urged his German colleagues to consider

> that the world is divided into two camps, that one camp is represented by black reaction, by barbarism, by an ideology of hatred of humanity and militarism, while the other camp is represented by millions of simple human beings who live for peace, who fight for peace. . . . I call upon you to insure that German writers and the German people find their place in the ranks of these simple people, these simple democrats.[39]

Wishnevsky's harsh attack on "the American reaction" and "the British reaction" was hardly destined to contribute to international harmony and sounded more like a battle cry than the call to peace and reconciliation that the conference planners had hoped for. Annelie Hartmann has argued that the Soviet delegation to the Berlin writers conference had probably received specific instructions from Moscow on how to behave; in her view, "only the trained and accurate observer could discern with what unanimity and precision the Soviet delegates represented the newest political guidelines."[40]

In a vigorous response to Wishnevsky's attack on the United States and Great Britain, Lasky insisted that the most important task of writers was to fight for cultural freedom.[41] It was not enough to condemn Nazi tyranny, which was over and done with; one must condemn tyranny everywhere and at all times, because freedom could exist only as the result of continuing struggle and constant vigilance. If German writers under the Nazi state had betrayed democratic ideals and put themselves at the service of a totalitarian state, then any writers who betrayed the ideals of cultural freedom could make themselves equally guilty. While Lasky earned applause at the conference for his criticism of political propaganda on the part of American writers — examples he gave were propaganda campaigns against Republican Spain during the 1930s and an all-too great willingness on the part of journalists to toe the pro-Soviet party line of the U.S. government during the Second World War — he scandalized many left-wing participants with his strong criticism of the contemporary Soviet Union:

> And I would like . . . to say that in this international spirit we feel solidarity
> with the writers and artists of Soviet Russia. They too know pressure and
> censorship. They too are fighting the battle for cultural freedom, and I be-
> lieve that we all should offer them our open-hearted sympathy.[42]

Reminding his listeners of the persecution of the great Soviet filmmaker Ser-
gei Eisenstein as well as of writers like Akhmatova and Zoschenko, Lasky
urged participants at the Berlin conference to condemn tyranny everywhere,
not just in Nazi Germany. With his condemnation of the contemporary Soviet Union, Lasky had accepted the gauntlet thrown down by Wishnevsky
and made the growing tensions between the Soviet Union and the United
States an explicit part of the postwar political debate among German writers.
In the words of the scholar Bernard Genton, Lasky's intervention "was certainly courageous. This twenty-seven-year-old man had given the congress a
significance which no one had foreseen."[43] Likewise Saunders notes dramatically that "to disrupt the proceedings" of the conference "was an act of either madness or courage, or both."[44] Genton has suggested that Lasky "was
the only person" at the conference "who expressed his viewpoint in complete freedom."[45] It is worthwhile noting, however, that far from taking a
stand against politicized literature, Lasky was in complete agreement even
with his Soviet counterparts about the essentially political responsibilities of
the writer. Not only did "the writer, the publisher, and the reader have certain inalienable rights," all three also had "in their own hands the responsibility . . . for the vigilant defense and uncompromising preservation of these
rights and these freedoms."[46] The American journalist insisted that writers
committed to freedom were necessarily governed by a spirit of nonconform-
ism and opposition to any political status quo.

Through his forceful participation in the Berlin writers congress, which
prompted the Soviet delegation to walk out of the room, Lasky had earned
himself, as Saunders reports, the sobriquet "Father of the Cold War in Berlin."[47] As Ruth Rehmann puts it, "the cat was out of the bag."[48] Less than
two months after the end of the Berlin writers' conference, Lasky proposed
to American military occupation officials the creation of a new journal of
opinion as part of a broad-based campaign to persuade German intellectual
elites to support American foreign policy. With the backing of military governor General Lucius Clay the journal, *Der Monat,* began publication a year
after the Berlin writers congress, in October, 1948, during the middle of the
Berlin air lift; the first issues of the new journal had to be flown to Berlin
along with food, medicine, and other supplies.[49] Max Frisch's important essay on "culture as alibi" appeared in one of those early issues of *Der Monat*
in April of 1949. Lasky's invocation at the Berlin writers' congress of the
"principles of cultural freedom" also prefigured the creation, three years
later, of the Congress for Cultural Freedom, whose founding conference

took place in Berlin in June of 1950, with Lasky's active participation and leadership; throughout the 1950s and for most of the 1960s, the Congress was an anti-Communist forum through which intellectuals from around the world sought to renew liberal thought, condemning the problematic situation of their colleagues in the Soviet bloc.[50] Saunders has called the Congress for Cultural Freedom "the centerpiece" of the covert cultural campaign carried out with the assistance and frequently at the behest of the United States government at the height of the cold war.[51]

Of course Lasky's intervention in Berlin in 1947 did not go unanswered. He was labeled "a living arsonist of war" and compared to "the late Dr. Goebbels" by the distinguished Soviet writer Valentin Petrovich Katayev, who went so far as to claim that "today people's decency and honesty is determined by their relationship to democracy, and specifically to the Soviet Union."[52] Anyone who criticized the Soviet Union was thus ipso facto an evil person, and anyone who defended it was good.

Against the increasing polarization of ideological perspectives so obvious in this controversy, several writers at the conference insisted on the preservation at the very least of German — if not international — cultural unity. In particular the patriotic Becher argued against "a division of Germany" that could threaten "the peace of the world."[53] All Germans belonged together in the unity of German culture, Becher insisted, "and therefore there is . . . no West German or East German literature, no South German or North German literature: there is only one . . . German literature, which will not allow itself to be circumscribed by zonal boundaries."[54]

By the fall of 1947 such sentiments were little more than wishful thinking, because they failed to grasp the way in which most German intellectuals — including Becher himself — had already become caught up in the cold war. The day after Lasky's and Becher's speeches, Becher's Kulturbund, one of the organizers of the Berlin writers conference, was banned in the western zones of occupation. Half a year later, when writers from the three western occupation zones gathered together in Frankfurt, the political situation in Germany had changed so dramatically that few of the writers present even bothered to protest against the coming division of their nation. Moreover, many of the writers at the Frankfurt congress explicitly criticized what they viewed as the overly political message of the writers in Berlin, and they questioned why there were no writers from the Soviet zone at the Frankfurt congress. The essayist and poet Wilhelm Emanuel Süskind, an editor at the *Frankfurter Zeitung* and, together with Gerhard Storz and Dolf Sternberger, one of the authors of *Das Wörterbuch des Unmenschen* (The Dictionary of the Human Beast) in the journal *Die Wandlung* — along with Victor Klemperer's *LTI*, one of the most important early examinations of Nazi language — complained that at the Berlin Congress "it sometimes seemed as if

I were in a course of indoctrination" because so much had been said about "the writer's ideological, political, and antifascist duties."[55]

One of the severest critics of writers in the eastern zone was Kurt Marek. Marek suggested that the division between political and antipolitical writers was increasingly becoming a division between the German East and the German West. In his view, the eastern part of Germany was becoming a zone of politicized literature, featuring writers who saw their function explicitly as supporters of propagandistic political campaigns. Far from being objective realists, Marek claimed, the proponents of activist realism "gather their facts according to an agreed-upon plan, which excludes very specific facts." In doing so,

> They bury reality in the coffins of their terminology. Literature like this is subject to party discipline, and these writers obey the literary commands of the group. No longer do they describe the events, states of affairs, and interconnections offered to them by reality; instead, they describe only those that they accept.[56]

In his own contribution to the Frankfurt debate, the poet and writer Rudolf Alexander Schröder argued that great works of art spoke to eternity, not to the moment. In contrast to Eliot's description of art and culture as organic developments, Schröder insisted that works of art have "no part in the organic life cycle of nature"; on the contrary, they are timeless and permanent. "That is, indeed, the peculiar characteristic of the genuine and truly valid poetic language of truth," Schröder argued: "it does not grow old, as works of specialized scholarship necessarily grow old."[57] Given the timeless nature of great poetry, the writer contended, for authors to seek momentary political advantage through their writing was a pathetic betrayal of that which was greatest in art.

Although most of the writers in attendance at the Frankfurt congress agreed with Schröder, several voiced dissent. In contrast to most of his colleagues, Hans Mayer urged greater understanding for an ethically motivated political literature, while Walter Kolbenhoff, suggesting that writers were the "conscience of their time," declared that a politicized literature was the only genuine possibility for meaningful literary activity in the postwar period.[58] And while he was critical of the Berlin congress, Süskind nevertheless distanced himself from what he called the "priestly fussiness" of his more radical antipolitical colleagues. It was an undeniable fact, he argued, that writers, like all other human beings, were bound up in history, and that their profession changed over time. The profession of the writer was a sociological category like any other, he insisted, and it had to be understood as such. It was no longer possible for writers to live cut off from society and to create autonomous worlds of their own. On the contrary, he argued, "the writer stands more obviously and raises his voice more decisively in public life" now than ever before.[59] Even though the apolitical, "idyllic conception of the writer . . . [is] still widespread among us," Süskind argued, "I still consider it to be false and even dangerous." Suggesting that his own development was probably symptomatic of a more general trend among postwar German writers, Süskind declared: "as a writer I am now focused less than before on a *literary* and more than before on a *journalistic* accent."[60] Writers were more and more activists and less and less seers and priests. German writers were therefore necessarily becoming more political, more concerned with the issues of the day.

Only one month after the Frankfurt writers' congress, the western German occupation zones initiated a currency reform, creating the Deutsche Mark and, virtually overnight, ending, at least in the west, the hoarding and black market trading that had dominated the German economy during the first three postwar years. In protest against what its leaders viewed as a major step on the road to a separate West German state, the Soviet Union immediately blocked off the roads, waterways, and railways into West Berlin, thus cutting off the half-city from western supplies. In response, the western Allies — primarily Great Britain and the United States — initiated an air lift which, for the next eight months, supplied the citizens of the beleaguered city with the most basic necessities, as well as with printed material like Lasky's *Der Monat*. Among the millions of Germans trapped in West Berlin was Gottfried Benn, an early supporter of the Nazis who later became an embittered inner emigrant fervently opposed to any intermingling of literature and politics. Benn, whose influential book of poems *Statische Gedichte* was published in that same momentous year, was to dominate much of West German literary sensibility during the first two decades after the Second World War. As Jürgen Schröder has suggested, Benn's fierce disdain for the Nazis during the late 1930s and 1940s made it possible, after the end of the war, for Germans who admired him to view themselves, with Benn, as "a nation of retroactive resisters and inner emigrants."[61] One month after the beginning of the Berlin air lift, Benn addressed the problem of literature and politics, a problem that had played such an important role at the Berlin and Frankfurt writers' congresses — although he had not attended either one. At the height of the cold war, while the very future of the city in which he was writing hung in the balance, Benn wrote in a letter to a friend in the western zones that it was not so much the Nazis or the Communists who were ruining European culture as literary intellectuals willing to prostitute themselves to politics:

> The fact is that in my view the West is doomed not at all by the totalitarian systems or the crimes of the SS, not even by its material impoverishment or the Gottwalds and Molotovs, but by the abject surrender of its intelligentsia to political concepts. The *zoon politikon* [political animal], that Greek blunder, that Balkan notion — *that* is the germ of our

impending doom. The primary importance of these political concepts has long ceased to be doubted by this brand of club-and-congress intelligentsia; its efforts now are limited to tail-wagging and making itself as acceptable as possible.[62]

Curiously enough, even so vigorous an antipolitical stance as Benn's nevertheless ascribed to writers a power so tremendous that it could cause the permanent decline of the West. The politicization of Western intellectuals, Benn argued, lay at the root of cultural decay. Benn believed that the real problem of Western intellectuals was their lack of self-confidence and pride, a lack which in turn led to intellectuals' inability to maintain their independence from the political world. Benn envisioned a future governed by a stark contrast between those leading an active and those leading a contemplative life:

> The coming century will exert a compulsion on the world of men, will confront it with a decision one can neither dodge nor emigrate from — it will permit no more than two types, two constitutions, two forms of reaction: the active and ambitious and those waiting in silence for the transformation, the historical type and the profound type, criminals and monks — and I plead for the black cowls.[63]

In various forms, the juxtaposition between monks and soldiers was to play an important role in the immediate postwar period. The German exile Arthur Koestler's book *The Yogi and the Commissar,* published in the United States in 1945 and widely discussed in Germany shortly thereafter, seemed to formulate concisely many of the basic problems facing western culture at the end of the war. For Alfred Andersch, Koestler was the most important representative of the younger German emigrants. "In his life and in his work he has become a figure of worldwide significance," Andersch declared in the pages of his new journal *Der Ruf* (The Call) in August of 1946.[64] Because of Andersch's fascination with Koestler, one reviewer in Berlin's *Tagesspiegel* suggested that the first issue of *Der Ruf* had been entirely constructed around Koestler's ideas.[65] In *Merkur* Koestler was described in the same year as belonging to an elite group of European intellectuals unafraid to draw unpleasant conclusions from the lessons of the past. "It is the very best spirits who gather together here. They come from the left and the right, from a battle in which there was no victory, but only sacrifice," declared *Merkur.*[66] Himself a disillusioned former Communist, whose novel *Darkness at Noon* was one of the great literary condemnations of Stalinism, Koestler invoked in *The Yogi and the Commissar* a "fraternity of pessimists" skeptical of the promises made by politicians to create a better world. Experience all too often shows, Koestler suggested, that such utopian plans ultimately lead to horrifying repression and misery; therefore Koestler pleaded for more modesty and for an end to utopian illusions. "Today we are farther than twenty years ago from the realisation of a truly new human climate," Koestler declared, adding that "the next decade or two" will "not be an era of long-term solutions but an intermediate, transitory period, an *interregnum* of half-truths and twilight."[67] In Koestler's view the real tension in debates about the human future existed "between the Yogi and the Commissar, between the fundamental conceptions of Change from Without and Change from Within."[68] For the furtherance of his own vision of a better future, the Commissar was willing to commit any crime; his own and every other human life was subordinate to his political end. The Yogi, in contrast, recognized that happiness lies not in the realm of politics but in the realm of the spirit, and he understood that attempts to solve spiritual problems by ruthless political means can lead only to further misery. Contemporary European leftists, Koestler argued, were overcome by what he called a "pink hangover," the realization that their utopian dreams had led primarily to "serial defeats" and thus to "disgust . . . with plans and promises, ideas and ideals, and most of all with one's own foolish and frustrated hopes."[69] Because of the obvious catastrophe of totalitarianism demonstrated by both Nazism and Communism, Koestler suggested, the postwar age had become "allergic to the rationalism, the shallow optimism, the ruthless logic, the arrogant self-assurance, the Promethean attitude of the nineteenth century; it is attracted by mysticism, romanticism, the irrational ethical values, by mediaeval twilight."[70] Even optimistic science, Koestler insisted, had come to recognize the limitations of its own methodology and was therefore making "room again for the other way of knowing, whose place it usurped for almost three centuries."[71] Contemplation and meditation were once more coming into their own right. It was clear that Koestler himself was on the side not of the Commissar but of the Yogi, because "when all is said, contemplation still remains the only source of guidance in ethical dilemmas where the rule-of-the-thumb criteria of social utility fail."[72]

Like Koestler, Hans Zehrer — a former radical conservative of the 1920s, whose journal *Die Tat* had been one of the most important forums for debate among non-Nazi right-wing intellectuals during the late 1920s and early 1930s — suggested that postwar European intellectuals needed to free themselves from the dictates of politics and come to an understanding that it was only in the inner, spiritual realm that the real problems of human beings could be addressed. After the obvious political disasters of the recent past, Germans and other Europeans were becoming increasingly skeptical of the possibilities of politics, Zehrer believed. Hence, he suggested, "the end of the political" was drawing ever nearer. "There is no doubt about it: the political has lost its powers of recruitment, it is no longer able to arouse people's hopes and expectations in the same way as before."[73] Increasingly, Zehrer reasoned, people were coming to understand that politics could not answer the truly important questions — questions about the meaning of life and God's purpose in the world.

> More and more individuals are forsaking the "isms" of the collectives and becoming marginal "outsiders," bitterly persecuted by their former followers and risking life and limb; this is true of Theodor Plivier and Arthur Koestler, as well as of the leading intellectuals in the USA, not to mention Russia.[74]

During the same month that Zehrer's words were published in book form (in May of 1949), the division of Germany became a reality. On May 12, 1949 the Soviet Union ended the blockade of West Berlin, and eleven days later, on May 23, the parliamentary council of the three western occupation zones promulgated a Basic Law, creating a Federal Republic of Germany consisting of nine *Länder*. Five months later, on October 7, the German Democratic Republic came into existence in the Soviet occupation zone. Two months after the founding of the GDR, Brecht commemorated the division of Germany in a poem whose ferocity gave voice both to the tensions of the cold war and to Brecht's conviction that national disunity was the direct result of capitalist perfidy:

> Germany, Germany, above all —
> Not above our money, though;
> Even if Germany must fall
> Apart for the sake of our dough.

> From Elbe to Rhine we came,
> And we're singing the western score.
> Our goal is always the same:
> For the rich man even more![75]

Most forms of military, political, economic, and cultural cooperation between the Soviet Union and its former western allies had ceased, and the Germany that western and eastern Allies had defeated together was now itself as divided as its conquerors. The Iron Curtain that Röpke had already invoked in the first half of 1945 now ran through the middle of Germany and its capital, Berlin, which had, in the words of the American sociologist James Burnham, become "the traumatic synecdoche of the cold war."[76] In addition to the political division of Germany, there was now also a literary and cultural division of the nation that was to characterize German cultural development for more than a decade, and in many ways even for the next half century. Referring back to the ancient border between the Roman Empire and barbarian tribes to the east, Röpke had described the Iron Curtain as "a *limes* of the Western world, carrying with it complete segregation in the matter of moral, political, social, and economic principles."[77] The cold war was eating away at the fundaments of the very *Kulturnation* that had comforted so many intellectuals both inside and outside Germany during the period of Nazi rule. The overwhelming evil of Nazi tyranny had enabled intellectuals to conjure up the unified, unchanging spirit of a different Germany embodied in the highest accomplishments of the *Kulturnation*. But as the German *Staatsnation* now reemerged in bifurcated form at the end of the Nuremberg interregnum, *Kultur* itself became increasingly fragmented and polarized. In the East, proponents of politicized socialist realism held sway, insisting on a socially relevant and easily accessible literature. In the West, the dominant perspective among cultural elites was that of Zehrer and Benn: that art in general and literature in particular should be free and independent of contamination by politics. For them, in the words of Benn's "Statische Gedichte" ("Static Poems"), "representing opinions/acting/ coming and going/is the sign of a world/that does not see clearly."[78] These thinkers believed that, as a spiritual and cultural pursuit demanding the utmost integrity, literature should remain a relatively isolated "Glass Bead Game" preserving its independence from the corruptions of politics. As early as 1947 the theater and film critic Friedrich Luft — a commentator for Berlin's RIAS — had warned of the danger of a "second inner emigration" in which disappointed intellectuals would leave "politics to the politicians" and beat a retreat back "to the book chest with Hölderlin and the late prose of Goethe."[79] By the end of the 1940s Luft's vision had become a reality. However, for its western proponents the "second inner emigration" was the necessary precondition for aesthetic and spiritual independence in a world dominated by repressive politics. Friedrich Meinecke had proclaimed in 1946: "Everything, yes everything depends upon an intensified development of our inner existence."[80] Philipp Lersch echoed Meinecke's words only a few months after Luft's condemnation of the "second inner emigration," arguing that the "call to inwardness" was the most fundamental message of the era. In his view, the fate of mankind rested not with large political collectives but with the individual human being. "Humanity's hope lies today in the individual, and only in him, in the 'innermost heart of his heart,'" Lersch insisted.[81] If independence, exclusivity, and rigor meant that literature must remain incomprehensible and inaccessible to the unwashed masses, then so be it. As the Catholic intellectual Karl Thieme had already suggested in 1945, "it is rootless mass man — as follower and as leader — who threatens Western civilization with destruction."[82] The Western response to that rootlessness was withdrawal from politics and an affirmation of inner values. In the East the commissars, in the West the yogis: not only a geographical division, but a deep cultural divide.

Notes

[1] "Was wir zu fragen haben, ist nicht mehr oder noch nicht so sehr die Frage, wie es habe geschehen können, sondern die Frage: Was ist, und was sollen wir tun?" Ernst Wiechert, "Über Kunst und Künstler," *Aufbau,* January 1946, 1–8, here 3. Unless otherwise specified, all translations from German in this book are my own; the German appears in the notes, followed by sources. I have added the notation "my translation" in a limited number of cases where confusion might otherwise occur.

[2] "Was können die Schriftsteller, was können die Dichter tun, um dem deutschen Volk auf den Weg zu einer wahren, wirklichen, verinnerlichten Demokratie zu helfen?" Hermann Brill, "Literatur und Demokratie," in *Der Frankfurter Schriftstellerkongreß im Jahr 1948,* ed. Waltraud Wende-Hohenberger, 52–56; here, 52 (Frankfurt: Peter Lang, 1989).

[3] "Die Frage nach den deutschen Intellektuellen und ihrem Verhältnis zur Politik ist mehr als eine literarische oder akademische Angelegenheit; sie ist noch niemals zuvor in Deutschland derart eine Gewissensfrage gewesen wie gerade heute." Gert H. Theunissen, "Der deutsche Intellektuelle und die Politik," *Die Weltbühne,* 1, no. 2 (24 June 1946), 41–44; here, 44.

[4] On the institutionalization of German writers in the Nazi period, see Jan-Pieter Barbian, *Literaturpolitik im "Dritten Reich": Institutionen, Kompetenzen, Betätigungsfelder* (Munich: Deutscher Taschenbuch, 1995).

[5] "Eroberung der Wirklichkeit über das Denken und die Erkenntnis." Kurt W. Marek, "Der Schriftsteller und die Wirklichkeit," in Wende-Hohenberger, *Der Frankfurter Schriftstellerkongreß im Jahr 1948,* 45–51; here, 50.

[6] "Durch alle Höllen glitt die Stimme hin, / In ihren Schleiern wandelt die Gestalt, / Wie Lufthauch raunend deutet sie den Sinn / Des Guten, das nicht endet, nicht verhallt. . . . / Ob Satan lauert auch in seiner Schlucht, / Sein Ohr vernimmt nur seinen eignen Sang, / Sein Auge sieht nur was ihn selber sucht; — / An ihm vorüber wallt der reine Klang. / Dank dir, die doch in Gottes Namen spricht, / Daß du uns bliebest, da das Unheil droht, / Daß du nicht ließest die im Untergehen / Noch Heilung, Tröstung suchten im Gedicht. / Du neigtest dich gedrängter Brüder Not, / Und Freiheit brachte deines Geistes Wehen." Dorothea Taeger, "Der Deutschen Dichtung," in *De Profundis: Deutsche Lyrik in dieser Zeit — Eine Anthologie aus zwölf Jahren,* ed. Gunter Goll, 417 (Munich: Kurt Desch, 1946). Loosely translated.

[7] "Denn kein anderer als er ist mehr berufen, uns eine Deutung der menschlichen Existenz zu geben. Er verdichtet Sein und Werden zum allgemeingültigen Erlebnis durch das Medium des Wortes. Er allein vermag es, im Rausch und Taumel der Geschehnisse das Bleibende zu halten und erhebt es in seinem Werk zum ruhenden Sein, das über den Zeiten steht." Werner Jahn, "Von der neuen deutschen Dichtung," cited in Volker Christian Wehdeking, *Der Nullpunkt: Über die Konstituierung der deutschen Nachkriegsliteratur in den amerikanischen Kriegsgefangenenlagern* (Stuttgart: Metzler, 1971), 48.

[8] "Alle höhere Entwicklung der Menschheit verknüpft sich für die Geistesgeschichte und die Entwicklung menschlicher Gesittung mit dem Wirken von Schriftstellern.

Die Philosophen haben selten regiert, was wohl kein Nachteil war; aber es hat kaum eine nach vernünftigen Grundsätzen aufgebaute Gesellschafts- und Lebensform gegeben, die sich nicht auf Gedanken und Träume der Dichter und Deuter berufen hätte." Hans Mayer, "Der Schriftsteller und die Krise der Humanität," in Wende-Hohenberger, *Der Frankfurter Schriftstellerkongreß im Jahr 1948*, 77–82; here, 82.

[9] "Es ist das geistige Deutschland, das noch Kredit in der Welt genießt, und auf ihm ruht unsere Hoffnung, wenn es noch Hoffnung gibt." Alfred Kantorowicz, "Schriftsteller in der Emigration," in *Erster Deutscher Schriftstellerkongreß 4.–8. Oktober 1947*, ed. Ursula Reinhold, Dieter Schlenstedt, and Horst Tanneberger, 142–47; here, 146 (Berlin: Aufbau, 1997).

[10] "Am Steingeröll der großen Weltruine [vorbei]." "Poems," trans. Karl F. Ross, in Benn, *Prose, Essays, Poems*, ed. Volkmar Sander (New York: Continuum, 1987), 218–19. (Dual-language edition.).

[11] "Kündern des Wahren und Gültigen." Klaus R. Scherpe, "Erzwungener Alltag: Wahrgenommene und gedachte Wirklichkeit in der Reportageliteratur der Nachkriegszeit," in *Nachkriegsliteratur in Westdeutschland 1945–1949: Schreibweisen, Gattungen, Institutionen*, ed. Jost Hermand, Helmut Peitsch, and Klaus R. Scherpe, 35–102; here, 36 (Berlin: Argument, 1982).

[12] "eine Versammlung von Männern," "würdige Gewänder," "in einem feierlichen, gemessenen Tanz." Hermann Kasack, *Die Stadt hinter dem Strom* (Frankfurt: Suhrkamp, 1947), 546–47. This entire passage is eliminated from Peter de Mendelssohn's English translation, *The City Beyond the River* (London: Longmans, Green and Co., 1953).

[13] "die dreiunddreißig Weltenwächter, die Hüter der goldenen Waage," "den Gang der Menschheit." Kasack, *Die Stadt hinter dem Strom*, 547.

[14] "Sie . . . hielten das Schöpfungsspiel im Gang." Kasack, *Die Stadt hinter dem Strom*, 549. This passage is also eliminated from the English translation.

[15] "Sie griffen nicht aktiv ein, aber sie ließen es auch nicht bei einer kontemplativen Betrachtung bewenden; sie halfen durch bloßes Dasein." Kasack, *Die Stadt hinter dem Strom*, 550. This passage is also eliminated from the English translation.

[16] Kasack, *The City Beyond the River*, 349. German original: "Hockende, starrende, sammelnde Menschen an unaufgeräumten Straßen." Kasack, *Die Stadt hinter dem Strom*, 577.

[17] Kasack, *The City Beyond the River*, 348. German original: "Zu tief war er in dem Zeitlosen verbannt gewesen, um noch an den Augenblicken des Zeitlichen Genüge zu finden." Kasack, *Die Stadt hinter dem Strom*, 575. In his 1956 revisions, Kasack made Lindhoff's alienation from the world of the living even clearer by eliminating many references to current conditions in Germany. See Kasack, *Die Stadt hinter dem Strom* (Frankfurt: Suhrkamp, 1994 [originally 1956]), as well as Mathias Bertram, "Literarische Epochendiagnosen der Nachkriegszeit," in Heukenkamp, *Deutsche Erinnerung*, 11–99; here, 46.

[18] "ich gehöre nicht mehr zu euch." Kasack, *Die Stadt hinter dem Strom*, 576.

[19] Jean-Paul Sartre, "The Responsibility of the Writer," trans. Betty Askwith, in *Reflections on Our Age: Lectures Delivered at the Opening Session of UNESCO at the Sorbonne University Paris*, with an introduction by David Hardman and a foreword by

Stephen Spender (New York: Columbia UP, 1949), 67–83; here, 70–71. Many of Sartre's reflections in this speech prefigured his ideas in *Situations II* (Paris: Gallimard, 1948); English translation as *What is Literature?* trans. Bernard Frechtman (New York: Philosophical Library, 1949). For more on Sartre's concept of commitment in literature, see Michael Scriven, *Jean-Paul Sartre: Politics and Culture in Postwar France* (New York: St. Martin's Press, 1999); and Christina Howells, *Sartre's Theory of Literature* (London: The Modern Humanities Research Association, 1979).

[20] T. S. Eliot, *Notes towards the Definition of Culture* (New York: Harcourt, Brace and Company, 1949), 123. The appendix to this book, entitled "The Unity of European Culture," was published in Germany in a dual language edition as *Die Einheit der europäischen Kultur* (Berlin: Carl Habel, 1946).

[21] For more information on socialist realism, see: Régine Robin, *Socialist Realism: An Impossible Aesthetic,* trans. Catherine Porter (Stanford: Stanford UP, 1992); *Zur Theorie des sozialistischen Realismus,* ed. Institut für Gesellschaftswissenschaften beim ZK der SED (Berlin: Dietz, 1974); and Thomas Lahusen and Evgeny Dobrenko, eds., *Socialist Realism Without Shores* (Durham, NC: Duke UP, 1997).

[22] "die moderne minderwertige bürgerliche Literatur des Westens," "Kriecherei und Katzbuckelei vor der spießbürgerlichen ausländischen Literatur." A. A. Shdanow, "Referat über die Zeitschriften 'Swesda' und 'Leningrad,' 1946," in *Beiträge zum Sozialistischen Realismus: Grundsätzliches über Kunst und Literatur,* with an introduction by Wilhelm Girnus, 20–42; here, 28 (Berlin: Kultur und Fortschritt, 1953).

[23] "fürchten den Sozialismus, sie fürchten unser sozialistisches Land, das ein Vorbild für die gesamte Menschheit ist." Shdanow, "Referat über die Zeitschriften 'Swesda' und 'Leningrad,'" 39.

[24] Cited in David Pike, *The Politics of Culture in Soviet-Occupied Germany, 1945–1949* (Stanford: Stanford UP, 1992), 224.

[25] On East German writers and the emergence of the cold war in the late 1940s, see Anne Hartmann and Wolfram Eggeling, *Sowjetische Präsenz im kulturellen Leben der SBZ und frühen DDR 1945–1953* (Berlin: Akademie, 1998).

[26] Reinhold and Schlenstedt, "Vorgeschichte, Umfeld, Nachgeschichte des Ersten Deutschen Schriftstellerkongresses," 49. This open letter by Soviet writers to their American colleagues was published in the *Tägliche Rundschau* and in *Neues Deutschland* on 2 October 1947.

[27] "daß das große amerikanische Volk viel verlieren und viel riskieren würde, wenn es irgend jemandem erlaubte, den freien Wettbewerb der Ideen auf kulturellem Gebiet einzuschränken." Werner Hecht, *Brecht Chronik 1898–1956* (Frankfurt: Suhrkamp, 1997), 795.

[28] Cited in Frances Stonor Saunders, *Who Paid the Piper? The CIA and the Cultural Cold War* (London: Granta, 1999), 199.

[29] Saunders, *Who Paid the Piper?* 17, 18.

[30] Wolfgang Koeppen, *Pigeons on the Grass,* trans. David Ward (New York: Holmes & Meier, 1988), 188. In German: "das einzige wärmende Licht in der Welt." Koeppen, *Tauben im Gras* (Frankfurt: Suhrkamp, 1951), 196.

[31] See Taylor D. Littleton and Maltby Sykes, *Advancing American Art: Painting, Politics and Cultural Confrontation* (Alabama: U of Alabama P, 1989) and Stephen J. Whitfield, *The Culture of the Cold War* (Baltimore: Johns Hopkins UP, 1991).

[32] Wilhelm Röpke, *The German Question,* trans. E. W. Dickes (London: George Allen & Unwin, 1946), 90. German original: "Sie waren nur vom geübten Auge zu erkennen, und auch dieses konnte nicht immer unterscheiden, ob es sich nicht um eine optische Täuschung oder um bloße Unkrautkeime handelte." Wilhelm Röpke, *Die deutsche Frage* (Erlenbach-Zurich: Eugen Rentsch, 1945), 103.

[33] See Helmuth Kiesel, "Ernst Jüngers 'Marmor-Klippen,'" in *Internationales Archiv für Sozialgeschichte der deutschen Literatur,* vol. 14 (1989), 126–64.

[34] Ernst Jünger, *Auf den Marmorklippen* (Frankfurt: Ullstein, 1995 [originally 1939]). English translation as Ernst Juenger, *On the Marble Cliffs,* trans. Stuart Hood (New York: New Directions, 1947).

[35] "wenn ich auf diese Literatur allein angewiesen wäre, hätte ich ganz gut ein strammer SS-Mann werden können." "überhaupt nicht irgendein Gegengift gegen den Faschismus in uns erzeugen konnte und uns immun machen konnte gegen diese Zeit." Wolfgang Harich, in Reinhold et al., eds., *Erster Deutscher Schriftstellerkongreß,* 159.

[36] On the Kulturbund, see Schivelbusch, *Vor dem Vorhang,* 115–68; English transla-tion: Schivelbusch, *In a Cold Crater: Cultural and Intellectual Life in Berlin, 1945–1948,* trans. Kelly Barry (Berkeley: U of California P, 1998), 72–106. On the SDA, see Carsten Gansel, "Vom Schutzverband Deutscher Autoren (SDA) zum Deutschen Schriftstellerverband (DSV): Zu Aspekten von literarischer Gruppenbildung zwischen 1945 und 1956," in *Literatur im politischen Spannungsfeld der Nachkriegszeit: Protokoll der internationalen Konferenz anläßlich des 50. Jubiläums des 1. Deutschen Schriftstellerkongresses vom Oktober 1947,* ed. Ursula Heukenkamp and Ursula Rein-hold, 147–67 (Berlin: Institut für deutsche Literatur, 1998) (unpublished conference proceedings).

[37] "heute aber den Weg in die Realität zu verlegen beginnt." Stephan Hermlin, "Wo bleibt die junge Dichtung?" in Reinhold et al., eds., *Erster Deutscher Schriftsteller-kongreß,* 307–11; here, 308–9.

[38] "Wir leben in einer Gesellschaft, in der die sozialen Konflikte eine solche Spannung erreicht haben, daß dem Schriftsteller gar nichts anderes übrigbleibt, als sich sehr scharf einer Stellung innerhalb dieser Konflikte bewußt zu werden, ob er das will oder nicht." Hans Mayer, "Der Schriftsteller und die Gesellschaft," in Reinhold et al., *Erster Deutscher Schriftstellerkongreß,* 208–12; here, 209.

[39] "daß die Welt sich in zwei Teile teilt, daß der eine Teil vertreten wird durch die schwarze Reaktion, durch die Barbarei, durch die Ideologie des Menschenhasses und des Militarismus und der andere Teil durch Millionen einfache Menschen, die für den Frieden leben, für den Frieden kämpfen, . . . und ich rufe Sie auf dazu, daß die deutschen Schriftsteller und das deutsche Volk sich in die Reihen dieser einfachen Menschen, dieser einfachen Demokraten befinden." Wishnewsky, in Reinhold et al., eds., *Erster Deutscher Schriftstellerkongreß,* 245.

[40] "nur der genaue und geschulte Beobachter konnte erkennen, mit welcher Geschlossenheit und Präzision die sowjetischen Delegierten die neuesten Richtlinien der Politik vertraten." Annelie Hartmann, "Die Rolle der sowjetischen Delegierten in

Berlin (1947) und Wroclaw (1948)," in Heukenkamp and Reinhold, *Literatur im politischen Spannungsfeld der Nachkriegszeit,* 43–58; here, 51.

[41] Lasky claims that his intervention was prompted by the writer Walter Birkenfeld, who was chairing that particular session of the conference. See Ruth Rehmann, *Unterwegs in fremden Träumen,* (Munich: Carl Hanser, 1993), 146–48.

[42] "Und ich möchte . . . sagen, daß wir in diesem internationalen Geist uns solidarisch fühlen mit den Schriftstellern und Künstlern Sowjetrußlands. Auch sie kennen den Druck und die Zensur. Auch sie stehen im Kampf um die kulturelle Freiheit, und ich glaube, wir alle müssen ihnen unsere offenherzige Sympathie entgegenbringen." Lasky, Reinhold et al., eds., *Erster Deutscher Schriftstellerkongreß,* 300. Lasky's criticism of the United States in his speech is generally ignored in the secondary literature on the conference.

[43] "Es war durchaus mutig. Dieser siebenundzwanzigjährige Mann hatte dem Kongress einen Sinn gegeben, den keiner vorausgesehen hatte." Bernard Genton, "Melvin J. Lasky und der 1. Deutsche Schriftstellerkongreß," in Heukenkamp and Reinhold, *Literatur im politischen Spannungsfeld der Nachkriegszeit,* 59–70; here, 69.

[44] Saunders, *Who Paid the Piper?* 27.

[45] Genton, "Melvin J. Lasky und der 1. Deutsche Schriftstellerkongreß," 67.

[46] "der Schriftsteller, der Verleger und der Leser gewisse unverletzliche Rechte haben," "die Verantwortung in ihren eigenen Händen . . . für die wachsame Verteidigung und kompromißlose Aufrechterhaltung dieser Rechte und dieser Freiheiten." Reinhold et al., eds., *Erster Deutscher Schriftstellerkongreß,* 295.

[47] Saunders, *Who Paid the Piper?* 28.

[48] "Die Katze ist aus dem Sack!" Rehmann, *Unterwegs in fremden Träumen,* 151.

[49] Saunders, *Who Paid the Piper?* 28–30.

[50] See Peter Coleman, *The Liberal Conspiracy: The Congress for Cultural Freedom and the Struggle for the Mind of Postwar Europe* (London: Free Press, 1989); Michael Hochgeschwender, "Der 'Kongreß für kulturelle Freiheit' und die Deutschen," in Heukenkamp and Reinhold, *Literatur im politischen Spannungsfeld der Nachkriegszeit,* 71–83; and Saunders, *Who Paid the Piper?* During the mid-1950s, Lasky became one of the editors of the journal *Encounter.* In 1967 the Congress for Cultural Freedom became the International Association for Cultural Freedom, which was active until 1970.

[51] Saunders, *Who Paid the Piper?* 1.

[52] "Heute wird die Anständigkeit und Ehrlichkeit der Leute durch die Beziehung zur Demokratie und im einzelnen zu der Sowjetunion bestimmt." Valentin Katayew, Reinhold et al., eds., *Erster Deutscher Schriftstellerkongreß,* 336.

[53] "eine Teilung Deutschlands," "den Weltfrieden." Johannes R. Becher, "Wie kämpft der Schriftsteller für den Frieden?" in Reinhold et al., eds., *Erster Deutscher Schriftstellerkongreß,* 362–69; here, 363.

[54] "und somit gibt es auch in diesem Sinne keine westdeutsche und ostdeutsche Literatur, keine süddeutsche und norddeutsche, sondern nur eine, eine deutsche, die sich nicht in Zonengrenzen bannen läßt." Becher, "Wie kämpft der Schriftsteller für den Frieden?" in Reinhold et al., eds., *Erster Deutscher Schriftstellerkongreß,* 365.

[55] "ich mir manchmal vorkam wie auf einem Schulungskurs," "den weltanschaulichen, politischen und antifaschistischen Pflichten des Schriftstellers." Wilhelm Emanuel Süskind, "Wandlung des Schriftstellers," in Wende-Hohenberger, *Der Frankfurter Schriftstellerkongreß im Jahr 1948,* 39–45; here, 43.

[56] "Sie sammeln ihre Fakten nach vorgenommenem Plan, der ganz bestimmte Fakten ausschließt," "Sie begraben die Wirklichkeit in den Särgen der Terminologien. Solche Literatur unterliegt einer Parteidisziplin und diese Schriftsteller einem literarischen Fraktionszwang. Sie beschreiben nicht mehr die Ereignisse, die Verhältnisse und die Zusammenhänge, die die Wirklichkeit ihnen bietet, sondern die, die sie billigen." Marek, "Der Schriftsteller und die Wirklichkeit," 47.

[57] "keinen Anteil an dem organischen Wechselleben der Natur," "das ist ja das eigentümlichste Charakteristikum des echten, des vollgültigen dichterischen Wahrwortes," "es veraltet nicht, wie etwa die Werke der Fachwissenschaft mit Notwendigkeit veralten." Rudolf Alexander Schröder, "Aufgaben der Dichtung in der Zeit," in Wende-Hohenberger, *Der Frankfurter Schriftstellerkongreß im Jahr 1948,* 23–30; here, 28.

[58] "Gewissen seiner Zeit." Cited in Wende-Hohenberger, *Der Frankfurter Schriftstellerkongreß im Jahr 1948,* 45.

[59] "priesterliches Getu," "Der Schriftsteller steht mit alledem viel sichtbarer im öffentlichen Leben und spricht viel entscheidender mit als einst." Süskind, "Wandlung des Schriftstellers," 42.

[60] "die idyllische Auffassung vom Schriftsteller . . . immer noch weit verbreitet bei uns [ist]," "Ich halte sie gleichwohl für falsch und sogar für gefährlich." "ich bin ein Schriftsteller weniger als früher mit einem *literarischen* und mehr als früher mit einem *publizistischen* Akzent." Süskind, "Wandlung des Schriftstellers," 44.

[61] "ein Volk von nachholenden Widerständlern und Inneren Emigranten." See Jürgen Schröder, "'Wer über Deutschland reden und richten will, muss hier geblieben sein': Gottfried Benn als Emigrant nach innen," in *Literatur in der Diktatur: Schreiben im Nationalsozialismus und DDR-Sozialismus,* ed. Günther Rüther, 131–44; here, 144 (Paderborn: Schöningh, 1997).

[62] Gottfried Benn, "Letter from Berlin, July 1948," trans. Ernst Kaiser and Eithne Wilkins, in *Prose, Essays, Poems,* 79–83; here, 80. In German: "Das Abendland geht nämlich meiner Meinung nach gar nicht zugrunde an den totalitären Systemen oder den SS-Verbrechen, auch nicht an seiner materiellen Verarmung oder an den Gottwalds und Molotows, sondern an dem hündischen Kriechen seiner Intelligenz vor den politischen Begriffen. Das Zoon politikon, dieser griechische Mißgriff, diese Balkanidee — das ist der Keim des Untergangs, der sich jetzt vollzieht. Daß diese politischen Begriffe die primären seien, wird von dieser Art Intelligenz der Klubs und Tagungen schon lange nicht mehr bezweifelt, sie bemüht sich vielmehr nur noch, um sie herumzuwedeln und sich von ihnen als tragbar empfinden zu lassen." Gottfried Benn, "Berliner Brief, Juli 1948," in *Sämtliche Werke,* 5:56–61; here, 57–58.

[63] Benn, "Letter from Berlin, July 1948," 82. In German: "Das kommende Jahrhundert wird die Männerwelt in einen Zwang nehmen, vor eine Entscheidung stellen, vor der es kein Ausweichen und keine Emigration gibt, es wird nur noch zwei Typen, zwei Konstitutionen, zwei Reaktionsformen zulassen: diejenigen, die handeln

und hochwollen und diejenigen, die schweigend die Verwandlung erwarten, die Geschichtlichen und die Tiefen, Verbrecher und Mönche — und ich plädiere für die schwarzen Kutten." Benn, "Berliner Brief, Juli 1948," 60.

[64] "Mit seinem Leben und seinem Werk ist er zu einer Figur von weltweiter Bedeutung aufgestiegen." Alfred Andersch, "Das junge Europa formt sein Gesicht," in *Der Ruf: Eine deutsche Nachkriegszeitschrift,* ed. Hans Schwab-Felisch, 21–26; here, 25 (Munich: Deutscher Taschenbuch Verlag, 1962). From *Der Ruf,* 15 August 1946.

[65] Jérôme Vaillant, *Der Ruf — Unabhängige Blätter der jungen Generation (1945–1949): Eine Zeitschrift zwischen Illusion und Anpassung,* trans. Heidrun Hofmann and Karl Heinz Schmidt (Munich: K. G. Sauer, 1978), 84.

[66] "Es sind die besten Geister, die sich hier sammeln. Sie kommen von links und rechts, und alle kommen sie aus einem Kampf, in dem es keinen Sieg gab, sondern nur das Opfer." "Die Bruderschaft der Pessimisten," *Merkur,* 1, no. 1 (1947), 131–37; here, 131; the author is probably Hans Paeschke, editor of *Merkur.*

[67] Arthur Koestler, *The Yogi and the Commissar* (New York: Macmillan, 1945), 103.

[68] Koestler, *The Yogi and the Commissar,* 4.

[69] Koestler, *The Yogi and the Commissar,* 10.

[70] Koestler, *The Yogi and the Commissar,* 13.

[71] Koestler, *The Yogi and the Commissar,* 245.

[72] Koestler, *The Yogi and the Commissar,* 245.

[73] "Es ist keine Frage: das Politische hat seine werbende Kraft verloren, es vermag die Erwartungen und Hoffnungen der Menschen nicht mehr in gleicher Weise zu wecken, wie bisher." Hans Zehrer, "Das Ende des Politischen," in *Aufsätze zur Zeit,* 61–65; here, 61 (Hamburg: Rowohlt, 1949).

[74] "Immer mehr Einzelne verlassen die 'Ismen' des Kollektivs und werden zu abseitigen 'Außenseitern,' die von der ehemaligen Gefolgschaft erbittert verfolgt werden und Kopf und Kragen riskieren, ob nun Theodor Plivier und Arthur Koestler, oder die führende Intelligenz in USA, von Rußland ganz zu schweigen." Hans Zehrer, "Die Wandlung der Intelligenz," in *Aufsätze zur Zeit,* 151–56; here, 152. After publishing his novel *Stalingrad,* Plievier, who had once been the chairman of the Kulturbund in Weimar, rejected the Soviet Union and Communism in 1947 and went to live in Wallhausen on the shore of Lake Constance in southwestern Germany.

[75] "Deutschland, Deutschland über alles/Nur nicht über unser Geld!/Wenn es auch gegebenen Falles/Dadurch auseinanderfällt//Ja, vom Rhein bis an die Elbe/Sind wir westlich eingestellt/Ist das Ziel doch ganz dasselbe:/Für den reichen Mann mehr Geld!" Bertolt Brecht, "Bonner Bundeshymne," *Werke,* ed. Werner Hecht et al., vol. 15, *Gedichte* 5 (Berlin, Weimar, and Frankfurt: Aufbau and Suhrkamp, 1993), 207. Loosely translated.

[76] Cited in Saunders, *Who Paid the Piper?* 10.

[77] Röpke, *The German Question,* 203. Original German: "So ist die Elbe zu einem *Limes* des Abendlandes geworden, der die vollkommene Scheidung der moralischen, politischen, sozialen und wirtschaftlichen Grundsätze bedeutet." Röpke, *Die deutsche Frage,* 248–49.

[78] "Richtungen vertreten,/Handeln,/Zu- und Abreisen/ist das Zeichen einer Welt,/die nicht klar sieht." Gottfried Benn, "Statische Gedichte," in Benn, *Sämtliche Werke,* ed. Gerhard Schuster, 1:224 (Stuttgart: Klett-Cotta, 1986). For an alternative English-language translation, see Benn, "Static Poems," in Benn, *Poems 1937–1947,* trans. Simona Draghici, 103 (Washington, DC: Plutarch Press, 1991).

[79] "Er überläßt Politik den Politikern. Er emigriert erneut nach innen. Der Rückzug an den Bücherschrank zu Hölderlin und Goethes Altersprosa." Friedrich Luft, "Zweite Emigration nach innen?" *Neue Zeitung* [Berlin edition], 20 May 1947, 2.

[80] Friedrich Meinecke, *The German Catastrophe: Reflections and Recollections,* trans. Sidney B. Fay (Cambridge, MA: Harvard UP, 1950), 115. German original: "Auf eine Verinnerlichung unseres Daseins kommt heute alles, alles an." Meinecke, *Die deutsche Katastrophe: Betrachtungen und Erinnerungen* (Brockhaus: Wiesbaden, 1946), 168.

[81] "Im einzelnen und nur in ihm, in seines 'Herzens tiefsten Herzen' liegt heute die Chance der Menschheit." Philipp Lersch, "Ruf nach Verinnerlichung," *Neue Zeitung,* 25 August 1947, 3.

[82] "Es ist der entwurzelte Massenmensch — als Geführter und als Führer —, der die abendländische Zivilisation mit dem Untergang bedroht." Karl Thieme, *Das Schicksal der Deutschen: Ein Versuch seiner geschichtlichen Erklärung* (Basel: Kobersche Verlagsbuchhandlung, 1945), 6.

6: A German Generation Gap?

GIVEN THE APPARENT moral bankruptcy of several generations of German leaders culminating in the cultural, political, military, and economic disaster of the Third Reich, it was only natural that the end of the Second World War saw a widespread interest in the search for a younger generation untainted by association with Nazi crimes. As Rudolf Schneider-Schelde, a Munich writer and the editor of a 1946 collection of essays devoted to the problem of youth, put it, "the world is worried about the subject of youth."[1] The supposed historical superiority of the younger generation in Germany in 1945 found expression two generations after the end of the war in a scene from Serbian author Milorad Pavic's novel *Landscape Painted With Tea*. One of the novel's characters describes a uniquely positive position for young people in Germany in the wake of the lost war, suggesting that, because of the older generation's failure, German youth are in a position to dominate national culture for many decades to come. In Germany, according to Pavic's character, "they'll be looking for younger people, who bear no responsibility for the defeat; the generation of fathers has lost the game there; there it's your generation's move."[2] The defeated nation, in other words, may have been a good country in which to be young after 1945.

On the surface this evaluation of the post-1945 situation might seem to have validity; it certainly corresponds to the idea of a zero hour in which there must be a radical new beginning that sweeps aside all associations with an unpleasant past. As the main character in Kolbenhoff's *Heimkehr in die Fremde* asserts, "my generation has the best chances of liberating itself and seeing clearly" in order to create a new world.[3] Ilse Aichinger's novel *Die grössere Hoffnung* is centered around the hopes and fears of the fifteen-year-old Ellen and her youthful friends, all of whom, in contrast to the adult world around them, have maintained their purity and innocence; although Ellen dies at the end of the novel, her hopes point to a better future. The words of Pavic's character — "no responsibility" — suggest that the search for a younger generation is governed by a need to escape a sense of guilt by ascribing all "responsibility for the defeat" — whether military, political, or moral — to an older generation that has, precisely because of its supposedly unique association with guilt, "lost the game." In Kolbenhoff's novel this accusation is articulated by a depressed returning soldier who declares to a wealthy older man, "you are guilty," insisting that he is responsible for the fact that "the buildings are nothing but rubble now and that the children are hungry. Your entire accursed generation has brought us to this, and now you're sitting here and ought really to be hanging on the gallows!"[4] In Aichinger's novel, the world of adults is ultimately a world of hard-heartedness and brutality, and guilt and the perception of guilt are passed down through the generations: "The older ones are guilty of us."[5] Three decades after the end of the war — during the same decade in which Pavic wrote his novel — the belief that the younger generation was free of guilt for the crimes of the Second World War was reiterated in Chancellor Helmut Kohl's invocation of a "Gnade der späten Geburt" (grace of late birth) which allegedly liberated younger Germans from the guilt of their fathers. Behind this version of a zero hour lies the implicit or explicit belief that what is being consigned to nonexistence and nontime before the zero is German guilt. Alfred Andersch made this banishment of guilt explicit as early as 1946, when he insisted that the younger generation was "separated from older people through their non-responsibility for Hitler."[6]

Not quite two decades after the end of the war, Heinz Friedrich lent weight to this idealized version of a zero hour in a heroic retrospective on postwar writing by members of the younger generation who formed Gruppe 47. Friedrich declared: "If after May 8, 1945 there was a group of people . . . who had the right to speak their mind and put their fingers on the cancerous sores of Europe, it was the younger generation, those who were then between twenty and forty."[7] In Friedrich's scenario, this younger generation had both the right and the duty to speak out because — in contrast to their elders, who he believed were largely to blame for the national disaster — German youth had experienced and come to terms with the senselessness of war and totalitarianism. After the end of the war, Friedrich declared, the younger generation of war veterans returned to Germany "without illusions." In Friedrich's account, this generation hated both nationalism and nostalgic humanism. Young people wanted, he claimed, "to make a clean break with the past. . . . Energetically and uncompromisingly they demanded a unified Europe without national resentments and prejudices."[8] Such a picture suggests a younger generation unaffected by Nazi propaganda and untouched by German guilt. In Friedrich's optimistic vision, German writers of the younger generation knew exactly where they stood after the end of the war and immediately took advantage of their position.

Of course, Friedrich's heroic picture neglects the younger generation's own conformism during the Nazi period. Moreover, Friedrich glosses over the Nazis' self-representation as a youth movement. Less than two decades earlier, it was they who had characterized their predecessors as old-fashioned members of an outdated generation. In 1946 Friedrich Meinecke reminded his fellow countrymen that Hitler had come "to power through a typical but dazzled and blinded youth movement."[9] The American historian Robert Wohl notes that "it became part of the mythology of the regime that the

Nazi leadership represented the essence of youth," the culmination of the diverse youth movements that had preceded it.[10] George Mosse has written that the Nazi "movement stressed youth, at the expense of the older generation, which might still harbor vestiges of liberalism or even socialism."[11] And Alexander Mitscherlich has described National Socialism as in part a revolution "of youth against authoritarian but weak fathers."[12] The Nazis themselves had declared that "National Socialism is the organized will of the youth."[13] In Nazi ideology the *Führer* and his followers represented youth, while the proponents of Weimar democracy embodied decrepitude. In his own 1946 contribution to the postwar debate on German youth, Rudolf Schneider-Schelde noted: "It is easy to see what role Hitler and National Socialism played in the most recent developments. They were the representatives of youth." Indeed, for Schneider-Schelde "Hitler's cause was the cause of youth, just as every revolution is an affair for youth."[14] The collapse and defeat of Germany had not been the fault of a supposedly guilty older generation, Schneider-Schelde claimed, because "the collapsing 'achievement' was itself to a large extent the work of youth." Hence the German collapse was also "the collapse of youth itself. It is the collapse . . . of the belief in youth and the beliefs of youth."[15] The Nazi catastrophe was only the last and worst example of the devastation wrought by decades of youthful ideology in European culture: "One hundred and fifty years of youthful energy have sufficed to lay waste to the western world."[16] It was now, Schneider-Schelde believed, time for older, wiser figures to take the lead.

Thomas Mann made the problem of German youth a central theme in his novel *Doktor Faustus*. In the idealistic world of the German youth movement, which plays a major role in the socialization of the novel's hero Adrian Leverkühn, youth and Germanness are essentially interchangeable quantities. In the words of the aptly named student Deutschlin (little German), with whom the future composer Leverkühn studies theology at the University of Halle, "the German is the eternal student, the eternal striver among the nations."[17] Indeed, the very concept of youth as a category separate from old age is, Deutschlin believes, specifically German: "The concept of youth is a privilege and advantage of our people, the Germans." In Deutschlin's view "German youth, precisely as youth, represents the spirit of the people itself, the German spirit, which is young and forward-looking . . . immature, if you want, but what is that supposed to mean!"[18] German youthfulness produced Martin Luther's Reformation against the decrepit Roman Catholic church, Deutschlin argues, and it continues to provide a necessary antidote to staid conservatism in the rest of the world. "Where would the world be if maturity were the last word! In our immaturity we still have many innovations, many revolutions to give the world."[19] The result of this youthful revolution is precisely the Nazi ascension, to which, during the first half of 1943, the novel's narrator Serenus Zeitblom refers as "the supposedly purifying new beginning, the rebirth of the people ten years ago."[20] Because of the Nazi indoctrination of youth, Zeitblom, a teacher, now no longer knows how to approach his own students, or even his own sons, who are both obedient servants of their *Führer* and who, he believes, would not hesitate to betray him to the Gestapo if they were to find written proof of his anti-Nazi sentiments.[21]

Like Mann's fictional Serenus Zeitblom, many real-life older Germans were concerned about the effect of Nazi propaganda on German youth. At the end of the Second World War Ernst Wiechert suggested in a much-discussed speech, the "Rede an die deutsche Jugend" (Speech to German Youth) of 1945, that the perversion of youth had been the most important goal of Nazi ideology. One of the worst crimes of the Nazis, Wiechert believed, had been the theft of German youth: "In these twelve years an entire nation was robbed of that which was most precious and specific to it, that which it had always possessed: its youth, and with youth the guarantee of any future."[22] In Wiechert's view almost the entire German people had been "ruined and poisoned" during the Third Reich, but German young people had been particularly vulnerable to the Pied Pipers of the Nazi Party.

Such critiques were not merely the gift of hindsight after the defeat of the Third Reich. By the late 1930s anti-Nazi writers had begun to recognize the insidious effectiveness of the National Socialist youth policies that Mann later diagnosed in *Doktor Faustus*. In 1937, one year before his country's *Anschluß* with Germany, the Austrian writer Ödön von Horváth published the novel *Jugend ohne Gott* (Youth Without God, translated into English as *The Age of the Fish*), which described young people growing up under the influence of a racist and nationalist ideology. Brecht's short play *Der Spitzel* (The Informer), part of the collection of one-act plays *Furcht und Elend des Dritten Reiches* (Fear and Misery of the Third Reich, 1938), also depicts the Nazi emphasis on youth from an antifascist perspective. Like von Horváth and Brecht, anti-Nazi activists recognized the danger of National Socialist policies towards youth. In his anti-Nazi manifesto *Zero Hour* (1944) Karl Becker wrote that "the greatest crime committed by the Nazis against the German people was their treatment of German youth," adding sadly that the Nazis "still hold . . . German youth . . . in their iron grip."[23] The Communist exile Paul Merker wrote that "German youth was influenced by Nazi ideology more deeply than any other section of the people," asserting that the "morally degenerate young generation came to be one of the strongest pillars of the Nazi Army, and was to furnish cadres for the S.S. and the Gestapo."[24]

Hence when Victor Klemperer, who survived inside the Nazi Reich as an ethnic Jew, declared in 1946 that the most critical problem facing postwar Germany was the younger generation, he was echoing concerns that had been growing for many years. In Klemperer's words,

The thinking and feeling of this generation has been poisoned from their ABC's on, it has never learned, seen, or inhaled anything but Nazism; in itself it is completely free of guilt, but at the same time it is utterly immersed in the original sin of Nazism and utterly saturated with it.[25]

Klemperer's words suggest that far from being in a clearly superior position with respect to old age after 1945, youth may well have been at a distinct disadvantage. Significantly, Roberto Rosselini's *Germania, anno zero* (Germany, Year Zero, 1947), a film which probably contributed more than any other to the establishment of the year 1945 as a zero hour in German cultural memory, dealt not with the superiority but with the weakness and endangerment of the younger generation. Like many other works of postwar literature and film, *Germania, anno zero* reverses the National Socialist topos of the deserved moral triumph of youth over old age, characterized by the martyrdom of a virtuous boy. In Rosselini's film the fourteen-year-old anti-hero winds up — like the nihilists of Russian literature — killing his father not out of any desire for a new spiritual beginning but because his Nazi teacher has filled him with social Darwinist platitudes about the superiority of the strong over the weak. Ultimately, the boy kills himself as well, and his death, unlike that of Nazi boy-martyrs, is offset by no images of youthful resurrection in a triumphantly marching collectivity that carries the memory of the dead hero into eternity. Instead, the young anti-hero's death is as senseless as his life, and the film's zero hour is a dead end.

One of the first works of the "new" German literature by a — relatively — younger generation to appear after the war's end was thirty-eight-year-old Walter Kolbenhoff's 1946 novel *Von unserem Fleisch und Blut* (From Our Flesh and Blood), which, like Rosselini's film, reversed some of the main topoi of National Socialist youth mythology. This novel, written during Kolbenhoff's sojourn in the United States as a prisoner of war in the mid-1940s, told the story of seventeen-year-old Werwolf — the name given to German terrorists resisting the Allies even after the German surrender on May 8, 1945 — and fanatical Nazi Hans; like Heini Volker in the 1933 Nazi film *Hitlerjunge Quex,* Hans is deeply resentful of his working class father, who is a member of the Social Democratic Party. At the end of the war, Hans fights a bitter rear-guard action against the defeatism of his recalcitrant German elders; this doomed struggle leads to the brutal murder of two people. During the period of Nazi rule Hans triumphantly declares to his father, "You have lost; we have won! We will show you!"[26] The "you" to which Hans is referring is not just the Social Democrats but the entire older generation, and the "we" is not just the Nazis but the younger generation with which they are so strongly identified. Even after the war is clearly lost, Hans continues to insist that he is right and the entire opportunistic older generation wrong: "All your laws have no validity for me any more," declares Hans rebelliously, insisting "I have to separate myself totally from everything." Hans's more mature brother Paul tells him, "You are sick. . . . You are the best proof of how horrible is the plague with which they have infected you," but Hans is unwilling to listen to the voice of reason.[27] His idea of a tabula rasa — rhetorically similar to postwar invocations of a zero hour — is the desire that all of Germany should be destroyed completely if it fails to put up a sufficiently heroic fight against the advancing Allies: "If we go down, then everything must go down too, he thought."[28] Citing the slogan his Nazi leaders have brainwashed him with, he declares, "After us the deluge. And then the desert."[29] As with Rosselini's *Germania, anno zero,* this novel's zero hour is a senseless dead end, the result of a wanton break with traditional structures of morality and authority. As the novel's title suggests, the fanatical Hans is anything but an incomprehensible alien; he is the prodigal German son who fails to seek salvation and forgiveness. Although the main character in this book is certainly a victim of National Socialist brainwashing, he is nevertheless at least partially responsible for his own fate, because he repeatedly rejects other people's efforts to save and enlighten him. The same is true of Hans Bachem, a major character in Heinrich Böll's unpublished first novel *Kreuz ohne Liebe* (Cross Without Love, written in 1946–1947 but not published until 2002), who, in contrast to his pious mother and brother, becomes a Nazi and realizes only too late the extent of the guilt he has heaped upon himself.[30] And even in Aichinger's *Die grössere Hoffnung,* in which children are generally seen as not sharing the guilt of adults, there is a band of Hitler Youth children who torment and persecute the Jewish and "half-Jewish" children around the heroine Ellen, and who thus heap upon themselves the same guilt as many adults.

In a controversial 1946 article in *Aufbau,* the writer Manfred Hausmann (born in 1898) described the situation of postwar youth in profoundly negative terms. Far from being plagued by skepticism and doubt, Hausmann claimed, German youth were still scarred by their fanatical devotion to Nazism. "When was youth ever so unconditionally trusting, credulous, and obedient as in the Third Reich?" Hausmann asked. "Never before anywhere in the world. And what became of it? Death, dismemberment, starvation, imprisonment, hopelessness, impotence, and despair."[31] Virtually everyone in Germany, especially Germany's youth, Hausmann argued, had been struck by "an uncanny disease" in 1933, the year of Hitler's rise to power. "People did not want to think any more, they simply wanted to believe with their eyes closed and obey." As much as Germans in the older generation were to blame for this uncanny disease, however, German youth also bore a terrible burden of guilt, because they had thrown away their moral independence. "German youth surrendered passively and thoughtlessly to the temptations and threats of those obsessed with power. In spite of all the justifications that can doubtlessly be brought forward, this was their fault," Hausmann declared.[32] Moreover, even after the end of the Hitler dictatorship in 1945 German youth were still demonstrating their inability to recognize the profound depth of their moral failure. Instead of admitting their mistakes, young people no longer wanted to hear about the problems of the past. It was, suggested Hausmann, a strange paradox that the same youth who had demonstrated such perverse bravery in fighting for the Nazis now showed a pathetic lack of courage in facing the moral and spiritual problems of the present. "Up to the present moment, German youth have still apparently not discovered themselves," the writer insisted. "Today it looks as if they were lacking in courage."[33] Kolbenhoff's novel about the fanatical Werwolf Hans and Hausmann's article about the postwar situation of German youth — both appeared in 1946 — pointed in the same direction, suggesting that German youth were still profoundly under the influence of Nazism and had not recognized the moral possibilities arising from the German defeat.

In a blistering response to Hausmann that clearly demonstrated the difficulties of communication between the older and younger generations after the war, Rolf Pabst acknowledged that a great many young people had blindly followed the Nazis on the path to catastrophe, but he insisted that "one can't place the blame for this on youth," since the young people of the immediate postwar period had not even reached their second decade of life when Hitler came to power in 1933. This generation simply "believed . . . what it was told was true, it learned nothing else and therefore was unable to form its own opinion," Pabst insisted. "The guilty ones," he argued, "can be found among those who failed so miserably in 1933," a generation of older people who had neglected to set a good example for the children entrusted to them. Alas, Pabst noted, Hausmann himself had participated in this failure: in 1940 he had published a letter celebrating war as the apotheosis of human game-playing. "Now perhaps you will understand, Herr Dr. Hausmann," Pabst wrote, "that for all these reasons I cannot grant you the right to suck up to youth today and try to pass out good advice. In 1940 you proclaimed to youth that war liberated, and today you dare to condemn the very same youth for having fought."[34]

Pabst was not the only spokesperson for youth who resented advice, however well-meant, from the older generation. In an article published in the *Süddeutsche Zeitung* in February of 1946 the twenty-five-year-old essayist Anna Ozana complained: "In the recent past there has been so much nauseating sermonizing going on that we are now alienated by the didactic, pseudo-democratic moralizing tone of the licensed pedagogues."[35] Such complaints sometimes met with understanding among older writers. In a response to Ozana, Wilhelm Emanuel Süskind admitted that "we licensed sermonizers simply could not keep ourselves from preaching, imploring, and demanding," and at the same time he acknowledged "that it is nonsense for us now to approach youth with a ceaseless 'Thou shalt.'" While it was true,

Süskind believed, that German youth were the "educational product of National Socialism," it was also true that this generation had long since ceased believing in Nazi ideology.[36] Like Süskind, many older Germans had great sympathy with the situation of German youth. Elisabeth Bamberger, head of the municipal office for youth in Munich, declared in 1946 that the spiritual problems of German youth were far greater than their material needs. After years of Nazi brainwashing young people now stood alone, without role models and ideals. "The values hammered into them for twelve years have proved themselves to be false," Bamberger noted. "The gods whom they had to worship for twelve years are dead. The ideals in which they believed for twelve years lie shattered on the ground." In what sounded like a response to Hausmann's criticisms of an all-too-gullible youth, Bamberger asked: "But who wants to blame youth for being credulous?"[37]

In a 1946 article in the *Deutsche Rundschau*, Rudolf Pechel agreed that "the question of German youth" was "the most difficult problem that we have . . . to solve," but he insisted that it was pointless and unfair "to blame youth for its mistakes."[38] German youth had honestly believed in the ideals preached to them by the Nazis, Pechel argued. Intellectually and spiritually, Pechel believed, postwar German youth were faced with a landscape of ruins just as desolate as the physical landscape of Germany's devastated cities. All the values that German young people had learned in childhood were now discredited; and their previous good-faith service to those ideals was now suddenly declared to have been a crime. It was not scolding and preaching that German youth needed, Pechel believed, but rather understanding and help. Today's youth was "a lost jumble of shot-up cripples, the spiritually broken, the tired, disappointed, and embittered."[39] It was true that there were still "spiritual Werwolf nests" among the ranks of German youth, but it should be left to youth itself to eliminate those nests.[40] While postwar politics and culture were still largely dominated by older figures like Pechel himself, the journalist concluded, most older intellectuals longed in their hearts to hand over the reins of power as soon as possible to a wiser and more mature youth.

Although Zuckmayer's play *Des Teufels General* does not directly address the problems of youth in the postwar period, it touches critically on the situation of youth in Nazi Germany. *Des Teufels General,* one of the most popular plays of the postwar period, was performed 2069 times in Germany in the 1948/1949 season alone — and this in spite of the fact that it was banned in the Soviet zone due to its supposedly sympathetic portrait of a Wehrmacht officer.[41] Two of the play's major figures are indoctrinated young people: the air force officer Hartmann and his erstwhile girlfriend Waltraut von Mohrungen, nicknamed Pützchen, the daughter of a German industrialist. In a conversation with air force general Harras, the play's eponymous protagonist, Hartmann describes his childhood as that of a half-orphan alienated from his mother and ultimately saved from isolation by the Nazis.

He had been homeless, he declares, "until I came to the Hitler Youth. My home was the training camp. The citadel of the order."[42] In a society in which parental authority had disappeared or been discredited, the National Socialist Party and its youth organizations took on the role of primary adult care-giver, supplying role models and camaraderie. Pützchen, too, is presented as a child essentially reared not by her widower father but by the Nazis. Pützchen's father admits that after his wife's death he had little time to take care of his wayward daughter, implying that her sexual and moral looseness are a result of unhealthy Nazi influences.[43]

For both Pützchen and Hartmann, Nazi youth organizations have replaced the missing same-sex parent. Hartmann ultimately recognizes the true nature of Nazi tyranny when, during a military action in the Polish city of Lodz, he observes his comrades shooting innocent civilians; as an honorable soldier, he realizes that atrocities of this sort have "nothing to do with war any more," and he therefore comes to understand that previously unbelievable rumors about Nazi crimes are based on fact. Hartmann's non-Nazi commanding officer, General Harras, is ultimately able to displace the Nazis as Hartmann's chief source of paternal authority; at the end of the play the wounded Hartmann returns to Harras and acknowledges that the older man's criticisms of the Nazis, which he had previously rejected, had been entirely correct. However Hartmann's former girlfriend Pützchen is presented as irretrievably lost: when her attempts to seduce General Harras fail, she threatens to expose him as sympathetic to Jews and antifascists. She is the epitome of the indoctrinated, amoral, unredeemed Nazi young person.

Zuckmayer participated in many public discussions of his play in 1947 and 1948, particularly with German young people. In June of 1947 students in Switzerland met with students from Germany to discuss the play after a performance in Zurich; their discussions showed that they clearly recognized the parallels between Zuckmayer's figure Hartmann and postwar German youth. For the Swiss student Willfried Rohr, "Hartmann is the embodiment of the German youth of our time."[44] During the same discussion a German student named Wolfgang Lindner declared that "at least German youth are trying to find a new path. We see with open eyes the mistakes and crimes of our nation's past."[45]

After witnessing the discussions between Swiss and German students following the presentation of Zuckmayer's play in Zurich, Erich Kästner wrote in Munich's *Neue Zeitung* that such discussions filled him with hope for the future and led him to doubt the most pessimistic assessments of contemporary German youth: "If young Germans who were trained like animals from childhood on in the cage of the dictatorship can today participate with such distinction in a group of students educated in freedom, then the dreaded thesis that twelve years were enough to spiritually and morally castrate Germany's youth simply cannot be true!"[46] Partially in response to such reactions, Zuckmayer himself wrote that he had intended the figure of Hartmann as "a ray of light in this darkened world," and that without such a representative of hope he would have been incapable of writing the play. His postwar experiences with German youth had taught him, he claimed, that his fictional character Hartmann had a great deal to do with postwar German reality: "Today I know that he existed and still exists, and that he is identical to a large part of German youth," the playwright declared in the pages of *Die Wandlung* in 1948.[47] German reality was thus, in his opinion, imitating dramatic art.

Like *Des Teufels General,* Plievier's *Stalingrad* is full of references to the moral indoctrination of youth by the Nazi party. To a great extent the Sixth German Army surrounded and trapped by the Soviet Red Army at Stalingrad is composed of young men who, like Zuckmayer's Hartmann, have been brainwashed by the Nazis. Some of these young men are ultimately able to free themselves from such mind control; others remain trapped in a Nazi worldview; and all must suffer as a consequence of their participation in an immoral war. Particularly representative of misguided youth is Lieutenant Wedderkop, a young man who from the very beginning had been brainwashed to think like a Nazi: "as a stripling in camp he had read the inscription: WE ARE BORN TO DIE."[48] By the end of Plievier's novel, Wedderkop, like so many other thousands of young men at Stalingrad, has paid the ultimate price — already foretold by the camp slogan that was part of his childhood indoctrination — for his fanatical Nazism. He is summarily shot by a member of his own army for stealing food from fellow soldiers. Such a miserable death is hardly the glorious martyrdom of Nazi mythology. Plievier's depiction of the catastrophe of the German Wehrmacht at Stalingrad suggests that the situation of German youth in 1945 is anything but the triumph of a younger generation over its elders. German youth were not just fresh-faced and idealistic Hitler Youth boys but also members of an army that had covered itself with shame in the occupation of foreign countries and the mistreatment of foreign populations — "tens of thousands, hundreds of thousands of victims in two or three thousand kilometers of countryside they had driven through," as Plievier puts it.[49] In spite of the multiple crimes against civilians they have witnessed — and in many cases committed — most of these soldiers fail to draw self-critical moral consequences; their devotion to an evil cause leads them into catastrophe and defeat.

Wolfgang Borchert's 1947 play *Draußen vor der Tür* (The Man Outside) — by far the most popular and influential dramatic work by a young German nonemigrant in the immediate postwar period — depicts the difficult position of the younger generation in Germany after the end of the war in a less stringent, if equally depressing way. Borchert himself was only twenty-six when he wrote the play and therefore a member of the younger generation about which he was writing. Like Borchert himself, the play's chief figure

Beckmann is a young German soldier who returns to Hamburg after the war's end only to find that there is no one waiting for him, and that he must therefore remain indefinitely on the margins, a man who belongs nowhere. Postwar Hamburg in Borchert's play is governed not by the younger generation represented by Beckmann but by such figures as Beckmann's former colonel, who had ordered a military action that led to the decimation of Beckmann's unit during the war, but who now plays the role of bourgeois family man; and a cabaret director who — although he invokes the need for a hard-nosed, realistic youth — turns Beckmann away because of his all-too realistic poetic depiction of the lost war. "You see, the field of Art is just where youth's needed again, a youth that takes its stand in all problems. A courageous, sober," even a "revolutionary youth," declares the director hypocritically; but he means the opposite of what he says.[50] At the end of the play, shortly before he presumably commits suicide by throwing himself into the Elbe River, Beckmann paints a picture of himself and his entire generation as victims of an older generation that has once again taken control and shown no mercy for the young people whom it has betrayed. When his generation became old enough to fight, Beckmann cries, "they thought out a war for us too. And they packed us off to it." Without questioning the responsibility of young people themselves in allowing the war to happen and actively contributing to it, Beckmann ascribes blame solely to the older generation:

> And at last came the war. And they packed us off to it. And they said to us — Make a job of it, boys! They said. Make a job of it, boys. That's how they betrayed us. Yes, betrayed us. And now they're sitting behind their doors. The Professor, the Director, the Judge, the Doctor. No one's packed us off this time. No, no one. They're all sitting behind their doors and the doors are firmly shut. And we're outside. And from their pulpits and their armchairs they point their fingers at us. That's how they've betrayed us. Betrayed us terribly. And now they ignore their murder, simply ignore it. They ignore the murder they've committed.[51]

The mention of an older generation sitting comfortably in armchairs and pointing its fingers at a guilty younger generation was possibly a reference to critiques of the kind Manfred Hausmann had published a year earlier in *Aufbau*. As understandable as Borchert's resentment against such criticisms was, however, his depiction of victimized young German men was problematic, because it removed from youthful soldiers any personal responsibility for their own fate and ignored the tremendous enthusiasm of many German young people for the Nazi party. In direct contrast to Plievier in *Stalingrad* and to Zuckmayer in *Des Teufels General*, Borchert made no mention of the many murders committed by German soldiers in foreign countries; instead, in Borchert's melodramatic and self-pitying view it was German soldiers themselves who were victims of the barbarous war they fought, and of the older generation which made them fight. The murder to which Beckmann refers in the last line of the passage is not the killing of civilian Russians, Poles, or Jews. Rather, it is the death in war of German soldiers, specifically eleven men in Beckmann's troop for whom he considers himself responsible. What his men were doing in Russia in the first place and why Beckmann chose to obey the colonel whose order he so resents is never discussed; and the crimes that may or may not have been committed by Beckmann and his soldiers against Russian civilians are left unmentioned, as if the only deaths that really matter for Beckmann are those of German soldiers. In spite of his attempt to foist responsibility off onto his commanding officer, Beckmann is haunted by a sense of guilt that prevents him from sleeping at night. The language of Borchert's play suggested the frustration of young men who lost an immoral war and returned home to find the chief positions in society already occupied by their elders; but the same language also suggested young people's profound unwillingness to accept individual responsibility, let alone guilt. Borchert's words incriminated an older generation for Nazi crimes — even though the only crimes mentioned in the play were crimes against German youth — and suggested that youth, far from sharing part of the responsibility for those crimes, were in fact the primary victim of those crimes. Borchert's understanding of guilt was, hence, far removed from Hausmann's declaration that "guilt always remains guilt," no matter who else or what else may also be depicted as sharing responsibility.[52] The fact that the older generation participated equally or even more in German guilt did not relieve the younger generation from its burden of guilt, and vice versa. However, much of the intergenerational debate that occurred in the wake of 1945 can be understood as an attempt on the part of the younger generation to assign blame to its elders, thus exculpating itself. Indeed, it is in precisely this context that Gruppe 47, later understood as the champion of a zero hour, got its start.

Hans Werner Richter, the founder of Gruppe 47, published an anthology of poems by German veterans in 1947, the year that saw the end of Richter's and Andersch's editorship of the journal *Der Ruf* and the subsequent beginning of Gruppe 47, as well as the premiere of Borchert's play. Many of the poems in this anthology employ self-exculpating rhetorical tropes similar to those used by Borchert. For instance in a poem entitled "Deutsches Soldatenlied" (Song of the German Soldier) one veteran writing under the pseudonym "Vitalis" proclaims:

> They say we are a disgrace,
> we're in the black book of the human race
> for the damage and the bloody dawns
> we inflicted! They say we must atone:
> In the book of guilt we stand alone —
> *But we were only soldiers, only pawns!*

Although "Vitalis" explicitly admits that "we" soldiers inflicted "damage" on other peoples, he disclaims all responsibility, because "no one asks soldiers," and "we were only slaves."[53] Like Borchert's Beckmann, the poet fails to ask why soldiers allowed themselves to be mistreated and made into slaves, and why they obeyed the orders of their tormentors. He bemoans the "armies of millions of dead," but does not ask why German soldiers were apparently willing to sacrifice their lives for a political system they supposedly hated rather than for the freedom and decency they supposedly longed for. The poet concludes:

> Together with our nation we
> suffer hunger, scorn, and infamy.
> We're summoned as the day of judgment dawns
> and silently, with patience we
> bear the debts, but not the guilt, you see!
> We were only soldiers, only pawns.[54]

Such self-exculpation was intolerable to many both inside and outside Germany. In an open letter to a German student published in 1946, the Swiss writer Ernst von Schenck reminded young German men of their own responsibility in helping Hitler to prosecute the Second World War. Even many young Germans who rejected Nazism had, von Schenck believed, made themselves culpable by allowing themselves to be used as Hitler's tools: "All of you who did not want to know anything about Nazism, or who wanted to know very little about it, were nevertheless among the followers of your fanatical former school comrades," he argued. It may have been true that many individual German young people had, in their own minds, distanced themselves from Nazi ideology, von Schenck acknowledged,

> But still you fought the battles of National Socialism. It was you who were the heroes of Warsaw, Narvik, and Flanders, of Tobruk and Moscow. You marched through the world as the victorious bearers of the swastika. With you the Nazis attacked one country after another, and even after the world had long since recognized how hopeless it was, it was you who, with unprecedented bravery and horrific casualties, lost one battle after another against an enemy who was becoming more overpowering with each passing day.

Indeed, von Schenck concluded, in some ways the heroic bravery of Germany's non-Nazi youth was even more terrible than "the loud proclamations of the fanatical Hitler youths," because it was a heroism without belief or conviction.[55] In sum, von Schenck noted, German youth had been trained from childhood on to shut themselves off from the wellsprings of their own individuality; as a result they had become rigid conformists.

In spite of such warnings from inside and outside Germany, many of the writings of the postwar younger generation betray an unwillingness to accept personal responsibility, an unwillingness similar to that of Borchert and "Vitalis," suggesting that Hausmann was at least partially right in his criticisms of German youth. In a poem entitled "Jugend der Städte" (Youth of the Cities), read at a meeting of the nascent Gruppe 47 during a conference near Ulm in 1947, Wolfgang Bächler described the situation of the German youth for whom Gruppe 47 considered itself to be the forum as one of helplessness and lack of volition:

> Over life's raging fires
> We stand, sane or insane,
> Listening to hear if our sires
> Fathered us in vain.
>
> We've smelled the blood,
> The sweat of fear, the ire.
> Our bridges lie in the mud,
> In the sluggish, rotting mire.
>
> Chimneys point askew
> Into the tattered gray.
> Only the vultures stay
> In an unmarred blue.
>
> The windows are broken
> Through which we looked at life.
> The buildings built for us
> Were torn down in all the strife.
>
> Our world is a creation
> Out of which darkness spreads.
> Over the rubble desperation
> weaves its air-tight threads.[56]

This poem describes a landscape of devastation, but it never identifies who is responsible for the destruction. Who destroyed the bridges and the chimneys, why are the windows broken, and why have houses been torn down? Youth — the poem's "we" — is presented as a passive victim seemingly free from responsibility for its own situation. The only verbs associated with youth are "stand," "listen," "smell," and "look at," suggesting that youth is helpless to do anything but observe. It is the "sires" who have brought "us" into existence, probably "in vain, and "we" are simply observers, peering into the ruins of the cities. All that youth can do is "stand" and "listen"; who actually destroyed the cities or the windows, and why, remains unclear;

youth itself seems to have done nothing. This was a far cry from Plievier's devastating depiction of German youth at Stalingrad.

Not surprisingly, it was generally members of the older generation, such as Hausmann and Zuckmayer, who were more clearly able to recognize the morally precarious situation of German youth in the postwar years. However, older people's greater willingness to understand the true ethical situation of German youth only increased the perceived gap between the two generations. Given the extent to which the discussion around youth in the postwar period involved members of the older generation discussing — "with the self-assurance of professors," as the annoyed Hans Werner Richter put it — the future of a presumably endangered younger generation deprived, in Richter's words, of "all spiritual and moral capacities," it is perhaps not surprising that some members of the younger generation, including Richter himself, responded in anger to such concerns.[57] Two years after Wiechert's 1945 "Rede an die deutsche Jugend," on the occasion of the writer's sixtieth birthday, the older writer received a nasty answer in the form of "The First and Only Speech of German Youth to Their Poet," published in *Der Ruf* by Erich Kuby, born in 1910. Claiming to speak for Germany's younger generation against Wiechert and the older generation he represented, the thirty-seven-year-old Kuby denounced what he saw as the older generation's hypocrisy, implying that the essence of the postwar German generation gap was the opposition between elderly mendacity and youthful honesty. "That a God allowed you to speak about sufferings you never experienced is your own affair," Kuby declared. "But that you dare to speak about our suffering moves us to this disclaimer. Can't you finally keep your promise and leave us out of it?"[58] With reference to a man who had spent two months in Buchenwald, Kuby's reference to "sufferings you never experienced" was impertinent and unfeeling. Like so many other German writers of the self-described younger generation, Kuby seemed determined, regardless of facts, to portray German youth as the victim of domineering old age. Like so many other self-conscious interventions by younger German writers in the postwar years, Kuby's language suggested an unwillingness to accept moral responsibility; speaking only about "our suffering," he remained silent about the suffering of anyone else, and he once again presented youth as a passive victim of the older generation. Kolbenhoff was less offensive but equally dismissive when he allowed the main character of his novel *Heimkehr in die Fremde* to ruminate, after reading an article by Wiechert: "You are too educated, Mr. Poet, you don't speak our language. Your article doesn't speak to us, because the fate you're talking about isn't our fate."[59]

General concern for the situation of youth in postwar Germany and the postwar world culminated in an international youth conference that took place in Munich at the end of June 1947. In a speech at that conference the French writer André Gide declared that during the Nazi dictatorship German youth had "suffered under a superiority complex" and "made other people suffer under it as well." But in the period after the war's end, Gide argued, it was important for German youth not to make the opposite mistake and fall prey to an inferiority complex. As someone old enough to have experienced both world wars, Gide proclaimed:

> The war of 1914 did not have the unsettling consequences we are registering today. Then, there was not really a break with the past. Now the bond between the generation coming and the generation going appears to be broken. Young people today are burning bridges behind them and refusing to take the hand reached out to them by their elders.[60]

Erich Kästner compared the gap between young and old people in Germany to the Great Wall of China, suggesting that "this line of separation is unquestionably of decisive significance."[61] In a satirical poem written in 1946 and performed in a Munich cabaret, Kästner poked fun at the postwar German generation gap and especially at older people's obsession with the problem of youth. The very title of the poem, "Die Jugend hat das Wort" ("Youth Are Allowed to Speak") responds to a situation in which youth are talked about a great deal but do not have the opportunity to speak for themselves.

> We have youth. You have age.
> You stand on the sidelines and give advice.
> With fingers pointed and words that are sage,
> You show us how to make the future nice.

Kästner's poem also makes fun of the speed with which the older generation is perceived to have changed its ideological orientation:

> Your advice is always in season.
> A year ago you were still screaming "Heil!"
> We are amazed that you now preach reason,
> Just as before you were preaching bile.

Moreover, Kästner suggests that the older generation bears much greater responsibility for German guilt than the younger generation:

> We grew up in your cage.
> Along with your cult we grew stronger.
> We have youth. You have age.
> Those with age are blamed for longer.[62]

As accurately as he located many of the problems of postwar German discourse on youth, Kästner here clearly demonstrated his problematic belief that the younger generation was, unlike the older generation, largely free of blame. In his words, the younger generation was still essentially a victim of the older generation, trained like dogs to respond to commands and with no more guilt than a trained animal would have. As he had written in response to *Des Teufels General,* Kästner simply did not want to believe "that twelve years were enough to spiritually and morally castrate Germany's youth." But this refusal to believe was perhaps more wishful thinking than hard-headed realism.

Expressions of protest against a perceived takeover by the older generation at the expense of the younger generation became increasingly frequent by 1947 and 1948, when the cold war confrontation between East and West helped to strengthen a restoration of traditional political forces in both the eastern and western occupation zones. As Heinz Friedrich was to write in his heroic recollections a decade and a half later, "by the year 1947 the battle of youth for a spiritual and political new dispensation in our shaken-up postwar world was already lost."[63] It was to a great extent the frustration with a perceived restoration of traditional privileges that led members of the self-proclaimed younger generation of writers such as Richter and Andersch to insist, during the first postwar years, on a complete break with the past and with what they identified as the older generation. Richter and Andersch, both former members of the German Wehrmacht, had spent time as prisoners of war in the United States, where they had worked on the prisoner-of-war journal *Der Ruf.*[64] After their return to Germany in 1946, they were entrusted with the editorship of a Munich journal with the same title — *Der Ruf: Unabhängige Blätter der Jungen Generation* (The Call: Independent Journal of the Young Generation) — and this journal became an important forum for public opinion in the immediate postwar period. Not only Richter and Andersch but also Friedrich Minssen, Karl Krolow, Walter Kolbenhoff, Erich Kuby, and Gustav René Hocke, among others, published in *Der Ruf.* It was largely in these younger writers' polemical insistence on a complete break with the past that the concept of a zero hour was subsequently located by literary historians. However in the immediate aftermath of the war such declarations were governed not by a triumphant conviction that the older generation was finished and that the younger generation would control the German future but, rather, by the fear that no real break with the past had taken place, and that, on the contrary, traditional privileges and elites had largely been restored. Many of Richter's and Andersch's zero hour declarations can be understood as literary-political attempts by a younger generation symbolically to kill an older generation and thus to escape from what Harold Bloom has called the "anxiety of influence."[65] In their championship of a younger generation, Richter and Andersch were frequently just as blind as any of their peers to the moral problems of youth raised by older writers such as Hausmann, Plievier, Wiechert, and Mann. While it would probably be unfair to call *Der Ruf* "a positive glossary and index of Fascist language," as W. G. Sebald has done, its editors were no more immune to the problems of the German past than many of their targets in the older generation.[66] As Karl Korn put it in a generally positive early review of *Der Ruf* in 1946, its editors, themselves former German soldiers, were in danger of creating a new "myth of the warriors at the front," ignoring the problem of German political and moral responsibility and causing an unproductive break between a supposedly guilty older generation and a supposedly innocent younger generation.[67] In the immediate postwar period the fatal history of German acquiescence in Nazi crimes may have given this younger generation a potentially powerful weapon to use against the older generation; but the use of that weapon meant that the younger generation had to view itself as guilt-free.

Der Ruf was full of declarations by self-styled representatives of the younger generation — although in fact most of the contributors were already well into their thirties — decrying the bankruptcy of the older generation and of the entire German cultural tradition. "Our hatred, the hatred of the younger generation, has the justification of unconditional necessity," declared Andersch during the Nuremberg Trials in 1946, trying to separate himself and the younger generation for which he claimed to speak from the crimes being prosecuted at Nuremberg.[68] "The fighters of Stalingrad, El Alamein, and Cassino, who were well respected by their opponents, are innocent of the crimes of Dachau and Buchenwald," Andersch insisted.[69] Andersch's picture of Stalingrad was clearly more forgiving than that of Plievier, from whom one could hardly imagine a description of the hundreds of thousands of German soldiers senselessly obeying absurd orders in the doomed Volga encampment as somehow nevertheless "well respected" by their Russian opponents. For Andersch, it was the Nazis in the older generation who had misused German youth and the entire German people as a weapon in their dirty war. Hence the younger generation needed to make a total break from the corruption of its elders.

Declarations such as Andersch's have come to be seen as part of a literary-political zero hour associated with *Der Ruf* and the loose association of writers called Gruppe 47 centered around and called into being by Richter after he and Andersch had been removed from the editorship of *Der Ruf* — partly at the behest of the same American occupation authorities of whom Richter and Andersch had been critical, and partly because of differences of opinion between the two editors and their publishing company — in the spring of 1947.[70] Among the most famous of these declarations of the moral bankruptcy of an older generation was Richter's own 1946 juxtaposition of a corrupt but all too voluble older generation with a morally intact but silent younger generation. "Rarely in the history of any country . . . has such a spiritual gap between two generations opened up as now in Germany," wrote Richter.[71] While the older generation sought to disguise the enormity of the destruction that has taken place, Richter argued, "even the prettiest professorial speeches cannot close our eyes to the continuing disintegration of a well-ordered human picture."[72] In the meantime, the younger generation must "now silently allow itself to be inundated by a never-ending flood of well-meaning speeches."[73] Admitting that his younger generation was as yet relatively silent, Richter wrote:

> Yes, this generation is silent, but it is silent not because it is without a clue, it is silent not because it has nothing to say or can not find the words that are necessary in order to say what has to be said. It is silent because it has the definite feeling that the discrepancy between a human existence that is threatened and the comfortable problems of the older generation that has emerged from its Olympian silence after twelve years is too big to be bridged. It knows that the image of human existence that the older generation inherited from its forefathers and which it would now like to erect again can no longer be built. It knows that this image is permanently destroyed.[74]

This was a remarkably loquacious declaration of silence. Richter's specific claim that the purported silence of the younger generation was *not* a result of having nothing to say or being "clueless" suggested precisely the opposite: that in fact the younger generation was without a spiritual compass and unable to say anything meaningful about the situation in which it found itself. Moreover, Richter's insistence that the world of yesterday could "no longer be built" belied an underlying but unspoken fear that, on the contrary, older structures were indeed rapidly being rebuilt, leaving the self-styled spokesmen of the younger generation powerless and frustrated. Of course the younger generation was not alone in its inability to understand the current situation. But in his declarations about a praiseworthy silence, Richter was probably trying to make a virtue out of an unpleasant necessity. He painted a picture of a profound break in the cultural tradition that precisely described the most radical vision of a zero hour:

> Faced with the smoke-blackened picture of this European landscape of ruins, in which human beings wander aimlessly, cut loose from all outdated bonds, the value systems of the past turn pale and lifeless. Any possibility of connecting up with what went before, any attempt to begin again where the older generation left its continuous developmental path in 1933 in order to surrender to an irrational adventure, seems paradoxical in the face of this European picture.[75]

Like so many other self-styled representatives of the younger generation, Richter was careful to separate youth from any guilt for the "irrational adventure" that had begun in 1933; he associated this catastrophe exclusively with "the older generation." The writer concluded:

> Because of the dislocation of life, because of the violence of the experiences that have become a part of and that have shaken the younger

generation, this generation believes that the only possible source for a spiritual rebirth lies in an absolute and radical new beginning.[76]

While Richter's words were noteworthy for the radicality of their intention to break with tradition, the writer made no attempt to describe precisely how such a break could be accomplished, let alone to address the question of whether a beginning *ex nihilo* was humanly possible or even desirable. For all his intention to break with the older generation and with tradition, Richter's vision of a radical new beginning was not substantively different from Wiechert's noble but vague 1945 address to German youth, in which the older writer had also urged: "Let us make a new beginning, mark a new borderstone for a new field."[77] Paradoxically, Richter's 1946 call for a radical new beginning was already itself outdated; a fifty-eight-year-old had beaten him to the starting gate.

Two weeks earlier, in the programmatic essay with which he inaugurated the first issue of *Der Ruf* in the middle of August, 1946, Andersch had suggested that the protagonists of what he saw as "this reawakening of Europe" were generally young, unknown people like the existentialists in France and independent writers like himself in Germany.[78] These young people, Andersch believed, were governed by "a new humanism that departs from all tradition."[79] In Germany, Andersch believed, former members of the Hitler Youth could form a coalition with the former inmates of German concentration camps in the struggle against "the thinking of the older generation, which, in the weakness of its conception of tolerance, and in its fear of making the ultimate sacrifice, paved the monster's path to power."[80] Such language suggested that the primary reason for Hitler's rise to power had been the humanist cowardice of an older generation. In spite of that older generation, Andersch believed, "a new, virginal Athenian spirit with the freshness of youth" was spreading over Europe, just as the Greek goddess of wisdom had sprung full-grown from the head of Zeus in Greek mythology.[81] The new Europe could not survive without the new Germany, Andersch averred, and the new Germany would be created by a younger generation without help either from its elders or the conquerors of Germany. The slogan of this younger generation was: "The educators must be overtaken."[82]

In October of 1946 Richter suggested that the destruction of Germany during the war might well have been a paradoxical blessing, because it had eliminated "all the ballast of the past" which still burdened other countries.

In Germany all of that has been smashed. Germany has neither a state nor an economic order. The younger generation can make a new beginning, starting off from the point toward which developments are now leading. The younger generation does not need to make renovations. It can build new things.[83]

Given Goebbels's Nazi celebrations of destruction and Holthusen's negative poetic view of the German "tabula rasa" only a year earlier, such words were highly problematic, betraying a lack of awareness of the many cultural problems associated with massive destruction and radical new beginnings. In view of the Nazis' repeated insistence that it was they who were breaking with the outdated past and creating a new epoch, such statements were also paradoxical as demonstrations of a will to break with Nazism. As Urs Widmer wrote two decades later in his critique of postwar zero hour rhetoric, "twelve years of cliché language seem to be a heavy burden on the young journalists. They are unable to free themselves from the nebulous ideas that the 'Third Reich' had created." Indeed, Widmer claimed, "they continue to write in the same diffuse style — it is only the pluses and minuses that have changed."[84] The members of the younger generation after 1945 seemed unable to understand that the very desire for a complete break with the past had itself become historically problematic in view of Nazi insistence on youth and newness. In Zuckmayer's *Des Teufels General* the younger man finally learns to understand the older man's skepticism. But neither Richter nor Andersch seemed to have absorbed such skepticism into their postwar writings.

Richter's and Andersch's use of words such as "compulsion" and "necessity" suggests that the much-ballyhooed new beginning was not just a question of volition; rather, it was felt to be an assignment. The renewal of German intellectual life and the original act of creation appeared more as unpleasant necessities than as longed-for events. As Erich Kuby — who replaced Andersch and Richter as editor of *Der Ruf* in 1947 — said in his belated reply to the older writer Wiechert, "We did not choose to live in this era. We have to deal with it as we have found it."[85] The emphasis was on an undesirable situation that the younger generation was forced to deal with against its will. While younger writers proclaimed their belief that the older generation would be no help in creating a new German culture, the contours of their own desires remained nebulous and vague. At the same time, Richter's and Andersch's insistence on the necessity of a new beginning suggested their fear that such a beginning was not, in fact, taking place in the postwar years.

It was probably because of Richter's and Andersch's harsh criticism of the United States and the Soviet Union and their often soldierly glorifications of Germany as predestined to mediate between East and West that the U.S. military government ultimately cancelled Richter's and Andersch's permit to publish *Der Ruf,* a step which then led to Richter's invitation to German writers to meet with him at the Bannwaldsee in Bavaria in September of 1947. This meeting went down in literary history as the birth of Gruppe 47. Hans Magnus Enzensberger was later to call Gruppe 47 "the central café of a literature without a capital city."[86] Over the course of its two decades of existence Gruppe 47 was to attract not only Richter and Andersch but also Enzensberger, Peter Rühmkorf, Hans Mayer, Marcel Reich-Ranicki, Ingeborg Bachmann, Günter Grass, Heinrich Böll, Martin Walser, and many others who were to help determine the direction of postwar culture in the German-speaking countries of Europe for decades to come.

In raising the question of literary politics, writers for *Der Ruf,* like so many others, harked back to the debate about exile and inner emigration that had taken place in the second half of 1945. Gustav René Hocke and others developed a critique of what they perceived as an ongoing inner emigration which sought to avoid political concreteness in literature. Hocke argued that even if a literary flight from political reality had been justified during the years of the Hitler dictatorship, such escapism was by no means desirable in the relatively free conditions of the postwar period.[87] For Hocke, much of postwar German literature was growing in a "subtropical hothouse climate" separated from cold, hard reality.[88] In its flights of fancy the literature of the older generation in Germany avoided simple, direct statements, he believed, declaring:

> We are groping our way through a fearsome thicket of loquacious sentences, which usually lack two things: clarity of form and immediacy of message. One encounters a bizarre craftsmanship characterized by the ability to create marginally or completely useless things with brilliant means.[89]

Such literature did not really try to *say* anything; it simply tried to be beautiful. With reference to a turn-of-the-century Italian literary movement, Hocke identified such writers as "calligrafisti" or calligraphers, meaning that they sought only beauty and not truth; much of postwar German literature, he argued, was "deutsche Kalligraphie" (German calligraphy). In contrast to the "calligraphers" of the older generation, the younger generation preferred simple, direct realism, Hocke argued. Young writers tended to view the aesthetic complexity of the "calligraphers" as "simulated profundity," and they were determined to confront the "social and psychological reality of today" directly.[90] Although Hocke admitted that German literary production was still largely dominated by the "calligraphy" of an older generation, he asserted that in journals like *Der Ruf* the younger generation was already beginning to create new, starkly realistic literary forms, especially journalistic reports on journeys through Germany. Through such reports reality was once again being won back for literature: "in rubble one discovers the first new laws of the sociological and psychological reality of today, above all the clarity and simplicity of suffering, and the multiplicity of reactions to it."[91]

Such simple, concrete reports on life in postwar Germany, with all its blemishes and piles of rubble (Trümmer) led to the mocking designation of such literature as "Trümmerliteratur" (rubble literature). But for Hocke the refusal of many younger writers to paint a more beautiful picture of postwar Germany, far from being an aesthetic weakness, was in fact a moral strength, because such writers were presenting a true picture of a Germany that lay in ruins. As Richter had argued at the beginning of September 1946, it was important for Germans' perception of the world to correspond to the reality of a landscape "whose profile is marked by the ruins and rubble of the great cities."[92] Hocke was insisting on the validity of a literature that acknowledged the need for such correspondence.

In a 1947 summary of postwar literary development published in *Der Ruf*, the writer and critic Horst Lange was even harsher in his criticisms of literary escapism, subtly associating inner emigration with the Nazi journal *Das innere Reich*. "Enchanted Seville orange trees bloomed there, wafting odors, and idyllic landscapes of the soul unfolded, full of tasteful classicism," Lange wrote mockingly, arguing that even as they sought to demonstrate their aesthetic independence through works of apolitical fancy the writers of the inner emigration had been useful marionettes for their Nazi masters:

> The official guards, who kept intellectual life in our country under their control, tolerated and promoted these idyllic poets. While the outer Reich descended ever more strongly and exclusively into barbarism, they were supposed to help cultivate the inner Reich — until marching orders took the place of hexameters, Wehrmacht reports took the place of odes, and judgments by the People's Court took the place of sonnets.[93]

The criticism that the literature of inner emigration had in fact served as a fig leaf behind which Nazi leaders were able to hide their crimes took away one of the major moral arguments of the inner emigrants: that their apolitical literature had been a necessary response to Nazi cooptation of literature. Lange was not even willing to acknowledge that the apolitical nature of the inner emigration had served a useful function during the Nazi dictatorship; for him, it had been out of place then, and it was still out of place now. Like Hocke, he argued for a straightforward, simple, unpretentious literature that acknowledged and dealt with the fundamental realities of life in postwar Germany, however difficult or unpleasant. However, Lange's argument conveniently ignored the fact that it was not just members of the older generation but also many of their young attackers, including Richter and Andersch, who had conformed during the years of the Third Reich.

The ideal of a literature that is both honest and simple became one of the themes of Kolbenhoff's *Heimkehr in die Fremde*, whose main character is a writer seeking, in the midst of postwar chaos, to create a truthful book that will give Germans a mirror in which to view the reality of their own lives. "Be honest, I thought, as I began to write, don't let yourself be bought off by pretty words. Write honestly and tell your story very simply, try to tell your story as simply as possible."[94] At the end of Kolbenhoff's novel this writer is still working on his book, in spite of loneliness and hunger: "I checked the drawer, but there was no more bread there. Then I sat down at the table and began to write."[95]

One of the most famous invocations of the new literary style favored by such representatives of the younger generation was made by the writer Wolfgang Weyrauch in an afterward to the anthology *Tausend Gramm* (One Thousand Grams), a collection of short stories by younger German writers that was published in 1949. In language reminiscent of Hocke's "fearsome thicket of loquacious sentences," Weyrauch described escapist literature as full of hothouse trees and plants. Many contemporary German writers, he believed, were lost in a literary jungle; they "are groping around and don't know what to do." In particular, Weyrauch argued, too few writers understood "that reality and literature communicate with each other."[96] The response of the younger generation to the hothouse literature of inner emigrants was a "clear-cutting in our thicket."[97] Just as the path of civilization was marked by the clearing away of dense primeval forests in order to create arable land, so younger writers today were clearing away massive stands of useless — and artificial — verbiage to make way for simplicity and functionality. The writers whom he referred to as "clear-cutters" ("Kahlschlägler"), Weyrauch argued, "begin from the beginning in language, substance, and conception."[98] Such writers "record reality. Since they do it for the sake of truth, they do not take photographs. They make X-rays. Their precision is surgical."[99] The "clear-cutters" absolutely rejected any return to German calligraphy, he insisted:

> By . . . beginning from the beginning, from the very beginning, with the addition of parts and sub-parts of the plot, with the ABC of sentences and words, with the state of anabasis, they contradict, sometimes definitively, the continuation of calligraphic . . . literature in Germany, the imposition and the calamity of a new fog among us in which the vultures and the hyenas nest and grope. And wait. Wait for our permanent dismemberment, so that they can establish their old, inhuman empire. . . .[100]

Like Lange, Weyrauch was suggesting that the calligraphers were in fact playing into the hands of the Nazis, creating a jungle of words in which wild beasts could hunt for prey. Such inhumane literature could ultimately help to create yet another political nightmare in which people preyed on other people like the animals of the jungle. And also like Lange, Weyrauch was neglecting to account for the younger generation's own previous complicity with Nazism. To continue Weyrauch's metaphor, some of the underbrush being cleared away by the "Kahlschlägler" was the evidence of their own complicity with the Nazis.

As an example of the kind of straightforward, simple literature written by the "clear-cutters," Weyrauch cited a poem by Günter Eich which, partly because of Weyrauch's attention, was later to become one of the most famous documents of a supposed literary zero hour. Weyrauch's invocation of Eich as a representative figure of the purported zero hour is undercut by a fact that Eich sought to suppress after the end of the war: that he had previously been a relatively successful author during the Third Reich, and that some of his writings had at the very least reflected National Socialist ideology.[101] For such a writer an aesthetic of stark simplicity, of mere naming, along with the attendant refusal of interpretation, was perhaps all too convenient. Eich's poem "Inventur" (Inventory, 1947), originally published in Richter's anthology of poetry by veterans, was the apparently simple listing by a soldier — perhaps, like Eich himself, a prisoner of war — of his few possessions:

> This is my cap,
> this is my greatcoat,
> and here's my shaving kit
> in its linen bag.[102]

This kind of simple listing was what Weyrauch meant when he referred to "Kahlschlag" literature as a simple addition of parts. For him such simplicity was far preferable to what he saw as the elegant refusal of hothouse literature to face up to reality. Writers like Eich, Weyrauch predicted, were paving the way for Germany's literary future. However a less charitable reading of Weyrauch's "beginning from the beginning," based on what we now know about the history of Eich and several other supposed zero-hour writers, is that they simply wanted to suppress the past, including, in the case of Eich, "his involvement with the Nazi radio and his accommodation of fascist ideology and other propagandistic aims" (Cuomo).[103]

As Weyrauch saw it, German "Kahlschlag" literature was helping to fill a gap that had come into existence in German culture as a result of Nazi barbarity. What Weyrauch called "immediate realism" was, in his view, the particular specialty of American literary modernism, with Ernest Hemingway as "the most consistent realist of immediacy."[104] Other important American realist authors he identified were John Steinbeck and Thomas Wolfe. Such writers, he believed, sought to depict human reality in simple, unadorned prose. In contrast, he believed, German authors tended to make their writing unnecessarily complex. German literature, he argued, was so full of philosophy that the real world got lost; contemporary American writers, on the other hand, were unafraid to show the world as it is. For Weyrauch, postwar German literature should follow the path already cleared by the Americans:

> To bundle reality and language, to connect both to the cataracts of the earth surrounding us, will be a hellish task for German writers and poets. The task will be easier if one considers that this, too, is a kind of restitution.[105]

The word "restitution"(Wiedergutmachung) suggests that the literary change Weyrauch favors will, in part, be a way of exorcising German wartime guilt. Weyrauch presents the development in Germany of an authentically realist literature as one path toward making up not just for literary-cultural but also for political mistakes of the past.

Although the dominant tone in West German literature throughout the last half of the 1940s and well into the 1950s continued to be set by proponents of the separation between literature and politics, the arguments of Weyrauch, Hocke, and Lange, together with the critiques of Andersch and Richter, helped to create a nascent opposing tendency. All five of these writers, however, had themselves spent the years of the Third Reich in Germany, and therefore they were, in some ways, almost as much members of the presumably apolitical inner emigration as Frank Thiess and Walter von Molo, even if they had published far less. Prefiguring some of the findings of Germanists half a century later, Weyrauch admitted this problem as early as 1948, acknowledging in an open letter to Johannes R. Becher that he had identified Hitler with Germany during the Nazi dictatorship and therefore acted against the demands of his own conscience.[106]

It would not be correct to say that Weyrauch and others from the self-appointed younger generation were the only German writers insisting on a new literary realism. In 1946 the exile Alfred Döblin had insisted that what German culture most needed was "a new realist literature that clears away the residues of the old literature of lies and repression." As Döblin hoped, such a literature would be "clear and formulated without frills"; it would be critical but not bound by any particular party program.[107] Richter and his colleagues were by no means the only writers in the western zones to address political and historical questions of vital importance to postwar Germany. But Andersch, Richter, and others used their role as self-appointed spokesmen for a younger generation to further a cautious modernization and partial politicization of literature still largely rejected by most of the major writers and inner emigrants in the western zones. As Döblin noted, much of the German literature published during the "Third Reich" had become "slack and soft," characterized by "out-of-the-way themes, distant stories." Pressured by the cultural barbarism of the Nazis, many German writers had produced "a tedious belletristic literature," and even in the freedom of the postwar period they brought "the old attitudes of pussyfooting and wretchedness with them."[108] As Döblin saw it, much of the writing of inner emigrants had in fact been "brown" (i.e., Nazi), not so much in spite of as because of its attempted escape from political significance. "But the fact that the authors are unaware of their own political nature makes neither them nor their works unpolitical."[109] It is noteworthy that younger nonconformists in the west joined not only with Döblin but also with intellectuals like Harich and Hermlin in the East to condemn a purely apolitical literature. While such condemnations did not receive widespread attention in the west during the Nuremberg interregnum, they became part and parcel of literary debates decades later.

If during the first part of the cold war politicized literature was associated with the Eastern bloc, while an apolitical literature of pure form was associated with the West, self-proclaimed nonconformists in the West, such as Hocke and Lange, insisted on a conscious synthesis of literature and politics. Just as Richter and Andersch envisioned Germany as a synthesis between Eastern socialism and Western freedom, so literary theorists like Weyrauch sought, in accordance with Sartre's precepts, to combine artistic freedom with social commitment. They wanted realistic and relevant literature, but at the same time they insisted on the value of individual freedom, and on stylistic excellence. Although literature must concern itself with human reality and therefore also with politics, Weyrauch argued, it must also remain independent and free: "No one can take from them [the literatures of the world] their autochthony." Indeed, literature can only be literature "when it is bound through the means of absolute literature."[110] Such writers insisted on realism and on a political mission for literature, but simultaneously they also insisted on an outsider status for literature not completely alien to aestheticism. Nevertheless the writers of the younger generation in the West seemed to recognize far more clearly than writers like Harich in the East what Sartre had seen as the fundamental tension between conflicting notions of freedom. As proponents of a nonconformist stance insisting on both personal freedom and social relevance, the *Kahlschlag* writers sought to steer between the opposing political and aesthetic fronts of the emerging cold war. In the literary history of postwar Germany, Weyrauch's primarily literary *Kahlschlag* came to be inextricably associated with Richter's and Andersch's insistence on a cultural-political and generational *tabula rasa*, conflating the primary areas of German culture, from politics to literature to morality, in an attempted — but failed — radical new beginning.

In 1952, well after the initial debates about postwar literary politics were over, one young member of Gruppe 47, the short story writer and novelist Heinrich Böll, defended "Trümmerliteratur" against its attackers by arguing that aesthetic solipsism was the work of the "blindman's-buff writer" ("Blindekuh-Schriftsteller") who, instead of reflecting human reality in his work, tries to create with his work a new reality. "The blindman's-buff writer sees into himself, he builds a world to suit himself," Böll wrote, claiming that the most egregious example of such writing was Hitler with his book *Mein Kampf*.[111] In suggesting this Böll was, like Lange five years earlier, clearly connecting pure aestheticism in its German incarnation with National Socialism. At the time, this viewpoint was a minority position. However given the fact that Böll was arguably to become the most influential representative of postwar West German literature, one cannot simply discard such sentiments as being out of touch with the dominant impulses of literature during the early 1950s. No matter how opportunistic or self-serving it may initially have been, the literary opposition embodied by Andersch and Richter in *Der Ruf* and, later, in Gruppe 47, did ultimately prove to be the birthplace of a more politicized approach to literature that would exercise significant influence in the coming decades, even if it remained a minority position in the late 1940s and throughout most of the 1950s. Although Richter styled his generation as heroic losers in his 1949 novel *Die Geschlagenen* (The Defeated, translated into English as *The Odds Against Us*), the defeat was not to be permanent; and the very invocation of a noble defeat helped to pave the way for victory decades later. If nothing else, these writers' futile and often self-serving calls for a radical cultural-political new beginning after the Second World War became the mythic prehistory for much of the unrest and agitation of the 1960s and 1970s, when a new younger generation insisted on a realization of the supposedly failed zero hour of 1945. "The intellect coped with the situation, but it did not change it," Andersch had noted as early as February of 1947, lamenting young intellectuals' inability to change the course of political events in the immediate postwar period. "The intellect is moving, it is striking out, it is proliferating. But it is useless, because it exists in an air-tight chamber. It is unable to realize itself and come to fruition in praxis." Such complaints were the beginning of critiques of a West German restoration that were to grow stronger in the coming decades. For Andersch the primary problem was "intellect without power."[112] Deprived of the power to create, Andersch warned, "freedom seeks refuge in criticism. It has its last position there."[113] These sentences, written less then two years after the end of the Second World War, described the way that many subsequent German writers, including particularly Böll and Grass, would understand their moral mission to be a critique of political power. The suggestion that the longed-for zero hour had in fact been a German restoration lent powerful ethical legitimacy to voices arguing for a radical change, while incriminating those who argued for preservation and conservatism. The seeds that were being sown in the second half of the 1940s may not have come to fruition immediately, but they did ultimately bear fruit in a general politicization of German literature during the 1960s and 1970s. Figures like Hans Egon Holthusen, who argued against a tabula rasa, are now almost forgotten, while Andersch and Böll are remembered as the fathers of postwar West German literature. In this sense, the character from Pavic's *Landscape Painted With Tea* who argues that postwar Germany was an excellent place to be young may, belatedly — and notwithstanding all of the contrary arguments about stasis and impotence to be found in the pages of *Der Ruf* — have been right. However much their self-positioning served to obscure the problems of their own and the German past, Richter and Andersch may nevertheless have fulfilled the role seen for German youth in the vision of Pavic's fictional character four decades after the end of the war. The historical irony is that by the time Pavic's character was proved right, the self-styled rebels of the 1940s had become the elder literary statesmen of the 1960s and 1970s.

Notes

[1] "Das Thema der Jugend beschäftigt die Welt." Rudolf Schneider-Schelde, "Vorbemerkung des Herausgebers," in *Die Frage der Jugend*, ed. Schneider-Schelde, 7–8; here, 7 (Munich: Kurt Desch, 1946). Unless otherwise specified, all translations from German in this book are my own; the German appears in the notes, followed by sources. I have added the notation "my translation" in a limited number of cases where confusion might otherwise occur.

[2] Milorad Pavic, *Landscape Painted with Tea* (New York: Knopf, 1990), 41.

[3] "Meine Generation hat die besten Voraussetzungen, sich am ehesten zu befreien und klar zu sehen." Walter Kolbenhoff, *Heimkehr in die Fremde* (Frankfurt: Suhrkamp, 1988), 65.

[4] "Sie sind schuld . . . daß die Häuser nur noch in Ruinen sind und daß die Kinder hungern. Ihre ganze verfluchte Generation hat es uns eingebrockt, und jetzt sitzen Sie hier und sollten eigentlich am Galgen hängen." Kolbenhoff, *Heimkehr in die Fremde*, 72.

[5] "Schuld sind die Alten an uns. . . ." Ilse Aichinger, *Die grössere Hoffnung* (Amsterdam: Bermann-Fischer/Querido, 1948), 70.

[6] "getrennt von den Älteren durch ihre Nicht-Verantwortlichkeit für Hitler." Alfred Andersch, "Das junge Europa formt sein Gesicht," *Der Ruf*, no. 1 (15 August 1946), reprinted in *Der Ruf: Eine deutsche Nachkriegszeitschrift*, ed. Hans Schwab-Felisch (Munich: Deutscher Taschenbuch Verlag, 1962), 21–26; here, 25.

[7] "Wenn eine Gruppe von Menschen nach dem 8. Mai 1945 das Recht . . . hatte, sich zu Wort zu melden und mit dem Finger auf die Krebsschäden Europas hinzuweisen, dann war es die junge Generation der damals Zwanzig- bis Vierzigjährigen." Heinz Friedrich, "Das Jahr 47," in *Almanach der Gruppe 47 1947–1962*, ed. Hans Werner Richter, 15–21; here, 16 (Reinbek: Rowohlt, 1962).

[8] "ohne Illusionen," "Die Zwanzig- bis Vierzigjährigen wollten reinen Tisch machen mit der Vergangenheit . . ., mit Energie und kompromißlos forderten sie das vereinte Europa ohne nationale Ressentiments und ohne Vorurteile." Friedrich, "Das Jahr 47," 16.

[9] Friedrich Meinecke, *The German Catastrophe: Reflections and Recollections*, trans. Sidney B. Fay (Cambridge, MA: Harvard UP, 1950), 45. In German: "Hitler ist, kann man sagen, durch eine typische, aber zugleich verblendete Jugendbewegung zur Macht gekommen." Friedrich Meinecke, *Die deutsche Katastrophe: Betrachtungen und Erinnerungen* (Brockhaus: Wiesbaden, 1946), 71.

[10] Robert Wohl, *The Generation of 1914* (Cambridge, MA: Harvard UP, 1979), 72.

[11] George Mosse, ed., *Nazi Culture: A Documentary History* (New York: Schocken, 1981), 263.

[12] "der Jugend gegen autoritäre, faktisch aber schwache Väter." Alexander Mitscherlich, *Ein Leben für die Psychoanalyse: Anmerkungen zu meiner Zeit* (Frankfurt: Suhrkamp, 1980), 75.

[13] Cited in Karl Dietrich Bracher, *The German Dictatorship: The Origins, Structure, and Effects of National Socialism*, trans. Jean Steinberg (New York: Praeger, 1970), 146.

[14] "Es ist leicht zu sehen, welche Rolle Hitler oder der Nationalsozialismus in der letzten Entwicklung gespielt haben. Sie waren die Repräsentanten der Jugend."

"Hitlers Sache war die Sache der Jugend, so gut jede Revolution eine Angelegenheit der Jugend ist." Rudolf Schneider-Schelde, "Jugenddämmerung," in *Die Frage der Jugend,* ed. Rudolf Schneider-Schelde, 84–102; here, 95 (Munich: Kurt Desch, 1946).

[15] "das zusammenbrechende 'Werk' war ja weitgehend Jugendtat." "der Zusammenbruch der Jugend selbst. Er ist der Zusammenbruch . . . des Glaubens an die Jugend und der Jugend." Schneider-Schelde, "Jugenddämmerung," 97.

[16] "Einhundertfünfzig Jahre jugendlicher Tat haben ausgereicht, um die abendländische Welt in Schutt und Asche zu legen." Schneider-Schelde, "Jugenddämmerung," 91.

[17] "der Deutsche [ist] der ewige Student, der ewig Strebende unter den Völkern." Thomas Mann, *Doktor Faustus: Das Leben des deutschen Tonsetzers Adrian Leverkühn, erzählt von einem Freunde* (Frankfurt: Fischer, 1998), 160. My translation. In the Lowe-Porter translation: Mann, *Doctor Faustus: The Life of the German Composer Adrian Leverkühn As Told by a Friend,* trans. H. T. Lowe-Porter. (New York: Alfred Knopf, 1948), 118.

[18] "Der Jugendgedanke ist ein Vorrecht und Vorzug unseres Volkes, des deutschen." "Die deutsche Jugend repräsentiert, eben als Jugend, den Volksgeist selbst, den deutschen Geist, der jung ist und zukunftsvoll, — unreif, wenn man will, aber was will das besagen!" Mann, *Doktor Faustus,* 159. My translation. For the Lowe-Porter translation, see Mann, *Doctor Faustus,* 117.

[19] "Wo bliebe die Welt auch, wenn Reife das letzte Wort wäre! Wir werden ihr in unserer Unreife noch manche Erneuerung, manche Revolution bescheren." Mann, *Doktor Faustus,* 160. My translation. For the Lowe-Porter translation, see Mann, *Doctor Faustus,* 117.

[20] "den vermeintlich reinigenden Neubeginn, die völkische Wiedergeburt von vor zehn Jahren." Mann, *Doktor Faustus,* 234. My translation. For the Lowe-Porter translation, see Mann, *Doctor Faustus,* 175.

[21] Mann, *Doktor Faustus,* 665, 43. My translation. For the Lowe-Porter translation, see Mann, *Doctor Faustus,* 505, 31.

[22] "In diesen zwölf Jahren hatte man einem Volk das Eigenste und Kostbarste genommen, das es zu allen Zeiten besaß: seine Jugend und mit ihr die Gewähr aller Zukunft." "verdorben und vergiftet." Ernst Wiechert, *Rede an die deutsche Jugend 1945* (Munich: Zinnen, 1945), 18.

[23] Karl Becker, *Zero Hour for Germany* (London: I.N.G. Publications, 1944), 59, 63.

[24] Paul Merker, *Germany Today . . . and Germany Tomorrow?* (London: I.N.G., 1943), 7–8.

[25] "Dieser Generation ist das Denken und Fühlen vom Abc an vergiftet worden, sie hat nie etwas anderes gelernt, gesehen, in sich eingeatmet als Nazismus; sie ist von sich aus vollkommen unschuldig und ist doch ganz eingetaucht in die Erbsünde des Nazismus und ganz durchtränkt von ihr." Victor Klemperer, *Kultur: Erwägungen nach dem Zusammenbruch des Nazismus* (Berlin: Neues Leben, 1946), 54.

[26] "Ihr habt verloren: Wir haben gesiegt! Wir werden es euch zeigen!" Walter Kolbenhoff, *Von unserem Fleisch und Blut* (Munich: Nymphenburger Verlagshandlung, 1946), 160.

[27] "Alle eure Gesetze haben für mich keine Gültigkeit mehr," "Ich muß mich ganz lösen von allem." "Du bist krank. . . . Du bist der beste Beweis dafür, wie fürchterlich die Pest ist, die sie in dich hineingeimpft haben." Kolbenhoff, *Von unserem Fleisch und Blut*, 170, 180, 147.

[28] "Wenn wir untergehen, soll alles andere auch untergehen, dachte er." Kolbenhoff, *Von unserem Fleisch und Blut*, 21.

[29] "Nach uns die Sintflut. Und dann die Wüste." Kolbenhoff, *Von unserem Fleisch und Blut*, 60.

[30] Heinrich Böll, *Kreuz ohne Liebe*, in *Werke*, ed. J. H. Reid, 2:149–425; see especially 371 (Cologne: Kiepenheuer & Witsch, 2002).

[31] "Wann hat eine Jugend jemals so bedingungslos vertraut, geglaubt und gehorcht wie in den Zeiten des Dritten Reiches?" "Nie zuvor irgendwo auf der Welt. Und was ist daraus geworden? Tod, Verstümmelung, Hunger, Gefangenschaft, Ausweglosigkeit, Unvermögen und Verzweiflung." Manfred Hausmann, "Jugend zwischen gestern und morgen," *Aufbau* 2, no. 7 (1946), 667–74; here, 668.

[32] "eine unheimliche Krankheit," "Man wollte nicht mehr denken, man wollte nur noch geschlossenen Auges glauben und gehorchen." "Daß die deutsche Jugend sich so willenlos und so gedankenlos den Lockungen und Drohungen der Machtbesessenen auslieferte, war trotz aller Entlastungen, die zweifelsohne vorgebracht werden können, ihre Schuld." Hausmann, "Jugend zwischen gestern und morgen," 669.

[33] "Bislang hat die deutsche Jugend offenbar sich selbst noch nicht entdeckt." "Heute sieht es so aus, als fehle ihr der Mut." Hausmann, "Jugend zwischen gestern und morgen," 671.

[34] "hielt dann für wahr, was man ihr als wahr erzählte, sie hatte nichts anderes kennengelernt und konnte sich deshalb kein selbständiges Urteil bilden," "Die Schuldigen . . . sind bei jener Generation zu suchen, die 1933 so kläglich versagte," "Sie werden nun vielleicht verstehen, Herr Dr. Hausmann . . . daß ich Ihnen aus all diesen Gründen das Recht abspreche, sich heute als guten Freund bei der Jugend anbiedern und ihr gute Ratschläge erteilen zu wollen. 1940 riefen Sie der Jugend zu, allein der Krieg mache den Menschen frei, und heute wagen Sie es, der gleichen Jugend vorzuwerfen, daß sie damals kämpfte. . . ." Rolf Pabst, "Ein Brief an Dr. Manfred Hausmann: Die Problematik zweier Generationen," *Neue Zeitung* [Berlin edition], 15 August 1947, 2. Although Hausmann is now largely forgotten, he still comes in for criticism occasionally. See especially Arn Strohmeyer, *Der Mitläufer: Manfred Hausmann und der Nationalsozialismus* (Bremen: Donat, 1999).

[35] "Die letzten Jahre hindurch wurde so viel und uns so sehr zum Ekel erzogen, daß uns der anscheinend jetzt unvermeidliche, demokratisch verbrämte, pädagogisch-moralisierende Ton der lizenzierten Pädagogen befremdet." Cited in W. E. Süskind, "An die Jugend," in Schneider-Schelde, *Die Frage der Jugend*, 55–63; here, 60.

[36] "wir lizenzierten Prediger eben einfach nicht anders könnten als predigen, flehen und fordern," "daß es unsinnig ist, wenn wir der Jugend nun in einem fort mit einem 'Du sollst' begegnen." "Erziehungsprodukt des Nationalsozialismus." W. E. Süskind, "An die Jugend," 61.

[37] "Die Werte, die ihr 12 Jahre lang eingehämmert wurden, haben sich als falsch erwiesen," "Die Götter, die sie 12 Jahre lang anbeten mußte, sind tot. Die Ideale, an die sie 12 Jahre lang geglaubt hat, liegen zerbrochen am Boden." "Wer aber will die Jugend dafür tadeln, daß sie gläubig war?" Elisabeth Bamberger, "Not," in Schneider-Schelde, *Die Frage der Jugend,* 39–48; here, 47.

[38] "die Frage der deutschen Jugend," "das schwerste Problem, dessen Lösung unser Auftrag ward," "der Jugend die Schuld an ihrem Irrtum geben zu wollen." Rudolf Pechel, "Unsere vordringlichste Aufgabe," in Pechel, *Deutsche Gegenwart: Aufsätze und Vorträge 1945–1952,* 28–35; here, 28 (Stuttgart: no publisher, 1952). Originally in the *Deutsche Rundschau,* April 1946.

[39] "ein verlorener Haufe von zusammengeschossenen Krüppeln, seelisch Gebrochenen, Müden und Enttäuschten und Verbitterten." Pechel, "Unsere vordringlichste Aufgabe," 30.

[40] "geistige Werwolfnester" Pechel, "Unsere vordringlichste Aufgabe," 32.

[41] Dirk Niefanger, "Die Dramatisierung der 'Stunde Null,'" in *Zwei Wendezeiten: Blicke auf die deutsche Literatur 1945 und 1989,* ed. Erhart and Niefanger (Tübingen: Niemeyer, 1997), 47–70; here, 49.

[42] "bis ich zur Hitler-Jugend kam. Meine Heimat war das Schulungslager. Die Ordensburg." Zuckmayer, *Des Teufels General* (Stockholm and Vienna: Bermann-Fischer and Schönbrunn, 1947), 76.

[43] Zuckmayer, *Des Teufels General,* 37.

[44] "Hartmann ist die Verkörperung der deutschen Jugend unserer Zeit." Hay, Rambaldo, and Storck, eds., *"Als der Krieg zu Ende war,"* 430.

[45] "Die deutsche Jugend bemüht sich immerhin um einen neuen Weg. Sie sieht offenen Auges die Fehler und die Verbrechen der Vergangenheit ihres Landes." Gerhard Hay, Hartmut Rambaldo, and Joachim W. Storck, eds., *"Als der Krieg zu Ende war": Literarisch-politische Publizistik 1945–1950* (Marbach: Deutsche Schillergesellschaft, 1995), 430.

[46] "Wenn junge Deutsche, die von Kind auf im Zwinger der Diktatur dressiert wurden, heute im Kreise freiheitlich erzogener Studenten so glänzend bestehen, dann kann die gefürchtete These, daß es in zwölf Jahren gelungen sei, Deutschlands Jugend geistig und moralisch zu sterilisieren, ganz einfach nicht wahr sein!" Erich Kästner, "Reise in die Zukunft: Über Studenten und Kinder," *Neue Zeitung* [Berlin edition], 4 July 1947, 6.

[47] "ein Lichtblick in dieser verfinsterten Welt," "Heute weiß ich, daß es ihn gab und gibt, daß er mit einem großen Teil der deutschen Jugend identisch ist." Hay, Rambaldo, and Storck, eds., *"Als der Krieg zu Ende war,"* 434.

[48] Theodor Plievier, *Stalingrad,* trans. Richard and Clara Winston (New York: Appleton-Century-Crofts, 1948), 92. In German: "schon als Kind hatte er die Lagerinschrift über sich: "WIR SIND GEBOREN, UM ZU STERBEN!" Theodor Plievier, *Stalingrad* (Berlin: Aufbau, 1984), 138.

[49] "Zehntausende, Hunderttausende Opfer auf zweitausend und dreitausend Kilometern durchfahrenen Landes." Plievier, *Stalingrad,* 241. This passage is eliminated from the published English-language translation.

[50] "Sehen Sie, gerade in der Kunst brauchen wir wieder eine Jugend, die zu allen Problemen aktiv Stellung nimmt. Eine mutige, nüchterne" "revolutionäre Jugend." Wolfgang Borchert, *The Man Outside,* trans. David Porter (New York: New Directions, 1971), 106. In German: Wolfgang Borchert, *Draussen vor der Tür* (Reinbek: Rowohlt, 1992), 28, 29. The play was first performed in Hamburg one day after Borchert's premature death on 20 November 1947.

[51] Wolfgang Borchert, *The Man Outside,* trans. David Porter (New York: New Directions, 1971), 130. In German: "da haben sie auch für uns einen Krieg ausgedacht. Und da haben sie uns dann hingeschickt." "Und dann war der Krieg endlich da. Und dann haben sie uns hingeschickt. Und sie haben uns nichts gesagt. Nur — Macht's gut, Jungens! haben sie gesagt. Macht's gut, Jungens! So haben sie uns verraten. So furchtbar verraten. Und jetzt sitzen sie hinter ihren Türen. Herr Studienrat, Herr Direktor, Herr Gerichtsrat, Herr Oberarzt. Jetzt hat uns keiner hingeschickt. Nein, keiner. Alle sitzen sie jetzt hinter ihren Türen. Und ihre Tür haben sie fest zu. Und wir stehen draußen. Und von ihren Kathedern und von ihren Sesseln zeigen sie mit dem Finger auf uns. So haben sie uns verraten. So furchtbar verraten. Und jetzt gehen sie an ihrem Mord vorbei, einfach vorbei. Sie gehen an ihrem Mord vorbei." Wolfgang Borchert, *Draussen vor der Tür* (Reinbek: Rowohlt, 1992), 49.

[52] "Aber darum bleibt Schuld in jedem Falle doch Schuld." Hausmann, "Jugend zwischen gestern und morgen," 670.

[53] "Wir sollen vor die Hunde gehn,/im schwarzen Buch der Menschheit stehn/für all den blutigen Schaden,/den wir den Völkern angetan!/wir stehn im Schuldbuch obenan — /*und waren nur Soldaten.*" "Soldaten werden nicht gefragt," "wir waren ja nur Sklaven." Vitalis, "Deutsches Soldatenlied," in *Deine Söhne, Europa: Gedichte deutscher Kriegsgefangener,* ed. Hans Werner Richter, 96–98; here, 96 (Munich: Nymphenburger Verlagshandlung, 1947).

[54] "Millionenheere//von Toten," "Wir leiden Hunger, Haß und Hohn,/wir sind mit unserer Nation/vors Weltgericht geladen/und tragen schweigend, mit Geduld/die Schulden, aber nicht die Schuld!/Wir waren nur Soldaten." Vitalis, "Deutsches Soldatenlied," in Richter, *Deine Söhne,* 98.

[55] "Ihr alle, die ihr vom Nazismus nichts oder doch nicht viel wissen wolltet, standet dennoch im Gefolge der Fanatisierten unter euern ehemaligen Schulkameraden," "Aber ihr habt doch dem Nationalsozialismus seine Schlachten geschlagen. Ihr waret doch die Helden von Warschau, Narvik und Flandern, von Tobruk und Moskau. Ihr habt die Welt durchzogen als die siegreichen Träger des Hakenkreuzes. Mit euch haben die Nazis ein Land ums andere überfallen, und ihr habt, als die Welt schon längst wußte, wie hoffnungslos es war, mit unerhörter Bravour und grauenhaften Verlusten eine Schlacht um die andere gegen eine täglich unvorstellbarer werdende Übermacht verloren." "die lauten Deklamationen der überzeugten Hitlerjungen." Ernst von Schenck, "An einen Studenten," in Schneider-Schelde, *Die Frage der Jugend,* 23–33; here, 27.

[56] "Auf den Balkonen des Lebens/stehn wir, hinabgebeugt,/und lauschen, ob uns vergebens,/vergebens die Eltern gezeugt.//Wir haben das Blut gerochen,/die schweißige Angst, den Haß./Die Brücken liegen zerbrochen/im trägen, fauligen Naß.//Kamine bohren geborsten/hinein ins zerschlissene Grau./Nur die Geier horsten/in ungetrübtem Blau.//Die Fenster sind eingeschlagen,/durch die wir ins

Leben geschaut./Die Häuser sind abgetragen,/die man um uns erbaut.//Die Welten sind für uns die Fassaden,/aus denen das Dunkel grinst./Die Not zieht über Kaskaden/von Schutt ihr dichtes Gespinst." Wolfgang Bächler, "Jugend der Städte," in Richter, *Almanach der Gruppe 47,* 76–77. Loosely translated.

[57] "mit professoraler Selbstverständlichkeit," "jede geistige und sittliche Fähigkeit." Hans Werner Richter, "Warum schweigt die junge Generation?" *Der Ruf,* no. 2 (1 September 1946), reprinted in Schwab-Felisch, *Der Ruf: Eine deutsche Nachkriegszeitschrift,* 29–33; here, 29.

[58] "Daß Dir ein Gott gab, zu sagen, was Du nicht leidest, ist Deine Sache." "Daß Du Dich aber vermißt zu sagen, was wir leiden, veranlaßt uns nun unsererseits zu diesem Dementi. Möchtest Du doch endlich Dein Versprechen wahrmachen und uns aus dem Spiel lassen!" Alexander Parlach [pseudonym for Erich Kuby], "Die erste und einzige Rede deutscher Jugend an ihren Dichter," *Der Ruf* 2, no. 25, 10, cited in *Auf der Suche nach der Stunde Null: Literatur und Alltag 1945,* ed. Hartwin Gromes and Hans-Otto Hügel (Bad Salzdebfurth: Barbara Franzbecker, 1991), 18–20; here, 19.

[59] "Sie sind zu sehr gebildet, Herr Dichter, Sie sprechen nicht unsere Sprache. Ihr Artikel erreicht uns nicht, denn das Schicksal, von dem Sie reden, ist nicht das unsere." Kolbenhoff, *Heimkehr in die Fremde,* 19.

[60] "der Krieg von 1914 nicht die beunruhigenden Folgen gehabt [habe], die wir heute feststellen. Es gab damals nicht eigentlich einen Bruch mit der Vergangenheit. Jetzt sieht es so aus, als sei das Band zwischen der Generation, die kommt, und der, die geht, zerrissen. Die jungen Leute von heute brechen die Brücken hinter sich ab und stoßen die Hand zurück, die ihnen von den Älteren gereicht wird. "André Gide an die Jugend: Der Wortlaut seiner Münchner Rede," *Neue Zeitung* [Berlin edition], 4 July 1947, 6.

[61] "dieser Trennungsstrich ist ohne Frage von entscheidender Bedeutung." Erich Kästner, "Die chinesische Mauer," in Schneider-Schelde, *Die Frage der Jugend,* 64–68; here, 64.

[62] "Ihr seid die Ält'ren. Wir sind jünger./Ihr steht am Weg' mit gutem Rat./Mit scharfgespitztem Zeigefinger/weist ihr uns auf den neuen Pfad." "Ihr habt das wundervoll erledigt./Vor einem Jahr schriet ihr noch 'Heil!'/Man staunt, wenn ihr jetzt 'Freiheit' predigt/wie kurz vorher das Gegenteil." "Wir wuchsen auf in eurem Zwinger./Wir wurden groß mit eurem Kult./Ihr seid die Ält'ren. Wir sind jünger./Wer älter ist, hat länger schuld." Erich Kästner, "Die Jugend hat das Wort," in *Der tägliche Kram,* 91–92 (Berlin: Atrium, 1948). Loosely translated.

[63] "Im Jahre 1947 war eigentlich der Kampf der Jungen um eine geistige und politische Neuordnung unserer zerrütteten Nachkriegswelt schon verloren." Friedrich, "Das Jahr 47," 17.

[64] On the literary activities of German POW's in the United States, see Volker (Christian) Wehdeking, *Der Nullpunkt: Über die Konstituierung der deutschen Nachkriegsliteratur in den amerikanischen Kriegsgefangenenlagern* (Stuttgart: Metzler, 1971).

[65] Harold Bloom, *The Anxiety of Influence: A Theory of Poetry* (New York: Oxford UP, 1973).

[66] Sebald, "Between the Devil and the Deep Blue Sea: On Alfred Andersch," in his *On the Natural History of Destruction,* 125. In German: "ein wahres Glossarium und Register der faschistischen Sprache." Sebald, *Luftkrieg und Literatur,* 141–43. Klaus

Briegleb, however, not only subscribes to Sebald's description but actually uses it as a chapter title; see Klaus Briegleb, *Mißachtung und Tabu: Eine Streitschrift zur Frage: "Wie antisemitisch war die Gruppe 47?"* (Berlin: Philo, 2003), 229.

[67] "Frontkämpfermythos." Karl Korn, "Karl Korn über den 'Ruf': Rufer oder Jugend in der Igelstellung," in Jérôme Vaillant, *Der Ruf — Unabhängige Blätter der jungen Generation (1945–1949): Eine Zeitschrift zwischen Illusion und Anpassung,* trans. Heidrun Hofmann and Karl Heinz Schmidt, 200–201 (Munich: K. G. Sauer, 1978). From *Der Kurier,* 6 November 1946.

[68] "Unser Haß, der Haß der jungen Generation, besitzt die Rechtfertigung der unbedingten Notwendigkeit." Alfred Andersch, "Notwendige Aussage zum Nürnberger Prozeß," *Der Ruf,* no. 1 (15 August 1946); reprinted in Schwab-Felisch, *Der Ruf: Eine deutsche Nachkriegszeitschrift,* 26–29; here, 26.

[69] "Die Kämpfer von Stalingrad, El Alamein und Cassino, denen auch von ihren Gegnern jede Achtung entgegengebracht wurde, sind unschuldig an den Verbrechen von Dachau und Buchenwald." Andersch, "Notwendige Aussage," 27.

[70] For the most thorough account of the circumstances under which Richter and Andersch left the journal, see Vaillant, *Der Ruf,* 106–49. Vaillant's account clears up some of the inaccuracies that continue to crop up.

[71] "Selten in der Geschichte eines Landes . . . hat sich eine derartige geistige Kluft zwischen zwei Generationen aufgetan wie heute in Deutschland." Richter, "Warum schweigt die junge Generation?" 29.

[72] "über diesen immer noch andauernden Zerfall eines wohlgeordneten menschlichen Bildes können auch die schönsten Professorenreden nicht hinwegtäuschen." Richter, "Warum schweigt die junge Generation?" 31.

[73] "nun schweigend eine unendliche Flut von wohlgemeinten Reden über sich ergehen lassen." Richter, "Warum schweigt die junge Generation?" 31.

[74] "Ja, diese Generation schweigt, aber sie schweigt nicht, weil sie etwa ratlos wäre, sie schweigt nicht, weil sie nichts zu sagen hätte oder die Worte nicht fände, die notwendig wären, um das zu sagen was gesagt werden muß. Sie schweigt aus dem sicheren Gefühl heraus, daß die Diskrepanz zwischen der bedrohten menschlichen Existenz und der geruhsamen Problematik jener älteren Generation, die aus ihrem olympischen Schweigen nach zwölf Jahren heraustrat, zu groß ist, um überbrückbar zu sein. Sie weiß, daß jenes Bild des Menschen, das die ältere Generation von ihren Vorvätern ererbt hat und das sie nun wieder errichten möchte, nicht mehr aufgebaut werden kann. Sie weiß, daß dieses Bild endgültig zerstört ist." Richter, "Warum schweigt die junge Generation?" 31.

[75] "Vor dem rauchgeschwärzten Bild dieser abendländischen Ruinenlandschaft, in der der Mensch taumelnd und gelöst aus allen überkommen Bindungen irrt, verblassen alle Wertmaßstäbe der Vergangenheit. Jede Anknüpfungsmöglichkeit nach hinten, jeder Versuch, dort wieder zu beginnen, wo 1933 eine ältere Generation ihre kontinuierliche Entwicklungslaufbahn verließ, um vor einem irrationalen Abenteuer zu kapitulieren, wirkt angesichts dieses Bildes wie eine Paradoxie." Richter, "Warum schweigt die junge Generation?" 32.

[76] "Aus der Verschiebung des Lebensgefühls, aus der Gewalt der Erlebnisse, die der jungen Generation zuteil wurden und die sie erschütterten, erscheint ihr heute die

einzige Ausgangsmöglichkeit einer geistigen Wiederbegurt in dem absoluten und radikalen Beginn von vorne zu liegen." Richter, "Warum schweigt die junge Generation?" 32.

[77] "Laßt uns einen neuen Anfang setzen, einen neuen Grenzstein vor einem neuen Feld." Wiechert, *Rede an die Deutsche Jugend 1945,* 33.

[78] "dieses europäischen Wiedererwachens." Andersch, "Das junge Europa formt sein Gesicht," 21.

[79] "ein neuer, von aller Tradition abweichender Humanismus." Andersch, "Das junge Europa formt sein Gesicht," 22.

[80] "dem Denken der älteren Generation, die in der Unverbindlichkeit ihres Toleranz-Begriffs, ihrem Zurückschrecken vor dem letzten Einsatz, dem Unhold seinen Gang zur Macht erlaubte." Andersch, "Das junge Europa formt sein Gesicht," 23–24.

[81] "ein neuer, jugendfrischer, jungfräulich-athenischer Geist." Andersch, "Das junge Europa formt sein Gesicht," 21.

[82] "Die Erzieher müssen überholt werden." Andersch, "Das junge Europa formt sein Gesicht," 26.

[83] "dem ganzen Ballast der Vergangenheit," "In Deutschland ist das alles zerschlagen. Es hat weder einen Staat noch eine Wirtschaftsordnung. Die junge Generation kann ganz von vorn und dort beginnen, wo die Entwicklung bei den andern hindrängt. Sie braucht nicht umzubauen. Sie kann neu bauen." Hans Werner Richter, "Deutschland — Brücke zwischen Ost und West," *Der Ruf,* no. 4 (1 October 1946), reprinted in Schwab-Felisch, *Der Ruf: Eine deutsche Nachkriegszeitschrift,* 46–49; here, 48.

[84] "Zwölf Jahre Klischeesprache scheinen schwer auf den jungen Journalisten zu lasten. Sie können sich von den vernebelten Begriffen, die das 'Dritte Reich' geschaffen hat, nicht lösen." "Im gleichen diffusen Stil wird weitergeschrieben — nur die Vorzeichen haben sich geändert." Widmer, *1945 oder die "neue Sprache,"* 198.

[85] "Wir haben uns unser Zeitalter nicht ausgesucht. Wir müssen mit ihm, so wie es ist, fertig werden." Gromes and Hügel, eds., *Auf der Suche nach der Stunde Null,* 19.

[86] "das Zentralcafé einer Literatur ohne Hauptstadt." Hans Magnus Enzensberger, "Die Clique," in Richter, *Almanach der Gruppe 47 1947–1962,* 22–27; here, 27.

[87] Gustav René Hocke, "Deutsche Kalligraphie oder: Glanz und Elend der modernen Literatur," *Der Ruf,* no. 7 (15 November 1946), reprinted in Schwab-Felisch, *Der Ruf: Eine deutsche Nachkriegszeitschrift,* 203–8; here, 204.

[88] "subtropischen Treibhausklima." Hocke, "Deutsche Kalligraphie," 205.

[89] "Wir tasten uns durch beängstigendes Gestrüpp wortreicher Perioden durch, die meist zweierlei vermissen lassen: Klarheit der Form und Unmittelbarkeit der Aussage. Eine eigengeartete kunstgewerbliche Fertigkeit, dadurch gekennzeichnet, daß mit brillanten Mitteln halb oder ganz Unnützes gebastelt wird, tritt einem entgegen." Hocke, "Deutsche Kalligraphie," 203.

[90] "vorgetäuschten Tiefsinn," "soziologischen und psychologischen Wirklichkeit von heute." Hocke, "Deutsche Kalligraphie," 206.

[91] "in Trümmern entdeckt man die ersten neuen Gesetze der soziologischen und psychologischen Wirklichkeit von heute, vor allem Eindeutigkeit und Einfachheit des

Leids und doch die Mannigfaltigkeit der Reaktion darauf." Hocke, "Deutsche Kalligraphie," 207

[92] "deren Profil von den Ruinen und Trümmern der großen Städte gezeichnet ist." Richter, "Warum schweigt die junge Generation?" 31.

[93] "Da blühten und dufteten magische Pomeranzenzweige, da entfalteten sich idyllische Seelenlandschaften von geschmackvollem Klassizismus," "Die offiziellen Wächter, welche das geistige Leben bei uns unter ihrer Kontrolle hielten, duldeten und förderten diese Idylliker — während das äußere Reich immer stärker und ausschließlicher der Barbarei verfiel, sollten sie das innere Reich kultivieren helfen — so lange, bis an die Stelle der Hexameter Marschbefehle, an die Stelle der Oden der Wehrmachtsbericht und an die Stelle der Sonette Volksgerichtshof-Urteile zu treten hatten." Horst Lange, "Bücher nach dem Kriege: Eine kritische Betrachtung," in *Der Ruf*, no. 10 (1 January 1947), reprinted in Schwab-Felisch, *Der Ruf: Eine deutsche Nachkriegszeitschrift*, 216–23; here, 218, 219.

[94] "Ehrlich sein, dachte ich, als ich anfing zu schreiben, nicht sich bestechen lassen durch schöne Worte. Schreib ehrlich, erzähle ganz einfach, versuche so einfach zu erzählen wie möglich." Kolbenhoff, *Heimkehr in die Fremde*, 192.

[95] "Ich untersuchte die Schublade, aber es war kein Brot mehr drin. Dann setzte ich mich an den Tisch und begann zu schreiben." Kolbenhoff, *Heimkehr in die Fremde*, 224.

[96] "tappen herum und wissen nicht, was tun." "daß Realität und Literatur kommunizieren." Wolfgang Weyrauch, "Nachwort," in *Tausend Gramm: Sammlung neuer deutscher Geschichten*, ed. Weyrauch, 207–19; here, 211 (Hamburg: Rowohlt, 1949).

[97] "Kahlschlag in unserem Dickicht." Weyrauch, "Nachwort," 213.

[98] "fangen in Sprache, Substanz und Konzeption, von vorn an." Weyrauch, "Nachwort," 214.

[99] "fixieren die Wirklichkeit. Da sie es wegen der Wahrheit tun, photographieren sie nicht. Sie röntgen. Ihre Genauigkeit ist chirurgisch." Weyrauch, "Nachwort," 217.

[100] "Indem . . . [sie] von vorn anfangen, ganz von vorn, bei der Addition der Teile und Teilchen der Handlung, beim A-B-C der Sätze und Wörter, beim Stand der Anabasis, widerstreiten sie, manchmal sogar ultimativ, der Fortsetzung der kalligraphischen . . . Literatur in Deutschland, der Verhängung und dem Verhängnis eines neuen Nebels bei uns, worin die Geier und die Hyänen nisten und tappen. Und warten. Warten auf unsre endgültige Zerstückelung, damit sie ihr altes, außermenschliches Reich der Gefräßigkeit des Menschen gegen den Menschen errichten können." Weyrauch, "Nachwort," 216.

[101] See Glenn Cuomo, *Career at the Cost of Compromise: Günter Eich's Life and Work in the Years 1933–1945* (Amsterdam: Rodopi, 1989).

[102] "Dies ist meine Mütze,/dies ist mein Mantel,/hier mein Rasierzeug/im Beutel aus Leinen." Günter Eich, "Inventory," trans. Michael Hamburger, in *Pigeons and Moles: Selected Writings of Günter Eich* (Columbia, SC: Camden House, 1991), 3. Cited in Weyrauch, "Nachwort," 215; originally published as "Inventur" in Richter, *Deine Söhne, Europa*, 17.

[103] Cuomo, *Career at the Cost of Compromise*, 138.

[104] "unmittelbarer Realismus," "der konsequenteste Realist des Unmittelbaren." Wolfgang Weyrauch, "Realismus des Unmittelbaren," *Aufbau*, 2 no. 7 (1946), 701–6; here, 702, 703.

[105] "Wirklichkeit und Sprache zu bündeln, sie beide mit den Katarakten der uns umgebenden Erde zu kommunizieren, wird eine höllische Aufgabe für die deutschen Schriftsteller und Dichter sein. Die Aufgabe wird leichter sein, wenn sie bedenken, daß auch dies eine Wiedergutmachung ist." Weyrauch, "Realismus des Unmittelbaren," 706.

[106] Hans Dieter Schäfer, "Kultur als Simulation: Das Dritte Reich und die Postmoderne," in *Literatur in der Diktatur: Schreiben im Nationalsozialismus und DDR-Sozialismus*, ed. Günther Rüther, 215–45; here, 231–32 (Paderborn: Schöningh, 1997). See *Aufbau*, 4, no. 7 (1948), 588–89.

[107] "eine neue realistische Literatur, welche mit den Rückständen der alten Lug- und Verdrängungsliteratur aufräumt." Alfred Döblin, "Die beiden deutschen Literaturen," in *Schriften zu Ästhetik, Poetik und Literatur*, 364–67; here, 367 (Olten: Walter, 1989).

[108] "schlaff und weich," "abseitige Themen, entfernte Historie." "ein langweiliges, schöngeistiges Schrifttum," "die alte Duck- und Kümmerhaltung mit." Döblin, "Die beiden deutschen Literaturen," 366.

[109] "Aber daß die Autoren ihren eigenen politischen Charakter nicht kennen, macht weder sie noch ihre Werke unpolitisch." Alfred Döblin, "Die literarische Situation," in *Schriften zu Ästhetik, Poetik und Literatur*, 409–87; here, 451. Originally published in 1947.

[110] "Keiner kann ihnen ihre Autochthonie wegnehmen, keiner darf sie ihnen wegnehmen." "wenn sie mit den Mitteln der absoluten Literatur verpflichtet ist." Weyrauch, "Nachwort," 216.

[111] "Der Blindekuh-Schriftsteller sieht nach innen, er baut sich eine Welt zurecht." Heinrich Böll, "Bekenntnis zur Trümmerliteratur," in *Erzählungen Hörspiele Aufsätze*, 339–43; here, 342 (Cologne: Kiepenheuer & Witsch, 1961).

[112] "Der Geist hat die Situation bewältigt, aber er hat sie nicht verändert," "Der Geist bewegt sich, er schlägt um sich, er wuchert. Aber er ist zu nichts nutze, denn er bewegt sich im luftleeren Raum. Er kann sich nicht in der Praxis verwirklichen und vollenden." "Geist ohne Macht." Alfred Andersch, "Aktion oder Passivität," *Der Ruf*, no. 12 (1 February 1947), reprinted in Schwab-Felisch, *Der Ruf: Eine deutsche Nachkriegszeitschrift*, 132–36; here, 133.

[113] "Die Freiheit flüchtet sich in die Kritik. Sie hat dort ihre letzte Position." Alfred Andersch, "Aktion oder Passivität," 134.

7: The Darkening of Consciousness

ERNST JÜNGER WAS one of the first Germans to speak consistently of the period around the end of the Second World War as a *Nullpunkt* (zero point) in modern history. For Jünger, and for many other German conservatives, the zero of the *Nullpunkt* implied nothingness and its philosophical counterpart, nihilism: the belief in nothing and no one. In an attempt to describe the basic premise of this world view, the Munich psychologist Philipp Lersch declared in 1947 that nihilism is "the conviction that behind everything that human beings can desire and expect from life stands the cheerless emptiness of absolute absurdity."[1] Nihilism meant the rejection of a conventional morality based on the existence of a supernatural being — God — and, at an extreme, a glorification of the relentlessly negative spirit articulated by Mephistopheles in Goethe's *Faust:* "I am the Spirit of Eternal Negation." From the point of view of Mephistopheles, this negation is quite justified, as "all that gains existence/is only fit to be destroyed."[2] In its nihilistic meaning, the postwar German conception of a *Nullpunkt* came to imply that the Germany of the "Third Reich" had reached an absolute negation of morality and ultimately, of all existence; and that the troubled nation had embarked upon a path that led, ultimately, to self-destruction. The nadir of self-negation corresponded with national defeat in 1945 and was, hence, a spiritual, military, and political *Nullpunkt*.

Among major German intellectuals in the immediate postwar period, only Gottfried Benn celebrated his nihilism, declaring that it was so deep and pervasive that, far from creating a vacuum into which he might fall and be destroyed, it provided him with an anchor.[3] Other German intellectuals believed nihilism to be a profound danger and explored various ways of overcoming that danger, of which the two most prominent were, for the most part, mutually exclusive: the return to Christianity on the one hand or the adherence to existentialist philosophy on the other. After a brief look at the philosophical roots of postwar diagnoses of nihilism, I will in this chapter explore the diagnosis itself, then the Christian response to that diagnosis, frequently already inherent in the diagnosis, and, last, the existentialist response. Since it is my contention that aspects of the Christian diagnosis of and response to the problem of nihilism are shared by unlikely representatives of both the right and the left, that section includes an exploration of the occasionally convergent views of Jünger on the one hand and the sociologists Max Horkheimer and Theodor W. Adorno on the other.

The Roots

In the philosophy of Friedrich Nietzsche and the novels of Fyodor Dostoyevsky, postwar Germans found two divergent nineteenth-century approaches to the problem of nihilism. According to Nietzsche, the philosophy of rationalism and technological optimism is based on a shaky foundation and therefore doomed to collapse; since post-Renaissance European culture is founded on optimistic rationalism, the inevitable collapse of this philosophy means that all received Western values have become worthless. No matter how much success they have in trying to uncover the secrets of the world by means of science and logic, Western intellectuals all too quickly come to understand that their tools are limited. Skeptical rationalism has already destroyed the foundations of the Christian religion — what remains of Christianity is a mere shell, Nietzsche believes — but in the end rationalism also self-destructs, leaving its adherents alone and unsupported. When all received values have become worthless, what remains is nihilism. For Nietzsche, modern European history — and the European future — is therefore the history of the confrontation with nihilism: "What I relate is the history of the next two centuries. I describe what is coming, what can not be avoided: *the rise of nihilism.*"[4] But Nietzsche believes that history does not end with the emergence of nihilism as the primary mental force; beyond nihilism lies human beings' autonomous creation of their own values. The task of humanity in the future will be to emerge beyond nihilism, freed from both irrational superstition and the superstitions of rationalism. The creation of the new values of the future is the task of Nietzsche's *Übermensch* (overman or superman).

Whereas Nietzsche insisted that the only approach to the problem of nihilism was to accept its irresistible power and therefore the inevitable destruction of all traditional religious and philosophical values, Dostoyevsky believed that the solution to the problem of nihilism was a reaffirmation of religious tradition. If Nietzsche had sought to pass through the dangers of nihilism and emerge transformed and strengthened on the other side — "beyond good and evil," in the philosopher's words — Dostoyevsky insisted that the only safe course was a return to the religious verities of the past. For Dostoyevsky, loss of faith in God leads directly to nihilism and is, quite literally, the work of the devil. In Dostoyevsky's *The Brothers Karamazov*, the brother Mitya reasons that without God "all things are lawful, that one may do anything one likes."[5] In the absence of God, the novel suggests, there is no crime that cannot and will not be contemplated and even carried out. God is the only guarantor of decency and morality; if human beings dispose of God, then they have disposed of all self-restraint. The patricide around which the novel revolves signals nihilism's disdain for all established traditions and certainties. The nihilist longs for absolute independence and self-creation, and therefore he seeks to destroy everything that connects him to a prior world. But ultimately this murderous disdain is self-destructive: the nihilist undermines the very foundations of his own existence. In Dostoyevsky's 1873 novel *Demons,* his most extended rumination on the problem, the nihilist Nikolai Vsevolodovich Stavrogin, although beautiful and charismatic, ultimately commits suicide after causing both the death of his own wife and the suicide of a little girl he raped. In the same novel the nihilist Alexei Nilych Kirilov declares "If there is no God, then I am God," and insists that "Man has done nothing but invent God, so as to live without killing himself; in that lies the whole of world history up to now." In order to kill off the need for God, Kirilov kills himself, thus demonstrating his own absolute autonomy. "I kill myself to show my insubordination and my new fearsome freedom."[6] And yet in killing himself, Kirilov is also demonstrating his inability to live without God. For Dostoyevsky, nihilism is a Mephisto-phelean philosophy which seeks to negate the value of God's creation; those infected with nihilism are possessed by demons. Only God's love can exorcise those demons.[7] Dostoyevsky's reflections on God and nihilism are echoed in much of the Christian fiction of German-speaking writers during the postwar period, as when, in Ilse Aichinger's *Die größere Hoffnung,* God is referred to as a "fremder Sender" (foreign radio station of the kind the Nazis had forbidden), and the novel's characters come to the realization: "If there is no foreign radio station, then we are nothing but a bad joke!"[8]

The Diagnosis

In approaching the problem of nihilism after the end of the Second World War, Germans could, like Nietzsche, accept the collapse of all established values as a *fait accompli* and seek to create new values out of the rubble; or, like Dostoyevsky, they could come to the recognition that religious and moral tradition offer the only security against chaos. Both approaches were in fundamental agreement on the diagnosis of nihilism as a profound problem in contemporary Western civilization, and as the primary reason for the triumph of Hitlerism; and both sought to overcome nihilism by insisting on humanity's need for moral values. In broad terms, the adherents of a Dostoyevskian position with respect to the problem of nihilism tended to favor a revival of the Christian church in both its Catholic and its Protestant German incarnations, while the adherents of a Nietzschean position were attracted to the philosophy of existentialism — articulated in Germany by the philosophers Martin Heidegger and Karl Jaspers and popularized in France in the novels and plays of Jean Paul Sartre, which were imported into Germany with great success during the first two postwar decades.

In geographical terms, the word *Nullpunkt* can also indicate sea level: that point at which measurements of topographical height and depth typi-

cally begin. The nihilistic and topographical meanings of the term come together metaphorically in a much-noticed 1950 volume about the concept of
a *Nullpunkt,* a work in which Jünger compares nihilism to a vast ocean that
threatens to engulf the dry land of civilization and the human psyche. For
Jünger, nothingness is not just a threat but also a profound temptation:
"Whoever has not felt the enormous power of nothingness in himself and
has not succumbed to its temptation knows our age but little."[9] For
Nietzsche, nihilism had been "a stream that wants to get *to the end*," suggesting both a tremendous power and a goal-oriented linearity with a definite point of rest.[10] In Jünger's metaphors, however, nothingness is an
amorphous ocean with ebbs and floods, suggesting a circularity with no
definite goal. In Nietzsche's imagery, nihilism is part of human history; for
Jünger, nihilism is beyond history. Jünger's nihilism is primarily part of the
individual human psyche. For him, nothingness also contains hidden "treas-
ures" that can be salvaged if nothingness is overcome.

Although Jünger insisted that a surrender to nihilist temptations was
necessary in order to understand the temper of the times — and believed
that those who triumphed in the struggle with nihilism would emerge
stronger after their victory — it was clear to many German intellectuals that
their nation, far from triumphing in the battle with nihilism, had been
shamefully defeated and made weaker as a result. In the words of a character
from a story-within-the-story in Jünger's 1949 novel *Heliopolis,* "We have
summoned tremendous powers; we were not strong enough for their answer. We are overcome by terror. We are faced with a choice: to enter into
the realms of the demons or to withdraw to the weakened domains of the
humane."[11] The latter was by far the most popular option for Germans after
1945. For them nihilism was a dangerous phenomenon that needed to be
resisted, not succumbed to. Faced with what Jünger described as a choice
between "conservative and nihilist currents," they chose conservatism.[12]

The epitome of German nihilism was Hitler and his National Socialist
German Workers Party, whose philosophy Friedrich Meinecke described as "a
fundamentally nihilist striving, for which any ideology was all right, if only it
brought power quickly."[13] An important precursor to postwar interpretations
of the role of nihilism in Hitler's rise to power was the former Nazi Hermann
Rauschning's 1938 study *Die Revolution des Nihilismus* (The Revolution of
Nihilism), which interpreted National Socialism as a nihilist attack on civilization. Meinecke's and Rauschning's interpretation of Nazism seemed quite
plausible to many Germans in the years following the end of the war. In his
book *Die deutsche Frage* Röpke described National Socialism as the most extreme form of "modern tyranny," characterized "by the *entire dissolution of
the values and standards* without which our society, or any other, cannot exist
in the long run." It was anything but an exaggeration, Röpke argued, to refer
to Nazism "literally as Satanism and Nihilism."[14] Many thinkers like Röpke

believed that Hitler represented the apotheosis of nihilism: a belief in and a radical will to nothingness that, true to form, had ultimately self-destructed. For Christoph Bachem, the protagonist of Böll's *Kreuz ohne Liebe*, Hitler is "Satan himself"; and for Christoph's pious mother the Nazi "Third Reich" is quite literally the "Reich of the devil."[15] Hitler, Jünger argued during the war, "is probably the person at whose behest the greatest mass of killing and leveling that history has ever seen was carried out."[16] For the Catholic Reinhold Schneider, writing in 1946, Hitler was a fundamentally nameless man with "always changing, dissolving features," an instrument of the devil coming "from a different dimension."[17] Schneider concluded: "Here another was acting through and over the head of the man who believed that he was leading."[18] For many of the characters in Böll's *Kreuz ohne Liebe*, Hitler's face is obviously the face of the Antichrist, "the real two-faced nebulous visage of catastrophe."[19] In the words of Koeppen's *Tod in Rom*, Hitler was "the Devil's chosen tool, a magical zero, a chimera of the people, a bubble that ultimately burst."[20] Jünger described the German people's enthusiasm for Hitler as "applause at the prospect of self-destruction, a highly nihilistic act," and believed that "the destruction of the synagogues, the elimination of the Jews, the bombing of London, the buzz bombs" had shown ordinary Germans "that such deeds are thinkable and possible," thus destroying ethical safeguards and giving the masses a first-hand experience of what happens when all moral values are eliminated.[21] In Jünger's *Heliopolis*, it is the proletarians attacking the helpless "Parsis" who take on the role of such an amoral mass, giving their support to the nihilistic *Landvogt* (governor), who is described as one of the "Calibans . . . in whom the masses immediately recognized embodiments and idols of . . . animalistic nature. . . ."[22] The connection between Jünger's "Parsis" and European Jews, although not directly articulated in the text, is clear enough.

During the last years of the war the sociologist Alfred Weber — whose brother Max had been the most famous representative of German sociology — attempted a philosophical-historical interpretation of Nazism in which he claimed that European history itself had come to an end with the rise and fall of National Socialist nihilism. His book, *Abschied von der bisherigen Geschichte* (A Farewell to Previous History), was subtitled in the form of a question: *Überwindung des Nihilismus?* (Overcoming Nihilism?). Weber proclaimed "the end of History as we know it, that is to say, history as moulded by the civilization of the West."[23] What follows the end of conventional Western history, Weber believes, will be qualitatively different. In Weber's view, nihilism is "the deep-seated cause . . . of the historical catastrophe which we of the West, and particularly we Europeans, have brought upon the world."[24] According to Weber, Nazism was a result of a nihilistic European philosophical movement that had destroyed all previous values;

the most important representative of this corrosive movement had been the very Nietzsche who claimed falsely to be involved in overcoming nihilism.

In essential agreement with such voices, Döblin described Nazism as a process leading "to the reckless negation and disposal of received moral values, whether formulated only in religion or given more concrete legal or social form." Because of this nihilist decadence, in Döblin's view, "people sanctioned things which under the rule of the moral values now disposed of would have seemed to be tremendous brutalities and cruelties." The medical doctor Döblin described nihilism as a dangerous infection, "a mass sickness of the paranoid kind" that started with a small group of people but then "won the entire country and caused the outbreak of a mass epidemic."[25] In Döblin's view, non- and anti-Nazi German writers could be used in the postwar situation to inoculate Germans against a recurrence of the nihilist epidemic. As part of his own response to the dangers of nihilism, Döblin realized that his own need for order had become overpowering; he converted to Roman Catholicism in 1941. "Life had to have a system of coordinates," he believed, "and not just a lifeless framework."[26] For him, the Roman Catholic church represented the monumental achievement of centuries of Western culture, "the invisible community of the devout and the wise, the pious and the holy."[27] If National Socialism represented part of a nihilist epidemic, then "Christianity set upon humanity as a higher state of well-being, the true well-being of humankind."[28] Döblin was not the only German to turn to religion in the wake of the "Third Reich." The young Heinrich Böll was also convinced of the need for a revival of Christianity, arguing in a letter to his wife that one of Germany's major problems was its virtually complete alienation from Christianity, and allowing his protagonist in *Kreuz ohne Liebe,* Christoph Bachem, to declare that religion now has the task of replacing politics itself.[29] In general, as Jerry Muller has argued, "the return to religion was among the most striking aspects of German culture in the decade after the war."[30]

One of the most influential examinations of the Hitler phenomenon after the end of the war was Max Picard's study *Hitler in uns selbst* (Hitler in Our Selves, 1945), the very title of which suggested that Hitler, far from being primarily a political or economic problem, had been a kind of Dostoyevskian demon taking possession of the human soul. In Picard's reflections, National Socialism appears as the consequence of many decades of movement away from God in the Western world.[31] For Picard, the National Socialist dictatorship clearly shows "what happens when man lives in disunion with the things of this world, with his fellow men, with himself, with God."[32] It can thus serve as a warning to the European world. What happened in Germany could happen anywhere in the Western world, because the same kind of nihilistic discontinuity and absurdity is present everywhere. The collapse of the nothingness that was Hitler has left an empty space that can be filled either by further nothingness or — if Europeans recognize the danger of nihilism and the promise of Christian faith — by a return to God's grace.

The conservative journalist Hans Zehrer's diagnosis of contemporary European nihilism was fundamentally similar to that of Picard. Zehrer, the former revolutionary conservative, was to become the editor of the daily newspaper *Die Welt* in the 1950s. His path from insurrectionary anger to conservative cultural critique is typical of many former opponents of the Weimar Republic during the formation and early history of the Federal Republic.[33] In his book *Der Mensch in dieser Welt* (Man in this World, 1948), Zeher declared that "Western man finds himself in the great historic crisis of his culture. The crisis began with the falling away of Western man from God."[34] The path away from God is the true origin of what Zehrer calls the darkening ("Verfinsterung") of European consciousness, leading to guilt and the death of the human conscience, which, for Zehrer, is identical to the consciousness of God working within the soul.

The explanation of Nazism as an outgrowth of philosophical nihilism offered several advantages to Germans in the immediate postwar period. Ignoring specific political, economic, and social factors that might have contributed to the disaster of the "Third Reich," the nihilist explanation raised discussion to an abstract metaphysical plane that avoided questions of individual — or even group — guilt or responsibility. If Nazism was nothing more or less than a particularly virulent political embodiment of nihilism, and if nihilism was part of contemporary Western culture more generally, then neither individual Germans nor Germany as a whole could be held responsible for the disasters that had happened between 1933 and 1945. Likewise, if the nihilism of the Nazis was simply a dangerous epidemic, as Döblin argued, the infectious "invasion of a foreign mass of ideas," then the German people could no more be considered guilty for being infected than a doctor would consider a patient morally guilty for having contracted a disease.[35] The physically sick person needs a physician; the social body infected by the demons of nihilism needs either an exorcist or a good metaphysician. Indeed, the nihilistic explanation for Nazism gave Germans the opportunity to see themselves as spiritual mine-sweepers for the rest of Europe, showing others the philosophical and political paths that must be avoided in the future. "It very much appears," declared Lersch in 1947, "that the German fate of the most recent past — as certainly as it is also the expression of specifically German dangers — above and beyond that is simultaneously an example of world history, demonstrating the dangers that threaten modern existence more generally."[36]

One of the many problems that the focus on nihilism made it possible to avoid was the issue of class domination and economic polarization — what during the years of the *Kaiserreich* and the Weimar Republic had been called the "social question" (soziale Frage). The so-called Dimitrov thesis of European Communists — named after its formulator Georgi Mikhailov Dimitrov, the major twentieth-century leader of the Bulgarian Communist Party and a functionary of the Communist International — held that the National Socialist dictatorship was "the open terrorist dictatorship of the most reactionary, chauvinist, and imperialist elements of finance capitalism," who turned to Hitler in a desperate effort to save themselves from an impending socialist revolution.[37] In the Marxist scheme there were specific and identifiable social reasons for the Hitler dictatorship; and the transfer of power to Hitler could be attributed to the self-defensive actions of German capitalists. If, however, Nazism was simply one variety of ongoing European nihilism, then such Marxist explanatory schemes fell apart. The belief that Nazism was the result primarily of philosophical nihilism implied that it had had little to do with social and class structures; this in turn meant that any changes in such structures became unnecessary in the postwar world. For this reason theories of the nihilistic origins of Nazism had far wider currency in the three western occupation zones than in the Soviet zone.

Issues of class structure were not the only problems exempted from critical examination in theories of Nazism as an expression of nihilism. At root, theories of nihilism excised Nazism from German and European history, declaring the Hitler phenomenon to be essentially ahistorical and alogical and thus immune to historical analysis and explanation. In such theories, Nazism was primarily a metaphysical or theological conundrum, not a concrete research problem for historians or political scientists. A primary focus on nihilism as the origin of Nazi barbarity implied that problems associated with German national traditions could largely be excluded from culpability. If nihilism was the complete rejection of all previous traditions, as Rauschning had argued, then the disaster of Nazism, far from implicating German conservatives or the traditions they valued, in fact vindicated them. The stylization of Hitler as a revolutionary nihilist meant that an anti-Nazi policy in the wake of the Third Reich could be constructed along the lines of a restoration of traditional values. If Hitler had been the revolutionary destroyer of hallowed German conservative traditions, then such a policy of restoration, far from being negatively reactionary, was in fact positively progressive, an appropriately measured, constructive response to self-destructive National Socialist radicalism. As Rauschning had already written in the 1930s, the response to a "revolution that has wrecked the social order, overthrown every standard, and rejected every ideology" should lie "in the forces of true Conservatism and in the healing restoration of the spiritual and social forces of our historic past."[38]

The concept of Nazism as a revolutionary nihilism that had ultimately led to a *Nullpunkt* in German history implied a radical discontinuity between the years of the Third Reich and both the prewar and postwar years, a discontinuity which, paradoxically, allowed the postwar years to be constructed as a philosophical continuity with earlier, non-nihilistic German traditions. Before the zero of 1945 came a nothingness that did not need to be examined as part of a problematic continuity with post-1945 or pre-1933 structures of power and domination. Most attractively, the idea of Nazism as a force coming out of nowhere and disappearing into nothingness, like anti-matter, implied that survival itself was clear proof of moral superiority. Anyone who had preceded or, more importantly, survived the Nazi catastrophe had obviously neither come from nowhere nor disappeared into nothingness; the very existence of such a person indicated a will to self-preservation directly in conflict with Nazi destructiveness. The fact of having escaped the Nazi catastrophe could thus become a moral virtue. Reconstruction and restoration could be interpreted as a post-facto act of anti-Nazi resistance. If Nazism was a Mephistophelean "Spirit of Eternal Negation," then a postwar spirit of affirmation and rebuilding was ipso facto morally justified. This vindication applied not just to individual Germans but also to the nation as a whole, which had survived a Hitler ultimately bent on the destruction of Germany itself.

Hence postwar culture was filled with the pathos of rebuilding. When he returned to Germany in 1945, Döblin noted that he was amazed by the way Germans, far from falling into despondency, "are running around in the ruins like overwrought, industrious ants on a crushed anthill."[39] Döblin believed that "it will be much easier to rebuild their cities than to get them to comprehend what it was they have experienced, and to understand how it all came to pass." The *Trümmerfrau* (rubble woman), who gathers together the bricks and stones of destroyed buildings in order to pave the way for the construction of new ones, became the embodiment of this pathos among what Döblin called a still "industrious, orderly people."[40] The cheerful woman with the positive outlook was an emblem of postwar German reconstruction. Wolfgang Staudte's 1946 film *Die Mörder sind unter uns* (The Murderers Are Among Us), the first postwar German feature film and easily the most famous of so-called *Trümmerfilme* (rubble films), tells the story of precisely such a heroic woman, whose will to survive stands in positive contrast to the cynical, self-destructive skepticism of her male counterpart — whom she is ultimately able to convert.

The Christian Response

Not surprisingly, German theologians were among the most fervent supporters of an interpretation of Nazism based on the analysis of nihilism. Many theologians followed Picard's lead in positing Nazism as a nihilistic Antichrist whose essence lay in the denial of God. Protestant Bishop Theophil Wurm declared at a church conference in 1945 that as a result of increasing secularization and materialism Germany had descended into nihilism; as Wurm made clear four years later in an article for *Die Zeit*, this ethical decline had left Germans vulnerable to demonic influences.[41] The Protestant theologian Heinrich Vogel showed after the war how it was possible to transform religious interpretations of Nazism-as-nihilism into a call for a return to traditional church doctrine and institutions. Vogel declared that nihilism sought to wrest human beings from allegiance to their true creator, God, and instead to assert allegiance to nothingness: "*to put man at the mercy of nothingness as his supposed creator and savior.*"[42] In agreement with Dostoyevsky, Vogel contended that nihilism was "the last step in the process of secularization. We will have to understand this belief in nothingness as the last, consciously demonic turn of man after he has delivered himself to a belief in things and ideologies and no longer wants to hear the word of the living God."[43]

Theological and Christian interpretations of nihilism as the root cause of the German catastrophe were not without concrete political correlates in Western and even Eastern Germany during the immediate postwar period. The most important and long-lasting consequence of such interpretations was the foundation of two new Christian parties in the Western zones, the Christian Social Union in Bavaria and the Christian Democratic Union in the rest of Western Germany. The CDU, which was to become the governing party in the Federal Republic for most of the post-1945 period, brought Catholics from the former *Zentrum* party of the Weimar Republic together with Protestants in a unified Christian *Volkspartei* (people's party) proclaiming fundamental occidental principles. As Maria Mitchell has noted, "the year 1945 marked the first time in German history that Catholics and Protestants, divided by decades of mutual political antagonism, sought consciously to design an avowedly democratic, interconfessional political platform."[44] The CDU sought to achieve what the Swiss theologian Emil Brunner called a "rechristianization of the dechristianized society."[45] In the words of Theodor Scharmitzel, an early activist in the CDU, "the German people has been dechristianized to a great extent," and the path to recovery could occur only "if we once again become a Christian people."[46] This rechristianization was an explicit goal of the CDU and of many German-speaking Christian writers.

Although Ernst Jünger maintained his distance from explicitly Christian solutions to the problem of nihilism, he nevertheless agreed on the importance of a return to God. Jünger's conception of the nihilist "Nullpunkt" was one of the most influential in postwar German culture. In alignment with Weber's notion of the end of history, Jünger described the time before 1945 and the time after 1945 as divided by an absolute zero defined by nihilism. In his book *Über die Linie* (Across the Line, 1950), he conceived of the zero point in navigational terms, describing the zero as a meridian, the zero longitudinal marker running from the North to the South Pole, which is connected on the other side of the earth with the meridian known today as the International

Date Line — a meridian sought with determination by eighteenth-century explorers. Just as such explorers and scholars had disputed the precise location of the meridian, so too modern intellectuals sought, perhaps in vain, to locate the nothingness of nihilism: "the intellects are divided by a Babylonian confusion whose theme is the exact position of the zero point."[47] In Jünger's metaphor, human history after 1945 is in the position of a ship that has passed over meridian 180, except that this passage entails the beginning not just of a new day but of an entirely new history. It marks the mid-point on the journey through the sea of nihilism, but not the end: "The crossing of the line, the passage over the zero point, *divides* the drama; it marks the middle, but not yet the end."[48] Jünger believed that in the contemporary world "nihilism is not just dominant but, even worse, has become the normal state of affairs."[49] According to Jünger, "with the passage over the zero meridian the old numbers are no longer correct, and a new reckoning must begin."[50] This new position will also, paradoxically, be old: freed from the destructive radicalism of the past decades and focused on the conservative preservation of western values. "The path to God is enormously long in our time," Jünger had argued in his notebooks before the end of the war, "as if man had gotten lost in the unlimited spaces invented by his genius." In view of the current horrors, however, "God must be conceived anew."[51]

Like other commentators, Jünger described the advent of Hitler as a product of the philosophical movement of the previous century, suggesting that "in the hothouse of wars and civil wars the great theories of the previous century bore fruit by turning to praxis."[52] In an attack on the concept of progress that was as pessimistic as Nietzsche's had been over half a century earlier, Jünger suggested that the ultimate teleology of Western civilization had been Hitler's concentration camps: "There progress ended with its thoughts and ideas; it was into these swamps that the all too clever inventive era led."[53] By the end of the Second World War, Jünger — who had previously welcomed the development of technology and science enthusiastically — had become a historical pessimist. Increasingly, he was "convinced of the wrongness and hopelessness of this historical period," writes Helmuth Kiesel.[54] For Jünger, scientific progress and barbarity are by no means mutually exclusive. In the novel *Heliopolis,* technology is used in the service of barbarity, far outpacing "the boldest dreams of the old tyrants." In a world dominated by inhumane technology, "the old measures returned with new names — torture, serfdom, slavery."[55] A primary representative of this demonic technology is Dr. Mertens, head of the "Toxicological Institute" where human beings are experimented on and murdered. Like Dr. Mertens, Dr. Thomas Becker, who runs the "Department of Foreign Peoples" at the *Landvogt*'s "Central Agency" — and who is thus responsible for collecting information and performing research on peoples and races considered to be inferior — also represents the intertwining of enlightenment and barbarity.

Dr. Becker's office is decorated with the shrunken heads of the victims of his scientific interest. For him, "old Francis Bacon's 'Knowledge is power' had been simplified to 'Knowledge is murder.'"[56] He represents a science disdainful of humanity and morality and obsessed with notions of "progress" abstracted from any nonscientific concerns. For him, science does not serve to create a more humane life for human beings; rather, human beings are tools to be used in the creation of a more powerful science.

In 1947 Max Horkheimer and Theodor W. Adorno published their *Dialektik der Aufklärung* with the small Querido publishing company in Amsterdam, an important outlet for German emigrants. This book, which was later to exercise considerable influence on the German student movement of the 1960s and 1970s, took the discussion of enlightenment, liberalism, and nihilism to a new level of sophistication. As Jeffrey Herf has aptly noted, "despite vastly different starting points, the right wing and the left wing of the German *Bildungsbürgertum*," including Horkheimer and Adorno along with Ernst Jünger and his brother Friedrich Georg Jünger, shared "considerable common ground and some common inspiration" in their postwar critiques of social and technological progress.[57] Fascinated by the seeming paradox that the human species appears to "other species as the highest evolutionary and therefore most fearsome destructive power," Horkheimer and Adorno explored the reasons for human beings' "urge to destroy."[58] Their deliberations circled around the dialectical interconnection between human progress and inhuman destruction. In their view the dialectic of enlightenment was the dialectic of history itself; they conceived of enlightenment not just as a specific intellectual movement of the eighteenth century but as a general, ongoing human path away from primitive superstition to the rule of reason and purposive logic. For them, what is called history is none other than the complex and twisted path of enlightenment itself. At one level, Horkheimer and Adorno conceived of enlightenment as a liberating force by means of which people free themselves from superstition and fear, making themselves the rulers of both nature and their own destinies.

However the price that human beings pay for control of nature is rigid self-control to the point of self-denial. In order to survive in a hostile outward environment, human beings rein in their natural desires; thus the imitation of death is the price of life. As Horkheimer and Adorno put it, "men pay for the increase of their power with alienation from that over which they exercise their power."[59] It is not just from nature itself that human beings alienate themselves; they also become alienated from everything natural within them. Ultimately, the very same rationalizing techniques used to dominate nature are used to dominate the self and other people. "For enlightenment, whatever does not conform to the rule of computation and utility is suspect."[60] Those aspects of nature that do not conform to the dictates of enlightenment are pushed aside; so too nonconformist human beings and the nonconformist aspects of one's own nature are eliminated. Hence enlightenment necessarily tends toward brutality and control: "Enlightenment is totalitarian."[61] Enlightenment is thus not just the path toward human liberation but also the path toward repression; as part of the process of enlightenment, human beings begin to imitate the very violence from which they are trying to escape. "The curse of irresistible progress is irresistible regression," the two writers declare.[62]

In Horkheimer's and Adorno's view, Nazism is a product not of primitivism or backwardness but rather of the progress of enlightenment itself. It is an expression of "that destructive lust of civilized men who could never fulfill the painful process of civilization."[63] Far from being a return to original superstition, they believe, Nazism is a fundamentally modern rebellion against and simultaneous expression of the brutality of enlightenment. In their view, "fascism is also totalitarian in that it seeks to make the rebellion of suppressed nature against domination directly useful to domination."[64] What Horkheimer and Adorno mean by this is that the rebellion of nature against the violence perpetrated by enlightenment is understandable and even justified; however Nazism transforms rebellion against violence into an apotheosis of violence. Far from annihilating enlightenment, Nazism becomes enlightenment as annihilation.

Horkheimer's and Adorno's dictum that "the dialectic of enlightenment is transformed objectively into madness"[65] converges with conservative diagnoses of nihilism in the sociologists' belief that the apotheosis of inhumane enlightenment represented by Nazism is made possible in part by the destruction of previous European value systems. "In accordance with its principle, enlightenment does not stop at the minimum of belief without which the bourgeois world cannot exist."[66] In a chapter on the Marquis de Sade and enlightenment in the realm of sexual mores, Horkheimer and Adorno suggest that it is impossible to ground ethical or moral systems purely on the basis of logic or reason. In their view "reason is the organ of calculation, of planning; it is neutral in regard to ends."[67] Because reason is neutral with respect to goals, it can be instrumentalized in the service of any goal. Reason is a tool that can be used by anyone; it has become "a purposeless purposiveness which might thus be attached to all ends."[68] Sade's works, the two sociologists write, make "the scientistic the destructive principle." Sade's Juliette "is by no means fanatical"; on the contrary, "her procedure is enlightened and efficient as she goes about her work of sacrilege."[69] The sexual predators described by Sade behave reasonably and logically, given the prior deconstruction of all received social morality. Whereas traditional sexual morality oppresses women by making them subordinate to and dependent on their fathers and husbands, the elimination of traditional sexual morality, far from freeing women from oppression, plunges them even deeper into helplessness, because it does away with the feelings of responsibility and commitment previously demanded of men in return for the submission of women. Men are now free to use women as instruments of work and pleasure, relieved from all moral commitments. In general, Horkheimer and Adorno believe, it is the weak who suffer most from the inhumane underside of enlightenment, because in the naked struggle for power that follows in the wake of moral collapse it is they who cannot defend themselves. The two sociologists offer no fail-safe solution to the problem of enlightenment in their study; its tendency toward self-destruction, they suggest, is necessary and inevitable. However they insist that since enlightenment always also contains its own negation the only possibility for true liberation from the dialectic of enlightenment must come through more enlightenment, in a complex process of negation and self-reflection.

Probably the most important postwar Christian exploration of nihilism and salvation in German literature of the immediate postwar period was Langgässer's *Das unauslöschliche Siegel,* which the German critic Ursula Reinhold has called "*the* literary sensation" of the era.[70] This novel, greeted by contemporary critics as a signal of German literature's renewed claim to world significance, tells the story of Lazarus Belfontaine, a Jew half-heartedly converted to Catholicism who, together with his devout wife Elisabeth and his daughter Elfriede, lives in a small town in the Rhineland, where he operates the grocery store previously owned by his deceased father-in-law. In May of 1914, seven years after his baptism and marriage, the restless Belfontaine suddenly departs for France, leaving his family behind. After the outbreak of the First World War in late August of 1914, Belfontaine is interned in France as an enemy alien; upon his release at war's end, he stays in France, becomes a French citizen, and marries a dissolute but wealthy French woman named Suzette — thus becoming a well-to-do bigamist, although Belfontaine's German wife and daughter both die of flu not long after. In May of 1925, eighteen years after his German marriage and baptism, eleven years after his departure from Germany, and seven years after his release from the French internment camp, Belfontaine's wife Suzette is robbed and murdered by a wandering criminal whom she had previously invited into her home. On the same day, Belfontaine is overwhelmed and transformed by the love of God; for the first time in Belfontaine's life his conversion to Christianity becomes a spiritual reality. From now on Belfontaine devotes his life to prayer, becoming a charismatic religious figure. Belfontaine departs for Germany; because of his Jewish background, he is shipped off by the Nazis a decade and a half later to a concentration camp in Poland, from which he ultimately escapes, one of few survivors. On his journey back into Germany in the wake of the victorious Red Army, Belfontaine emerges as a renowned and much sought-after figure, "blessed with the gift of healing and the charisma of awakening."[71]

The indelible seal of the novel's title is the sign of the cross under which the baptism of Belfontaine was carried out.[72] In spite of Belfontaine's efforts to escape from his Christianity — i.e., from the recognition of the divine nature of Christ — he is unsuccessful. His baptism plants a seed of spiritual life in him that ultimately comes to fruition. Belfontaine's first name is a reference to the man whom Christ raises from the dead in the Gospels; it is the words of Christ from the Bible (John 11:43–44) that Belfontaine hears on the day of his spiritual resurrection in 1925: "LAZARUS! COME OUT!"[73] The name Belfontaine (beautiful fountain) suggests both the baptismal water with which Belfontaine has been consecrated and Belfontaine's status as a caught fish, wriggling and twisting but unable to escape from the grace of Christ.

Langgässer's novel is fundamentally modern, full of a great many disparate elements and making jumps in time and place that become clear only in light of the work in its entirety.[74] In the first part of the novel, which takes place primarily in Germany in May of 1914 and tells the story of Belfontaine's decision to leave the small town where he has become a successful businessman and citizen, there are three episodes whose structural relationship to the rest of the story is initially unclear. The first such episode — which takes the form of a discussion between two old men in Paris on the same night in May of 1914 — tells the story of Saint Bernadette and the miracles at Lourdes in 1858, especially of a blind man healed by the water of the holy spring and then blinded again, in answer to his own prayers, by the power of God. As it turns out, this blind man, fondly but somewhat mockingly named "Blind Faith" by those who know him, is none other than the beggar encountered by Belfontaine immediately after his baptism in 1907 and on each succeeding anniversary of his baptism; the beggar's death in May of 1914, in Belfontaine's small Rhineland town, coincides with the seventh anniversary of Belfontaine's baptism and with the telling of his story on the same night in Paris by a man who had encountered "Blind Faith" as a youth, and who dreams of his death as an old man. The second episode takes the form of a conversation between two Catholic priests sometime in 1925 about the double life of Lazarus Belfontaine; one of the priests, Jacques Le Roy, had been a friend of Belfontaine during his residence in Senlis, France; it is this residence that forms the subject matter of the novel's third part. The third structurally mysterious episode, which forms the conclusion of the novel's first part, once again takes place in Paris on the same night in 1914 and is focused on the prayer of a Catholic missionary who has just returned to France from an unsuccessful trip to China in order to train young priests for missionary work. This missionary, named Lucien Benoît, is the holy man whose prayer, eleven years later, results in the spiritual awakening of Belfontaine; Benoît is also the former fiancé of Hortense de Chamant, best friend of Suzette Bonmarché, Belfontaine's future wife. The novel's second part tells the story of Hortense de Chamant's downfall and suicide and thus also of Suzette's spiritual degradation, which ends with her murder on the day of Belfontaine's spiritual awakening.

As this brief summary of the novel's first part indicates, the narrative structure of *Das unauslöschliche Siegel* is complex, featuring extensive jumps in space and time and requiring a good deal of patient work on the part of readers. Langgässer herself stated that she wished to achieve an "existential representation of objective understanding of the world and anti-psychological religiosity."[75] As Catherine Gelbin has noted, Langgässer clearly perceived herself as "an avant-garde writer."[76] Her modernist techniques and depictions of sexuality and perversion earned attacks from many critics and readers, including some devout Roman Catholics who wished to see the novel placed on the church's index of forbidden books.[77] At first glance, entire sections of *Das unauslöschliche Siegel* appear to be random montage. However such disorder ultimately dissolves, revealing an underlying order guaranteed by the grace of God. Langgässer uses many of the techniques of the modern novel — interior monologue, uncertainty, montage — in order to reveal that underneath the seeming chaos of modern life there is a deep, abiding order. If, according to György Lukács, the novel as a literary genre tells the story of man's transcendental homelessness, with more modern novels becoming ever more radical in their aesthetic approach to such homelessness, then Langgässer uses the tools of the modern novel in order to reverse such homelessness and lead her primary figure to unity with God.[78] Most of the novel still deals with Belfontaine's spiritual despair, thus confirming Lukács's thesis; but the thrust of the novel is towards an overcoming of that despair. Although many of the novel's events appear to be random coincidences, it becomes evident by the end of the story that there are no coincidences; everything is structured according to God's plan. As the critic Mathias Bertram has written, "every name, every physiognomic detail, every gesture . . ., and certainly every action" in the novel prove ultimately "to be a sign . . . pointing to a higher reality."[79] Likewise the novel's occasionally confusing chronological structure, which entails sometimes abrupt jumps in time, reflects the divine presence of God, for whom chronological differentiation dissolves into an eternal present — "Now."[80]

What makes God's plan so complex and difficult for humans to understand is human freedom of choice and the existence of the devil, who seeks to destroy creation itself. The devil is the lord of the world and of the history of the world, and at any given time he is always triumphant over God. It is only at the end of history that God triumphs over Satan. Human beings cannot affect the outcome of the battle itself; but they are given the freedom to choose sides. The devil is an anti-God, a master of mimicry; in all of his workings he resembles God as a kind of reversed mirror image. In Langgässer's novel the devil takes the form of Belfontaine's former teacher Grandpierre; of the French wine merchant Tricheur, who induces Belfontaine to leave his wife and children and come to France in 1914; and of the criminal sailor who has sex with and then murders Belfontaine's second wife

Suzette in 1925 at the end of the novel's third part. In Belfontaine's mind the devil is associated with the Greek god-satyr Pan. Whereas for Nietzsche the death of Pan had prefigured the death of God, for Langgässer Pan's death is the death of the devil and the triumph of God in Belfontaine's soul. The devil is ubiquitous and can take on many shapes. Asked to describe Tricheur, Belfontaine's first wife Elisabeth finds that he resembles everyone and no one; he is a protean form, capable of his own satanic transubstantiation. The novel is full of references to the Nietzschean image of the snake biting its own tail; for Langgässer this is a symbol of the devil's devious and labyrinthine "logic of sin" from which there is no internal escape.[81] The only escape lies in the sudden external intervention of grace.

For Langgässer, the devil of modernity is no longer the horrific, animalistic demon of medieval imagery but rather a reasonable bourgeois spirit, the dark side of enlightenment. He is the ghost of reason and reason as ghost. As Hortense de Chamant's father says to Belfontaine on the day of the latter's spiritual resurrection, the devil today is "a friend of the status quo, a man of reason, a man of the lectern, the genuine citizen, the subject and foundation stone of our savings banks, offices, and schools."[82] The logic of reason is satanic, because it seeks to block off access to God. Stuck in history, it leads nowhere, like Nietzsche's circular snake. Contemporary science and technology are a kind of modern alchemy, creating a devious mechanical progress that is in fact nothing but a standstill. The sterilized gods of modernity leave human beings filled with the boredom, tiredness, and sadness that overcome Belfontaine at the beginning of the novel, and which lead to his desire for nothingness at the novel's end. Blocked from access to both the past and the future, civilized human beings live in an endless empty present of ennui in which, like Belfontaine, they become reverse mirror images of their true selves, actors performing a role whose substance has become lost. "You were probably never yourself?" Belfontaine is asked in the first part of the novel by the pharmacist Mösinger, himself a tormented bourgeois who has come to understand that the contemporary man of affairs "gradually becomes the echo of his own self and the mirror image of his own person."[83] The contemporary bourgeois is, in other words, possessed by — all too logical and seemingly harmless — demons. His self-mimicry is itself nothing but a small-scale imitation of Satan's mimicry of the divine. Just as Satan has alienated himself from God, so too the contemporary bourgeois has become alienated from the true source of his being. Disgusted with life, he longs to escape from his superstitious and unsatisfying "cult of reason," and this escape can take two possible paths: the path toward Satan or the path toward God.[84] Satan's is the path of nothingness and the erasure of creation. For Langgässer as for Dostoyevsky, liberalism and the Enlightenment ultimately pave the way for nihilism. The representative figure of such nihilism is Hortense de Chamant, who commits suicide at the end of the novel's second part, after she learns that she has become the victim of a cruel joke. In the frenzy of her despair she explains her nihilistic credo to an apparently chance acquaintance, the aspiring young writer Camille Descha-teaux, who will later appropriate her words in his own writing:

> Isn't nothingness . . . stronger and larger than all content, hence stronger than heaven and hell, because it is not and therefore cannot suffer, cannot begin, cannot end? I want to tell you something, sir, but don't tell anyone else: nothingness is greater than this God with the terrible urge to create, for which He even expects thanks and worship from His creatures. Why are we not nothing?[85]

For Hortense the gargoyles and chimeras on Gothic cathedrals have become symbols of the nihilistic rejection of creation. Whereas the Virgin Mary bears God into flesh, the chimera bears human beings into nothingness. Nothing-ness is the great temptation:

> Come, let us be nothing! Let us leave the womb of nature and of that which is above nature, this drivel and old wives' tale about birth and rebirth. Why does the circle hold us? Only because we do not dare to step over the edge.[86]

All three parts of *Das unauslöschliche Siegel* end with the death of a woman who surrenders to the temptation of nothingness. At the end of the novel's first section the adulteress Helene Gitzler, like Tolstoy's Anna Karenina, throws herself into the path of an oncoming train after her lover has left her. At the end of the second section, the virgin Hortense de Chamant, diaboli-cally deceived and debased by the evil father of her best friend, throws her-self into the River Seine. And at the end of the novel's third section Suzette Belfontaine — who intentionally takes the risk of associating herself with a criminal sailor because, more than life itself, she desperately wants the pearl necklace he is hocking — is strangled in her bed after having engaged will-ingly in sexual intercourse with her murderer.

However the satanic nothingness to which these figures surrender is sim-ply a perverse reflection of the divine nothingness to which Belfontaine himself submits at the novel's end. This divine nothingness eliminates Belfontaine's secondary, inauthentic life, with its reasonable demons, making way for the fullness of God, who, because He himself is everything, can tolerate nothing which is not part of Him. At the end of the novel's third part Belfontaine is not even an empty vessel into which God is poured; rather, his secondary, dia-bolical existence has been completely obliterated. "Great Pan has died. Great Pan is dead."[87] What for Nietzsche had been the death of God is, for Lang-gässer, the death of Satan. The nothingness into which Belfontaine's despair has thrust him ultimately clears the way for unity with God.

In addition to being the story of one man's spiritual transformation, *Das unauslöschliche Siegel* is also a reflection on the path of German and European religious history, which receives extensive attention at the beginning of the novel's second part, in the form of a visit by two German military officers to the cathedral of Senlis in September of 1914. In Langgässer's conception, France is the country of the Enlightenment, and Germany is the home of Martin Luther's Protestant Reformation. Both of these intellectual movements represent paths away from God. As one of the two military officers, a young nobleman, reads through the pages of an old book from the Senlis library, he is confronted with the words of the Spanish diplomat, politician, and religious writer, Donoso Cortés, from the middle of the nineteenth century. For Langgässer, as for the historical Donoso, the history of Prussia is the history of Protestantism, which is the history of a "falling away from God."[88] If the Holy Roman Empire had constituted part of a Christendom that encompassed all of Western Europe in a unified Catholic faith, then Prussia — and the second, Bismarckian empire whose core it later became — emerged as the Protestant embodiment of a cleavage in Christianity.[89] "Freedom is dead," Donoso declares, suggesting that "the world is racing in seven-mile boots toward despotism, toward a regime more violent and destructive than human beings have ever seen."[90] In the context of the year 1946, when Langgässer's novel was published, it becomes clear that this despotic regime has already become a reality in Hitler's dictatorship, with the "Third Reich" as the diabolically logical extension of the path away from God initiated by Luther and furthered by Bismarck's second empire.[91] If Protestantism splits Christianity in half, distancing Christians from God, then Nazism seeks to kill God entirely, establishing an empire of absolute nihilism. The Third Reich is thus the logical extension of the second Reich, itself a product of the destruction of the Catholic Holy Roman Empire, or first Reich.[92]

Relatively few of the figures of postwar German literature find the kind of spiritual resurrection granted to Langgässer's Lazarus Belfontaine. Many works by authors of the younger generation during this period suggest that any return to traditional Christian faith will be difficult if not impossible. In Borchert's *Draussen vor der Tür* the veteran Beckmann, upon his return to Hamburg, finds himself confronted with a series of dreamlike figures, including a fat, burping undertaker and a sad old man. As it turns out, the old man is "the God no one believes in now," while the undertaker is death personified. In the postwar world Europeans believe in the latter, not the former. As the old man complains to his competitor: "Death? You're all right. You're the new God. They believe in you. They love you. They fear you. You can't be deposed. You can't be denied."[93] For Beckmann the Christian God has become a pathetic fiction. "Oh, you are old, God, you're old-fashioned, you can't cope with the long lists of our dead and our agonies. We no longer really know you, you're a fairytale God."[94] The old man replies to Beckmann's accusations by insisting that it is not he who has turned away from human beings but human beings who have turned away from him; and he insists that there is nothing he can do to make things better. "I cannot help it. I cannot, cannot help it."[95] God, in other words, is just as helpless as Beckmann himself. The all-powerful divinity of Christian theology has become a helpless, sniveling old man, no longer loved or feared by Beckmann's contemporaries. Like Beckmann himself, he is a "man outside."

In Wolfdietrich Schnurre's short story "Das Begräbnis" (The Burial, 1946), Borchert's powerless old man has given up the ghost, thus fulfilling the Nietzschean dictum "God is dead" three-quarters of a century late. Whereas Borchert's play is full of the pathos of Expressionism, Schnurre's prose is understated and matter-of-fact. At the beginning of this laconic short story the first-person narrator receives a black-bordered death announcement: "LOVED BY NO ONE, HATED BY NO ONE, HE DIED TODAY AFTER LONG SUFFERING, BORNE WITH HEAVENLY PATIENCE: GOD."[96] The rest of the story describes God's burial, which takes place in an urban cemetery in the middle of the night during pouring rain; hardly any mourners come. During the course of the burial God falls out of the coffin; it turns out that God is nothing but an unremarkable, pale man, with a bit of blood on his mouth and beard. When God is finally buried, the pastor finds himself unable to make a speech; no one wants to listen, and at any rate he has nothing to say. The great theological constructions of European civilization have ended — first in stuttering and then in silence. The point of Schnurre's story is its lack of drama and excitement. During the nineteenth century Nietzsche had still managed to wind up emotions with the earth-shattering revelation of God's death; Schnurre is suggesting that in Germany in the late 1940s the death of God is no longer news.

The Existentialist Response

If the path to Christianity was blocked for many members of the younger generation, then the problem of nihilism needed to be solved in another way. One of the most common responses was existentialism, which the Marburg philosopher Julius Ebbinghaus — himself an opponent of existentialism — described in a 1947 article for the *Neue Zeitung* as "a phenomenon which we encounter with such intensity in our social reality that a palpable . . ., urgent need exists to become enlightened about it."[97] For Lersch existentialism was one of the key words of the era, mirroring "its view of the world and of existence."[98] In a response to Ebbinghaus's largely negative interpretation of existentialism, Alfred Andersch acknowledged that existentialism truly was a "philosophy of fashion," but only inasmuch "as it gets its exciting relevance from the apocalyptic situation of this era." In Andersch's view, existentialism, in accordance with the spirit of the times, articulates "the radical questioning of all 'objective' values."[99] Whereas Christian authors like Langgässer had sought an essentially Dostoyevskean response to the problem of nihilism, insisting on the continuing validity of the Christian faith, existentialist authors like Andersch agreed with Nietzsche that traditional religious values could no longer be revived. Out of the fearsome freedom — and loneliness — that emerges from the death of God, such authors, like Nietzsche, wanted to create new human values. Andersch was particularly enthusiastic about the writing of Sartre, whose play *Les mouches* (The Flies) — although initially banned in the Western zones because of its purported immorality — became one of the most influential theatrical works in Germany during the immediate postwar period. In September of 1947 Gustaf Gründgens produced the play in Düsseldorf, and in January of 1948 the play had its Berlin premiere at the Hebbel Theater, in the presence of Sartre and his companion Simone de Beauvoir, for whom Russian officials gave a reception at a local arts club — even though Alexander Dymschitz, the chief Russian cultural officer in Berlin, had already published an article in Berlin's *Tägliche Rundschau* at the end of November, 1947 explaining that he disliked Sartre's play because of its individualism and disdain for the masses.[100] It was from *Les mouches* and German writers' interpretations of French and German existentialist philosophy that ordinary Germans and even most intellectuals in the second half of the 1940s learned about existentialism — not from difficult philosophical tomes like Heidegger's *Sein und Zeit* (Being and Time) or Sartre's *L'être et le néant* (Being and Nothingness), which — even if Germans had the patience to work their way through them — were generally unavailable in the occupied country during the immediate postwar period. As Henri Nannen of Hannover's *Abendpost* complained, "Sartre is being performed in all the theaters, but Heidegger's works can only be found in France."[101] But the fact that existentialist philosophy was primarily available to Germans as a literary or theatrical phenomenon does not seem to have lessened its impact. For Andersch, existentialist literature became philosophically effective "by putting a face in the place of the problem" and thus "making the problem transparent."[102]

Sartre's *Les mouches* is essentially a retelling of Aeschylus's *The Libation Bearers,* the second play in the *Oresteia,* but with an existentialist twist. In killing his mother Clytemnestra and her lover Aegisthus, the hero Orestes is also killing off the gods to whom he had previously sworn fealty. The warmth and comfort of the gods and of the value systems set up around them are hence gone for him; he now lives alone and for himself. "I am free, Electra. Freedom has crashed down on me like a thunderbolt," he declares.[103] To regret the crime that he has committed would be a denial of himself and thus of his own freedom; Orestes therefore refuses repentance, declaring allegiance to his crime as his only real possession. "I have done *my* deed, Electra, and that deed was good," he declares. "I shall bear it on my shoulders as a carrier at a ferry carries the traveler to the farther bank . . . The heavier it is to carry, the better pleased I shall be; for that burden is my freedom."[104] Orestes becomes "a king without a kingdom" and understands that "all here is new, all must begin anew."[105] A hero of the zero hour, Orestes leaves Argos pursued by the spirits of the old order that he has destroyed.

In a brief introduction to the German edition of *Les mouches,* Sartre indicated that he had originally written the play in response to the German invasion of France, after which "our past no longer existed." In Sartre's description, the citizens of German-occupied France were faced with a clear choice: they could succumb to unproductive regret and self-hatred, or they could choose a new life of freedom. It is this freedom from the past and from self-hatred that Orestes represents. Germans after the end of the Second World War, Sartre believes, are faced with a similar situation. "For the Germans, too, I believe, self-denial is unfruitful," he writes.[106]

For Andersch, Sartre's philosophy embodied the new freedom of both Germany and German literature, severed from ties to the past and facing a self-created future. In Andersch's view Germans must, like Orestes, sever themselves from all ties to the harmful past, but they must do so without self-hatred and false repentance. The catastrophe of Nazism demonstrated the complete bankruptcy of German idealism, Andersch argued: "How good it would have been if, in the last twelve years, the Germans had escaped the suggestive powers of a philosophy that revealed its essence precisely in its degeneration."[107] American occupation authorities were hostile to the philosophy of existentialism, Andersch argued, because it did not fit their neat, optimistic plans for reeducating the German people. But a return to previous idealistic naiveté would be harmful if not downright impossible. In contrast to an idealistic philosophy that sought to bind human beings to objective values, existentialism offered freedom in and for itself, total freedom. "Do we not understand the divine serenity that this freedom gives us?" Andersch asked.[108] If Germans did not accept this freedom, then they would probably soon find themselves once again waging war and killing other people who did not share their supposedly higher ideals.

In his programmatic essay *Die deutsche Literatur in der Entscheidung,* presented at the second gathering of Gruppe 47 writers in Herrlingen in November of 1947 — and published as a pamphlet in 1948 — Andersch argued that because of the brittleness of previous cultural and literary values and the "dictates of a completely unprecedented situation, the younger generation stood before a tabula rasa, before the necessity of achieving, through an original act of creation, a renewal of German spiritual life."[109] A "temporary nihilism," Andersch argued, could be quite useful for postwar German culture, because it could help to eliminate the remains of an aged, weak culture. "In its appeal to the personal decision," Andersch believed, existentialism proclaims human freedom to be the most important value. Like Orestes in Sartre's *Les mouches,* he saw human beings generally and Germans specifically as being damned to freedom.[110]

In his 1952 memoir *Die Kirschen der Freiheit* (The Cherries of Free-dom) Andersch described his desertion from the German army as just such a moment of pure, existential freedom. Human beings can never be free for more than a moment, Andersch believes, but it is for just such moments of freedom that they live. "My book has only one task: to describe a single moment of freedom."[111] It is this single moment of freedom — Andersch's desertion from the German army in Italy on June 6, 1944 — that, Andersch believes, "gave meaning to my life."[112] In leaving the German army Andersch is breaking his bonds to his comrades and to the national community, as well as to the oath of allegiance he had sworn. But "the oath can only be sworn by believers to other believers."[113] Once a person has freed himself from be-lief, then he is no longer bound by such oaths. Freedom, Andersch writes, is aloneness in the face of either God or nothingness, and "deserters are people who send themselves into the desert."[114] As Erhard Schütz has suggested, significant sections of *Die Kirschen der Freiheit* are a "variation on themes of Sartre."[115] In Sartre's existentialist philosophy Andersch sees the opportunity for personal rebirth. Andersch sums up his vision of human freedom by de-scribing the brief span of time between his desertion from the German army and his surrender to the Americans. Instead of immediately surrendering to the opposing army, whose tanks he can hear in the distance, the liberated soldier does something "massively corny" — but it is precisely this pathos of freedom that Andersch celebrates. He throws away his weapons and walks through the Italian countryside. In a valley he finds a wild cherry tree, and he begins to pluck the cherries, which he calls "the deserted cherries, the de-serter-cherries, the wild desert cherries of my freedom." As long as he is eat-ing these cherries, Andersch believes, time belongs to him. The cherries taste "fresh and tart."[116] Amidst the collapse of the old world, Andersch celebrates a new kind of nonconformist heroism: the heroism of the zero hour whose reward is the bitter sweetness of freedom.

Andersch's description of his imaginary, idyllic moment of freedom is, as he himself admits, full of pathos. It is easy to understand how a writer who had more or less conformed during the years of the Third Reich, and who had divorced a wife whom the Nazis deemed "half-Jewish" at the very mo-ment when the Nazis' so-called "Final Solution of the Jewish Question" be-gan to be carried out, could be attracted to Sartre's philosophy of absolute, existential freedom, accompanied by the absence of regret and self-castigation. As Andersch's biographer Stephan Reinhardt has written, "his own development was more important for him" than any moral qualms.[117] Contemporary scholars seeking to understand German literary culture at the so-called zero hour are faced with a seemingly insoluble dilemma, apparently forced to choose between the generally conservative upholders of tradition on the one hand and the self-aggrandizing and frequently dishonest propo-nents of a tabula rasa on the other. The socialist writers of the nascent German Democratic Republic, who at first glance appear to offer a solution to this dilemma, are in fact mostly, like Johannes R. Becher, upholders of an essentially traditional and conservative notion of culture.

Fortunately, one does not have to accept the terms of this double-bind. One can refuse to accept the choice between two equally unacceptable solutions to the dilemma of German culture at the zero hour. With the benefit of hindsight, one is not forced to take sides in the literary battles of the zero hour. One can, rather, seek what is useful from both sides and reject the rest. I reject both restoration and a radical new beginning. The synthetic solution to this problem moves beyond "either-or" to an amalgam of "neither-nor" and "both-and." Specifically, the conservative upholders of tradition must be rejected, but their insistence on the presence of the past must be maintained, for it is only where there is an awareness of the past and one's obligations to memory that a sense of ethical and cultural responsibility can be maintained. Likewise, the bathos of Andersch and Richter's zero hour cannot be accepted at face value, but their criticism of traditional culture and their insistence that German — and Western — culture is faced with a radical — and radically new — challenge must be preserved. The zero hour was always imaginary, but as imagination it becomes real: a continuing burden imposed by Germany's literary culture on the nation's identity. The tabula rasa was not a clean slate but a palimpsest, and onto that palimpsest German intellectuals helped to write the history of postwar culture.

Notes

[1] "die Überzeugung, daß hinter allem, was der Mensch wollen und vom Leben erwarten kann, die trostlose Leere absoluter Sinnlosigkeit steht." Philipp Lersch, "Über den Nihilismus," *Neue Zeitung,* 10 October 1947, 3. Unless otherwise specified, all translations from German in this book are my own; the German appears in the notes, followed by sources. I have added the notation "my translation" in a limited number of cases where confusion might otherwise occur.

[2] Johann Wolfgang von Goethe, *Faust I & II,* trans. Stuart Atkins (Boston: Suhrkamp/Insel, 1984), 36. In German: "Ich bin der Geist, der stets verneint!/ . . ., denn alles, was entsteht,/Ist wert, daß es zugrunde geht. . . ." Goethe, *Faust, der Tragödie erster Teil* (Stuttgart: Reclam, 1980), 40.

[3] Gottfried Benn, "Berliner Brief, Juli 1948," in Benn, *Sämtliche Werke,* ed. Gerhard Schuster, 5:284 (Stuttgart: Klett-Cotta, 1991).

[4] "Was ich erzähle, ist die Geschichte der nächsten zwei Jahrhunderte. Ich beschreibe, was kommt, was nicht mehr anders kommen kann: *die Heraufkunft des Nihilismus.*" Friedrich Nietzsche, *Der Wille zur Macht: Versuch einer Umwerthung aller Werthe (Studien und Fragmente),* ed. Elisabeth Förster-Nietzsche (Leipzig: Naumann, 1901), 5. Emphasis in the original.

[5] Fyodor Dostoyevsky, *The Brothers Karamazov,* trans. David McDuff (London: Penguin, 1993), 679.

[6] Fyodor Dostoevsky, *Demons,* trans. Richard Pevear and Larissa Volokhonsky (New York: Knopf, 1994), 617–18, 619.

[7] For an analysis of Dostoyevsky's account of nihilism in *Demons,* see Ina Fuchs, *Die Herausforderung des Nihilismus: Philosophische Analysen zu F. M. Dostojewskijs Werk "Die Dämonen"* (Munich: Otto Sagner, 1987).

[8] "Wenn es keinen fremden Sender gibt, sind wir nichts als ein schlechter Witz!" Ilse Aichinger, *Die grössere Hoffnung* (Amsterdam: Bermann-Fischer/Querido, 1948), 140.

[9] "Der kennt am wenigsten die Zeit, der nicht die ungeheure Macht des Nichts in sich erfahren hat, und der nicht der Versuchung unterlag." Ernst Jünger, *Über die Linie* (Frankfurt: Vittorio Klostermann, 1950), 44. Jünger wrote this essay for a Festschrift in honor of Martin Heidegger: *Anteile: Martin Heidegger zum 60. Geburtstag* (Frankfurt: Vittorio Klostermann, 1950), 245–84.

[10] "Strom, der *ans Ende* will. . . ." Nietzsche, *Der Wille zur Macht,* 5. Emphasis in the original.

[11] "Wir haben die ungeheuren Mächte angerufen, deren Antwort wir nicht gewachsen sind. Da faßt uns das Grauen an. Wir stehen vor der Wahl, in die Dämononreiche einzutreten oder uns auf die geschwächte Domäne des Menschlichen zurückzuziehen." Ernst Jünger, *Heliopolis: Rückblick auf eine Stadt* (Stuttgart: Ernst Klett, n.d. [Jünger, *Werke,* vol. 10, *Erzählende Schriften* II]), 150.

[12] "konservative und nihilistische Strömungen." Jünger, *Heliopolis,* 35.

[13] "ein im Grunde nihilistisches Streben, dem jede Ideologie recht war, wenn sie nur rasch Macht brachte." Friedrich Meinecke, "Zusammenarbeit," in Paetel, *Deutsche innere Emigration,* 86–88; here, 87.

[14] Wilhelm Röpke, *The German Question,* trans. E. W. Dickes (London: George Allen & Unwin, 1946), 38. Emphasis in the original. Original German: "der modernen Tyrannis," "die *vollkommene Auflösung der Werte und Normen,* ohne die unsere oder irgendeine andere Gesellschaft auf die Dauer nicht bestehen kann," "was man mit durchaus sachlichen Ausdrücken als Satanismus und Nihilismus bezeichnen kann." Wilhelm Röpke, *Die deutsche Frage* (Erlenbach-Zurich: Eugen Rentsch, 1945), 35.

[15] "Satan selbst," "Reich des Teufels." Heinrich Böll, *Kreuz ohne Liebe,* in Böll, *Werke,* ed. J. H. Reid 2:149–425; here, 241 and 193 (Cologne: Kiepenheuer & Witsch, 2002).

[16] "ist wohl überhaupt derjenige, auf dessen Gebot hin das größte Maß von Tötung und Einebnung vollzogen wurde, das man je in der Geschichte sah." Ernst Jünger, *Strahlungen* (Tübingen: Heliopolis, 1949), 553.

[17] "die immer wechselnden, verfließenden Züge," "aus einer andern Dimension." Reinhold Schneider, *Der Mensch vor dem Gericht der Geschichte* (Augsburg-Göggingen: Johann Wilhelm Naumann, 1946), 8.

[18] "Hier handelte ein andrer durch den, der zu führen glaubte, und über ihn hinweg." Schneider, *Der Mensch vor dem Gericht der Geschichte,* 17.

[19] "Die richtige zweigesichtige Dämmervisage des Untergangs." Böll, *Kreuz ohne Liebe,* 170; see also 169, 258, and 489.

[20] Wolfgang Koeppen, *Death in Rome,* trans. Michael Hofmann (London: Hamish Hamilton, 1992), 42. Original German: "des Teufels auserwähltes Werkzeug, eine

magische Null, eine Schimäre des Volkes, eine Luftblase, die schließlich platzte."
Koeppen, *Der Tod in Rom* (Frankfurt: Suhrkamp, 1975), 42. There is another translation of the same title by Mervyn Savill (New York: Vanguard, 1961).

[21] "die Akklamation zur Aussicht auf Selbstvernichtung, ein hochnihilistischer Akt," "die Sprengung der Synagogen, die Ausrottung der Juden, die Bombardierung Londons, die fliegenden Bomben," "daß solche Taten ausdenkbar und möglich sind." Jünger, *Strahlungen,* 562.

[22] "Kalibane . . ., in denen die Masse sogleich Verkörperungen und Idole des Animalischen erkannte." Jünger, *Heliopolis,* 242.

[23] Alfred Weber, *Farewell to European History, or The Conquest of Nihilism,* trans. R. F. C. Hull (London: Kegan Paul, Trench, Trubner & Co., 1947), ix. In German: "Ende der bisherigen Art der Geschichte, der Geschichte nämlich, die wesentlich vom Abendland her bestimmt war." Weber, *Abschied von der bisherigen Geschichte: Überwindung des Nihilismus?* (Hamburg: Claassen & Goverts, 1946), 10. For more on the influential concept of an end of history in the immediate postwar years, see Lutz Niethammer, *Posthistoire: Has History Come to an End?* trans. Patrick Camiller (London: Verso, 1992).

[24] Weber, *Farewell to European History,* xi. In German: "die tiefere Ursache . . . für den katastrophalen geschichtlichen Zusammenbruch . . ., den wir Abendländer, insbesondere wir Europäer, über die Welt gebracht haben." Weber, *Abschied von der bisherigen Geschichte,* 12–13.

[25] "zu dem rücksichtslosen Verneinen und Beseitewerfen der übernommenen moralischen Werte, ob sie nun bloß religiös formuliert oder sich in gesetzlichen oder gesellschaftlichen Formen befestigt hatten." "man billigte Dinge, die anderswo, unter der Herrschaft der jetzt abgelegten moralischen Werte, als ungeheuerliche Brutalitäten und Grausamkeiten erschienen." "eine Massenerkrankung paranoider Art," "das ganze Land gewann und eine Massenepidemie zum Ausbruch brachte." Alfred Döblin, "Die literarische Situation," in *Schriften zu Ästhetik, Poetik und Literatur,* 38 (Olten: Walter, 1989).

[26] "Ein wirkliches Koordinatensystem mußte das Leben haben, und keinen bloßen, leblosen Rahmen." My translation, from Alfred Döblin, *Schicksalsreise,* in *Autobiographische Schriften und letzte Aufzeichnungen* (Olten: Walter, 1980), 103–426; here, 344. For an alternative English translation, see Döblin, *Destiny's Journey,* trans. Edna McCown (New York: Paragon House, 1992), 246.

[27] Döblin, *Destiny's Journey,* 250. Original German: "die unsichtbare Gemeinschaft der Gläubigen und der Wissenden, der Frommen und der Heiligen." Döblin, *Schicksalsreise,* 348.

[28] Döblin, *Destiny's Journey,* 253. Original German: "Das Christentum befiel die Menschheit als eine höhere Gesundheit, als die wahre Gesundheit der Menschen." Döblin, *Schicksalsreise,* 354. The word translated here as "well-being" is "Gesundheit," which of course also means "health."

[29] Böll, *Kreuz ohne Liebe,* 479 and 408.

[30] Jerry Z. Muller, *The Other God That Failed: Hans Freyer and the Deradicalization of German Conservatism* (Princeton: Princeton UP, 1987), 336.

[31] Picard had already described this process in *Die Flucht vor Gott* (Erlenbach-Zurich: Eugen Rentsch, 1934).

[32] Max Picard, *Hitler in Our Selves,* trans. Heinrich Hauser (Hinsdale, IL: Henry Regnery, 1947), 248. German original: "was geschieht, wenn der Mensch ohne Zusammenhang ist mit den Dingen, mit den Menschen, mit sich selbst, mit Gott." Picard, *Hitler in uns selbst* (Erlenbach-Zurich: Eugen Rentsch, 1946), 246.

[33] See Ebbo Demant, *Von Schleicher zu Springer: Hans Zehrer als politischer Publizist* (Mainz: v. Hase & Koehler, 1971), 124–48, especially 132–41 on *Der Mensch in dieser Welt;* and Muller, *The Other God That Failed,* 399–401.

[34] "Der abendländische Mensch befindet sich in der großen geschichtlichen Krise seiner Kultur. Die Krise hat ihren Anfang genommen mit dem Abfall des abendländischen Menschen von Gott." Hans Zehrer, *Der Mensch in dieser Welt* (Hamburg: Rowohlt, 1948), 57; my translation. This book was published in an abridged English translation as *Man in this World* (New York: New York UP, 1955). For a more explicitly theological exploration of similar themes, see Walter Künneth, *Der große Abfall: Eine geschichtstheologische Untersuchung der Begegnung zwischen Nationalsozialismus und Christentum* (Hamburg: Friedrich Wittig, 1947).

[35] "Eindringen einer fremden Ideenmasse" Döblin, *Die literarische Situation, 27.* Friedrich Meinecke also suggested that "the German people were not fundamentally diseased with criminal sentiments but were only suffering for a while with a severe infection from poison administered to it. If the poison had been allowed to work a long time in the body, then indeed the case might have become hopeless." Friedrich Meinecke, *The German Catastrophe: Reflections and Recollections,* trans. Sidney B. Fay (Cambridge, MA: Harvard UP, 1950), 95. Original German: — "Das deutsche Volk war nicht etwa von Grund aus an verbrecherischer Gesinnung erkrankt, sondern litt nur an einer einmaligen schweren Infektion durch ein ihm beigebrachtes Gift. Hätte sich dieses noch lange im Körper auswirken können, so hätte allerdings der Fall hoffnungslos werden können." Friedrich Meinecke, *Die deutsche Katastrophe: Betrachtungen und Erinnerungen* (Brockhaus: Wiesbaden, 1946), 140. Similarly, Wilhelm Röpke likened Germany to a "patient . . . suffering from a highly infectious disease." Röpke, *The German Question,* 16. German original: "einen Patienten . . ., der mit einer höchst ansteckenden Krankheit behaftet ist." Röpke, *Die deutsche Frage,* 8.

[36] "Es hat ganz den Anschein . . . als ob das deutsche Schicksal der jüngsten Vergangenheit, so gewiß es auch der Ausdruck spezifisch deutscher Gefahren ist, darüber hinaus doch zugleich wie in einem Beispiel der Weltgeschichte die Gefahren demonstriert, von denen das moderne Dasein überhaupt bedroht ist." Philipp Lersch, "Ruf nach Verinnerlichung," *Neue Zeitung,* 25 August 1947, 3.

[37] "die offene terroristische Diktatur der am meisten reaktionären, chauvinistischen und imperialistischen Elemente des Finanzkapitals." Cited in *Historisch-Kritisches Wörterbuch des Marxismus,* ed. Wolfgang Fritz Haug (Hamburg: Argument, 1999), 4:157. This definition of fascism became official at the thirteenth plenum of the Executive Committee of the Communist International in December 1933.

[38] Hermann Rauschning, *The Revolution of Nihilism,* trans. E. W. Dickes (Garden City: Garden City Publishing, 1942), 120. Original German: "da sich in dem totalen Umkehrungsprozeß unter der Auflösung aller Normen im Ideologieverdacht," "bei den Kräften echten Konservatismus und in der Verbindung mit einer heilenden Restauration der geistigen, sozialen, der historischen Mächte unserer Herkunft." Hermann Rauschning, *Die Revolution des Nihilismus: Kulisse und Wirklichkeit im dritten Reich*

(Zurich: Europa, 1938); here, 210. First English-language edition published as *Germany's Revolution of Destruction*, trans. E. W. Dickes (London: Heinemann, 1939). Note that in the first section the published English-language translation, while accurately reflecting Rauschning's thinking, is not an exact translation of his German-language text.

[39] Döblin, *Destiny's Journey*, 279. German original: "daß die Menschen hier wie Ameisen in einem zerstörten Haufen hin und her rennen." Döblin, *Schicksalsreise*, 376.

[40] Döblin, *Destiny's Journey*, 280. German original: "Es wird viel leichter sein, ihre Städte wieder aufzubauen als sie dazu zu bringen, zu erfahren, was sie erfahren haben und zu verstehen, wie es kam." "hier lebt unverändert ein arbeitsames, ein ordentliches Volk." Döblin, *Schicksalsreise*, 377.

[41] Marcus Holz, *Christliche Weltanschauung als Grundlage von Parteipolitik: Eine Analyse des genuin Christlichen in der frühen CDU/CSU (1945–50) aus der Betrachtung des christlichen Menschenbildes und seiner ideengeschichtlichen Hintergründe* (doctoral dissertation, Universität der Bundeswehr, Munich, 1992), 64–65.

[42] "*den Menschen dem Nichts als seinem angeblichen Schöpfer und Heiland auszuliefern.*" Heinrich Vogel, *Nihilismus und Nationalismus* (Berlin: Evangelische Verlangsanstalt, 1948), 14. Emphasis in the original.

[43] "den letzten Schritt der Säkularisierung. Wir werden jenen Glauben an das Nichts verstehen müssen als die letzte, dämonisch-bewußte Wendung des Menschen, der sich dem Glauben an die Washeiten, an die Ismen überantwortet hatte, nachdem er das Wort des lebendigen Gottes nicht mehr hören wollte." Vogel, *Nihilismus und Nationalismus,* 16.

[44] Maria Dee Mitchell, *Christian Democracy and the Transformation of German Politics, 1945–1949* (doctoral dissertation, Boston University, 1995), 152.

[45] "Rechristianisierung der entchristlichten Gesellschaft." Cited in Harry Noormann, *Protestantismus und politisches Mandat 1945–1949* (Gütersloh: Gerd Mohn, 1985), 1:43.

[46] "das deutsche Volk ist in hohem Maße entchristlicht," "wenn wir wieder ein christliches Volk werden." Theodor Scharmitzel, *Christliche Demokratie im neuen Deutschland*, vol. 1 of *Schriftenreihe der Christlich-Demokratischen Union, Landesverband Rheinland* (Cologne: Balduin Pick, 1946), 11.

[47] "Die Intelligenzen trennt eine babylonische Verwirrung, deren Thema die exakte Lage des Nullpunkts ist." Jünger, *Über die Linie,* 31.

[48] "Die Überquerung der Linie, die Passage des Nullpunkts *teilt* das Schauspiel; es deutet die Mitte, doch nicht das Ende an." Jünger, *Über die Linie,* 26. Emphasis in the original.

[49] "nicht nur herrschend, sondern, was schlimmer, auch zum Normalzustand geworden ist." Jünger, *Über die Linie,* 29.

[50] "mit dem Überqueren des Nullmeridians die alten Ziffern nicht mehr stimmen und eine neue Rechnung anzufangen ist." Jünger, *Über die Linie,* 29.

[51] "Der Weg zu Gott in unserer Zeit ist ungeheuer weit," "als hätte der Mensch sich in den grenzenlosen Räumen verirrt, die sein Ingenium erfunden hat." "Gott muß neu konzipiert werden." Jünger, *Strahlungen,* 325.

[52] "Im Treibhaus der Kriege und Bürgerkriege trugen die großen Theorien des vorigen Jahrhunderts Früchte, indem sie sich zur Praxis wendeten." Jünger, *Der Friede* (Stuttgart: Ernst Klett, 1965 [originally written 1943–44]), 17.

[53] "Dort endete der Fortschritt mit seinen Gedanken und Ideen; in diese Sümpfe mündete die allzu kluge, erfindungsreiche Zeit." Jünger, *Der Friede*, 21.

[54] "Mehr und mehr scheint er von der Verfehltheit und von der Heillosigkeit dieser geschichtlichen Periode überzeugt zu sein." Helmuth Kiesel, "Zwischen Kritik und Affirmation: Ernst Jüngers Auseinandersetzung mit dem Nationalsozialismus," in Rüther, *Literatur in der Diktatur*, 163–72; here, 169. See also Helmuth Kiesel, *Wissenschaftliche Diagnose und Dichterische Vision der Moderne: Max Weber und Ernst Jünger* (Heidelberg: Manutius, 1994), 146–92. For an account in English of Jünger's postwar views, see Jeffrey Herf, "Belated Pessimism: Technology and Twentieth Century German Conservative Intellectuals," in *Technology, Pessimism, and Postmodernism*, ed. Yaron Ezrahi, Everett Mendelsohn, and Howard Segal, 115–36; especially 120–24 (Amherst: U of Massachusetts P, 1995).

[55] "die kühnsten Träume der alten Tyrannen," "die alten Mittel kehrten mit neuen Namen wieder — die Folter, die Leibeigenschaft, die Sklaverei." Jünger, *Heliopolis*, 242.

[56] "Toxikologisches Institut," "Abteilung Fremdvölker," "Zentralamt," "Das 'Wissen ist Macht' des alten Francis Bacon hatte sich vereinfacht zum 'Wissen ist Mord.'" Jünger, *Heliopolis*, 247.

[57] Herf, "Belated Pessimism," 134, note 45.

[58] Max Horkheimer and Theodor W. Adorno, *Dialectic of Enlightenment*, trans. John Cumming (New York: Continuum, 1995), 190, 170. Original German: "Wie seit ihrem Aufstieg die species Mensch den anderen sich zeigt, als die entwicklungsgeschichtlich höchste und daher furchtbarste Vernichtung," "Vernichtungswillen." Max Horkheimer and Theodor W. Adorno, *Dialektik der Aufklärung: Philosophische Fragmente* (Frankfurt: S. Fischer, 1969), 199, 179. I have altered the translation somewhat, rendering "Vernichtung" as "destructive power" rather than "distinctive power."

[59] Horkheimer and Adorno, *Dialectic of Enlightenment*, 9. German original: "Die Menschen bezahlen die Vermehrung ihrer Macht mit der Entfremdung von dem, worüber sie die Macht ausüben." Horkheimer and Adorno, *Dialektik der Aufklärung*, 15.

[60] Horkheimer and Adorno, *Dialectic of Enlightenment*, 6. Translation slightly altered. German original: "Was dem Maß von Berechenbarkeit und Nützlichkeit sich nicht fügen will, gilt der Aufklärung für verdächtig." Horkheimer and Adorno, *Dialektik der Aufklärung*, 12.

[61] Horkheimer and Adorno, *Dialectic of Enlightenment*, 6. German original: "Aufklärung ist totalitär." Horkheimer and Adorno, *Dialektik der Aufklärung*, 12.

[62] Horkheimer and Adorno, *Dialectic of Enlightenment*, 36. German original: "Der Fluch des unaufhaltsamen Fortschritts ist die unaufhaltsame Regression." Horkheimer and Adorno, *Dialektik der Aufklärung*, 42.

[63] Horkheimer and Adorno, *Dialectic of Enlightenment*, 172. German original: "die Zerstörungslust der Zivilisierten . . ., die den schmerzlichen Prozeß der Zivilisation nie ganz vollziehen konnten." Horkheimer and Adorno, *Dialektik der Aufklärung*, 181.

[64] Horkheimer and Adorno, *Dialectic of Enlightenment*, 185. German original: "Der Faschismus ist totalitär auch darin, daß er die Rebellion der unterdrückten Natur

gegen die Herrschaft unmittelbar der Herrschaft nutzbar zu machen strebt." Horkheimer and Adorno, *Dialektik der Aufklärung,* 194.

[65] Horkheimer and Adorno, *Dialectic of Enlightenment,* 204. Translation slightly modified. German original: "Die Dialektik der Aufklärung schlägt objektiv in den Wahnsinn um." Horkheimer and Adorno, *Dialektik der Aufklärung,* 214.

[66] Horkheimer and Adorno, *Dialectic of Enlightenment,* 93. German original: "Aufklärung macht ihrem Prinzip nach selbst vor dem Minimum an Glauben nicht halt, ohne das die bürgerliche Welt nicht existieren kann." Horkheimer and Adorno, *Dialektik der Aufklärung,* 100.

[67] Horkheimer and Adorno, *Dialectic of Enlightenment,* 88. German original: "Vernunft ist das Organ der Kalkulation, des Plans, gegen Ziele ist sie neutral. . . ." Horkheimer and Adorno, *Dialektik der Aufklärung,* 95.

[68] Horkheimer and Adorno, *Dialectic of Enlightenment,* 89. German original: "Sie ist zur zwecklosen Zweckmäßigkeit geworden, die eben deshalb sich in alle Zwecke spannen läßt." Horkheimer and Adorno, *Dialektik der Aufklärung,* 96.

[69] Horkheimer and Adorno, *Dialectic of Enlightenment,* 94. German original: "In all dem verfährt Juliette keineswegs fanatisch . . ., sie besorgt nur aufgeklärt, geschäftig den Betrieb des Sakrilegs." Horkheimer and Adorno, *Dialektik der Aufklärung,* 101.

[70] "*dem* literarischen Ereignis der Nachkriegszeit." Ursula Reinhold, "Elisabeth Langgässers Berliner Jahre: Christliches Weltbild und zeitgeschichtliche Erfahrung," in *Unterm Notdach: Nachkriegsliteratur in Berlin 1945–1949,* ed. Ursula Heukenkamp, 317–54; here, 333 (Berlin: Erich Schmidt, 1996). Emphasis in the original. Reinhold gives an extensive survey of contemporary critical reaction to the novel in the pages that follow.

[71] "dem die Gabe der Heilung und das Charisma der Erweckung gegeben war." Elisabeth Langgässer, *Das unauslöschliche Siegel* (Hamburg: Claassen, 1959 [originally 1946]), 590.

[72] Catherine Susan Gelbin interprets the title, additionally, as a reference to Belfontaine's Jewish background. See Gelbin, *The Indelible Seal: Race, Hybridity and Identity in Elisabeth Langgässer's Writings* (dissertation, Cornell University, 1997), 123. Gelbin's dissertation also contains useful biographical information on Langgässer.

[73] "LAZARUS! KOMM HERAUS!" Langgässer, *Das unauslöschliche Siegel,* 582.

[74] I am in disagreement here with Mathias Bertram, who, because of Langgässer's Roman Catholic worldview, labels the novel modern only in a superficial sense. For Bertram only a complete negation of comprehension of the world is truly modern, and hence any literature based on Christian or any other religious faith is fundamentally unmodern. It appears that Bertram has taken one of the most common definitions of postmodernism — that it eliminates totalizing explanations and grand narratives — and applied it inadmissibly to modernism. Such an analysis, however, overlooks both powerful religious and messianic currents at the heart of literary and artistic modernism and powerful modernist currents in twentieth-century religious thought. To take two obvious counterexamples, one cannot label Arnold Schönberg's opera *Moses und Aaron* unmodern simply because it tells the story of the coming of monotheism to the Jews; and T. S. Eliot's late poems are hardly unmodern simply because they are Christian. See Mathias Bertram, "Literarische Epochendiagnosen der Nachkriegszeit," in *Deutsche*

Erinnerung: Berliner Beiträge zur Prosa der Nachkriegsjahre (1945–1960), ed. Ursula Heukenkamp, 11–99; here, 29 (Berlin: Erich Schmidt, 2000).

[75] "existentieller Darstellung objektiver Welterfassung und antipsychologisierender Religiosität." Cited in Angela G. Zimmer Lauman, *Elisabeth Langgässer (1899–1950) als christliche Dichterin und Schöpferin christlicher Frauengestalten* (dissertation, University of Maryland, 1994), 56.

[76] Gelbin, *The Indelible Seal,* 211.

[77] Reinhold, "Elisabeth Langgässers Berliner Jahre," 338.

[78] György Lukács, *Theory of the Novel* (Cambridge, MA: M.I.T. Press, 1971).

[79] "Jeder Name, jedes physiognomische Detail, jede Geste . . . und natürlich erst recht jede Handlung erweist sich als eine Chiffre, die . . . auf die höhere Wirklichkeit verweist." Bertram, "Literarische Epochendiagnosen," 29.

[80] "Jetzt." Langgässer, *Das unauslöschliche Siegel,* 576.

[81] "Logik der Sünde." Langgässer, *Das unauslöschliche Siegel,* 573.

[82] "ein Freund alles Bestehenden, ein Mann der Vernunft, ein Mann der Katheder, der wahrhafte Bürger, der Untertan und der Grundstein unsrer Sparkassen, Kanzeln und Schulen." Langgässer, *Das unauslöschliche Siegel,* 540.

[83] "Sie waren wohl noch niemals Sie selbst?" "allmählich zu seinem eigenen Nachhall und zum Spiegelbild seiner Person [wird]." Langgässer, *Das unauslöschliche Siegel,* 192, 193.

[84] "Kultus der Vernunft," Langgässer, *Das unauslöschliche Siegel,* 502.

[85] "Ist nicht das Nichts jenes Etwas, das stärker und größer als alle Inhalte ist, also auch stärker als Himmel und Hölle, weil es nicht ist und daher nicht leiden, nicht beginnen, nicht endigen kann? Ich will Ihnen etwas sagen, mein Herr, aber erzählen Sie es nicht weiter: das Nichts ist größer als dieser Gott mit dem entsetzlichen Trieb zu erschaffen, für den er von seinen Geschöpfen noch Dank und Anbetung erwartet. Warum sind wir nicht Nichts?" Langgässer, *Das unauslöschliche Siegel,* 474.

[86] "Komm, laß uns Nichts sein! Laß uns den Schoß der Natur und der Übernatur verlassen, dieses Geschwätz, dieses Ammengerede von Geburt und Wiedergeburt. Warum hält uns der Kreis? Nur, weil wir nicht wagen, über den Rand zu treten." Langgässer, *Das unauslöschliche Siegel,* 474.

[87] "Der große Pan ist gestorben. Der große Pan ist tot." Langgässer, *Das unauslöschliche Siegel,* 581.

[88] "Abfall von Gott." Langgässer, *Das unauslöschliche Siegel,* 324. Donoso Cortès lived from 1809 to 1853 and was the author of several works, including the *Ensayo sobre el catolicismo, el liberalismo y el socialismo* (Essay on Catholicism, Liberalism, and Socialism, 1851).

[89] Langgässer was not alone among German Catholic intellectuals in this negative diagnosis of Prussia. See Richard Faber, *Abendland: Ein "politischer Kampfbegriff"* (Hildesheim: Gerstenberg, 1979), 272.

[90] "Die Freiheit ist tot," "Die Welt eilt mit Siebenmeilenstiefeln der Despotie entgegen, einem Regime, wie gewaltiger und zerstörender es die Menschen noch niemals gesehen haben." Langgässer, *Das unauslöschliche Siegel,* 325.

[91] Langgässer was not the only German intellectual who viewed Donoso's nineteenth-century warnings as highly relevant for the twentieth century. For Carl Schmitt — whose essays on Donoso Langgässer might well have seen in the Catholic journal *Hochland* during the second half of the 1920s — Donoso was one of the most important and prescient historical thinkers of the nineteenth century, prefiguring much of Schmitt's own critique of liberalism. See Schmitt, *Donoso Cortès in gesamteuropäischer Interpretation: Vier Aufsätze* (Cologne: Greven, 1950), a collection of Schmitt's essays on Donoso from the 1920s through the 1940s.

[92] Langgässer was not alone in seeing Hitler's Third Reich as a godless perversion of the Holy Roman Empire. The Catholic intellectual Karl Thieme calls Hitler's Reich "a diabolical caricature of that empire" ("des diabolischen Zerrbildes jenes Reiches"). Karl Thieme, *Das Schicksal der Deutschen: Ein Versuch seiner geschichtlichen Erklärung* (Basel: Kobersche Verlagsbuchhandlung, 1945), 7. The word "diabolical" should be understood literally here.

[93] Wolfgang Borchert, *The Man Outside,* trans. David Porter (New York: New Directions, 1971), 84. German original: "der Gott, an den keiner mehr glaubt," "Der Tod? — Du hast es gut! Du bist der neue Gott. An dich glauben sie. Dich lieben sie. Dich fürchten sie. Du bist unumstößlich. Dich kann keiner leugnen!" Wolfgang Borchert, *Draussen vor der Tür* (Reinbek: Rowohlt, 1992), 10.

[94] Borchert, *The Man Outside,* 121–22. German original: "Ach, du bist alt, Gott, du bist unmodern, du kommst mit unsern langen Listen von Toten und Ängsten nicht mehr mit. Wir kennen dich nicht mehr so recht, du bist ein Märchenbuchliebergott." Borchert, *Draussen vor der Tür,* 42.

[95] Borchert, *The Man Outside,* 122. German original: "Ich kann es doch nicht ändern!" Borchert, *Draussen vor der Tür,* 42.

[96] "VON KEINEM GELIEBT, VON KEINEM GEHASST, STARB HEUTE NACH LANGEM, MIT HIMMLISCHER GEDULD ERTRAGENEM LEIDEN: GOTT." Wolfdietrich Schnurre, "Das Begräbnis," in *Erzählungen,* 11–18; here, 11 (Freiburg: Walter, 1966).

[97] "ein Faktum, dem wir in unserer sozialen Wirklichkeit so intensiv begegnen, daß ein fühlbares . . ., unaufschiebbares Bedürfnis besteht, darüber einigermaßen aufgeklärt zu werden." Julius Ebbinghaus, "Was ist Existentialphilosophie?" *Neue Zeitung,* 28 July 1947, 5.

[98] "ihre Sicht auf die Welt und auf das Dasein." Lersch, "Über den Nihilismus," 3.

[99] "Modephilosophie," "als sie allerdings ihre erregende Aktualität aus dem apokalyptischen Zustand dieser Zeit bezieht." "den radikalen Zweifel an allen 'objektiven' Werten." Alfred Andersch, "Die Existenz und die objektiven Werte: Eine Entgegnung," *Neue Zeitung,* 15 August 1947, 3.

[100] Hermann Glaser, *Kulturgeschichte der Bundesrepublik Deutschland: Zwischen Kapitulation und Währungsreform 1945–1948,* (Munich: Carl Hanser, 1985), 179, 178. On the views of Dymschitz, see Wigand Lange, "Die Schaubühne als politische Umerziehungsanstalt betrachtet: Theater in den Westzonen," in *Nachkriegsliteratur in Westdeutschland 1945–1949: Schreibweisen, Gattungen, Institutionen,* ed. Jost Hermand, Helmuth Peitsch, and Klaus R. Scherpe, 6–35; here, 27 (Berlin: Argument, 1982).

[101] "Sartre wird auf allen Bühnen gespielt, während Heideggers Werke nur in Frankreich zu haben sind." Glaser, *Kulturgeschichte der Bundesrepublik Deutschland,* 333.

[102] "indem sie an die Stelle des Problems die Gestalt setzt," "das Problem durchsichtig macht." Andersch, "Die Existenz und die objektiven Werte," 3.

[103] Jean-Paul Sartre, *The Flies,* in *No Exit and Three Other Plays* (New York: Vintage, 1955), 49–127; here, 108.

[104] Sartre, *The Flies,* 108.

[105] Sartre, *The Flies,* 127.

[106] "Auch für die Deutschen, glaube ich, ist Selbstverleugnung unfruchtbar." Jean-Paul Sartre, *Die Fliegen,* in *Gesammelte Dramen* (Reinbek: Rowohlt, 1984), 7–65; here, 9.

[107] "Wie gut wäre es gewesen, wenn die Deutschen in den letzten zwölf Jahren der Suggestion einer Philosophie entronnen wären, die gerade in ihrer Entartung ihr Wesen enthüllte." Andersch, "Die Existenz und die objektiven Werte," 3.

[108] "Begreifen wir nicht die göttliche Heiterkeit, die uns diese Freiheit gibt?" Andersch, "Die Existenz und die objektiven Werte," 3.

[109] "Aus dem Zwang einer völlig neuartigen Situation heraus, steht die junge Generation vor einer tabula rasa, vor der Notwendigkeit in einem originalen Schöpfungsakt eine Erneuerung des deutschen geistigen Lebens zu vollbringen." Alfred Andersch, *Deutsche Literatur in der Entscheidung: Ein Beitrag zur Analyse der literarischen Situation* (Karlsruhe: Volk und Zeit, 1948), 24.

[110] "temporärer Nihilismus," "In seinem Appell an die persönliche Entscheidung." Cited in Erhard Schütz, *Alfred Andersch* (Munich: Beck, 1980), 27.

[111] "Mein Buch hat nur eine Aufgabe: einen einzigen Augenblick der Freiheit zu beschreiben." Alfred Andersch, *Die Kirschen der Freiheit: Ein Bericht* (Zurich: Diogenes, 1972), 84. Originally published in 1952.

[112] "meinem Leben Sinn verlieh." Andersch, *Die Kirschen der Freiheit,* 71.

[113] "der Eid kann nur von Gläubigen einem Gläubigen gegenüber geleistet werden." Andersch, *Die Kirschen der Freiheit,* 107.

[114] "Deserteure sind Leute, die sich selbst in die Wüste schicken." Andersch, *Die Kirschen der Freiheit,* 128.

[115] "Variation auf Thesen Sartres." Schütz, *Alfred Andersch,* 36.

[116] "kolossal Pathetisches," "die verlassenen Kirschen, die Deserteurs-Kirschen, die wilden Wüstenkirschen meiner Freiheit," "frisch und herb." Andersch, *Die Kirschen der Freiheit,* 130.

[117] "andererseits war ihm seine eigene Entwicklung wichtiger." Stephan Reinhard, *Alfred Andersch: Eine Biographie* (Zurich: Diogenes, 1990), 82. On the recurring "legends" of Andersch-scholarship, see Friedrich Denk, *Die Zensur der Nachgeborenen: Zur regimekritischen Literatur im Dritten Reich* (Weilheim: Denk, 1996), 437–40.

Postscript: Revisiting the Zero Hour

Beyond the Zero Hour

URING THE IMMEDIATE postwar period no single phrase monopolized designations of the current era. Many phrases competed with each other, each suggesting a slightly different point of view. Jünger's "Nullpunkt" implied a spatial perspective. Words like "crisis" and "catastrophe" suggested a state of affairs, while noun forms derived from verbs, like "end," "decline," and "collapse," implied a process taking place over time, and hence focused attention on an earlier, no longer sustainable state of affairs. Holthusen's "tabula rasa" suggested a volumetric perspective, emphasizing not what had been eliminated but rather the infinite possibility of the new, an emptiness yet to be filled.

Roberto Rosselini's *Germania anno zero* popularized the chronological or calendrical perspective, at the same time reemphasizing the emptiness already present in the concepts of a "Nullpunkt" or a "tabula rasa." But the concept of a "year zero" did not, in the end, fare any better than most of the other terms used in the immediate postwar period. It too gradually disappeared, to be replaced by the seemingly greater immediacy and drama of the concept "Stunde Null." The calendar was replaced by the clock, the framework of the year by the framework of the day.

Originally a battlefield expression referring to the hour when a major military action is set to begin, the phrase "zero hour" was used during the 1930s and 1940s by anti-Nazi German exiles in order to rally the Western world to vigilance against Nazi Germany. It was not until well after the "zero hour" itself that the phrase became established as a designation for German history in the immediate postwar period. In adopting the term "Stunde Null," Germans were, in a sense, adopting the perspective of anti-Nazi German emigrants.

In 1945 the most common words used in Germany to refer to the end of the Second World War were "Zusammenbruch" (collapse) and "Katastrophe" (catastrophe); both terms implied a generally unspoken third term: "Niederlage" (defeat). Five decades after the end of the war, German politicians and the German media largely concurred that the most appropriate way to designate the end of the war was "Befreiung" (liberation). This radical terminological shift over the course of half a century once again indicates a shift in perspective: in the intervening period the German defeat had, to a remarkable extent, lost its negative connotations in national culture and acquired a positive significance. Implicit in the concept of liberation is the notion that Germany itself was an occupied country in the Second World War. A "liberated" Germany is therefore a Germany that can be compared to Czechoslovakia, Poland, and France, or to any of the other countries occupied by the Nazis during the Second World War. The shift from "collapse" to "liberation" indicates Germans' acceptance of membership in the community of democratic nations and determination to avoid the mistakes of the past; but at the same time, and more problematically, it also elides the concrete European situation in 1945, a year in which the other nations of Europe were liberated from German occupation while Germany was, quite simply, defeated and occupied by foreign armies. Indeed, on April 24, 1945 the Allies had explicitly declared that "Germany is not being occupied in order to be liberated but because it is a defeated country."[1] If, in spite of this declaration, Germany was liberated in 1945, then it was liberated — from occupation by itself.

Although not as clearly as the use of the term "liberation," the use of the term "Stunde Null" also seems to imply that the majority of the German people now see themselves — certainly in the present but perhaps also in the past — as anti-Nazis. The term "zero hour" unites its users over the intervening decades with those German emigrants who had first called for the overthrow of the Nazi dictator in the 1930s and 1940s — people like Erika Mann, Thomas Mann's daughter, who, in 1940, had urged Americans: "Act! This is your hour, it's the final hour — the Zero Hour!"[2] Decades after this call was first made by German emigrants, the term "Stunde Null" implies a radical, decisive, and above all immediate break with the Nazi dictatorship and the mentalities associated with it. An hour, after all, is far shorter than a year. Whereas Rosselini's film had painted the picture of a paralyzed or hysterical Germany, the concept of a "Stunde Null" implies clear-headedness and decisive action. Such qualities were rare in occupied Germany in 1945. In its connotations of a radical, immediate break and decisiveness, the concept of a "Stunde Null" is ahistorical, granting Germans of the postwar period a kind of heroic status in a country that, like the bloated movie star Alexander in Koeppen's novel *Tauben im Gras,* was "heroed out" (ausgeheldet).[3] Koeppen's Alexander plays heroic roles in melodramatic movies, but in real life he is a fat, sniveling buffoon. Nevertheless, his fans confuse him with his movie roles: "they mistook Alexander for his shadow."[4] In Koeppen's novel it is the writer Philipp who most clearly articulates his own lack of heroism: "the bell tolled not for me, I dodged my way through the dictatorship." As Philipp acknowledges, "with people like that you can never bring down a state either, no hope, none for me any more."[5] Philipp's morose honesty about his own lack of courage in the past and hopelessness in the present reflects more accurately the historical situation in German culture in 1945 than the heroic protestations of Hans Werner Richter and Alfred Andersch. Subsequent zero-hour mythmaking sought to cast postwar Germans in the kinds of roles that Koeppen's Alexander plays for an adoring audience that loves to be deceived.

Aside from its etymology and frequently ahistorical usage, the term "Stunde Null" does fit some aspects of the German situation in 1945 and the years which followed. Like Rosselini's "anno zero," "Stunde Null" is a chronological expression; but it refers to both an affirmation and a negation of time. The word "Stunde" expresses one of the basic measurements of human time, the hour, which can be multiplied or divided to create longer or shorter units. But the word "Null" negates precisely the measurement, division, and multiplication potentially embedded in the other term. Whereas an hour is part of the basic process of counting and measuring the passage of time over the course of the day, the concept of zero resists measurement and counting; it is, in fact, their negation. Whereas in quotidian life the hours of the day add up to a predictable routine, the concept of a zero hour signifies a radical break in that routine. The zero hour is thus a chronological expression of nonchronology, a historical term that defies history, implicitly invoking the divine. It is therefore not surprising that few literary or cultural historians are willing to accept the concept of a zero hour at face value — while at the same time contemporary German popular culture seems to have accepted the term as the definitive expression for the end of the Second World War and the beginning of the postwar period.

The zero hour has no definite contours. "But I gaze into the wet grayness," says the narrator of Nossack's *Nekyia*, "and there is nothing by which I could make measurements. It could be a beginning or an end."[6] "That is where the melted-down bells ring the beginning and the end simultaneously, that is where the seconds are revealed," declares Aichinger in *Die grössere Hoffnung,* invoking the sense of the divine.[7] Both Nossack's and Aichinger's sentences capture the disorientation so widespread in Germany during the immediate postwar years — a disorientation to which the term "Stunde Null" neatly corresponds. In keeping with its chronological indeterminacy, the zero hour can be conceived as both a beginning and an end: "To make an end. To set a beginning," Holthusen noted in the first lines of his poem "Tabula Rasa."[8] However those using the term "Stunde Null" tend to place primary emphasis more on one than on the other. In the context of the immediate postwar period the emphasis was naturally more on what had come to an end than on what was now beginning. The future — which seems so inevitable to those looking back from the perspective of hindsight — was not at all clear for those experiencing the zero hour itself. Instead, Germans in 1945 were confronted with the enormity of loss — of homes, cities, friends and relatives, and, many feared, of an entire civilization. Appropriate literary

metaphors for a society lost in contemplation of the horrors it had left behind were Orpheus on his way out of the underworld but irresistibly drawn
to look back; and his wife Eurydice, who must return to the world of the
dead because of her husband's backward-looking gaze. "Who is not Orpheus
today, and who is not Eurydice?" asks a character in Langgässer's *Märkische
Argonautenfahrt.*[9]

The past pervades postwar culture with a stubborn finality, proclaiming
the inevitability of its own past-ness. As Ernst R. Mellinghoff declared in his
poem "Zusammenbruch," "Germany is dead."[10] The finality of this statement was shared by many other authors of the immediate postwar period.
One despairing character in Kolbenhoff's *Heimkehr in die Fremde* declares to
his more optimistic friend that everyone in Germany and Europe is already
dead: "We're all of us no longer living. The stench of our bodies is beginning to spread, the pestilence is hovering over this entire accursed continent."[11] As they are crossing a body of water in Brandenburg, the seven
primary characters in Langgässer's *Märkische Argonautenfahrt* have a vision
of an even more apocalyptic ending, suggesting a Ragnarok of Western civilization: "In their mind's eye it was not just the shore that they had just left
that seemed to be burning; nor just the great city of their origin. Rather,
from Lisbon to Kiev and from Helsinki to Gibraltar, all of Europe seemed to
be burning."[12] Such images of the end of Western civilization were common
during the immediate postwar period: Alfred Weber was not alone in declaring the end of European history. Gottfried Benn's vision was less dramatic,
but even more all-encompassing. For him, it was not just Germany or
Europe but the human race itself that had come to an end.[13] Benn did not
mean that there would be no more biological hominids walking the face of
the earth in the third millennium; rather it was human beings as thinking,
reflective creatures who now faced their extinction. "A few lonely souls"
with a "deeply melancholy spirit" might still remain; "but the dogma about
homo sapiens was at an end."[14] Benn's vision was echoed several years later
in Walter Jens's novel *Nein.*[15]

In the immediate postwar period the zero hour — whether or not explicitly invoked in the various terminologies then available — primarily
marked the end of the Second World War and of the "Third Reich," and
possibly of Germany or even of Western or human history as a whole. But
the contours of any possible future remained inchoate. One of the most
striking images of historical uncertainty, from Langgässer's *Märkische
Argonautenfahrt,* is a variation on the concept of a "tabula rasa." The
novel's narrator describes Clio, the muse of history, sitting "half crazed by
despair" in front of a blank slate, stricken with a severe case of writer's block.
"She did not understand anything any more," the narrative voice of the
novel tells us. Even though Clio remembers a multitude of disasters that she
has recorded and interpreted in the past, she cannot find meaning in the pre-

sent situation of Germany and Europe. Far from making sense, the history that it is her duty to record and interpret has become utterly absurd. "But now she would write something down and then cross it out and then write something down again with a sense of hopelessness. Her toils were absurd; she sensed this, without knowing why."[16] The work of historiography produces only nonsense, because Western history has lost all meaning. Later on in Langgässer's novel one character asks scornfully if Clio, faced with the disasters of the immediate past, will now simply turn to a new, blank page and write "a new chapter on this page of innocence." In response he is informed that Clio "will write nothing at all any more."[17] History is over, and any "tabula rasa" will remain empty. There is nothing more to say.

One of the surest markers separating the mental attitude of the immediate postwar period from the period of "restoration" that followed it is the shift of emphasis from these declarations of a senseless ending to proclamations of a meaningful new beginning. With the reestablishment of social and political order in Germany's zones of occupation, the foundation of two German states in 1949, and ultimately the achievement of political sovereignty and the rearmament of the two Germanys in the mid-1950s, perceptions of the year 1945 changed radically. The zero hour no longer marked the end of Germany or of Western culture; instead it marked the beginning of a new, better Germany and of a more optimistic phase in European history. *Finis Germaniae* had been transformed into *Initium Germaniae*. Many of the best West German writers tended to view this shift in mood with skepticism. At the beginning of postwar reconstruction in 1947, Benn noted sarcastically: "The populace is peeking out of its windows eagerly: culture is once again on the advance, not much murder, more song and music." For Benn culture and art were a central part of the rebuilding process, offering the defeated nation reassuring values that helped to distract from the reality of its devastation: "a transatlantic bishop arrives and mumbles: my brothers; a humanist makes his appearance and murmurs: the Western world; a tenor whispers: O blessed art. The reconstruction of Europe is underway."[18] An eighteen-year old American soldier in Koeppen's *Tauben im Gras* expresses the spirit of reconstruction by demeaning what has been destroyed: "What had fallen here? A couple of old buildings had collapsed. They had long since been ready to come down." The American soldier would like to rebuild the city of Munich completely, making it modern and American: "What skyscrapers he would set on their rubble heaps! The whole place would take on a more progressive look."[19] In Koeppen's *Das Treibhaus* (The Hothouse, 1953) the main character is the politician Keetenheuve, a returned emigrant, whose "involvement in the reconstruction" and "eagerness to reinvent the nation as a liberal democracy" have won him a seat in the young West German parliament.[20] Unfortunately Keetenheuve cannot keep pace with the reconstruction of his nation; his deep pessimism draws him irresistibly to the past, making him unfit for the political life of the present. As early as 1945 Döblin had already expressed his amazement at the ant-like industriousness demonstrated by Germans in the clearing and rebuilding of their cities. Arthur Levi-Jeschower, a Jewish-born Catholic in Langgässer's *Märkische Argonautenfahrt*, is struck by the same phenomenon: "millions of ants have been squashed, millions of others are eager to take the place of those who have been stepped on; to lay eggs, to watch over the larvae and to succumb unconditionally to the terrible desire for reproduction and endless repetition."[21] Such images suggest that some West German writers viewed the rebuilding of their nation with profound skepticism.

The culture of the zero hour has a static, melancholy quality, giving voice to what Nossack called a "state of will-lessness"[22] The static quality of postwar culture is famously invoked in the title poem of Benn's collection *Statische Gedichte*, in which "estrangement from development" — words that one critic has interpreted as signifying "the poet's detachment from the arena of histori-cal" action[23] — is declared to be "the profundity of the wise man."[24] The static quality described by Nossack and recommended by Benn as the apotheosis of wisdom pervades many of the literary documents of the immediate postwar period, from Nossack's and Benn's own works through Borchert's *Draussen vor der Tür* to Koeppen's novels of the 1950s and Heinrich Böll's early novels and short stories. The anguished or numbed characters in these works are fun-damentally incapable of facing the future. Unable to cope with everyday life in a world that he perceives as ruined, Borchert's Beckmann presumably drowns himself in the Elbe river immediately after his return to Hamburg at the end of the war; while Koeppen's intellectual politician Keetenheuve, in *Das Treibhaus*, throws himself into the Rhine almost a decade later, after battling unsuccess-fully against West German rearmament and what he perceives as the all-too-vigorous spirits of an undead past. Like Borchert's Beckmann, Koeppen's Keetenheuve is a "man outside."

The main character of Böll's first published longer work, *Der Zug war pünktlich* (The Train Was On Time, 1949), finds it impossible to imagine a future beyond a zero hour he designates with one word: "Soon." "The future has no face now, it is cut off somewhere; the more he thinks about it, the more he realizes how close he is to this Soon."[25] This character's zero hour is the moment of his death; during the course of the narrative, his future shrinks literally to nothing, and any train heading into the uncharted territory of other people's future, no matter how punctual, will reach its destination without him. Feinhals, the primary character in Böll's *Wo warst du, Adam?* manages to make it home to Germany at the end of the war — only to be killed by venge-ful German snipers in a rearguard action at the threshold of his family home. Although the primary figure in Böll's novel *Der Engel schwieg* (The Silent An-gel) — written six years after the end of the war but not published until 1992, after Böll's death in 1985 — narrowly manages to escape death, he resents his continued existence and believes that he has been cheated out of the death that was his due. When he meets the widow of the man who sacrificed himself for him, he declares to her: "[your husband] stole my death."[26] This survivor is not just incapable of forming a positive attitude toward work, but is actually appalled by other people's ability to go about their daily business as if nothing had happened: "It seemed incredible, almost offensive, that there still should be people here who went to work, promptly and regularly, their satchels under their arms."[27] This character wants nothing better than to lie in bed all day, simulating the death that has been taken from him. Likewise, the main character in Böll's *Und sagte kein einziges Wort* (And Never Said a Word, 1953) — an alcoholic father who has left his wife and children because his sudden fits of rage make him a threat to them — is as unable to imagine a meaningful future as Langgässer's despairing muse Clio: "I felt lost, lethargically floating along on an endless current . . ."[28] And Nella Bach, the primary female character in Böll's *Haus ohne Hüter* (House Without a Keeper, 1954; translated as *The Unguarded House*), explicitly declares her hatred of those who allow quotidian life to continue after the German catastrophe: "Oh, I hate you all, because you allow life to go on. Strewing oblivion over murder as one strews ashes on icy pavements." Like Langgässer's Arthur Levi-Jeschower, Böll's Nella Bach envisions German reconstruction as part of an eternal vicious circle of creation and destruction: "to bring up new widows and new husbands who will be shot down in order to make more women into widows."[29] Böll's hatred of an attitude that allowed life simply to continue on as if nothing terrible had happened found expression as early as 1946–1947, in his first novel (not published until 2002) *Kreuz ohne Liebe*, in which both the protagonist and his mother feel that "this was the most remorseless thing: that life went on."[30]

In his anthem for the newly formed German Democratic Republic, Johannes R. Becher is far more positive about the rebuilding of Germany: "Resurrected from the ruins/And turned toward the future."[31] These words resonate with the force of a secular theology. Becher's resurrected Germany is not lost in melancholy contemplation of an awful past; rather, it faces the future with confidence and determination. In its resolute turning away from the horrors of the past, Becher's view of the fatherland stands in stark contrast not only to that of Langgässer's Clio but also to that of another personification of historical thought, Walter Benjamin's angel of history, who has his back to the future and faces the past in helpless anguish.[32] Benjamin's angel, with his skepticism about what we call progress, hovered over the immediate postwar period, giving it that sense of stasis and impotence invoked again and again by West German authors like Nossack, Benn, and Böll. When the formerly melancholy angels of the postwar period are left behind as their more optimistic companions turn — like the Germany of Becher's 1949 national anthem — to face the future, the zero hour itself is over.

Now, far from being a cause for despair, the devastation of Germany becomes the most powerful justification for the creation of a different, better nation. Anyone skeptical or even critical of the new beginning is an obstacle to this creative process and needs to make way for the new spirit. "Those are the old ones," declares the poetic voice of Becher's optimistic hymn "Strasse Frei!" (Clear the Street!), and they seek to hinder the construction of a new Germany. But "what grows old breaks in two," and ultimately the forces of conservatism must surrender to the youthful forces of change, who "want to live/But not as people lived before."[33] Becher's national anthem urges his fellow citizens to participate enthusiastically in national reconstruction: "Let us plough, let us build,/Learn and create as never before."[34] Once "Germany's new life" has become a reality, the devastation of the zero hour out of which it emerged becomes a standard against which to measure the progress made.[35] The more thoroughly the old Germany has been destroyed, the more brightly the better nation can shine. The flag of the Freie Deutsche Jugend (FDJ, Free German Youth), the youth group of the SED, featured the rising sun against a blue background. "And from the blue the sun is shining,/Shedding light, Germany, on you," run the triumphant words to Becher's "Lied von der blauen Fahne" (Song of the Blue Flag).[36] In Becher's national anthem "the sun shines more beautifully than ever/Over Germany."[37] Such invocations of a triumphant new beginning echo pre-1945 dreams of a better Germany, written at a time when the German zero hour still lay in the future, as in Becher's 1943 vision of the German people awakening at midnight to greet the triumph of freedom in "a German dawn."[38] But by the end of the 1940s and the beginning of the 1950s the zero hour invoked in the dark years of the war had come and gone. It now lay in the past, a reminder to Germans on both sides of the Iron Curtain of how far they had come — or, more pessimistically, of how little had changed.

One of the fundamental differences between the literature of the German Democratic Republic and the literature of the Federal Republic in the years following the foundation of the two German states was that the former celebrated reconstruction and renewal, while the latter did not. If the shift from melancholy contemplation of a failed history to celebration of a new German beginning marked the end of the zero hour itself, it also marked a literary split between the German West and the German East. While East German writers like Becher celebrated the new German beginning in the GDR, writers like Langgässer, Benn, Böll, and Koeppen tended to take a skeptical, critical, and even hostile attitude toward West German rebuilding and explicitly saw themselves as outsiders and nonconformists in the midst of heedless reconstruction. Their consciousness continued to be governed by the melancholy angels and the Eurydices of the zero hour. While West Germany as a political and economic entity turned its face to the future, West German literature remained fundamentally backward-looking, grounded in remembrance and mourning.

This program of remembrance is succinctly expressed by Joseph, one of the main characters in Böll's *Kreuz ohne Liebe,* who, in response to the question "My God, what are we to do?" responds:

> proclaim the truth; every day of our life remind ourselves that what happened in these seven years [from 1938–1945] was no dream but reality. People will forget it, the species of the clueless will once again sit on the throne, and even though it is almost certain that the clueless will be victorious again, we want to proclaim the truth.[39]

The end of the zero hour thus marked a profound split not only between East and West German culture but also between literature and politics in West Germany. West German authors, for the most part, continued to see themselves as defeated and humiliated throughout the late 1940s and 1950s, while East German authors tended to ally themselves with a party that defined itself as the victor of history, destined to rebuild a better Germany.

Anna Seghers's novella "Der Mann und sein Name" ("The Man and His Name," 1952) demonstrates that the pathos of rebuilding in the GDR did not have to be based on an erasure of the past. The central figure in this story is a former Nazi who has taken a new name and a new identity in order to escape punishment for his crimes. Armed with his new name, the man seeks to become part of East German reconstruction. But under the new name hides the old man, a Nazi and a criminal. A truly new man can emerge only after the old man has been dealt with. Hence the man's attempt at a new beginning is doomed to failure until he confronts the ghosts of his past. Only after he has publicly acknowledged his previous crimes can the man truly integrate himself into a new, better Germany. Seghers's invocation of postwar reconstruction is more muted and less triumphant than Becher's; but ultimately even her former Nazi is able to participate in the creation of the new Germany. If the main character never acknowledged his true name and the past for which it stands, the story could be read as an implicit critique of East German reconstruction, because it would suggest that unrepentant Nazis participated in that reconstruction; but the man's ultimate conscientiousness rehabilitates both him and the integrity of East German collective rebuilding.[40] At the same time Seghers's story accurately describes the extent to which, in both parts of Germany, the zero hour allowed individuals to erase their past and create new identities.[41]

The writer Franz Fühmann is an instructive counterpoint to Seghers's account of personal transformation. Himself the son of a right-wing, authoritarian father, as well as a former enthusiastic supporter of Hitler in his own right, Fühmann became a Soviet prisoner of war at the end of the Second World War, was reeducated in a prisoner of war camp, and returned to the nascent GDR in the late 1940s. Fühmann uses the history of his own transformation from a member of the Hitler Youth into a dedicated Communist in his short story collection *Das Judenauto* (The Jew-Car, 1962).[42] For Fühmann as for Seghers, East German reconstruction is based not on forgetting the Nazi past but on working through it towards a better future that will, as the title of the last story in Fühmann's collection indicates, be "Zum ersten Mal: Deutschland" ("For the First Time: Germany"). In these accounts, personal transformation mirrors the large-scale transformation of Germany itself. When Fühmann, Christa Wolf, Heiner Müller, and others began to doubt the integrity of East German transformation in the 1960s and 1970s, their work became more pessimistic and critical, taking on the skepticism characteristic of West German literature from the very beginning and helping to usher in an era of convergence between the two German literatures.[43] But in the late 1940s and throughout the 1950s that pessimism had yet to find a strong voice in East German literature. Nor was it just the future Minister of Culture Johannes R. Becher who wrote hymns for the new state at the end of the immediate postwar period. A year before the foundation of the GDR even the skeptical Brecht, never a member of the Communist Party or the SED, celebrated the youthful rebuilding of Germany:

> And so we'll first build a new state
> *Cart off the rubble and shoulder your weight!*
> *Build something new there!*
> *It's we who must master our own fate;*
> *And seek to stop us if you dare*[44]

Three years later Brecht was still enthusiastic about the newer, better Germany:

> But the new must conquer the old
> And the waves on the Rhine always flow.
> And we will win a Germany, youthful and bold;
> And it will be new and different, we know.[45]

After Wolfgang Weyrauch had called such lyrics a betrayal of the freedom of poetry and written to Brecht wondering whether he had become a schizophrenic lackey of the East German regime, Brecht replied: "I have my opinions not because I am here; rather, I am here because I have my opinions."[46]

    The incipient division between East German and West German literature in the late 1940s and early 1950s marked the difference between criticism and celebration of postwar reconstruction. However the divergence in explicit literary mood should not necessarily be perceived as a fundamental division in underlying attitudes: on one side happy East Germans participating in optimistic reconstruction and on the other side depressed West Germans passively reflecting on the horrific past. In fact reconstruction was occurring far more quickly and thoroughly in West Germany than in East Germany. Hence East German writers were invoking a reconstruction that was in reality slow and painful, while West German writers were attacking a reconstruction that occurred far more forcefully. Many of Becher's and Brecht's more private poems and notes, as well as ambiguities in Seghers's stories, suggest that all three writers were far more skeptical of East German reconstruction than they were willing to admit publicly.

Beyond the realm of high literature, West German culture of the postwar period did indeed include celebratory invocations of German reconstruction. W. G. Sebald has noted that many West German accounts of the devastation of Germany in the 1950s were governed by a longing for triumph over adversity, in much the same way as Becher's celebratory poems. In West German popular culture, as in East German literature, the new Germany would be better than the old Germany that had been destroyed. This spirit is captured by the image of a phoenix rising from the ashes on the wall of a postwar building in the central core of Frankfurt, one of the many cities devastated during the bombing raids of the Second World War. Like Becher's "Germany, unified fatherland," that Frankfurt phoenix is "resurrected from the ruins." The Frankfurt phoenix suggests that far from representing nothing but the work of a Communist party hack, poems like Becher's national anthem gave voice to a genuine, pan-German spirit of triumph over adversity. However in West Germany that optimistic spirit expressed itself primarily in politics and in popular culture — particularly film — while the most respected literary intellectuals remained pessimistic.

The central message of many West German *Trümmerfilme* is expressed in the words of the virtuous female lead in Harald Braun's 1947 film *Zwischen gestern und morgen* (Between Yesterday and Tomorrow), who, in spite of her many misfortunes and fears, affirms: "We have to go on living, don't we? There's no other alternative," words repeated at the end of the film by the more skeptical male lead. In Helmut Käutner's film *In jenen Tagen* (In Those Days, 1947) the optimistic message is proclaimed by a wrecked automobile which affirms the indestructible nature of positive humanity, in spite of human weakness; the last image of the film features flowers blooming in a desert of rubble. The message of Josef von Baky's *Und über uns der Himmel* (And above Us the Sky, 1947) is communicated in the final words of the movie's title song — "for above us the sky/will not let us fall" — and reaffirmed by the final words of the film's primary character: "Somehow there's always a way." The film ends with a shot of a crane being used to rebuild the devastated city of Berlin. Robert Stemmle's 1948 *Berliner Ballade* (Berlin Ballad) conveys the reassuring message that in spite of all adversity Otto Normalverbraucher (Otto the normal consumer) will not give up the ghost; he is literally resurrected during his own burial at the "Graveyard of the Resurrection."[47] Wolfgang Liebeneiner — who, during the "Third Reich," had directed the pro-euthanasia film *Ich klage an* (I Accuse) in 1941 — even managed to transform Wolfgang Borchert's depressing drama *Draussen vor der Tür* into the optimistic movie *Liebe 47* (Love 47) in 1949. As Sabine Hake has argued, the rubble films fought defeatism by offering "the promise of a new beginning captured in the myth of" a zero hour, thus helping to construct a more positive national identity. Hake notes that in spite of sometimes bitter pronouncements on "the inhumanity of the world," the rubble films generally reaffirmed "the essential goodness of humankind," generating "hope and confidence for the future."[48] Hake suggests that West German cinema during the period of the *Wirtschaftswunder* (economic miracle) propagated an optimistic dream image of national reconstruction, urging viewers to internalize the value of hard work. Hake's analysis suggests that in the West the split between mass culture and elite culture enabled a kind of cultural-political division of labor in the postwar period, with mass culture celebrating German reconstruction while elite literary culture tended to criticize and reject it.

In spite of the criticisms of many major West German authors, then, the phoenix rising from the ashes can be seen as the symbol of two German states, both determined to face the future and put the past behind them. In this sense Alfred Andersch's denigration of the old and insistence on the value of the new, far from being unambiguously nonconformist in the 1950s, resonated with a widespread feeling that the remains of the old needed to be eliminated and replaced with things that were new and progressive. In both East and West the pathos of reconstruction coexisted uneasily with an insistence on tradition and received values. The new Germany was, paradoxically, also a function of what was true and tested in German tradition. In both East and West, German elites tried to position themselves simultaneously, and impossibly, as heirs to Germany's great traditions and as daring innovators. To the melancholy angels of West German high literature, as custodians of the nation's conscience, fell the task of reminding Germans of what had been lost.

Back to the Zero Hour?

One of the primary tropes with which Germans described the radical changes that occurred in their nation in 1989–1990 was the comparison to the zero hour of 1945. Nineteen eighty-nine seemed to have summoned the zero hour from the distant past into the present. Ruth Rehmann, a West German writer who was doing research on the 1947 writers' conference in Berlin when the Wall opened, noted: "Now my topic has been broken open and is flowing everywhere into the present."[49] The comparison between 1945 and 1989 demonstrated that, in spite of all attempts by historians and literary scholars to debunk notions of a radical new beginning in 1945, the concept still had a powerful fascination for many Germans.

Of course some of the same arguments made against 1945 as a "Stunde Null" in German literature can also be made against 1989. In spite of Frank

Schirrmacher's insistence, in 1990, that the literature of the Federal Republic had come to an end, for instance, it is easy to demonstrate literary continuities between the 1980s and the 1990s, and beyond, from the continuing development of a "postmodern" literature in Germany through the continued vitality of older-generation authors such as Günter Grass and Martin Walser. Even the literature of the GDR did not come to a definitive end with the "dissolution" (Charles Maier) of the East German state in 1989–1990.[50] Not only have major authors, such as Christa Wolf, Volker Braun, Christoph Hein, and Wolfgang Hilbig, continued to publish important work, but a younger generation of "GDR" writers — including Thomas Brussig, Ingo Schulze, Kerstin Hensel, and Angela Krauß, among others — has emerged in the 1990s and in the first years of the twenty-first century; their work bears all the marks of what Ursula Heukenkamp has called a "regional" identity, suggesting that at least in literature there has been no absolute reunification, let alone a second zero hour.[51]

On the face of it, the concept of a second zero hour would seem absurd. Although Germany certainly did undergo radical change in 1989–1990, that change was by no means as far-reaching as the events of 1945. Nor could the brutality of the socialist dictatorship be compared meaningfully to the brutality of the Nazi regime. The GDR, after all, had neither initiated a world war nor murdered millions of men, women, and children. To state this fact is by no means to make light of the severity of political conditions in the GDR; it is to insist on the specific uniqueness of the Nazi dictatorship. Moreover, whereas the Nazi regime was supported or at least tolerated by the vast majority of Germans, the GDR regime was limited only to a part of Germany, and even in that part of Germany it was opposed, actively or passively, by large numbers of people. The Nazi dictatorship was indeed, as Karl Dietrich Bracher has noted, a "German dictatorship," emerging from within Germany and supported by Germans. The East German dictatorship, conversely, was imposed from the outside, by the Soviet Union, and it collapsed as soon as Soviet support disappeared. The GDR dictatorship was not conquered from the outside; it imploded from the inside. Hence its collapse does not pose the same ethical challenges with respect to collective guilt that are associated with the Nazi regime.

In spite of the radical differences between 1945 and 1989, however, some of the literary and cultural discussions that occurred in and around German reunification eerily echoed the debates of the late 1940s. There were, for instance, debates between writers who had remained in the GDR and those who had emigrated, as reflected in the dispute surrounding the publication of Christa Wolf's novella *Was bleibt* (What Remains) in 1990.[52] Those same debates frequently involved the politicization of literature, which was viewed as either positive or negative, depending on the standpoint of the critic. The revelations of several GDR writers' involvement with the secret police or Stasi (Staatssicherheit, state security) brought to the fore questions of literary conformism and ethics that seemed to echo earlier debates about writers' role in the Nazi dictatorship.[53] Just as writers had met in conferences in the late 1940s to discuss these issues, so too German writers of the 1990s argued in their PEN clubs and elsewhere about similar problems.

In many ways, however, the literary debates of the 1990s, far from repeating the debates of the late 1940s, appeared to be seeking to reverse them. The second zero hour, in other words, was envisioned more as an erasure of the phantasmatic first than as a reincarnation of it. This is particularly true of debates about the politicization of literature. For Karl Heinz Bohrer, Frank Schirrmacher, and other critics of GDR literature, the problem was not that this literature had, like the literature of the "inner emigrants" during the Nazi period, sought refuge from politics in a realm of literary-political indeterminacy; rather, the problem was that it had been overly politicized. As Rehmann has noted, "the object of desire in 1990 [an apolitical literature] comes dangerously close to the object of hatred in 1947," and vice versa.[54] In fact Karl Heinz Bohrer's arguments for the complete autonomy of literature are an echo not of German emigrants from the Nazis but of inner emigrants like Rudolf Alexander Schröder, who had argued at the 1948 writers conference in Frankfurt for the complete independence of literature from politics.[55]

If, as most scholars agree, there was no absolute zero hour in German literature in 1945, then there is little sense in claiming that there was a second zero hour in 1989/1990. How, after all, is it possible to repeat something that did not happen in the first place? A far more useful approach to the relationship between 1945 on the one hand and 1989/1990 on the other lies in the Freudian concept of the return of the repressed. The supposed "tabula rasa" of 1945 is, after all, precisely an attempt at erasure, and the events of 1989/1990 made such erasure visible. It is in this, and not as a supposed repeat of an event that never happened, that the significance of the "zero hour" for 1989/1990 must be seen.

Wolfgang Schivelbusch has written that the cultural legacy of the immediate postwar period is a kind of "time capsule" that was suddenly and unexpectedly unearthed by the events of 1989–1990; in his view, German intellectuals of the 1990s were, "with the self-assurance of sleepwalkers," shoving "this simultaneously archeological and futurist matter in front of them, without touching it." The phantom that emerged from the zero-hour time capsule, Schivelbusch believes, is "pan-German culture."[56] Schivelbusch's reflections suggest that the last apparition of an undivided German culture prior to national reunification in 1990 occurred not so much in the Nazi period — which would be reason enough for its suppression — as in the now largely forgotten years that immediately followed the defeat of the Third Reich. With the clear emergence of the cold war between the United

States and the Soviet Union, the apparition of a pan-German culture gradually disappeared, along with the memory of most of the writers who had invoked it; from then on political, social, and above all cultural history bifurcated, and subsequent German consciousness was fundamentally either West German or East German, repressing the memory of a lost cultural whole. If this account is accurate — and I believe that it is — then it was precisely the repression of the immediate postwar cultural situation carried out under the rubric of a supposed zero hour that laid the foundation for the development and subsequent narrative understanding of what became known as postwar German culture. The supposed zero hour marked the moment of erasure of the pan-German cultural identity still prevalent at war's end, enabling West and East Germans in later decades to imagine their own cultural history as a smooth and compelling transition from Nazi tyranny to postwar triumph over that tyranny. Harold James is thus probably right to note that "the theory of the 'Stunde Null' . . . stifled historical thought in order to provide that degree of effective amnesia necessary for the functioning of West German politics."[57] Postwar West German society seems to have needed a certain kind of historical-cultural repression. If what Wilhelm Röpke and Winston Churchill called the Iron Curtain marked the geographical divide between the two opposing political — and cultural — blocs, then the zero hour marked, for Germans on both sides, a chronological caesura protecting them from identification with a pan-German culture that would necessarily have included not only the ideological opponent on the other side of the border but also the legacy of National Socialist barbarity.[58] The zero hour thus traced in time the very same break marked in space by the Iron Curtain. In the ideology of the two German states that emerged in 1949, the ghosts of the past were located primarily on the other side of the Iron Curtain; on one's own territory there had been a radical new beginning that protected against contact with such ghosts.

The erasure of the specificity of the zero hour, which occurred at the levels of popular memory, literature, and literary scholarship, implied not just the refusal to recognize in the other Germany and its literature elements of one's own cultural identity, a refusal amply documented in West Germans' responses to the GDR and its literature. It also implied the refusal to recognize a common origin in a historical period whose memory had been reconceived as a nullity, a blank slate. It was not just the GDR and its "dubious geographical constructions" that were, in Patrick Süskind's words, more alien to him as a West German writer than "the Outer Hebrides."[59] Rather, it was the entirety of the German historical situation both invoked and erased by the concept of a zero hour that became, as Hans Magnus Enzensberger has put it, virtually "unimaginable."[60] As Sebald has suggested, the unimaginability of the zero hour, far from being a function simply of historical distance, resulted from a taboo. "The true condition . . . in which the entire country found itself" was simply too painful.[61] Sebald's specification of "the entire country" implies the specific unity of East and West Germany so obvious in the literary culture of the second half of the 1940s but subsequently repressed via the concept of two German literatures. One of the most telling signs of the way in which what Schivelbusch calls "pan-German culture" was repressed was that many Germans avoided the word "reunification" in referring to the events of 1989–1990, as if there had never previously been a unified German nation-state.[62]

The uncanniness that West Germans found in East Germany in and around German reunification corresponds to the uncanniness of a past whose essence is that "secret of identity" between good and evil invoked by Thomas Mann in *Doktor Faustus*. Whereas German division had made possible a mechanism of projection by means of which unwanted elements of identity could be foisted off onto an evil national alter-ego, German reunification forced a confrontation with the repressed self and its past. It is anything but a coincidence that the West German writer Rehmann's *Unterwegs in fremden Träumen* (A Journey Through Foreign Dreams, 1993), an exploration of the "other Germany" (i.e. the GDR), is also an exploration of the zero hour, and in particular of the 1947 writers conference. Although she does not explicitly articulate it, Rehmann views the GDR as a kind of state incarnation of the zero hour itself and the elimination of the GDR as a repetition of the "restoration" of the late 1940s. What Rehmann views as having been erased, in both instances, is the dream of a democratic socialism, a dream from which Rehmann is careful to distance herself: "I did not believe in Communism."[63] Because of this distancing, Rehmann is able to refer to the eponymous dreams as "foreign" or "strange," i.e. not a part of her own identity. However throughout the memoir, in Berlin and elsewhere, Rehmann is constantly confronted with the mystery of her own identity, suggesting that the "strangeness" or "foreignness" of these dreams conceals an uncanny familiarity. The "other" Germany and the "foreign" dreams are hence, in fact, her own. It is this recognition toward which she gropes, with different degrees of success, over the course of the memoir; and less sensitive West Germans are still groping toward an understanding of East Germany, and of the zero hour, as part of their own national identity. Along with the rediscovery of the "other" Germany has come a renewed interest in aspects of the German past, particularly the Nazi and the immediate postwar period. The simultaneity of these two paths of discovery — chronological and geographic — points to a common origin: the "other" Germany and the rediscovered past are interlinked.

One telling sign of the return of the repressed occurred in the wake of the publication, in the first months of 2002, of Günter Grass's best-selling novella *Im Krebsgang* (Crabwalk) about the sinking by the Red Army of the German ship *Wilhelm Gustloff*, filled with German refugees from the eastern

territories, in the Baltic Sea in January, 1945. As the narrator of Grass's novella is at pains to point out, this was probably the worst shipping catastrophe in history, far surpassing the number of casualties registered in the
catastrophe that sank the more famous *Titanic*. In the novella, Grass's fictional alter-ego, for whom the narrator functions as a ghost-writer and researcher, suggests that his generation's failure to tell the story of the more
general German catastrophe of which the sinking of the *Wilhelm Gustloff* was
only a small, albeit horrible part, constituted a terrible failure:

> We should never, he says, have remained silent about so much suffer-
> ing, silent only because our own guilt was overpowering and confes-
> sions of regret were more important in all those years; we should never
> have left the avoided topic to the right-wingers. This failure was pro-
> found. . . .[64]

Grass's novella is an attempt to compensate at least partly for this failure, and
to bring to the surface a forgotten but crucial part of German experience. With
the publication of his novella Grass touched a raw nerve. Throughout the
spring of 2002 the novella was hotly discussed in newspapers, magazines, and
on television; the newsmagazine *Der Spiegel* even devoted a four-part series,
including a cover story, to the collapse of Germany's eastern territories in the
first half of 1945. Germans were suddenly debating about whether it was acceptable for them to see themselves not just as perpetrators but also as victims;
about whether they could acknowledge other nations' suffering while also acknowledging their own. Events that had occurred more than half a century
earlier were treated almost as breaking news, as if Germans had not yet registered or understood them. The publication of Grass's novella caused a moment of national shock at the recognition of the strangeness of one's own
history. The respected German historian Hans-Ulrich Wehler described this
recognition as "liberating."[65] A year after the publication of Grass's novel,
Germans were debating about the idea of erecting a memorial to Europeans
expelled from their homelands in the twentieth century; the debate centered
around the problem of whether such a memorial should focus primarily on
Germans or should, instead, be pan-European in its outlook.[66]

It is important to acknowledge the strangeness, even the uncanniness
that many of the literary works and discussions of the immediate postwar period have for Germans and others today. But it is also important to explore
and question the reasons for this strangeness, which may lie precisely in an
act of repression. The past is not overcome simply by rejecting it or refusing
to acknowledge it; such reactions lead to the return of the repressed, as at
the end of Grass's novella, when the narrator declares in despair: "This will
never end. Never will this end."[67] Only those who face the past have a
chance of moving beyond it, Grass's novella suggests. Acknowledgement of
the strangeness of the past and its documents should occur not as a trium-

phalist celebration of how far "we" have come from an unwanted and unloved past but as a challenge from the past to our own conceptions and preconceptions. That past belongs, precisely because of its uncanniness, to us. If history has a value at all, that value lies not in history's status as an inert raw material that we can use to celebrate a supposedly enlightened present, but rather in its combustible potential to challenge our understanding of the present and to shed light on its hidden origins. "Why not until now?" asks Grass's alter ego at the beginning of the novella. And the narrator's attempt at an answer fades into an ellipsis: "Because not until now . . ."[68] Because now, finally, we can.

Notes

[1] "Deutschland wird nicht besetzt, um befreit zu werden, sondern weil es ein besiegtes Land ist." Cited in Barbro Eberan, *Luther? Friedrich "der Große"? Wagner? Nietzsche?. . .?. . .? Wer war an Hitler schuld? Die Debatte um die Schuldfrage 1945– 1949* (Munich: Minerva, 1983), 21. Unless otherwise specified, all translations from German in this book are my own; the German appears in the notes, followed by sources. I have added the notation "my translation" in a limited number of cases where confusion might otherwise occur.

[2] Stephen Vincent Benét, Erika Mann, et al., *Zero Hour: A Summons to the Free* (New York: Farrar & Rinehart, 1940), 76.

[3] Koeppen, *Pigeons on the Grass,* 134. In German: Koeppen, *Tauben im Gras,* 142.

[4] Koeppen, *Pigeons on the Grass,* 134. In German: "Man verwechselte Alexander mit seinem Schatten." Koeppen, *Tauben im Gras,* 142.

[5] Koeppen, *Pigeons on the Grass,* 133. In German: "mir schlug die Stunde nicht, ich drückte mich durch die Diktatur," "aber mit Leuten dieser Art ist auch kein Staat zu stürzen, keine Hoffnung, für mich nicht mehr." Koeppen, *Tauben im Gras,* 141.

[6] "und da ist nichts, wonach ich messen könnte. Es kann ein Anfang sein oder ein Ende." Hans Erich Nossack, *Nekyia: Bericht eines Überlebenden* (Frankfurt: Suhrkamp, 1961), 35.

[7] "Das ist dort, wo die geschmolzenen Glocken Anfang und Ende zugleich läuten, das ist dort, wo die Sekunden enthüllt sind. . . ." Aichinger, *Die grössere Hoffnung,* 71.

[8] Hans-Egon Holthusen, "Tabula Rasa," *Die Wandlung,* 1: 1 (November 1945), 65.

[9] "Wer ist nicht übrigens Orpheus heute, und wer nicht Eurydike?" Langgässer, *Märkische Argonautenfahrt* (Hamburg: Claassen, 1959), 235.

[10] "Deutschland ist tot." Ernst R. Mellinghoff, "Zusammenbruch," in *Deine Söhne, Europa: Gedichte deutscher Kriegsgefangener,* ed. Hans Werner Richter, 64–68; here, 65 (Munich: Nymphenburger Verlagshandlung, 1947).

[11] "Wir alle leben nicht mehr. Der Gestank unserer Leichen beginnt sich bereits auszubreiten, der Pestgeruch ruht über diesem ganzen verfluchten Kontinent." Kolbenhoff, *Heimkehr in die Fremde* (Frankfurt: Suhrkamp, 1988), 30.

[12] "In ihrer Vision schien nicht nur das Ufer, das sie verlassen hatten, zu brennen; auch nicht nur die große Stadt ihrer Herkunft, sondern von Lissabon bis nach Kiew und Helsingfors nach Gibraltar das ganze Abendland." Langgässer, *Märkische Argonautenfahrt*, 240.

[13] Gottfried Benn, "Der Ptolemäer: Berliner Novelle, 1947," in Benn, *Sämtliche Werke,* ed. Gerhard Schuster, 5:8–55; here, 20 (Stuttgart: Klett-Cotta, 1991).

[14] "Was sonst noch da war, würden ein paar Reste einsamer Seelen sein, etwas sehr bewußter, tief melancholischer, schweigend sich erlebender Geist —: aber das Dogma, das vom Homo sapiens, war zu Ende." Benn, "Der Ptolemäer: Berliner Novelle, 1947," 21.

[15] Walter Jens, *Nein: Die Welt der Angeklagten* (Munich: Piper, 1968).

[16] "halb wahnsinnig vor Verzweiflung," "Sie verstand nichts mehr," "Nun aber trug sie ein und strich aus und trug wieder von neuem ein mit der Empfindung der Hoffnungslosigkeit. Ihre Arbeit war sinnlos, sie fühlte es, ohne zu wissen, warum." Langgässer, *Märkische Argonautenfahrt*, 127.

[17] "ein neues Kapitel auf dieses Unschuldsblatt," "wird überhaupt nichts mehr schreiben." Langgässer, *Märkische Argonautenfahrt*, 269.

[18] "Die Bevölkerung sieht durch die Fenster gierig zu: die Kultur ist wieder im Vormarsch, wenig Mord, mehr Song und Klänge." "ein transatlantischer Bischof kommt angereist und murmelt: meine Brüder; — ein Humanist zeigt sich und flötet: das Abendland; — ein Tenor knödelt: oh holde Kunst —, der Wiederaufbau Europas ist im Gange." Benn, "Der Ptolemäer: Berliner Novelle, 1947," 25.

[19] Koeppen, *Pigeons on the Grass,* 105. In German: "Was war hier untergegangen? Ein paar alte Häuser waren zusammengebrochen. Sie waren längst untergangsreif gewesen." "Was für Hochhäuser würde er ihnen auf die Schutthalden setzen! Die Gegend würde ein fortschrittliches Gesicht bekommen." Koeppen, *Tauben im Gras,* 112.

[20] Wolfgang Koeppen, *The Hothouse,* trans. Michael Hofmann (New York: W. W. Norton, 2001), 34. In German: "seine Mitarbeit am Wiederaufbau, sein Eifer, der Nation neue Grundlagen des politischen Lebens und die Freiheit der Demokratie zu schaffen." Koeppen, *Das Treibhaus* (Frankfurt: Suhrkamp, 1978), 17.

[21] "Millionen Ameisen sind zertreten, Millionen andere warten begierig, den Platz der Zertretenen einzunehmen; Eier zu legen, die Larven zu hüten und dem schrecklichen Wunsch nach Vermehrung und ewiger Wiederholung bedingungslos nachzugeben." Langgässer, *Märkische Argonautenfahrt*, 76.

[22] "Zustand der Willenlosigkeit." Nossack, *Der Untergang* (New York: Harcourt, Brace & World, 1962), 36. Alternative translation: Nossack, *The Fall,* trans. Ronald Dale Tullius (M.A. Thesis, University of Texas at Austin, 1975), 48.

[23] Angelika Manyoni, *Consistency of Phenotype: A Study of Gottfried Benn's Views on Lyric Poetry* (Bern: Peter Lang, 1983), 223.

[24] "Entwicklungsfremdheit/ist die Tiefe des Weisen." Gottfried Benn, "Statische Gedichte," in Benn, *Sämtliche Werke,* ed. Gerhard Schuster, 1:224 (Stuttgart: Klett-Cotta, 1986). For an alternative English-language translation, see Benn, "Static Poems," in Benn, *Poems 1937–1947,* trans. Simona Draghici, 103 (Washington, DC: Plutarch Press, 1991).

[25] Heinrich Böll, *The Train Was On Time,* trans. Leila Vennewitz (London: Secker & Warburg, 1970), 5. Translation modified and punctuation changed. In German: "Die Zukunft hat kein Gesicht mehr, sie ist irgendwo abgeschnitten, und je mehr er daran denkt, um so mehr fällt ihm ein, wie nahe er diesem Bald ist." Heinrich Böll, *Der Zug war pünktlich,* in *Die Erzählungen* (Leipzig: Insel, 1966), 35–141; here, 39.

[26] Heinrich Böll, *The Silent Angel,* trans. Breon Mitchell (New York: St. Martin's Press, 1994), 42. In German: "Er hat mir meinen Tod gestohlen. . . ." Heinrich Böll, *Der Engel schwieg* (Cologne: Kiepenheuer & Witsch, 1992), 49.

[27] Böll, *The Silent Angel,* 35–36. In German: "Es schien unglaublich, fast widerwärtig, daß es hier noch Menschen geben sollte, die zur Arbeit gingen, pünktlich und regelmäßig, die Tasche unter dem Arm. . . ." Böll, *Der Engel schwieg,* 43.

[28] Heinrich Böll, *And Never Said a Word,* trans. Leila Vennewitz (New York: McGraw Hill, 1978), 191. "ich fühlte mich verloren, träge dahinschwimmend in einem unendlichen Strom." In German: Böll, *Und sagte kein einziges Wort* (Cologne: Kiepenheuer & Witsch, 1953), 211.

[29] Heinrich Böll, *The Unguarded House,* trans. Mervyn Savill (London: Arco, 1957), 89. Translation altered. In German: "Oh, ich hasse euch alle, weil ihr zulaßt, daß das Leben weitergeht. Vergessen streuen über den Mord, wie man Asche über Glatteis streut." "neue Witwen aufziehen, neue Männer, die abgeknallt werden und Frauen zu Witwen machen können." Böll, *Haus ohne Hüter* (Cologne: Kiepenheuer & Witsch, 1954), 113. For an alternative English-language translation, see Böll, *Tomorrow and Yesterday* [translator not identified] (New York: Criterion, 1957), 84.

[30] "das war das Unbarmherzigste: daß das Leben weiterging." Heinrich Böll, *Kreuz ohne Liebe,* in *Werke,* vol. 2, ed. J. H. Reid, 166. (Cologne: Kiepenheuer & Witsch, 2002). See also 234.

[31] "Auferstanden aus Ruinen/Und der Zukunft zugewandt." Johannes R. Becher, "Auferstanden aus Ruinen," in *Gesammelte Werke,* vol. 6, *Gedichte 1949–1958,* 61 (Berlin: Aufbau, 1973).

[32] Walter Benjamin, "Über den Begriff der Geschichte," in Benjamin, *Gesammelte Schriften,* ed. Rolf Tiedemann and Hermann Schweppenhäuser, 2:691–704; here, 697–98 (Frankfurt: Suhrkamp, 1980). In English: Benjamin, "Theses on the Philosophy of History," in Benjamin, *Illuminations,* ed. Hannah Arendt, 253–64; here, 257–58 (New York: Harcourt, Brace and World, 1968).

[33] "wollen leben/Nicht mehr so wie bisher." Becher, "Strasse Frei!" in *Gesammelte Werke,* vol. 6, *Gedichte 1949–1958,* 69–70.

[34] "Laßt uns pflügen, laßt uns bauen,/Lernt und schafft wie nie zuvor." Becher, "Auferstanden aus Ruinen," 61.

[35] "Deutschlands neues Leben." Becher, "Auferstanden aus Ruinen," 61.

[36] "Aus dem Blauen strahlt die Sonne,/Und sie leuchtet, Deutschland, dir." Becher, "Lied von der blauen Fahne," in *Gesammelte Werke,* vol. 6, *Gedichte 1949–1958,* 66.

[37] "die Sonne schön wie nie/Über Deutschland scheint." Becher, "Auferstanden aus Ruinen," 61.

[38] "ein deutsches Morgenrot." Johannes R. Becher, "Zeitenschlag," in *Gesammelte Werke,* vol. 5, *Gedichte 1942–1948,* 183–84; here, 184 (Berlin: Aufbau, 1967).

[39] "Mein Gott, was sollen wir tun?" "die Wirklichkeit verkünden; jeden Tag unseres Lebens daran denken, daß es kein Traum war, was in diesen sieben Jahren geschehen ist, sondern Wirklichkeit. Die Leute werden es wieder vergessen, das Geschlecht der Ahnungslosen wird wieder auf den Thron kommen, und obwohl es fast sicher ist, daß die Ahnungslosen wieder siegen werden, wir wollen die Wirklichkeit verkünden." Böll, *Kreuz ohne Liebe*, 423.

[40] Anna Seghers, "Der Mann und sein Name," in *Der Bienenstock: Gesammelte Erzählungen in drei Bänden*, 3:56–153 (Berlin: Aufbau, 1963).

[41] This aspect of the zero hour was reinforced in 1995, when the esteemed German literary scholar and Goethe specialist Hans Schwerte was publicly revealed to be identical to the SS officer Hans-Ernst Schneider, who had supposedly died in 1945. In that year the former Schneider reemerged with a new identity as Schwerte; he even married his own wife again, now the purported widow of Schneider. See Neal Ascherson, "The Art of Vanishing and Why the English Needn't Fear Identity Cards," *The Independent*, 14 May 1995, 26; and Alan Cowell, "German Scholar Unmasked as Former SS Officer," *The New York Times*, 1 June 1995, Section A, 2.

[42] Franz Fühmann, *Das Judenauto: Vierzehn Tage aus zwei Jahrzehnten* (Berlin: Aufbau, 1962). On Fühmann's life, see Hans Richter, *Franz Fühmann: Ein deutsches Dichterleben* (Berlin: Aufbau, 1992).

[43] See Stephen Brockmann, "Literature and Convergence: The Early 1980s," in *Beyond 1989: Re-Reading German Literature since 1945*, ed. Keith Bullivant, 49–67 (Providence: Berghahn, 1997).

[44] "Und so baun wir erst 'nen neuen Staat/*Fort mit den Trümmern Und was Neues hingebaut/Um uns selber müssen wir uns selber kümmern/Und heraus gegen uns, wer sich traut*." Bertolt Brecht, "Aufbaulied der F. D. J.," in Brecht, *Werke*, ed. Werner Hecht et al., vol. 15, *Gedichte* 5, 196–97; here, 196 (Berlin, Weimar, and Frankfurt: Aufbau and Suhrkamp, 1987–2000). Emphasis in the original.

[45] "Aber das Neue muß Altes bezwingen/Anders sind immer die Wellen im Rhein./Und wir werden ein Deutschland erringen/Und es wird neu und ein anderes sein." Bertolt Brecht, "Herrnburger Bericht," *Werke*, vol. 15, *Gedichte* 5, 246–53; here, 253.

[46] "Ich habe meine Meinungen nicht, weil ich hier bin, sondern ich bin hier, weil ich meine Meinungen habe." Bertolt Brecht, "Antworten auf Fragen des Schriftstellers Wolfgang Weyrauch," *Werke*, vol. 23, *Schriften* 3, 216–20; here, 220.

[47] Transcriptions and translations from these films are my own.

[48] Sabine Hake, *German National Cinema* (London: Routledge, 2001), 91, 92.

[49] "Nun ist mein Thema aufgebrochen und ergießt sich unübersichtlich in die Zeit." Ruth Rehmann, *Unterwegs in fremden Träumen* (Munich: Carl Hanser, 1993), 39.

[50] Charles S. Maier, *Dissolution: The Crisis of Communism and the End of East Germany* (Princeton: Princeton UP, 1997).

[51] Ursula Heukenkamp, "Ortsgebundenheit: Die DDR-Literatur als Variante des Regionalismus in der deutschen Nachkriegsliteratur," *Weimarer Beiträge*, 42, no. 1 (1996), 30–53.

[52] For an analysis of this dispute, see Stephen Brockmann, *Literature and German Reunification* (Cambridge: Cambridge UP, 1999), 64–70.

[53] For more on these debates, see Brockmann, *Literature and German Reunification*.

[54] "das Wunschbild von 1990 dem Ekelbild von 1947 gefährlich nahekommt." Rehmann, *Unterwegs in fremden Träumen*, 27.

[55] Karl Heinz Bohrer, "Die Ästhetik am Ausgang ihrer Unmündigkeit," *Merkur*, 44: 500 (1990), 851–65.

[56] "Zeitkapsel," "dieses gleichermaßen archäologische wie futuristische Material vor sich her, ohne es zu berühren," "Deutsche Gesamtkultur." Schivelbusch, *Vor dem Vorhang*, 289.

[57] Harold James, "The Prehistory of the Federal Republic," *The Journal of Modern History*, 63, no. 1 (March 1991), 99–115; here, 100.

[58] Röpke, *The German Question*, 197. German original: Röpke, *Die deutsche Frage*, 241.

[59] "dubiose Ländereien," "die Äußeren Hebriden." Patrick Süskind, "Deutschland, eine Midlife-Crisis," in *Angst vor Deutschland*, ed. Ulrich Wickert, 111–22; here, 118–19 (Hamburg: Hoffmann und Campe, 1990).

[60] "unvorstellbar." Hans Magnus Enzensberger, "Europa in Ruinen: Ein Prospekt," in *Europa in Ruinen: Augenzeugenberichte aus den Jahren 1944–1948*, ed. Enzensberger, 5–23; here, 7 (Frankfurt: Eichborn, 1990).

[61] "Der wahre Zustand . . ., in welchem das ganze Land sich befand." W. G. Sebald, *Luftkrieg und Literatur*, (Munich: Hanser, 1999), 18. Alternative English-language translation: Sebald, "Air War and Literature," *On the Natural History of Destruction*, trans. Anthea Bell (New York: Random House, 2003), 10.

[62] On the words "unification" and "reunification," see Erik J. Macki, "Semantics and the Ideological Lexicon of German (Dis)Unity," in *Germanics under Construction: Intercultural and Interdisciplinary Prospects*, ed. Jörg Roche and Thomas Salumets, 123–41 (Munich: Iudicium, 1996); and Brockmann, *Literature and German Reunification*, 166.

[63] "Ich habe nicht an den Kommunismus geglaubt. . . ." Rehmann, *Unterwegs in fremden Träumen*, 269.

[64] "Niemals, sagt er, hätte man über so viel Leid, nur weil die eigene Schuld übermächtig gewesen sei, schweigen, das gemiedene Thema den Rechtsgestrickten überlassen dürfen. Dieses Versäumnis sei bodenlos. . . ." Günter Grass, *Im Krebsgang* (Göttingen: Steidl, 2002), 99. Ellipsis in the original. English translation: Grass, *Crabwalk*, trans. Krishna Winston (Orlando: Harcourt, 2002).

[65] Hans-Ulrich Wehler, "Die Debatte wirkt befreiend," *Der Spiegel* no. 13, 25 March 2002, 61–64.

[66] See Gunter Hofmann, "Unsere Opfer, ihre Opfer: Erinnern an die Vertreibungen — national oder europäisch?" *Die Zeit*, 17 July 2003, 8; and Karl Schlögel, "Die Düsternis — in neuem Licht," *Die Zeit*, 24 July 2003, 9.

[67] "Das hört nicht auf. Nie hört das auf." Grass, *Im Krebsgang*, 216.

[68] "Weil jetzt erst . . ." Grass, *Im Krebsgang*, 7. Ellipsis in the original.

Works Cited

Adorno, Theodor W. "Auferstehung der Kultur in Deutschland?" In *Kritik: Kleine Schriften zur Gesellschaft*, 20–33. Frankfurt: Suhrkamp, 1971.

———. "Kulturkritik und Gesellschaft." In *Prismen: Kulturkritik und Gesellschaft*, 7–31. Frankfurt: Suhrkamp, 1976; English translation: "Cultural Criticism and Society." In *Prisms*, translated by Samuel and Shierry Weber, 17–34. Cambridge, MA: MIT Press, 1981.

Aichinger, Ilse. *Die grössere Hoffnung*. Amsterdam: Bermann-Fischer/Querido, 1948.

Alewyn, Richard. "Goethe als Alibi?" In Mandelkow, *Goethe im Urteil seiner Kritiker*, 333–35.

Andersch, Alfred. "Aktion oder Passivität." *Der Ruf*, no. 12 (1 February 1947). Reprinted in Schwab-Felisch, *Der Ruf: Eine deutsche Nachkriegszeitschrift*, 132–36.

———. *Deutsche Literatur in der Entscheidung: Ein Beitrag zur Analyse der literarischen Situation*. Karlsruhe: Volk und Zeit, 1948.

———. "Die Existenz und die objektiven Werte: Eine Entgegnung." *Neue Zeitung*, 15 August 1947, 3.

———. "Das junge Europa formt sein Gesicht." *Der Ruf*, no. 1 (15 August 1946). Reprinted in Schwab-Felisch, *Der Ruf: Eine deutsche Nachkriegszeitschrift*, 21–26.

———. *Die Kirschen der Freiheit: Ein Bericht*. Zurich: Diogenes, 1972 (originally 1952).

———. "Notwendige Aussage zum Nürnberger Prozeß." *Der Ruf*, no. 1 (15 August 1946). Reprinted in Schwab-Felisch, *Der Ruf: Eine deutsche Nachkriegszeitschrift*, 26–29.

Arendt, Hannah. *Eichmann In Jerusalem: A Report on the Banality of Evil*. New York: Viking, 1963.

———. "Organized Guilt and Universal Responsibility." In *The Jew as Pariah: Jewish Identity and Politics in the Modern Age*, edited by Ron H. Feldman, 225–36. New York: Grove Press, 1978. In German: "Organisierte Schuld." *Die Wandlung* 1: 4 (April 1946), 333–44.

Bächler, Wolfgang. "Jugend der Städte." In Richter, *Almanach der Gruppe 47*, 76–77.

Bamberger, Elisabeth. "Not." In Schneider-Schelde, *Die Frage der Jugend,* 39–48.

Barbian, Jan-Pieter. *Literaturpolitik im 'Dritten Reich': Institutionen, Kompetenzen, Betätigungsfelder.* Munich: Deutscher Taschenbuch, 1995.

Barnouw, Dagmar. *Germany 1945: Views of War and Violence.* Bloomington: Indiana UP, 1997.

Becher, Johannes R. "Aus: Der Befreier." In Mandelkow, *Goethe im Urteil seiner Kritiker,* 318–32.

———. "Deutschland klagt an!" *Der Aufbau* 2: 1 (January 1946), 9–18.

———. *Gesammelte Werke.* Berlin: Aufbau, 1973.

Becker, Karl. *Zero Hour for Germany.* London: I.N.G. Publications, 1944.

Benét, Stephen Vincent, Erika Mann, et al. *Zero Hour: A Summons to the Free.* New York: Farrar & Rinehart, 1940.

Benjamin, Walter. "Über den Begriff der Geschichte." In Benjamin, *Gesammelte Schriften,* edited by Rolf Tiedemann and Hermann Schweppenhäuser, 2:691–704. Frankfurt: Suhrkamp, 1980. English translation: "Theses on the Philosophy of History." In Walter Benjamin, *Illuminations,* edited by Hannah Arendt. New York: Harcourt, Brace and World, 1968, 253–64.

Benn, Gottfried. "Berliner Brief, Juli 1948." In Benn, *Sämtliche Werke,* edited by Gerhard Schuster, 5:56–61.

———. *Poems 1937–1947.* Translated by Simona Draghici. Washington, DC: Plutarch Press, 1991.

———. *Prose, Essays, Poems.* Edited by Volkmar Sander. New York: Continuum, 1987.

———. "Der Ptolemäer: Berliner Novelle, 1947." In Benn, *Sämtliche Werke,* edited by Gerhard Schuster, 5:8–55.

———. *Sämtliche Werke.* Edited by Gerhard Schuster. Stuttgart: Klett-Cotta, 1991.

Bertram, Mathias. "Literarische Epochendiagnosen der Nachkriegszeit." In Heukenkamp, *Deutsche Erinnerung,* 11–99.

Beutler, Ernst. "An Goethes hundertundzwölftem Todestage, dem 22. März 1944, starb auch das Haus seiner Kindheit, starb die Stadt seiner Jugend." In Mandelkow, *Goethe im Urteil seiner Kritiker,* 4:258–60.

———. *Besinnung: Ansprache zur Feier von Goethes Geburtstag.* Wiesbaden: Dieterich'sche Verlagsbuchhandlung, 1946.

Bloom, Harold. *The Anxiety of Influence: A Theory of Poetry.* New York: Oxford UP, 1973.

Bohrer, Karl Heinz. "Die Ästhetik am Ausgang ihrer Unmündigkeit." *Merkur,* 44: 500 (1990), 851–65.

Böll, Heinrich. "Bekenntnis zur Trümmerliteratur." In *Erzählungen Hörspiele Aufsätze,* 339–43. Cologne: Kiepenheuer & Witsch, 1961.

———. *Der Engel schwieg.* Cologne: Kiepenheuer & Witsch, 1992. English translation: *The Silent Angel.* Translated by Breon Mitchell. New York: St. Martin's Press, 1994.

———. *Haus ohne Hüter.* Cologne: Kiepenheuer & Witsch, 1954. English translations: *The Unguarded House.* Translated by Mervyn Savill. London: Arco, 1957; and *Tomorrow and Yesterday* (translator not identified). New York: Criterion, 1957.

———. *Kreuz ohne Liebe.* In Böll, *Werke,* edited by J. H. Reid, 2:149–425. Cologne: Kiepenheuer & Witsch, 2002.

———. *Und sagte kein einziges Wort.* Cologne: Kiepenheuer & Witsch, 1953. English translation: *And Never Said a Word.* Translated by Leila Vennewitz. New York: McGraw Hill, 1978.

———. *Wo warst du, Adam?* Leipzig: Reclam, 1985. English translations: *And Where Were You, Adam?* Translated by Leila Vennewitz. London: Secker & Warburg, 1970; and *Adam, Where Art Thou?* Translated by Mervyn Savill. London: Arco, 1955.

———. *Der Zug war pünktlich.* In Böll, *Die Erzählungen,* 35–141. Leipzig: Insel, 1966. English translation: *The Train Was On Time.* Translated by Leila Vennewitz, London: Secker & Warburg, 1970.

Borchert, Wolfgang. *Draussen vor der Tür.* Reinbek: Rowohlt, 1992. English translation: *The Man Outside.* Translated by David Porter. New York: New Directions, 1971.

Bracher, Karl Dietrich. *The German Dictatorship: The Origins, Structure, and Effects of National Socialism.* Translated by Jean Steinberg. New York: Praeger, 1970.

Brecht, Bertolt. "Antworten auf Fragen des Schriftstellers Wolfgang Weyrauch." In Brecht, *Werke,* edited by Werner Hecht et al., vol. 23, *Schriften 3,* 216–20.

———. "Bericht über die Stellung der Deutschen im Exil." In Brecht, *Werke,* edited by Werner Hecht et al., vol. 23, *Schriften 3,* 32–33.

———. *Die Gedichte von Bertolt Brecht in einem Band.* Frankfurt: Suhrkamp, 1981.

———. "The *Other* Germany 1943." Translated by Eric Bentley. In Brecht, *Werke,* edited by Werner Hecht et al., 23:24–30.

———. *Poems 1913–1956.* Edited by John Willett and Ralph Manheim. London: Methuen, 1987.

———. "Von der Jugend." In Brecht, *Werke,* edited by Werner Hecht et al., vol. 23, *Schriften 3,* 130–31.

————. *Werke: Große kommentierte Berliner und Frankfurter Ausgabe.* Edited by Werner Hecht, Jan Knopf, Werner Mittenzwei, and Klaus-Detlef Müller. Berlin, Weimar, and Frankfurt: Aufbau and Suhrkamp, 1987–2000.

Briegleb, Klaus. *Mißachtung und Tabu: Eine Streitschrift zur Frage: "Wie antisemitisch war die Gruppe 47?"* Berlin: Philo, 2003.

Broch, Hermann. *Der Tod des Vergil.* Zurich: Rhein, 1958.

Brockmann, Stephen. "Literature and Convergence: The Early 1980s." In *Beyond 1989: Re-Reading German Literature since 1945,* edited by Keith Bullivant, 49–67. Providence: Berghahn, 1997.

————. "German Culture at the 'Zero Hour.'" In Brockmann and Trommler, *Revisiting Zero Hour 1945,* 8–40.

————. *Literature and German Reunification.* Cambridge: Cambridge UP, 1999.

Brockmann, Stephen and Frank Trommler, eds. *Revisiting Zero Hour 1945: The Emergence of Postwar German Culture.* Washington: American Institute for Contemporary German Studies, 1996.

Busch, Stefan. *"Und gestern, da hörte uns Deutschland." NS-Autoren in der Bundesrepublik. Kontinuität und Diskontinuität bei Friedrich Griese, Werner Beumelburg, Eberhard Wolfgang Möller und Kurt Ziesel.* Würzburg: Königshausen & Neumann, 1998.

Celan, Paul. "Todesfuge." Translated by Christopher Middleton. In Michael Hamburger and Christopher Middleton, eds., *Modern German Poetry 1910–1960,* 318–21. London: Macgibbon & Lee, 1966.

Coleman, Peter. *The Liberal Conspiracy: The Congress for Cultural Freedom and the Struggle for the Mind of Postwar Europe.* London: Free Press, 1989.

Cuomo, Glenn. *Career at the Cost of Compromise: Günter Eich's Life and Work in the Years 1933–1945.* Amsterdam: Rodopi, 1989.

Curtius, Ernst Robert. "Aus: Goethe — Grundzüge seiner Welt." In Mandelkow, *Goethe im Urteil seiner Kritiker,* 308–13.

————. "Goethe oder Jaspers." In Mandelkow, *Goethe im Urteil seiner Kritiker,* 304–7.

Dahnke, Hans-Dietrich. "Humanität und Geschichtsperspektive: Zu den Goethe-Ehrungen 1932, 1949, 1982." *Weimarer Beiträge,* 28: 10 (1982), 66–89.

Delabar, Walter. *Was tun? Romane am Ende der Weimarer Republik.* Opladen: Westdeutscher Verlag, 1999.

Demant, Ebbo. *Von Schleicher zu Springer: Hans Zehrer als politischer Publizist.* Mainz: v. Hase & Koehler, 1971.

Demetz, Peter. *After the Fires: Recent Writing in the Germanies, Austria and Switzerland*. San Diego: Harcourt Brace Jovanovich, 1986.

Denk, Friedrich. *Die Zensur der Nachgeborenen: Zur regimekritischen Literatur im Dritten Reich*. Weilheim: Denk, 1996.

Dieckmann, Walter. "Diskontinuität? Zur— unbefriedigenden — sprachkritischen und sprachwissenschaftlichen Behandlung der Nachkriegssprache in Deutschland 1945–1949." In Hermand, Peitsch, and Scherpe, *Nachkriegsliteratur in Westdeutschland*, vol. 2, *Autoren, Sprache, Traditionen*, 89–100.

Döblin, Alfred. *Autobiographische Schriften und letzte Aufzeichnungen*. Olten: Walter, 1980.

———. "Die beiden deutschen Literaturen." In *Schriften zu Ästhetik, Poetik und Literatur*, 364–67. Olten: Walter, 1989.

———. *Destiny's Journey*. Translated by Edna McCown. New York: Paragon House, 1992.

———. "Die literarische Situation." In *Schriften zu Ästhetik, Poetik und Literatur*, 409–87.

———. *Schicksalsreise*. In *Autobiographische Schriften und letzte Aufzeichnungen*, 103–426.

———. *Schriften zu Ästhetik, Poetik und Literatur*. Olten: Walter, 1989.

Donahue, Neil H. *Voice and Void: The Poetry of Gerhard Falkner*. Heidelberg: Universitätsverlag C. Winter, 1998.

Dostoyevsky, Fyodor. *The Brothers Karamazov*. Translated by David McDuff. London: Penguin, 1993.

Dostoevsky, Fyodor (alternate spelling). *Demons*. Translated by Richard Pevear and Larissa Volokhonsky. New York: Knopf, 1994.

Drawert, Kurt. *Spiegelland: Ein deutscher Monolog*. Frankfurt: Suhrkamp, 1992.

Dubiel, Helmut. *Niemand ist frei von der Geschichte: Die nationalsozialistische Herrschaft in den Debatten des Deutschen Bundestages*. Munich: Carl Hanser, 1999.

Durzak, Manfred, ed. *Die deutsche Exilliteratur 1933–1945*. Stuttgart: Reclam, 1973.

Ebbinghaus, Julius. "Was ist Existentialphilosophie?" *Neue Zeitung*, 28 July 1947, 5.

Eberan, Barbro. *Luther? Friedrich "der Große"? Wagner? Nietzsche?...?...? Wer war an Hitler schuld? Die Debatte um die Schuldfrage 1945–1949*. Munich: Minerva, 1983.

Eckert, Brita, ed. *Goethe in Deutschland 1945–1982*. Frankfurt: Buchhändler-Vereinigung, 1982.

Eich, Günter. *Pigeons and Moles: Selected Writings of Günter Eich.* Columbia, SC: Camden House, 1991.

Eliot, T. S. *Die Einheit der europäischen Kultur.* Berlin: Carl Habel, 1946.

———. *Notes towards the Definition of Culture.* New York: Harcourt, Brace & Company, 1949.

Enzensberger, Hans Magnus. "Die Clique." In Richter, *Almanach der Gruppe 47 1947–1962.*

———. "Europa in Ruinen: Ein Prospekt." In *Europa in Ruinen: Augenzeugen-berichte aus den Jahren 1944–1948,* 5–23. Frankfurt: Eichborn, 1990.

Erhart, Walter, and Dirk Niefanger, eds. *Zwei Wendezeiten: Blicke auf die deutsche Literatur 1945 und 1989.* Tübingen: Niemeyer, 1997.

Faber, Richard. *Abendland: Ein "politischer Kampfbegriff."* Hildesheim: Gerstenberg, 1979.

Finney, Gail. *Christa Wolf.* New York: Twayne, 1999.

Frei, Norbert. *Vergangenheitspolitik: Die Anfänge der Bundesrepublik und die NS-Vergangenheit.* Munich: C. H. Beck, 1996.

Friedrich, Heinz. "Das Jahr 47." In Richter, *Almanach der Gruppe 47 1947– 1962,* 15–21.

Frisch, Max. *Als der Krieg zu Ende war.* New York: Dodd, Mead, 1967.

———. "Kultur als Alibi." *Der Monat,* 1: 7 (April 1949), 83–85.

Fromm, Erich. *Escape from Freedom.* New York: Farrar & Rinehart, 1941.

Fuchs, Ina. *Die Herausforderung des Nihilismus: Philosophische Analysen zu F. M. Dostojewskijs Werk "Die Dämonen."* Munich: Otto Sagner, 1987.

Fühmann, Franz. *Das Judenauto: Vierzehn Tage aus zwei Jahrzehnten.* Berlin: Aufbau, 1962.

Gansel, Carsten. "Vom Schutzverband Deutscher Autoren (SDA) zum Deutschen Schriftstellerverband (DSV): Zu Aspekten von literarischer Gruppenbildung zwischen 1945 und 1956." In Heukenkamp and Reinhold, *Literatur im politischen Spannungsfeld der Nachkriegszeit,* 147–67.

Garbe, Joachim. *Deutsche Geschichte in deutschen Geschichten der neunziger Jahre.* Würzburg: Königshausen & Neumann, 2002.

Gay, Peter. *Weimar Culture: The Outsider as Insider.* New York: Harper & Row, 1970.

Gelbin, Catherine Susan. *The Indelible Seal: Race, Hybridity and Identity in Elisabeth Langgässer's Writings.* Dissertation, Cornell University, 1997.

Genton, Bernard. "Melvin J. Lasky und der 1. Deutsche Schriftstellerkongreß." In Heukenkamp and Reinhold, *Literatur im politischen Spannungsfeld der Nachkriegszeit,* 59–70.

Gide, André. "André Gide an die Jugend: Der Wortlaut seiner Münchner Rede." *Neue Zeitung* (Berlin edition), 4 July 1947, 6.

Glaser, Hermann. *Kulturgeschichte der Bundesrepublik Deutschland: Zwischen Kapitulation und Währungsreform 1945–1948.* Munich: Carl Hanser, 1985.

Goethe, Johann Wolfgang von. *Faust, der Tragödie erster Teil.* Stuttgart: Reclam, 1980; In English: *Faust I & II.* Translated by Stuart Atkins. Boston: Suhrkamp/Insel, 1984.

Grass, Günter. *Im Krebsgang.* Göttingen: Steidl, 2002. In English: *Crabwalk.* Translated by Krishna Winston. Orlando: Harcourt, 2002.

Greiner, Bernd. "Mit Sigmund Freud im Apfelhain oder Was Deutsche in 45 Jahren über Henry Morgenthau gelernt haben." *Mittelweg* 36 (August/September 1992), 44–58.

Greschat, Martin, ed. *Die Schuld der Kirche: Dokumente und Reflexionen zur Stuttgarter Schulderklärung vom 18./19. Oktober 1945.* Munich: Kaiser, 1982.

Grimm, Reinhold. "Innere Emigration als Lebensform" In Grimm and Hermand, *Exil und Innere Emigration,* 31–73. Frankfurt: Athenäum, 1972.

Gromes, Hartwin, and Hans-Otto Hügel, eds. *Auf der Suche nach der Stunde Null: Literatur und Alltag 1945.* Bad Salzdetfurth: Barbara Franzbecker, 1991.

Grosser, J. F. G., ed. *Die grosse Kontroverse: Ein Briefwechsel um Deutschland.* Hamburg: Nagel, 1963.

Grotewohl, Otto. "Amboss oder Hammer: Rede an die deutsche Jugend zum Todestag von Goethe." In *Deutsche Kulturpolitik,* 57–79.

———. *Deutsche Kulturpolitik.* Dresden: Verlag der Kunst, 1952.

Hake, Sabine. *German National Cinema.* London: Routledge, 2001.

Hartmann, Annelie. "Die Rolle der sowjetischen Delegierten in Berlin (1947) und Wroclaw (1948)." In Heukenkamp and Reinhold, *Literatur im politischen Spannungsfeld der Nachkriegszeit,* 43–58.

Hartmann, Anne[lie], and Wolfram Eggeling. *Sowjetische Präsenz im kulturellen Leben der SBZ und frühen DDR 1945–1953.* Berlin: Akademie, 1998.

Haug, Wolfgang Fritz, ed. *Historisch-Kritisches Wörterbuch des Marxismus.* Hamburg: Argument, 1999.

Hausmann, Manfred. "Jugend zwischen gestern und morgen." *Aufbau,* 2: 7 (1946), 667–74.

Hay, Gerhard, ed. *Zur literarischen Situation 1945–1949.* Kronberg: Athenäum, 1977.

Hay, Gerhard, Hartmut Rambaldo, and Joachim W. Storck, eds. *"Als der Krieg zu Ende war": Literarisch-politische Publizistik 1945–1950.* Marbach: Deutsche Schillergesellschaft, 1995.

Hecht, Werner. *Brecht Chronik 1898–1956.* Frankfurt: Suhrkamp, 1997.

Herf, Jeffrey. "Belated Pessimism: Technology and Twentieth Century German Conservative Intellectuals." In *Technology, Pessimism, and Postmodernism*, edited by Yaron Ezrahi, Everett Mendelsohn, and Howard Segal, 115–36. Amherst: U of Massachusetts P, 1995.

———. *Divided Memory: The Nazi Past in the Two Germanys*. Cambridge, MA: Harvard UP, 1997.

Hermand, Jost. *Kultur im Wiederaufbau: Die Bundesrepublik Deutschland, 1945–1965*. Munich: Nymphenburger, 1986.

———. "Zum Vorverständnis." In Hermand and Lange, *"Wollt ihr Thomas Mann wiederhaben?" Deutschland und die Emigranten*, 7–55.

Hermand, Jost and Wigand Lange, eds. *"Wollt ihr Thomas Mann wiederhaben?" Deutschland und die Emigranten*. Hamburg: Europäische Verlagsanstalt, 1999.

Hermand, Jost, Helmut Peitsch, and Klaus R. Scherpe, eds. *Nachkriegsliteratur in Westdeutschland 1945–1949: Schreibweisen, Gattungen, Institutionen*. Berlin: Argument, 1982.

Hermlin, Stefan. "Aus dem Lande der Großen Schuld." In Hermlin, *Äußerungen 1944–1982*, 15–19.

———. *Äußerungen 1944–1982*. Berlin: Aufbau, 1983.

———. "Karl Jaspers 'Die Schuldfrage.'" In *Äußerungen 1944–1982*, 34–39.

———. "Die Zeit der Gemeinsamkeit." In *Erzählungen*, 135–204. Berlin: Aufbau, 1974.

Herzinger, Richard. "Ein extremistischer Zuschauer — Ernst von Salomon: Konservativ-revolutionäre Literatur zwischen Tatrhetorik und Resignation." *Zeitschrift für Germanistik* (Neue Folge), 8: 1 (1998), 83–96.

Heukenkamp, Ursula. "Ortsgebundenheit: Die DDR-Literatur als Variante des Regionalismus in der deutschen Nachkriegsliteratur." *Weimarer Beiträge*, 42: 1 (1996), 30–53.

———. "Vorwort." In *Deutsche Erinnerung*, 7–10.

Heukenkamp, Ursula, ed. *Deutsche Erinnerung: Berliner Beiträge zur Prosa der Nachkriegsjahre (1945–1960)*. Berlin: Erich Schmidt, 2000.

Heukenkamp, Ursula, and Ursula Reinhold, eds. *Literatur im politischen Spannungsfeld der Nachkriegszeit: Protokoll der internationalen Konferenz anläßlich des 50. Jubiläums des 1. Deutschen Schriftstellerkongresses vom Oktober 1947*. Berlin: Institut für deutsche Literatur, 1998 (unpublished conference proceedings).

Heuschele, Otto. "Sommer 1945." In *Betrachtungen und Deutungen: Neue Essays*, 79–89. Stuttgart: Hans E. Günther, 1948.

Hochgeschwender, Michael. "Der 'Kongreß für kulturelle Freiheit' und die Deutschen." In Heukenkamp and Reinhold, *Literatur im politischen Spannungsfeld der Nachkriegszeit,* 71–83.

Hocke, Gustav René. "Deutsche Kalligraphie oder: Glanz und Elend der modernen Literatur." *Der Ruf,* no. 7 (15 November 1946). Reprinted in Schwab-Felisch, *Der Ruf: Eine deutsche Nachkriegszeitschrift,* 203–8.

Hoffmann, E. T. A. "Die Abenteuer der Silvester-Nacht." In *Werke,* 1:205–32. Frankfurt: Insel, 1967. In English: Hoffmann. "A New Year's Eve Adventure." Translated by Alfred Packer. In *The Best Tales of Hoffmann,* edited by E. F. Bleiler, 104–29. New York: Dover, 1967.

Hofmann, Gunter. "Unsere Opfer, ihre Opfer: Erinnern an die Vertreibungen — national oder europäisch?" *Die Zeit,* 17 July 2003, 8.

Holthusen, Hans-Egon. "Tabula Rasa." *Die Wandlung,* 1: 1 (November 1945), 65.

Holz, Marcus. *Christliche Weltanschauung als Grundlage von Parteipolitik: Eine Analyse des genuin Christlichen in der frühen CDU/CSU (1945–50) aus der Betrachtung des christlichen Menschenbildes und seiner ideengeschichtlichen Hintergründe.* Doctoral dissertation, Universität der Bundeswehr, Munich, 1992.

Horkheimer, Max and Theodor W. Adorno. *Dialektik der Aufklärung: Philosophische Fragmente.* Frankfurt: S. Fischer, 1969; English translation: *Dialectic of Enlightenment.* Translated by John Cumming. New York: Continuum, 1995.

Howells, Christina. *Sartre's Theory of Literature.* London: The Modern Humanities Research Association, 1979.

Hüppauf, Bernd. "Krise ohne Wandel: Die kulturelle Situation 1945–1949." In *"Die Mühen der Ebenen,"* 47–112.

Hüppauf, Bernd, ed. *"Die Mühen der Ebenen": Kontinuität und Wandel in der deutschen Literatur und Gesellschaft 1945–1949.* Heidelberg: Carl Winter, 1981.

Hurwitz, Harold. *Die Stunde Null der deutschen Presse: Die amerikanische Pressepolitik in Deutschland 1945–1949.* Cologne: Wissenschaft und Politik, 1972.

Institut für Gesellschaftswissenschaften beim ZK der SED, collective editor. *Zur Theorie des sozialistischen Realismus.* Berlin: Dietz, 1974.

James, Harold. "The Prehistory of the Federal Republic." *The Journal of Modern History,* 63: 1 (March 1991), 99–115.

Jaspers, Karl. "Erneuerung der Universität." In *Philosophische Aufsätze,* 9–17.

———. "Geleitwort für die Zeitschrift 'Die Wandlung.'" In *Philosophische Aufsätze,* 18–20.

———. *Philosophische Aufsätze.* Frankfurt: Fischer, 1967.

————. *Die Schuldfrage: Von der politischen Haftung Deutschlands.* Munich: Piper, 1996. In English: *The Question of German Guilt.* Translated by E. B. Ashton. New York: Dial Press, 1947.

————. "Unsere Zukunft und Goethe." *Die Wandlung,* 2: 7 (October 1947), 559–78.

Jens, Walter. *Nein: Die Welt der Angeklagten.* Munich: Piper, 1968.

Jung, Carl Gustav. "Nach der Katastrophe." *Neue Schweizer Rundschau,* 13: 6 (1945/1946), 67–88. In English: "After the Catastrophe." In Jung, *Civilization in Transition,* translated by R. F. C. Hull. New York: Pantheon, 1964.

Jünger, Ernst. *Auf den Marmorklippen.* Frankfurt: Ullstein, 1995 (originally 1939). In English: *On the Marble Cliffs.* Translated by Stuart Hood. New York: New Directions, 1947.

————. *Der Friede.* Stuttgart: Ernst Klett, 1965.

————. *Heliopolis: Rückblick auf eine Stadt.* In *Werke,* vol. 10, *Erzählende Schriften* 2. Stuttgart: Ernst Klett, n.d.

————. *Strahlungen.* Tübingen: Heliopolis, 1949.

————. *Über die Linie.* Frankfurt: Vittorio Klostermann, 1950.

Kaes, Anton. "Literatur und nationale Identität: Kontroversen um Goethe 1945–49." In *Kontroversen, alte und neue (Akten des VII. Internationalen Germanisten-Kongresses Göttingen 1985,* vol. 10), edited by Albrecht Schöne. Göttingen: Niemeyer, 1986.

Kasack, Hermann. *Die Stadt hinter dem Strom.* Frankfurt: Suhrkamp, 1947; abridged English translation by Peter de Mendelssohn: *The City Beyond the River.* London: Longmans, Green and Co., 1953.

Kaschnitz, Marie Luise. "Rückkehr nach Frankfurt." *Die Wandlung,* 1: 10 (October 1946), 847–57.

Kästner, Erich. "Die chinesische Mauer." In Schneider-Schelde, *Die Frage der Jugend,* 64–68.

————. "Reise in die Zukunft: Über Studenten und Kinder." *Neue Zeitung* (Berlin edition), 4 July 1947, 6.

————. *Der tägliche Kram.* Berlin: Atrium, 1948.

Kiesel, Helmuth. "Ernst Jüngers 'Marmor-Klippen.'" *Internationales Archiv für Sozialgeschichte der deutschen Literatur.* 14 (1989), 126–64.

————. "Die Restaurationsthese als Problem für die Literaturgeschichtsschreibung." In Erhart and Niefanger, *Zwei Wendezeiten,* 13–45.

————. *Wissenschaftliche Diagnose und dichterische Vision der Moderne: Max Weber und Ernst Jünger.* Heidelberg: Manutius, 1994.

————. "Zwischen Kritik und Affirmation: Ernst Jüngers Auseinandersetzung mit dem Nationalsozialismus." in Rüther, *Literatur in der Diktatur,* 163–72.

Kinder, Hermann. *Der Mythos von der Gruppe 47.* Eggingen: Edition Isele, 1991.

Kleinschmidt, Erich. "Der vereinnahmte Goethe: Irrwege im Umgang mit einem Klassiker 1932–1949." *Jahrbuch der Deutschen Schillergesellschaft,* 28 (1984), 461–82.

Kleist, Heinrich von. "On the Puppet Theater." In Kleist, *An Abyss Deep Enough,* edited and translated by Philip B. Miller, 211–16. New York: E. P. Dutton, 1982.

Klemperer, Victor. *Kultur: Erwägungen nach dem Zusammenbruch des Nazismus.* Berlin: Neues Leben, 1946.

Knauth, Percy. *Germany in Defeat.* New York: Knopf, 1946.

Kocka, Jürgen. "Zerstörung und Befreiung: Das Jahr 1945 als Wendepunkt deutscher Geschichte." In *Geschichte und Aufklärung,* 120–39. Göttingen: Vandenhoeck und Ruprecht, 1989.

Koeppen, Wolfgang. *Tauben im Gras.* Frankfurt: Suhrkamp, 1951. In English: *Pigeons on the Grass.* Translated by David Ward. New York: Holmes & Meier, 1988.

———. *Der Tod in Rom.* Frankfurt: Suhrkamp, 1975. English translations as *Death in Rome* by: Michael Hofmann. London: Hamish Hamilton, 1992; and Mervyn Savill. New York: Vanguard, 1961.

———. *Das Treibhaus.* Frankfurt: Suhrkamp, 1978. In English: *The Hothouse.* Translated by Michael Hofmann. New York: W. W. Norton, 2001.

Koestler, Arthur. *The Yogi and the Commissar.* New York: Macmillan, 1945.

Kogon, Eugen. *Der SS-Staat: Das System der deutschen Konzentrationslager.* Munich: Kindler, 1974. Abridged English translation: *The Theory and Practice of Hell.* Translated by Heinz Norden. New York: Farrar, Straus & Cudahy, 1950.

Kolbenhoff, Walter. *Heimkehr in die Fremde.* Frankfurt: Suhrkamp, 1988.

———. *Von unserem Fleisch und Blut.* Munich: Nymphenburger Verlagshandlung, 1946.

Krenzlin, Leonore. "Große Kontroverse oder kleiner Dialog? Gesprächsbemühungen und Kontaktbruchstellen zwischen 'inneren' und 'äußeren' literarischen Emigranten." *Galerie: Revue culturelle et pédagogique,* 15: 1 (1997), 7–25.

Krenzlin, Leonore (Schiller-). "Hinter den Offenen Briefen: Initialzündung und Motivationsgeflecht des Streits zwischen innerer und äußerer Emigration." In Heukenkamp and Reinhold, *Literatur im politischen Spannungsfeld der Nachkriegszeit,* 169–86.

Kreuder, Ernst. *Die Gesellschaft vom Dachboden.* Frankfurt: Suhrkamp, 1986. In English: *The Attic Pretenders.* Translated by Robert Kee. London: Putnam & Co., 1948.

————. *Die Unauffindbaren.* Königstein: Athenäum, 1984.

Künneth, Walter. *Der große Abfall: Eine geschichtstheologische Untersuchung der Begegnung zwischen Nationalsozialismus und Christentum.* Hamburg: Friedrich Wittig, 1947.

Lahusen, Thomas, and Evgeny Dobrenko, eds. *Socialist Realism Without Shores.* Durham, NC: Duke UP, 1997.

Lang, Hans-Joachim. "Der letzte Deutsche." In Schröter, *Thomas Mann im Urteil seiner Zeit,* 365–74.

Lange, Horst. "Bücher nach dem Kriege: Eine kritische Betrachtung." In *Der Ruf,* no. 10 (1 January 1947). Reprinted in Schwab-Felisch, *Der Ruf: Eine deutsche Nachkriegszeitschrift,* 216–23.

Lange, Wigand. "Die Schaubühne als politische Umerziehungsanstalt betrachtet: Theater in den Westzonen." In Hermand, Peitsch, and Scherpe, *Nachkriegsliteratur in Westdeutschland 1945–1949,* 6–35.

Langgässer, Elisabeth. *Märkische Argonautenfahrt.* Hamburg: Claassen, 1959.

————. *Das unauslöschliche Siegel.* Hamburg: Claassen, 1959.

Leithäuser, Joachim G. "Das Goethejahr ist überstanden . . .: Rückblick und Bilanz." *Der Monat,* 2: 15 (1949/1950), 286–96.

Lersch, Philipp. "Ruf nach Verinnerlichung." *Neue Zeitung,* 25 August 1947, 3.

————. "Über den Nihilismus." *Neue Zeitung,* 10 October 1947, 3.

Littler, Margaret. *Alfred Andersch (1914–1980) and the Reception of French Thought in the Federal Republic of Germany.* London: Edwin Mellen Press, 1991.

Littleton, Taylor D. and Maltby Sykes. *Advancing American Art: Painting, Politics and Cultural Confrontation.* Alabama: U of Alabama P, 1989.

Luft, Friedrich. "Zweite Emigration nach innen?" *Neue Zeitung* (Berlin edition), 20 May 1947, 2.

Lukács, György. *Theory of the Novel.* Cambridge, MA: M.I.T. Press, 1971.

Macki, Erik J. "Semantics and the Ideological Lexicon of German (Dis)Unity." In *Germanics under Construction: Intercultural and Interdisciplinary Prospects,* edited by Jörg Roche and Thomas Salumets, 123–41. Munich: Iudicium, 1996.

Maier, Charles S. *Dissolution: The Crisis of Communism and the End of East Germany.* Princeton: Princeton UP, 1997.

Mandelkow, Karl Robert. *Goethe in Deutschland: Rezeptionsgeschichte eines Klassikers.* Vol. 2. Munich: Beck, 1989.

Mandelkow, Karl Robert, ed. *Goethe im Urteil seiner Kritiker: Dokumente zur Wirkungsgeschichte Goethes in Deutschland Teil IV 1918–1982.* Munich: C. H. Beck, 1984.

Mann, Erika and Klaus. *The Other Germany*. New York: Modern Age, 1940.

Mann, Thomas. *An die gesittete Welt: Politische Schriften und Reden im Exil*. Frankfurt: S. Fischer, 1986.

———. "Ansprache im Goethejahr 1949." In *Gesammelte Werke in Zwölf Bänden*, vol. 11, *Reden und Aufsätze 3*, 481–97.

———. *Deutsche Hörer! 25 Radiosendungen nach Deutschland*. Stockholm: Berman-Fischer, 1942.

———. *Doktor Faustus: Das Leben des deutschen Tonsetzers Adrian Leverkühn, erzählt von einem Freunde*. Frankfurt: Fischer, 1998. In English: *Doctor Faustus: The Life of the German Composer Adrian Leverkühn as Told by a Friend*. Translated by H. T. Lowe-Porter. New York: Alfred Knopf, 1948.

———. "Das Ende." in *Gesammelte Werke in Zwölf Bänden*, 12:944–51.

———. "Germany and the Germans," in *Thomas Mann's Addresses Delivered at the Library of Congress 1942–1949*, 45–66. Washington: Library of Congress, 1963.

———. *Gesammelte Werke in Zwölf Bänden*. Frankfurt: S. Fischer, 1960.

———. "Die Lager." In *Gesammelte Werke in Zwölf Bänden*, 12:951–53.

———. "Mario und der Zauberer." In *Die Erzählungen*, 2:502–42. Frankfurt: Fischer, 1967. English translation: *Mario and the Magician*. Translated by H. T. Lowe-Porter. London: Martin Secker, 1930.

———. "Schicksal und Aufgabe." In *Gesammelte Werke in Zwölf Bänden*, vol. 12, *Reden und Aufsätze 4*, 918–39.

———. *Tagebücher 1933–1934*. Edited by Peter de Mendelssohn. Frankfurt: S. Fischer, 1977.

———. *Tagebücher 1944–1.4.1946*. Edited by Inge Jens. Frankfurt: S. Fischer, 1986.

———. "Warum ich nicht nach Deutschland zurückgehe." In *Gesammelte Werke in Zwölf Bänden*, vol. 12, *Reden und Aufsätze 4*, 953–62.

Manyoni, Angelika. *Consistency of Phenotype: A Study of Gottfried Benn's Views on Lyric Poetry*. Bern: Peter Lang, 1983.

Marcuse, Herbert. "Über den affirmativen Charakter der Kultur." In *Kultur und Gesellschaft*. Frankfurt: Suhrkamp, 1965. English translation: Marcuse, "The Affirmative Character of Culture." In *Negations: Essays in Critical Theory*, translated by Jeremy J. Shapiro. Boston: Beacon Press, 1968.

Marcuse, Ludwig. *Mein zwanzigstes Jahrhundert: Auf dem Weg zu einer Autobiographie*. Munich: Paul List, 1960.

Mayer, Hans. "Konfrontation der inneren und äußeren Emigration: Erinnerung und Deutung." In Grimm and Hermand, *Exil und innere Emigration*, 75–87.

———. *Zur deutschen Literatur der Zeit*. Reinbek: Rowohlt, 1967.

Meier, Bettina. "Goethe in Trümmern: Der Streit um den Wiederaufbau des Goethehauses in Frankfurt." In Jochen Vogt, *Erinnerung ist unsere Aufgabe,"* 28–40.

———. *Goethe in Trümmern: Zur Rezeption eines Klassikers in der Nachkriegszeit.* Wiesbaden: Deutscher Universitäts-Verlag, 1989.

Meinecke, Friedrich. *Die deutsche Katastrophe: Betrachtungen und Erinnerungen.* Brockhaus: Wiesbaden, 1946. English translation: *The German Catastrophe: Reflections and Recollections.* Translated by Sidney B. Fay. Cambridge, MA: Harvard UP, 1950.

———. "Zusammenarbeit." In Paetel, *Deutsche innere Emigration,* 86–88.

Melchert, Monika. "Die Zeitgeschichtsprosa nach 1945 im Kontext der Schuldfrage." In Heukenkamp, *Deutsche Erinnerung,* 101–66.

Mellinghoff, Ernst R. "Zusammenbruch." In Richter, *Deine Söhne, Europa,* 64–68.

Merker, Paul. *Germany Today . . . and Germany Tomorrow?* London: I.N.G., 1943.

Mitchell, Maria Dee. *Christian Democracy and the Transformation of German Politics, 1945–1949.* Doctoral dissertation, Boston University, 1995.

Mitscherlich, Alexander. *Ein Leben für die Psychoanalyse: Anmerkungen zu meiner Zeit.* Frankfurt: Suhrkamp, 1980.

Mitscherlich, Alexander and Margarete Mitscherlich. *Die Unfähigkeit zu trauern: Grundlagen kollektiven Verhaltens.* Munich: Piper, 1991 (originally 1967).

Molo, Walter von. "Offener Brief an Thomas Mann." In Schröter, *Thomas Mann im Urteil seiner Zeit,* 334–36.

Morgenthau, Jr., Henry. *Germany is Our Problem.* New York: Harper & Brothers, 1945.

Mosse, George, ed. *Nazi Culture: A Documentary History.* New York: Schocken, 1981.

Muller, Jerry Z. *The Other God That Failed: Hans Freyer and the Deradicalization of German Conservatism.* Princeton: Princeton UP, 1987.

Neumann, Klaus. "Goethe, Buchenwald, and the New Germany." *German Politics and Society,* 17: 1 (Spring 1999), 55–83.

Nickel, Gunther, and Ulrike Weiß, eds. *Carl Zuckmayer 1896–1977: "Ich wollte nur Theater machen."* Marbach: Deutsches Literaturarchiv, 1996.

Niefanger, Dirk. "Die Dramatisierung der 'Stunde Null.'" In Erhart and Niefanger, *Zwei Wendezeiten,* 47–70.

Niemöller, Martin. "Die Erneuerung unserer Kirche." In *Reden 1945–1954,* 19–22.

———. *Reden 1945–1954.* Darmstadt: Stimme, 1958.

———. "Der Weg ins Freie." In *Reden 1945–1954,* 23–42.

———. "Zum Schuldbekenntnis." In *Reden 1945–1954,* 16–18.

WORKS CITED ♦ 277

Niethammer, Lutz. *Posthistoire: Has History Come to an End?* Translated by Patrick Camiller. London: Verso, 1992.

Nietzsche, Friedrich. *Der Wille zur Macht: Versuch einer Umwerthung aller Werthe (Studien und Fragmente).* Edited by Elisabeth Förster-Nietzsche. Leipzig: Naumann, 1901.

Noormann, Harry. *Protestantismus und politisches Mandat 1945–1949.* Gütersloh: Gerd Mohn, 1985.

Nossack, Hans Erich. *Nekyia: Bericht eines Überlebenden.* Frankfurt: Suhrkamp, 1961.

———. *Der Untergang.* New York: Harcourt, Brace & World, 1962. English-language translation: *The Fall.* Translation and introduction by Ronald Dale Tullius. M.A. Thesis, University of Texas at Austin, 1975.

"O Land, Land, höre des Herrn Wort!" *Die Zeit,* 4 November 1999, 55.

Pabst, Rolf. "Ein Brief an Dr. Manfred Hausmann: Die Problematik zweier Generationen." *Neue Zeitung* (Berlin edition), 15 August 1947, 2.

Padover, Saul K. *Experiment in Germany: The Story of an American Intelligence Officer.* New York: Duell, Sloan, & Pearce, 1946.

Paeschke, Hans. "Verantwortlichkeit des Geistes." *Merkur,* 1: 1 (1947), 100–110.

[Paeschke, Hans?]. "Die Bruderschaft der Pessimisten," *Merkur,* 1: 1 (1947), 131–37.

Paetel, Karl O. "Das Gesicht des innerdeutschen Widerstandes." In *Deutsche innere Emigration,* 32–38 .

Paetel, Karl. O., ed. *Deutsche innere Emigration: Anti-Nationalsozialistische Zeugnisse aus Deutschland.* New York: Friedrich Krause, 1946.

Parkes, Stuart, and John J. White. "Introduction." In *The Gruppe 47 Fifty Years On: A Re-Appraisal of its Literary and Political Significance,* edited by Parkes and White, i–xxiii. Amsterdam: Rodopi, 1999.

Parlach, Alexander. "Die erste und einzige Rede deutscher Jugend an ihren Dichter." *Der Ruf* 2, no. 25, 10. Cited in Gromes and Hügel, *Auf der Suche nach der Stunde Null: Literatur und Alltag 1945.*

Pavic, Milorad. *Landscape Painted with Tea.* New York: Knopf, 1990.

Pechel, Rudolf. *Deutsche Gegenwart: Aufsätze und Vorträge 1945–1952.* Stuttgart: no publisher, 1952 (private printing on the occasion of Pechel's seventieth birthday).

———. "Fragen um die deutsche Schuld." In *Deutsche Gegenwart: Aufsätze und Vorträge 1945–1952,* 39–46. Originally in the *Deutsche Rundschau,* August 1946.

———. "Unsere vordringlichste Aufgabe." In *Deutsche Gegenwart: Aufsätze und Vorträge 1945–1952,* 28–35.

Picard, Max. *Die Flucht vor Gott.* Erlenbach-Zurich: Eugen Rentsch, 1934.

———. *Hitler in uns selbst.* Erlenbach-Zurich: Eugen Rentsch, 1946. English translation: *Hitler in Our Selves.* Translated by Heinrich Hauser. Hinsdale, IL: Henry Regnery, 1947.

Pike, David. *The Politics of Culture in Soviet-Occupied Germany, 1945–1949.* Stanford: Stanford UP, 1992.

Plievier, Theodor. *Stalingrad.* Berlin: Aufbau, 1984. In English: *Stalingrad.* Translated by Richard and Clara Winston. New York: Appleton-Century-Crofts, 1948.

Rabinbach, Anson. *In the Shadow of Catastrophe: German Intellectuals between Apocalypse and Enlightenment.* Berkeley: U of California P, 1997.

Rauschning, Hermann. *The Revolution of Nihilism.* Translated by E. W. Dickes. Garden City: Garden City Publishing, 1942.

Rehmann, Ruth. *Unterwegs in fremden Träumen.* Munich: Carl Hanser, 1993.

Reinhardt, Stephan. *Alfred Andersch: Eine Biographie.* Zurich: Diogenes, 1990.

Reinhold, Ursula. "Elisabeth Langgässers Berliner Jahre: Christliches Weltbild und zeitgeschichtliche Erfahrung." In *Unterm Notdach: Nachkriegsliteratur in Berlin 1945–1949,* edited by Ursula Heukenkamp, 317–54. Berlin: Erich Schmidt, 1996.

Reinhold, Ursula, Dieter Schlenstedt, and Horst Tanneberger, eds. *Erster Deutscher Schriftstellerkongreß 4.–8. Oktober 1947.* Berlin: Aufbau, 1997.

Rhineland Conference. *The Signs of Awakening: German underground Speaks: The Peace Manifesto of the Rhineland Conference.* New York: German American, 1943.

Richter, Hans. *Franz Fühmann: Ein deutsches Dichterleben.* Berlin: Aufbau, 1992.

Richter, Hans Werner. *Briefe.* Edited by Sabine Cofalla. Munich: Hanser, 1997.

———. "Deutschland — Brücke zwischen Ost und West." *Der Ruf,* no. 4 (1 October 1946). Reprinted in Schwab-Felisch, *Der Ruf: Eine deutsche Nachkriegszeitschrift,* 46–49.

———. "Warum schweigt die junge Generation?" *Der Ruf,* no. 2 (1 September 1946). Reprinted in Schwab-Felisch, *Der Ruf: Eine deutsche Nachkriegszeitschrift,* 29–33.

Richter, Hans Werner, ed. *Almanach der Gruppe 47 1947–1962.* Reinbek: Rowohlt, 1962.

———, ed. *Deine Söhne, Europa: Gedichte deutscher Kriegsgefangener.* Munich: Nymphenburger Verlagshandlung, 1947.

Roberts, David. "Nach der Apokalypse: Kontinuität und Diskontinuität in der deutschen Literatur nach 1945." In Hüppauf, *"Die Mühen der Ebenen,"* 21–45.

Robin, Régine. *Socialist Realism: An Impossible Aesthetic.* Translated by Catherine Porter. Stanford: Stanford UP, 1992.

Rohrwasser, Michael. "Theodor Plieviers Kriegsbilder." In *Schuld und Sühne: Kriegserlebnis und Kriegsdeutung in deutschen Medien der Nachkriegszeit (1945–1961),* edited by Ursula Heukenkamp, 1:139–153. Amsterdam: Rodopi, 2001.

Roloff, Gerhard. *Exil und Exilliteratur in der deutschen Presse 1945–1949.* Worms: Georg Heintz, 1976.

Röpke, Wilhelm. *Die deutsche Frage.* Erlenbach-Zurich: Eugen Rentsch, 1945. English translation: *The German Question.* Translated by E. W. Dickes. London: George Allen & Unwin, 1946.

Rost, Nico. *Goethe in Dachau: Literatur und Wirklichkeit.* Berlin: Volk und Welt, 1948.

Rüther, Günther, ed. *Literatur in der Diktatur: Schreiben im Nationalsozialismus und DDR-Sozialismus.* Paderborn: Schöningh, 1997.

Sabrow, Martin. *Die verdrängte Verschwörung: Der Rathenau-Mord und die deutsche Gegenrevolution.* Frankfurt: Fischer, 1999.

Salomon, Ernst von. *Der Fragebogen.* Reinbek: Rowohlt, 1997. In English: *The Answers.* Translated by Constantine Fitzgibbon. London: Putnam, 1954.

Sartre, Jean-Paul. *The Flies.* In Sartre, *No Exit and Three Other Plays.* New York: Vintage, 1955. In German: *Die Fliegen.* In Sartre, *Gesammelte Dramen.* Reinbek: Rowohlt, 1984.

———. "The Responsibility of the Writer." Translated by Betty Askwith. In *Reflections on Our Age: Lectures Delivered at the Opening Session of UNESCO at the Sorbonne University Paris,* with an introduction by David Hardman and a foreword by Stephen Spender. New York: Columbia UP, 1949.

———. *Situations II.* Paris: Gallimard, 1948. English translation as *What is Literature?* Translated by Bernard Frechtman. New York: Philosophical Library, 1949.

Saunders, Frances Stonor. *Who Paid the Piper? The CIA and the Cultural Cold War.* London: Granta, 1999.

Schäfer, Hans Dieter. *Das gespaltene Bewußtsein: Über deutsche Kultur und Lebenswirklichkeit 1933–1945.* Munich: Hanser, 1981.

———. "Kultur als Simulation: Das Dritte Reich und die Postmoderne." In Rüther, *Literatur in der Diktatur.*

Scharmitzel, Theodor. *Christliche Demokratie im neuen Deutschland.* Vol. 1 of *Schriftenreihe der Christlich-Demokratischen Union, Landesverband Rheinland.* Cologne: Balduin Pick, 1946.

Schellworth, W. "Ein Tiefenpsychologe blickt in die deutsche Seele." *Aufbau*, 2: 7 (1946), 766–67.

Schenck, Ernst von. "An einen Studenten." In Schneider-Schelde, *Die Frage der Jugend*, 23–33.

Scherpe, Klaus R. "Erzwungener Alltag: Wahrgenommene und gedachte Wirklichkeit in der Reportageliteratur der Nachkriegszeit." In Hermand, Peitsch, and Scherpe, *Nachkriegsliteratur in Westdeutschland 1945–1949: Schreibweisen, Gattungen, Institutionen.*

Schiller, Friedrich. *Ueber die ästhetische Erziehung des Menschen in einer Reihe von Briefen.* In *Schillers Werke* (Nationalausgabe), vol. 20, part 1, *Philosophische Schriften*, ed. Benno von Wiese, 309–412. Weimar: Hermann Böhlaus Nachfolger, 1962. In English: *On the Aesthetic Education of Man in a Series of Letters.* Translated by Reginald Snell. Bristol: Thoemmes Press, 1994.

Schirrmacher, Frank. "Abschied von der Literatur der Bundesrepublik." *Frankfurter Allgemeine Zeitung*, 2 October 1990, L1–2.

Schivelbusch, Wolfgang. *Vor dem Vorhang: Das geistige Berlin 1945–1948.* Frankfurt: Fischer, 1995. English translation: Schivelbusch, *In a Cold Crater: Cultural and Intellectual Life in Berlin, 1945–1948.* Translated by Kelly Barry. Berkeley: U of California P, 1998.

Schlant, Ernestine. *The Language of Silence: West German Literature and the Holocaust.* New York: Routledge, 1999.

Schlenker, Wolfram. *Das "Kulturelle Erbe" in der DDR: Gesellschaftliche Entwicklung und Kulturpolitik 1945–1965.* Stuttgart: Metzler, 1977.

Schlögel, Karl. "Die Düsternis — in neuem Licht." *Die Zeit*, 24 July 2003, 9.

Schmitt, Carl. *Donoso Cortès in gesamteuropäischer Interpretation: Vier Aufsätze.* Cologne: Greven, 1950.

Schneider, Reinhold. *Der Mensch vor dem Gericht der Geschichte.* Augsburg-Göggingen: Johann Wilhelm Naumann, 1946.

Schneider-Schelde, Rudolf. "Jugenddämmerung." In *Die Frage der Jugend*, 84–102.

———. "Vorbemerkung des Herausgebers." In *Die Frage der Jugend*, 7–8.

Schneider-Schelde, Rudolf, ed. *Die Frage der Jugend.* Munich: Kurt Desch, 1946.

Schnurre, Wolfdietrich. "Das Begräbnis." In Schnurre, *Erzählungen.* Freiburg: Walter, 1966.

Schonauer, Franz. "Die Prosaliteratur der Bundesrepublik." In *Literatur nach 1945 I: Politische und regionale Aspekte*, edited by Jost Hermand. Wiesbaden: Akademische Verlagsgesellschaft, 1979.

Schornstheimer, Michael. *Bombenstimmung und Katzenjammer — Vergangenheitsbewältigung: Quick und Stern in den 50er Jahren.* Cologne: Pahl-Rugenstein, 1989.

Schröter, Klaus, ed. *Thomas Mann im Urteil seiner Zeit: Dokumente 1891–1955.* Hamburg: Christian Wegner, 1969.

Schütz, Erhard. *Alfred Andersch.* Munich: Beck, 1980.

Schwab-Felisch, Hans, ed. *Der Ruf: Eine deutsche Nachkriegszeitschrift.* Munich: Deutscher Taschenbuch Verlag, 1962.

Scriven, Michael. *Jean-Paul Sartre: Politics and Culture in Postwar France.* New York: St. Martin's Press, 1999.

Sebald, W. G. *Luftkrieg und Literatur.* Munich: Hanser, 1999. English translation containing two essays not in the German original: *On the Natural History of Destruction.* Translated by Anthea Bell. New York: Random House, 2003.

———. "Der Schriftsteller Alfred Andersch." In Sebald, *Luftkrieg und Literatur,* 121–60. English translation: "Between the Devil and the Deep Blue Sea: On Alfred Andersch." In Sebald, *On the Natural History of Destruction,* translated by Anthea Bell, 105–42. New York: Random House, 2003.

Seghers, Anna. "Der Mann und sein Name." In *Der Bienenstock: Gesammelte Erzählungen in drei Bänden,* 3:56–153. Berlin: Aufbau, 1963.

Shdanow, A. A. "Referat über die Zeitschriften 'Swesda' und 'Leningrad,' 1946." In *Beiträge zum Sozialistischen Realismus: Grundsätzliches über Kunst und Literatur,* with an introduction by Wilhelm Girnus. Berlin: Kultur und Fortschritt, 1953.

Sieburg, Friedrich. "Frieden mit Thomas Mann." In Schröter, *Thomas Mann im Urteil seiner Zeit,* 375–78.

Sontheimer, Kurt. *Thomas Mann und die Deutschen.* Munich: Nymphenburger Verlagshandlung, 1961.

Spitzer, Leo. "Zum Goethekult." *Die Wandlung,* 4 (Summer 1949), 581–92.

Sternberger, Dolf. "Thomas Mann und der Respekt." *Die Wandlung,* 1: 6 (June 1946), 451–59.

Srauß, Botho. "Am Rand. Wo sonst." Interview with Botho Strauß by Ulrich Greiner. *Die Zeit,* 31 May 2000, 55–56.

Strohmeyer, Arn. *Der Mitläufer: Manfred Hausmann und der National-sozialismus.* Bremen: Donat, 1999.

Süskind, Patrick. "Deutschland, eine Midlife-Crisis." In *Angst vor Deutschland,* ed. Ulrich Wickert, 111–22. Hamburg: Hoffmann und Campe, 1990.

Süskind, W. E. "An die Jugend." In Schneider-Schelde, *Die Frage der Jugend,* 55–63.

Taeger, Dorothea. "Der Deutschen Dichtung." In *De Profundis: Deutsche Lyrik in dieser Zeit — Eine Anthologie aus zwölf Jahren,* ed. Gunter Goll, 417. Munich: Kurt Desch, 1946.

Theunissen, Gert H. "Der deutsche Intellektuelle und die Politik." *Die Weltbühne,* 1: 2 (24 June 1946), 41–44.

Thieme, Karl. *Das Schicksal der Deutschen: Ein Versuch seiner geschichtlichen Erklärung.* Basel: Kobersche Verlagsbuchhandlung, 1945.

Thiess, Frank. "Die innere Emigration." In Schröter, *Thomas Mann im Urteil seiner Zeit,* 336–38.

Trommler, Frank. "Der 'Nullpunkt 1945' und seine Verbindlichkeit für die Literaturgeschichte." *Basis: Jahrbuch für deutsche Gegenwartsliteratur,* 1 (1970), 9–25.

———. "Die nachgeholte Résistance: Politik und Gruppenethos im historischen Zusammenhang." In *Die Gruppe 47 in der Geschichte der Bundesrepublik,* edited by Justus Fechter, Eberhard Lämmert, and Jürgen Schutte, 9–22. Würzburg: Königshausen & Neumann, 1991.

Vaillant, Jérôme. *Der Ruf — Unabhängige Blätter der jungen Generation (1945–1949): Eine Zeitschrift zwischen Illusion und Anpassung.* Translated by Heidrun Hofmann and Karl Heinz Schmidt. Munich: K. G. Sauer, 1978.

Vansittart, (Robert Gilbert) Lord. *Lessons of My Life.* New York: Alfred A. Knopf, 1945.

Vogel, Heinrich. *Nihilismus und Nationalismus.* Berlin: Evangelische Verlangsanstalt, 1948.

Vogt, Jochen. *"Erinnerung ist unsere Aufgabe" — Über Literatur, Moral und Politik 1945–1900.* Opladen: Westdeutscher Verlag, 1991.

Vormweg, Heinrich. "Deutsche Literatur 1945–1960: Keine Stunde Null." In *Deutsche Gegenwartsliteratur: Ausgangspositionen und aktuelle Entwicklungen,* edited by Manfred Durzak, 14–31. Stuttgart: Reclam, 1981.

———. "Gerechtigkeit über sich fühlend: Arnold Zweigs Roman 'Das Beil von Wandsbek.'" In Durzak, *Die deutsche Exilliteratur 1933–1945.*

Waine, Anthony. "Carl Zuckmayer's *Des Teufels General* as a Critique of the Cult of Masculinity." *Forum for Modern Language Studies,* 29: 3 (July 1993), 257–70.

Weber, Alfred. *Abschied von der bisherigen Geschichte: Überwindung des Nihilismus?* Hamburg: Claassen & Goverts, 1946. In English: *Farewell to European History, or The Conquest of Nihilism.* Translated by R. F. C. Hull. London: Kegan Paul, Trench, Trubner & Co., 1947.

Wehdeking, Volker. *Anfänge westdeutscher Nachkriegsliteratur: Aufsätze, Interviews, Materialien.* Aachen: Alano, 1989.

———. "Exilautoren und Aussenseiter in der frühen Gruppe 47 und Hans Werner Richters Schreibanfänge im Dritten Reich." Interview with Hans Werner Richter. In Wehdeking, *Anfänge westdeutscher Nachkriegsliteratur: Aufsätze, Interviews, Materialien,* 173–91.

———. "Mythologisches Ungewitter: Carl Zuckmayers problematisches Exildrama 'Des Teufels General.'" In Durzak, *Die deutsche Exilliteratur 1933–1945,* 509–19.

Wehdeking, Volker (Christian). *Der Nullpunkt: Über die Konstituierung der deutschen Nachkriegsliteratur in den amerikanischen Kriegsgefangenenlagern.* Stuttgart: Metzler, 1971.

Wehdeking, Volker. "Zwischen Exil und 'vorgeschobenem Posten' der Kulturnation: Thomas Mann als Projektionsfigur für die im Land gebliebenen Nichtfaschisten." In Rüther, *Literatur in der Diktatur,* 145–62.

Wende-Hohenberger, Waltraud, ed. *Der Frankfurter Schriftstellerkongreß im Jahr 1948.* Frankfurt: Peter Lang, 1989.

Werfel, Franz. "An das deutsche Volk." *Bayerische Landeszeitung,* 25 May 1945. Reprinted in Hay, Rambaldo, and Storck, *"Als der Krieg zu Ende war": Literarisch-politische Publizistik 1945–1950,* 23–24.

Weyrauch, Wolfgang. "Nachwort." In Weyrauch, *Tausend Gramm: Sammlung neuer deutscher Geschichten,* 207–19.

Weyrauch, Wolfgang. "Realismus des Unmittelbaren." *Aufbau,* 2: 7 (1946), 701–6.

Weyrauch, Wolfgang, ed. *Tausend Gramm: Sammlung neuer deutscher Geschichten.* Hamburg: Rowohlt, 1949.

Whitfield, Stephen J. *The Culture of the Cold War.* Baltimore: Johns Hopkins UP, 1991.

Widmer, Urs. *1945 oder die 'Neue Sprache.'* Düsseldorf: Schwann, 1966.

Wiechert, Ernst. *Rede an die deutsche Jugend 1945.* Munich: Zinnen, 1945.

———. *Der Totenwald: Ein Bericht.* Berlin: Union, 1977. In English: *Forest of the Dead.* Translated by Ursula Stechow. London: Victor Gollancz, 1947.

———. "Über Kunst und Künstler." *Aufbau,* January 1946, 1–8.

Wohl, Robert. *The Generation of 1914.* Cambridge, MA: Harvard UP, 1979.

Wolf, Friedrich. "Auch wir können nicht schweigen." *Aufbau,* 1: 3 (November 1945), 201–5.

Zehrer, Hans. *Aufsätze zur Zeit.* Hamburg: Rowohlt, 1949.

———. *Der Mensch in dieser Welt.* Hamburg: Rowohlt, 1948. Abridged English translation: *Man in this World.* New York: New York UP, 1955.

Zimmer Lauman, Angela G. *Elisabeth Langgässer (1899–1950) als christliche Dichterin und Schöpferin christlicher Frauengestalten.* Dissertation, University of Maryland, 1994.

Zuckmayer, Carl. *Des Teufels General.* Stockholm and Vienna: Bermann-Fischer and Schönbrunn, 1947.

Zweig, Arnold. *Das Beil von Wandsbek. Berlin: Aufbau, 1959.* In English: *The Axe of Wandsbek.* Translated by Eric Sutton. London: Hutchinson International Authors, 1948.

Index